Understanding *The* Bible: Head *and* Heart

Part Three: Romans through Revelation

Bob Dowell

WestBow Press books may be ordered through booksellers or by contacting:

WestBow Press
A Division of Thomas Nelson
1663 Liberty Drive
Bloomington, IN 47403
www.westbowpress.com
1-(866) 928-1240

ISBN: 978-1-4497-4283-6 (sc)
ISBN: 978-1-4497-4282-9 (e)

Library of Congress Control Number: 2012904460

Printed in the United States of America

WestBow Press rev. date: 07/03/2012

Contents

Dedication

in loving memory of my parents Alton and Valda

in loving appreciation for my wife Nancy

and our children: Stan, Dwight, and Brenda (Jimmy)
and our grandchildren: Will (Allison), Cale, Colton, Macy, Hailey, and Lori

ACKNOWLEDGMENTS

I wish to acknowledge those friends in the "Aldersgate Class," the "Friendship Class," and the evening bible study class "back to the Bible with Dr. Bob" for the enduring interest and the encouragement given this decade-long project. Week after week and year after they listened and responded to the prose summaries and poetic summaries that now comprise this book, *Understanding the Bible: Head and Heart.* They provided an immediate and critical audience for testing the work while in progress through the questions, they asked, the observations they voiced, and the praise they offered. Of course, I especially loved the praise; never did I tire of hearing, "this is great, you should publish it!" I pray that my friends who offered such praise prove to be prophets, and that anyone who peruses the pages of this book finds it a rewarding experience.

I wish also to acknowledge Cathe, Jerry, J'Nevelyn, and Kim, minister friends who, perusing the materials that comprise this work, offered many helpful suggestions, and to Ed, my tech friend, who provided vital computer assistance.

And I must not leave out two friends who volunteered their assistance in the preparation of Part Two and Part Three of this tripartite work: Judy, my university colleague, for her proofreading labors, and Paul, my co-presenter, who helped pilot these New Testament materials in "Back to the Bible with Dr. Bob" series.

Bob Dowell
McAllen, TX
(February, 2012)

INTRODUCTION

The Bible is a collection of materials usually referred to as books which were collected and assimilated over many centuries. Out of these collected books, believed to have been divinely inspired, emerges a story, but not one told in a straightforward manner. Sometimes events are arranged in chronological order and sometimes not; sometimes events move along rapidly and sometimes very slowly as digressions take precedent; sometimes chronological order is jumbled; and sometimes chronology goes on hold and theme orders events. But the story that emerges is the greatest of stories, for it is the story of the fall of man (male and female) and of the redemptive process that follows.

In the attempt to better understand this greatest of stories, I have spent the past decade (2000-2010) intensely reading and rereading the Bible word by word, sentence by sentence, book by book and then writing an interpretive summary of what I read, first summarizing in prose and then in poetry. Why the dual summaries? The prose summary serves to enhance cognitive comprehension by taking portions of the narrative and shaping characters, events, and concepts into a compact framework to aid in remembering the storied information. The poetic summary serves to enhance comprehension by shaping these same characters, events, and concepts into a framework which is by nature compact and dedicated to communicating experientially. Thus, the dual summaries serve memory and comprehension on dual levels: the cognitive and the experiential, the head and the heart.

In putting together my summaries, which I have entitled *Understanding the Bible: Head and Heart,* I have not included separate summaries of Leviticus, Numbers, I Chronicles, II Chronicles, Job, Psalms, Proverbs, Ecclesiastes, and the Song of Songs, but have included separate summaries of the other thirty books of the Old Testament and all twenty-seven of the New Testament. I felt that a narrative flow of the Old Testament was better served without separate summaries of the nine books listed above. Basically, I think of the Bible narrative as William Neil describes it: a drama with a prologue, three acts, and an epilogue. The creation and fall, related in Genesis, furnish the prologue and set the stage for three acts, the first act being the rest of the Old Testament telling the Israelite portion of the story, the second act being the gospels of the New Testament telling the Jesus Christ portion of the story, and the third act being Acts and the epistles telling the Church portion, and the epilogue being Revelation telling how the story ultimately ends.

Poetic Preface

We study the Bible to comprehend God's will;
There we read what He has chosen to reveal.
The more we read and study, the more we instill;
Ingesting the Bible's books transforms God into real.
Understanding its laws, its prophecies, its gospels, and its letters
Strengthens our spirit's capacity for breaking the world's fetters.

Where to start? Where to begin? Seekers ask that question again and again
In the very beginning, somewhere in the middle, or somewhere near the end?

This bible study begins at the beginning and follows the narrative thread
Summarizing first in prose, then poetry, inviting both heart and head.
When appealing to the head the effective mode is always prose,
But to the heart the effective mode is poetry, as the theory goes.
The head learns cognitively; the heart learns experientially
Depending on feeling and imagination, the stuff of poetry.

Our interpretive summary strives to be both informational and inspirational
Employing prose to address the factual, and poetry to address the spiritual

For there is the fact of the narrative, and there is the spirit of
the narrative.
To fully comprehend, the grasping of both fact and spirit is
imperative.
So, let us journey together through the Bible's enduring
narrative of events
And engage both head and heart in discerning its divinely
inspired contents.

Note to the Reader

The summaries that comprise this study follow the order of the Biblical books.

The longer books are divided into multiple parts.

Each part is given a title which serves for both the prose summary and the poetic summary; the prose summary always precedes the poetic summary.

The numbers in the parenthesis at the end of the titles listed in the table of contents indicate the Bible chapters and verses covered in the summaries.

The number following the numbers in parenthesis is the page number on which the prose summary for that particular part begins.

Theoretically, the reader would first read the Bible chapters and verses, then the prose summary followed by the poetic summary. But readers are, of course, free to read it in whatever order they choose.

It should be noted that, in most cases, the Biblical quotes in the prose summaries follow the New King James translation.

Romans Prose Summary One
Paul Introduces Himself

Why the Letter?

Most of the churches to whom Paul writes letters he has either founded or worked in them, but that is not the case with the church at Rome. He had neither founded the church there nor worked in it. Supposedly, he had never been to Rome. But for some time he had wanted to visit the church there and for good reason. He realizes the potential influence of a church located at the center of the known world. All roads leading to Rome meant roads that could carry the gospel to the ends of the earth. And by helping ground that church in sound Christian principles would insure that sound Christian principles would be flowing from Rome throughout the world. Thus, since Paul planned to visit Rome and wished to be well received, he, by letter, introduced himself and his beliefs as "a called apostle" before actually arriving in Rome. Also, Paul was thinking of the church at Rome as a potential supportive base for his intended missionary journey to Spain. (See 15:24).

Introduction and Greeting

The first seven verses may be said to be the "greeting" of the letter. It begins with the writer's name followed by a comma and a series of appositives defining himself: "Paul, a servant of Jesus Christ, called to be an apostle, separated to the gospel of God which He promised before through His prophets in the Holy Scriptures, concerning His Son Jesus Christ our Lord, who was born of the seed of David according to the flesh, and declared to be the son of God with power, according to the spirit of holiness, by the resurrection from the dead, through whom we have received grace and apostleship for obedience to the faith among all nations for His name" (1:1-5). Then, connecting himself to the recipients of the letter, he writes, "And you are also among those who are the called of Jesus Christ. To all who are in Rome, beloved of God, called to be saints: Grace to you and peace from God our Father and the Lord Jesus Christ" (1:6-7).

Common Interest

Paul congratulates the church saying, "I thank my God through Jesus Christ for you all that your faith is spoken of throughout the world . . . I make mention of you always in my prayers, making request if, by some means, now at last I may find a way in the will of God to come to you. For I long to see you, that I may impart to you some spiritual gift, so that you may be established—that is, that I may be encouraged together with you by the mutual faith both of you and me" (1:8-12). He goes on to say that he had often intended to come to them but had been hindered until now, that he had wanted to have fruit among them as among other Gentiles. Presumably, the church at Rome is primarily Gentile and he wants them to know that his major mission has been ministering to Gentiles.

Since reading Paul's letters is like listening to one side of a telephone conversation, the reader has to fill in through conjecture. So, let us conjecture. Though Paul had probably never been to Rome, no doubt he had met numerous persons from Rome who were Christians or who became Christians (e.g., Aquila and Priscilla) as his personal greeting to numerous persons in chapter sixteen suggests. And surely many of these acquaintances, as well as others, had mentioned Paul and his ministry to the Roman church. As Paul said to Agrippa, "this thing was not done in a corner," meaning the belief in Jesus. We cannot know for sure the feeling of the church at Rome about Paul; again, however, the personal greeting list suggests Paul was revered. And we know for sure that Paul knew about them and was very interested in sharing his ministry with them.

Thematic Concern of the Letter

Paul stresses that the gospel is for everyone, "for the Jew first and also for the Greek [Gentile]. For in it [gospel] the righteousness of God is revealed by faith, from first to last; as it is written, 'The just shall live by faith'" (1:17). In the gospel righteousness depends on faith. One can be righteous in God's sight only through faith.

Unrighteousness and Wrath

Violating the design of the Creator reveals the wrath of God because it suppresses the truth. "For since the creation of the world His invisible attributes are clearly seen, being understood by the things that are made, even His eternal power and Godhead, so that they are without excuse, because although they knew God, they did not glorify Him as God, nor were thankful, but became futile in their thoughts, and their foolish hearts were darkened . . . . Therefore God also gave them up to uncleanness, in the lusts of their hearts, to dishonor their bodies among themselves, who exchanged the truth of God for the lie, and worshiped and served the creature rather than the Creator, who is blessed forever. Amen" (1:20-25).

Consequently, "God gave them up to vile passions," meaning he let sin (actions contrary to His design for humanity) run its course as an act of judgment. As examples, Paul mentions women turning to women sexually and men turning to men sexually, turning from natural relations to unnatural ones, as contrary to God's design and "committing what was shameful, and receiving in themselves the penalty of their error which was due" (1:26-27). Paul continues saying that since they rejected God's design He "gave them over to a debased mind to do those things which are not fitting." Thus they became "filled with all kinds of unrighteousness, sexual immorality, wickedness, covetousness, maliciousness, envy, murder, strife, deceit, evil-mindedness . . . [thus becoming] backbiters, haters of God, violent, proud, boasters, inventors of evil things, disobedient to parents, undiscerning, untrustworthy, unloving, unforgiving, unmerciful" (1:29-31). And in thus defying God, knowing His righteous judgment, become worthy of death, yet continue to defy Him and to approve of others doing likewise. Can one read these passages without thinking of the judgment on Sodom and Gomorrah?

First, Paul spoke of righteousness through faith, how one gives oneself to God through faith and lives righteously, lives within God's design, that is to say, lives obedient to God's design. But to reject God and live by one's own design leads to unrighteousness and inevitably brings wrath and judgment. Since God is the Creator and we are the created, since God is infinite and we are finite, how could we presume not to follow the Creator's grand design? As finite creatures can we hope to know the infinite design. As Paul would say, "certainly not!" Thus, without God's guiding hand we self-destruct.

God's Righteous Judgment

Those who pass judgment on others pass judgment on themselves for at whatever point they judge others they condemn themselves, for they do the same things themselves. And since God's judgment is based on truth, they will not escape His judgment. Furthermore, showing contempt for God's tolerance and patience shows lack of understanding for that which leads to repentance. Stubbornness and a hard heart stores up wrath for the day of God's judgment. For God "will render to each one according to his deeds . . . tribulation and anguish, on every soul of man who does evil, of the Jew first and also of the Greek [Gentile]; but glory, honor, and peace to everyone who works what is good, to the Jew first and also to the Greek. For there is no partiality with God" (2:6-11).

Those who have sinned without the law will perish without the law and those who have sinned within the law will be judged by the law, for not the hearers of the law but the doers of the law will be justified in the sight of God. The Gentiles, not having the law, by nature do the things contained in the law, for "they are a law to themselves, who show the work of the law written in their hearts, their conscience also bearing witness, and between themselves their thoughts accusing or else excusing them in the day when God will judge the secrets of men by Jesus Christ, according to my gospel" (2:12-16).

Paul seems to be addressing these passages primarily to the Jews who generally would not be thinking of themselves among the unrighteous because of the covenant with Abraham and the law of Moses. But Paul makes a special case for the Gentile who without the law had a conscience and through faith could live in a right relationship with the Creator, thereby achieving righteousness. At the same time he warns the Jew that hearing the law is not the criterion for righteousness; the criterion is being a doer of the law whether written on a scroll or written on the heart. God judges according to truth, according to deeds, according to a person's light. It is faith that leads one to righteousness, and how well one lives by that faith is the criterion for judgment.

The Jews and the Law

Speaking from his own experience as a Jew, a self-righteous Pharisee, Paul challenges the Jews. You call yourself a Jew and boast about being God's for you know His will having been instructed out of the law "and are confident that you yourself are a guide to the blind, a light to those who are in darkness, an instructor of the foolish, a teacher of babes, having the form of knowledge and truth in the law," but do you, asks Paul, "teach another, do you not teach yourself? You who preach that a man not steal, do you steal? You who say, 'Do not commit adultery,' do you commit adultery? You who abhor idols, do you rob temples? You who make your boast in the law, do you dishonor God through breaking the law" (2:19-23)? Paul answers these rhetorical questions with Scripture: "The name of God is blasphemed among the Gentiles because of you" (Isa. 52:5).

About circumcision, he says that it is profitable only if you keep the law; if you are breaker of the law your circumcision becomes uncircumcision. And if one uncircumcised keeps the law will not his uncircumcision be counted as circumcision? "And will not the physically uncircumcised, if he fulfills the law, judge you who, even with your written code and circumcision, are a transgressor of the law? For he is not a Jew who is one outwardly, nor is that circumcision which is outward in the flesh; but he is a Jew who is one inwardly, and circumcision is that of the heart, in the Spirit, and not in the letter; whose praise is not from men but from God" (2:27-29).

What Advantage the Jews?

Paul argues that the Jews enjoy advantage "chiefly because to them were committed the oracles of God" (3:2). That some did not believe certainly does not render the faithfulness of God ineffective. God remains true though every one become a liar.

The Law Does not Justify

Then he addresses a real or potentially real heresy through rhetorical question and answer. "But if our unrighteousness demonstrates the righteousness of God, what shall we say? Is God unjust who inflicts wrath? Certainly not! For then how will God judge the world" (3:5-6)? Those who say let us do evil that good may result deserve condemnation. Are Jews better than the Gentiles because of the law? They are not says Paul: "We have already made the charge that Jews and Gentiles are all under sin" (3:9).

Justification through Faith Only

Are the Jews better than the Gentiles? Not at all says Paul. "For we have previously charged both Jews and Gentiles that they are under sin" (3:9). Then he goes on to say, "Now we know that whatever the law says, it says to those who are under the law, that every mouth may be stopped, and all the world may become guilty before God. Therefore by the deeds of the law no flesh will be justified in His sight, for by the law is the knowledge of sin" (3:19-20). The law reveals sin, but the law does not justify.

The righteousness of God apart from the law is revealed, testified to by the Law and the Prophets, the righteousness of God "which is through faith in Jesus Christ to all and on all who believe. For there is no difference; for all have sinned and fall short of the glory of God, being justified freely by His grace through the redemption that is in Christ Jesus, whom God set forth to be a propitiation by his blood, through faith, to demonstrate His righteousness, because in forbearance God had passed over the sins that were previously committed, to demonstrate at the present time His righteousness, that He might be *just* and the *justifier* of the one who has faith in Jesus" (3:22-26).

Thus, no one can boast, for justification comes through faith, apart from deeds of the law, apart from works. And since there is one God, He is God of both the Jews and the Gentiles, and He "will justify the circumcised *by* faith and the uncircumcised *through* faith" (3:30). Then, does faith void the law? Paul says certainly not, it upholds the law.

Romans Poetic Summary One
Paul Introduces Himself

He did not found the church at Rome, probably never been
to Rome, so why a letter to Rome?
Unlike most other of Paul's letters, this letter was not
written to address some specific wrong.
No, this letter is much more general, addressing the broadly
based question of righteousness.
The Jew could not presume because of Abraham and Moses
that he had title to exclusiveness.
The Gentile, though without Covenant and
Commandments, truly had an intuitive moral sense
Guided by the Creator's majesty embedded in his chest,
embedded there serving as recompense.

This matter of righteousness and as it pertained to both
Gentile and Jew, Paul the apostle knew
And he wanted to get the message spread worldwide rather
than merely circulated among a few.
Thus, he looked to Rome the world's great center of endless
commerce and communication
Knowing that a church grounded in this the world's solar
plexus would radiate to every nation.
So Paul by letter introduces himself and his beliefs, as called
apostle, before arriving in Rome
And a superb letter it is for it lays the foundation for Christian
doctrine as perpetually known.

The letter opens with its writer's name first followed by a
series of comma separated appositives
Defining him, "Paul, a servant of Jesus Christ, called to be an
apostle," holding holy perspectives.

Then he connects with the recipients including them among
those called of Jesus Christ saints to be
Congratulating them for their faith spoken of throughout
the world, thereby assigning responsibility
A responsibility that he wishes to share with them assuming
that they can share a mutual theology
An assumption he surely makes judging from the number of
persons greeted by name, some twenty.

Two things Paul wanted stated emphatically: the gospel is
for everyone, Gentile as well as Jew
And God's righteousness is revealed by faith, so says the
gospel and in the Scripture construed.
Paul also wants to address unrighteousness, how it is
offensive to creation thereby creating wrath.
So going back to the beginning he tells how man ignores his
Creator while traveling his own path.
Despite the Creator's righteous attributes, man did not
glorify Him as God, choosing the uncouth.
To violate God's glorious design inevitably elicits His wrath,
for to violate is to suppress the truth.

Since we exchanged the truth of God for the lie, and served
the creature rather than the Creator
The Creator let sin run its course as an act of judgment
allowing perversion of the natural to soar:
Women turning to women and men turning to men, turning
natural relations into unnatural ones
Not only sexually but in all ways, in all ways perverting
God's design to become perdition's sons.
Thus, Paul speaks first of righteousness and then of
unrighteousness defining the basis for the two
And it is unmistakably clear that righteousness and
unrighteousness applies to both Gentile and Jew.

Paul speaks of how one gives oneself to God through faith
and through this faith lives righteously

To reject God and live by one's own design is
unrighteousness that brings on wrath most grievously.
Because God is the Creator His grand design governs all and
any violation is met with wrath sure
God being Creator and infinite and man being created and
finite, how could he presume to abjure?
Thus, Paul makes it abundantly clear that judgment would
inevitably come and come for everyone
And the Jew need not think he was exempt because of having
been circumcised as Abraham's son.

Those who pass judgment on others pass judgment on
themselves, and thus themselves condemn
For they do the same themselves, and God's judgment being
based on truth also applies to them.
And contempt for God's tolerant patience reveals ignorance
for that which leads to repentance.
Hard hearted stubbornness stores up wrath for the day of
God's judgment, day of recompense:
Tribulation and anguish on every soul who chose evil, of the
Jew first and also of the Gentile;
Glory, honor and peace to every soul who chose good, of the
Jew first and also of the Gentile.

Those sinning without the law perish without the law, those
sinning within are judged by the law
For not the hearers of the law, but the doers of the law will
be justified in the eyes of God, yes all.
Gentiles, not having the law, by nature do things contained
therein, thus to themselves a law they
Who show the work of the law written in their hearts, their
conscience bearing witness day by day
Within themselves their thoughts accusing or excusing to be
judged by Jesus Christ, God's way.
Though music to Gentile ear, to the Jewish ear a sour note
sure, this new twist on judgment day.

Knowing the Jew to be thinking of himself as the only
righteous son of Abraham and Moses
Paul makes a case for Gentile righteousness, and thereby
Jewish self-righteousness exposes.
The Gentile though without the law had a conscience and
through faith could connect with God
Receiving righteousness through a right relationship with
the Creator, receiving affirmative nod.
Thus, Paul warns the Jew that righteousness requires being a
doer of the law, knowing is not enough
Faith leads us to righteousness, and how well we live that faith
determines God's judgment tough.

Speaking from his experience as a Jew, a self-righteous
Pharisee, Paul challenges his brethren boldly
Saying they think of themselves as being God's because they
have been instructed out of the law holy
And have become a guide for the blind, a light for those in
darkness, instructors of the foolish folk.
But Paul wants to know, "As you teach others, do you not
teach yourselves? Where is your yoke?
When you preach not to steal, not to commit adultery, do
you steal and commit adultery all the while?
Your boast is the law, but breaking it you dishonor God, who
is then blasphemed among the Gentile.

Circumcision is circumcision only if you keep the law;
otherwise, your circumcision is undone
If the uncircumcised keeps the law will not his
uncircumcision be counted as a circumcised one?
For he is not a Jew who is one outwardly; he is a Jew who is
one inwardly, circumcised of heart.
Circumcision is that of the heart, in the Spirit, not in the
letter. Such, God intended from the start.
The Jews, though misconstruing, enjoy advantage having
been first the oracles of God to receive
That some believed not does not render God's truth ineffective.
God is true though man a liar be.

Seeing a real or potential heresy in the making, Paul attacks
in his oft used analytical way:
"If our unrighteousness demonstrates the righteousness of
God, what then shall we say?
Shall we say God is unjust to inflict wrath on us since it is
our way that reveals His way?
Certainly not! Those who say let us do evil that good may
result deserve condemnation.
Are Jews better than Gentiles because of the law? Not! All
are under sin, all creation.
The law reveals sin, but deeds of the law do not justify; faith
alone brings justification."

Testified to in the Law and Prophets is the righteousness of
God apart from the law, says Paul
And the righteousness of God through faith in Jesus Christ
is for all who will believe, says Paul
For there is no difference, all have sinned and fall short of the
glory of God and need His grace
The redemption that is in Jesus Christ, sent by God to be
propitiation, by His blood sin replace.
God had in his forbearance passed over the sins that were
previously committed to demonstrate
At the present time His righteousness, that He might be the
just and the justifier of those of faith.

Thus, no man can boast, for justification comes through
faith, apart from deeds of the law
And being one God, He is God of both Gentile and Jew, and
justifies by faith, not the law.
He will justify the circumcised *by* faith and the
uncircumcised *through* faith, never the law.
Then, you may say, does faith void the law? Paul says
certainly not, faith upholds the law.

Romans Prose Summary Two
Abraham, Faith, and Righteousness

Righteousness Accounted to Abraham through Faith

First, Paul says that Abraham's faith was apart from works, thus he could not boast before God as Genesis 15:6 affirms, "Abraham believed God, and it was accounted to him for righteousness" (4:3). To him who works wages are not counted as grace but debt, says Paul. "But to him who does not work but believes on Him who justifies the ungodly, his faith is accounted for righteousness just as David [Ps 32:1-2] also describes the blessedness of the man whom God imputes righteousness apart from work: 'Blessed are those whose lawless deeds are forgiven, / And whose sins are covered; / Blessed is the man to whom the Lord shall not impute sin'" (4:5-8).

Second, Paul addresses faith apart from circumcision by asking when righteousness was accounted to Abraham, before or after circumcision. Of course, the answer is before circumcision. "And he received the sign of circumcision, a seal of the righteousness of the faith which he had while still uncircumcised, that he might be the father of all those who believe, though they are uncircumcised, that righteousness might be imputed to them also" (4:11). Thus, faith precedes circumcision and all who believe, the uncircumcised [Gentiles] and the circumcised [Jews], may "walk in the steps of the faith which our father Abraham had while still uncircumcised" (4:12).

Third, Paul addresses faith apart from the law saying that the promise to Abraham that he would be the heir to the world did not come through the law, "but through the righteousness of faith" (4:13). If righteousness came through the law, then faith would be void and of no effect.

Since Abraham's faith was apart from works, apart from circumcision, and apart from the law, it was through faith that righteousness was accounted to him "so that the promise might be sure to all the seed, not only to those who are of the law, but also to those who are of the faith of Abraham, who is father of all of us" (4:16). Against all hope Abraham in hope believed, disregarding his body, already dead at one-hundred years old, and also the deadness of Sarah's womb. "He did not waver at the promise of God through unbelief, but was strengthened in *faith* giving glory to God" (4:20). He was fully convinced and through his faith performed so that righteousness was accounted to him. Let it be noted that this accounting of righteousness was not written for his sake alone, "but also for us. It shall be imputed to us who believe in Him who raised up Jesus our Lord from the dead, who was delivered up because of our offenses, and was raised up for our justification" (4:24-25).

The Wonders of Faith, Hope, and Righteousness

"Having been justified by faith," Paul says, "we have peace through our Lord Jesus Christ through whom also we have access by faith into this grace in which we stand, and rejoice in hope of the glory of God" (5:1-2). Furthermore, "we also glory in tribulations, knowing that tribulation produces perseverance; and perseverance, character; and character, hope" (5:3-4). And hope does not disappoint, for out of love God poured the Holy Spirit into our hearts. And though we were ungodly, He sent His Son who died for us. And we having "now been justified by His blood, we shall be saved from wrath through Him" (5:9). What more could we hope for? Hardly would someone die for a righteous person, but when we were still sinners Christ died for us!

Death through Adam, Life through Jesus

Just as death came through Adam, life comes through Jesus. Through one man sin entered the world, and death through sin, and death spread to all men because all sinned. Though sin was not taken into account when there was not law, death reigned from Adam to Moses, who is a type of Him (Jesus) who was to come. "But the free gift is not like the offense. For if by the one man's offense many died, much more the grace of God and the gift by the grace of the one Man, Jesus Christ, abounded to many" (5:15). The judgment which came through one resulted in condemnation, but the free gift which came from many offenses led to justification. "As by one man's disobedience many were made sinners, so also by one Man's obedience many will be made righteous" (5:19). The law entered that the offense might abound, but where sin abounded grace abounded even more "so that as sin reigned in death, even so grace might reign through righteousness to eternal life through Jesus Christ our Lord" (5:21).

Dead to Sin, Alive in Christ

When we are baptized into Christ Jesus we are baptized into His death meaning we are buried with Him through baptism into death, and just as He was raised from the dead by the glory of the Father, so also are we to walk in newness of life. "For if we have been united together in the likeness of His death, certainly we also shall be in the likeness of His resurrection" (6:5). Christ having been raised from the dead dies no more; death no longer has dominion over Him. "Likewise you also, reckon yourselves to be dead indeed to sin, but alive to God in Christ Jesus our Lord" (6:11). Therefore, sin should not reign in our mortal bodies that we obey it in its lusts. We should present our mortal body to God as an instrument of righteousness. "For sin should not have dominion over you, for you are not under law but under grace" (6:14).

The Wages of Sin

Possibly to head off heresy, Paul asks, "What then? Shall we sin because we are not under the law but under grace" (6:15)? He answers emphatically: "certainly not." Having been set free of sin, we became slaves of righteousness. "Now having been set free from sin, and having become slaves of God, you have your fruit to holiness, the end, everlasting life. For the wages of sin is death, but the gift of God is eternal life in Christ Jesus our Lord" (6:23).

Marriage Metaphor to Explain Sanctification

In explaining the change from living under the law to living under grace, Paul uses a marriage metaphor and begins by saying that as long as one lives that person is bound by law. For example, the woman is bound by the law to her husband as long as he lives, but if the husband dies she is released from the law of her husband and can marry again without becoming an adulteress. Likewise, "my brethren you also have become dead to the law through the body of Christ, that you may be married to another, even to Him who was raised from the dead, that we should bear fruit to God" (7:4). When we were married to the law and under the dominion of sin we bore fruit to death. "But now we have been delivered from the law, having died to what we were held by, so that we should serve in the newness of the Spirit and not in the oldness of the letter" (7:6).

Is the Law Evil? Certainly Not

Paul uses the rhetorical question frequently and effectively. The device, posing a question, gets the reader's attention because we are conditioned to respond upon hearing a question. But in the case of the rhetorical question, the reader is manipulated because the writer intends to answer the question; he poses it only to get the reader's attention while he supplies the answer. Paul often follows the rhetorical question with an emphatic "certainly not" which adds authority to the answer that is then given in greater detail.

In this instance, Paul asks if the law is sin and then answers "certainly not" and goes on to explain saying that he would not have known sin except through the law. For example, he says he would not have known covetousness had not the law said, "You shall not covet." Thus, Paul says, "sin taking opportunity of the commandment produced in me all manner of evil desire. For apart from law, sin was dead" (7:8). It is the law that brings awareness to sin and to its power, its power of death. "Therefore, the law is holy, and the commandment holy and just and good" (7:12).

Struggle between Spirit and Flesh

Paul says, "the good that I will to do, I do not do, but the evil I will not to do, that I practice" (7:19). Then he explains that if he does that which he wills not to do then it is not he doing it but the sin that dwells within him. How can this be? Upon further examination, he finds the law of his members (his flesh) warring against the law of his mind (his spirit) and bringing him into captivity to the law of sin. But he knows the solution to the problem and expresses it dramatically and forcefully in a rhetorical question framework. The question: "O wretched man that I am! Who will deliver me from this body of death?" The answer: "I thank God—through Jesus Christ our Lord! So then with the mind I myself serve the law of God but with the flesh the law of sin" (7:24-25).

Free from the Law of Sin and Death

Paul says, "The law of the Spirit of life in Christ Jesus has made me free from the law of sin and death. For what the law could not do in that it was weak through the flesh, God did by sending His own Son in the likeness of sinful flesh, on account of sin: He condemned sin in the flesh, that the righteous requirement of the law might be fulfilled in us who do not walk according to the flesh but according to the Spirit. For those who live according to the flesh set their minds on the things of the flesh, but those who live according to the Spirit, the things of the Spirit" (8:2-5). Thus, if Christ is in you, the body is dead because of sin, but the Spirit is alive because of Him. And if the Spirit of Him who raised Jesus from the dead dwells in you, then He who raised Christ form the dead will also give you life.

Joint Heirs with Christ

If we live according to the flesh, we are dead, but if we live according to the Spirit we put to death the deeds of the body. "For as many as are led by the Spirit of God, these are sons of God" (8:14). In receiving the Spirit, we receive the Spirit of adoption, and the Spirit bears witness that we are God's children: "and if children, then heirs—heirs of God and joint heirs with Christ, if indeed we suffer with Him, that we may also be glorified together" (8:17).

Hope in the Glory to Come

Our sufferings now are not worthy to be contrasted to our glory to come. Creation awaits in eager expectation for the sons of God to be received because creation itself will be delivered from bondage, creation that groaned when Adam sinned subjecting it to futility also. Paul says "creation itself will be delivered from corruption into glorious liberty of the children of God," and that it "groans and labors with birth pangs" (8:21-22).

In this hope we are saved, but since hope is for something we do not see the Spirit helps us in our weakness for we do not know what we should pray for, "but the Spirit Himself makes intercession for us with groans [that words cannot express] . . . for He who searches the heart knows what the mind of the Spirit is, and He makes intercession for the saints [believers] according to the will of God. And we know that all things work together for good to those who love God, to those who are called according to His purpose" (8:26-28).

"If God is for Us, Who can be Against Us?"

All things work together for good to those who love God because to love God is be attuned to God's design for creation; to love God is to love righteousness. Paul says that those God foreknew "He predestined to be conformed to the image of His Son, that He might be the firstborn among many brethren" (8:29). Does this mean that God elects only certain ones? I think not. I think Paul is emphasizing the surety of faith and righteousness when he says whom God predestines, He calls, and whom He calls, He also justifies, and whom he justifies He also glorifies. Then he underscores it all with a rhetorical crescendo: "What then shall we say to these things? If God is for us, who can be against us" (8:31)?

Still sounding his assurances that those of faith are secure in their hope, Paul says, "He who did not spare His own Son, but delivered Him up for *us all*, how shall He not with Him also freely give us all things?" (8:32). And then, hyperbolically, adds, "For I am persuaded that neither death nor life, nor angels nor principalities nor powers, nor things present nor things to come, nor height nor depth, nor any other thing, shall be able to separate us from the love of God, which is in Christ Jesus our Lord" (8:38-39).

Romans Poetic Summary Two Abraham, Faith, and Righteousness

That righteousness comes through faith not law, Paul points
to Abraham where Scripture asserts
Because Abraham believed God, it was accounted to him for
righteousness: his belief not works.
And lest the Jew insist that circumcision essential to
righteousness, Paul poses the question true
With Abraham, which came first, belief or circumcision?
Faith step one, circumcision step two.
And how long between the promise and the giving of the
Law: promise to Abraham, law to Moses?
Righteousness through faith made Abraham the father of us
all reads the major premise Paul poses.

He did not waiver in unbelief at the promise of God, but
was buoyed by faith giving glory to God.
Abraham in hope believed, though Sarah's womb was dead
and his body too, being a hundred odd.
Through hope and faith our patriarch performed and
thereby righteousness was accounted to him
An accounting not confirmed for his sake alone, but for
everyone, Jew and Gentile, both of them
So that all could know righteousness available through faith,
imputed to anyone who would believe
Believe Jesus our Lord was raised up from the dead, thereby
furnishing sinners their only reprieve.

"Having been justified by faith, we have peace through our
Lord Jesus Christ," says apostle Paul,

"We rejoice in the hope of glory knowing that tribulation
now produces perseverance in saints all
And that perseverance produces character and that character
produces hope which disappoints not
For out of love God pours the Holy Spirit into our hearts
providing guide against old Adam's blot."
Could we ask for more? Not dying for righteous ones, but
for us, sinners all, He laid down His life:
As death came through Adam, so life comes through Jesus,
canceling the sin of old Adam and wife.

Through one man sin entered the world, and death through
sin, and spread to all because all sinned.
Since sin was not taken to account when there was no law,
death reigned from Adam to Moses then
Moses being a type of Him, Jesus Christ, who was to come
bringing His free gift for everyone
And His free gift reverses old Adam's offense, for sin and
death in the face of grace are undone.
The law was not enough; it only sin revealed leaving grace,
by faith, sin and death to overcome.
So as sin reigned in death, grace reigns in righteousness
through Jesus Christ, our beloved One.

When we are baptized into Christ we are baptized into His
death, buried into death with Him
And as He was raised in glory by the Father, so we also will
walk in newness of life with Him
For if we have been united together in the likeness of death,
so also in likeness of His resurrection.
Christ having been raised from the dead dies no more, for
death over Him no longer has dominion.
Likewise for us, we can reckon ourselves dead to sin but alive
to God in Jesus Christ our Lord
For sin no longer has dominion over us, we are not under law
but under the grace of our Lord.

Does that mean then that we can forget sin because we are
not under the law but under grace?
Certainly not, having been set free from sin we become
servants of God and enter a new race
Knowing that the wages of sin is death but the gift of God is
eternal life in Jesus Christ, Savior.
As the woman was bound to her husband under the law, but
upon his death is bound no more
So we have become dead to the law through the body of
Christ, making the future much better.
Having died to what held us, we now serve in newness of
spirit rather than in oldness of letter.

"Then is the law sin?" "Certainly not," answers Paul,
employing again his favorite rhetorical style:
Grab the reader's attention with a question, but answer for
him, hoping he remembers a long while.
How would you have known sin, had there not been
commandments, such as, "You shall not covet" ?
Apart from law sin was dead, but the law revealed all manner
of evil desires and said, "Do not love it."
It is the law that brings awareness to sin and its power of
death; otherwise we would do what we would.
It is the law that exposes old Satan by posting "you shall not"
into commandments holy, just, and good.

"The good that I will to do, I do not do, but the evil I will
not to do, that I practice," Paul sadly confesses.
If he is doing what he wills not to do, then it is not he doing
it but the sin that dwells within and possesses.
Thus, he says the law of his flesh wars against the law of his
spirit making him captive to the law of sin.
Sensing solution to his problem, he expresses it forcefully in
dramatic rhetorical framework, once again:
The rhetorical question posed: "Who will deliver me from
this body of death—I, oh wretched of men?"
Answer: "In my spirit I serve the law of God through our
Lord Jesus Christ, though my flesh seeks sin."

The law of the Spirit of life in Christ Jesus has made me free
from the law of sin and death in the flesh.
What the law could not do being weak through the flesh,
God did by sending His own Son in the flesh
That the righteousness of the law might be fulfilled in us
who walk according to the Spirit, not the flesh
For those who live according to the Spirit set their minds on
the Spirit, and not on the things of the flesh.
Thus, if Christ is in you, the body is dead because of sin, but
the Spirit is alive because of Him
And if the Spirit who raised Jesus dwells in you, then you also
will be given new life by Him.

Receiving the Spirit, we receive the spirit of adoption; we
become the children of God paternally
And thereby joint heirs with Christ to suffer with Him that
we may be glorified together eternally.
Creation awaits the children of God to be received because
creation itself will be bondage loosed.
Creation groaned when Adam sinned subjecting it to futility
also, to be loosed when man is loosed.
Paul says creation itself will be delivered from corruption
into glorious liberty of the children of God
And that it groans and labors with birth pangs in expectation
of the day, the day the Creator will nod.

In this hope we are saved, but since hope is something we do
not see, the Spirit sees to our weakness.
Since we know not what to pray for, He makes intercession
for us with groans words cannot express.
And He who searches the heart knows what the mind of the
Spirit is, and He makes intercession for us
According to God's will, knowing that all things work
together for good for those who love God thus.
All things work together for good because to love God is to
be attuned to His design, to His creation
Paul says that those God foreknew He predestined to be
conformed to the image of Jesus, His relation.

Thus, doing so God makes His Son firstborn among many
brethren all who love God and righteousness.
Does this mean no election no righteousness? I think not. I
think Paul is casting for rhetorical emphasis.
He says, "Whom God predestines, He calls, and whom calls
justifies, and whom justifies glorifies thus."
Then adds the rhetorical crescendo, "What shall we say to
this? If God is for us, who can be against us?"
Still giving assurances that those of faith are secure in their
hope, he again sounds the rhetorical chord
Declaring that nothing imaginable shall be able to separate us
from the love of God, in Christ our Lord.

Thus, Abraham is the epitome of faith, and grace comes
through faith not the law, a later addition
That reveals sin but cannot overcome that which Adam let
in; that is left for Jesus and crucifixion.
The law revealed sin to us but left us under the power of
death, for its letter was hardly enough.
Abraham knew faith before the law and lived by it, but later
the law of Moses became too tough
And its letter got the better of its spirit, and faith got lost
and man became lost to sin and death.
So sin and death to overcome, God sent His Son that
resurrection might restore faith and breath.

Romans Prose Summary Three Jew and Gentile, Salvation and Application

Paul Grieves for His Brethren of the Flesh

In a lyrical outburst, Paul laments the fact that his brethren of the flesh, the Jews, continue, for the most part, to reject Jesus as the promised Messiah. Continual grief weighs on his heart: "For I could wish that I myself were accursed from Christ for my brethren, my kinsmen according to the flesh, who are Israelites, to whom pertain the adoption, the covenants, the giving of the law, the service of God and the promises, of whom are the fathers and from whom according to the flesh, Christ came, who is over all, the eternally blessed God. Amen" (9:3-5).

God's Sovereignty

Paul takes consolation in the reality that God's word has taken some effect saying enigmatically, "they are not all of Israel who are of Israel" (9:6). Explaining, he says, "That is, those who are the children of the flesh [the circumcised], these are not the children of God; but the children of the promise are counted as the seed" (9:8). Those who follow the promise as Abraham followed, whether circumcised or uncircumcised, Jew or Gentile, are the children of God. For, says Paul, "this is the word of the promise: 'At this time I will come and Sarah shall have a son'" (9:9).

Paul explains God's sovereignty as evidenced in the promise to Abraham, saying, "For the children not yet being born, nor having done any good or evil, that the purpose of God according to election might stand, not of works but of Him who calls" (9:11). Continuing, Paul cites God's preference for Jacob over Esau, His telling Moses that He would have mercy on whomever He would, and His informing Pharaoh that He had raised him up that He might show His power in him that His name might be declared throughout the earth. "Therefore," says Paul, "He has mercy on whom He wills, and whom He wills He hardens" (9:18).

It is God's design and it is God who determines how it is to be followed, argues Paul: "Does not the potter have power over the clay, from the same lump to make one vessel for honor and another for dishonor?" (9:21). Paul is making the case for the inclusion of the Gentile into the promise. "What if God," says Paul, "wanting to show His wrath and to make His power known, endured with much longsuffering the vessels of wrath prepared for destruction, and that He might make known the riches of His glory on the vessels of mercy, which He had prepared beforehand for glory, even us whom He called, not of the Jews only, but also of the Gentiles" (9:22-24)? Adding the weight of Scripture, Paul quotes Hosea, "I call them My people, who were not my people," and Isaiah, "Though the number of the children of Israel be as the sand of the sea, [only] the remnant will be saved," and Isaiah again, "Unless the Lord . . . had left us a seed, we would have become like Sodom . . . and Gomorrah" (9:25-29).

Israel Stumbled

Thus, Paul concludes that the Gentiles who did not pursue righteousness have attained it through faith, but Israel who pursued righteousness through the law has not attained it. And they have not because they did not seek it by faith. "For they stumbled at the stumbling stone," says Paul, who then quotes supporting Scripture from Isaiah, "Behold, I lay in Zion a stumbling stone and rock of offense, / And whoever believes on Him will not be put to shame" (9:33).

Salvation through Faith

Paul reiterates that his heart's desire is that Israel will be saved. He says that he can bear witness that they have a zeal for God, "but not according to knowledge. For their being ignorant of God's righteousness, and seeking to establish their own righteousness, have not submitted to the righteousness of God. For Christ is the end of the law for righteousness to everyone who believes" (10: 2-4).

Paul lays out the means of salvation in its simplicity saying, "*If you confess with your mouth the Lord Jesus and believe in your heart that God has raised Him from the dead, you will be saved, for with the heart one believes to righteousness, and with the mouth confession is made to salvation" (10:9-10).* Referencing Isaiah again, Paul says that in the eyes of God there is no distinction between Gentile and Jew, *"for whoever calls upon the name of the Lord shall be saved" (10:13).*

A Remnant of Israel

Salvation is for whoever calls upon the name of the Lord, but Paul is thinking that for the Jews this will be difficult, for "the calling" raises several questions. How can the unknowing know who to call upon? Do they not first need to hear? And how shall they hear without a preacher? Israel had its prophet preachers, many of them, and Isaiah, one of its most noteworthy, said, "Lord, who has believed our report"(10:16). And the Lord Himself said through Isaiah, "All day long I have stretched out My hands / To a disobedient and contrary people" (10:21). But Paul believes God has not given up on the Israelites, and neither has he. "I also am an Israelite, of the seed of Abraham, of the tribe of Benjamin [and] God has not cast away His people whom He foreknew" (11:1-2). He gives the example of Elijah who tells God that his altars have been torn down and his prophets slain and that he is the only righteous one left in Israel. But God informs Elijah that He has preserved for himself seven-thousand men who have not bowed to Baal. Thus, says Paul, "at this present time there is a remnant according to the election of grace" (11:5). And he reasons that though "Israel has not obtained what it seeks . . . the elect have obtained it, and the rest were hardened" (11:7). God has seen to it that a remnant of Israel is saved.

Purpose for Israel's Stumbling

Paul surmises their fall serves two purposes: to extend salvation to the Gentiles, and to provoke the Jews out of jealousy to believe. He hopes that the Gentiles receiving salvation will cause the Jews, out of jealousy, to seek salvation through the same means: through faith in Jesus Christ. And he believes that the Jews are to be credited for the Gentile gain: "Now if their [the Jews] fall is riches for the world, and their failure riches for the Gentiles, how much more their fullness" (11:12)!

Gentiles, Jews, and the Olive Tree Metaphor

Paul emphasizes that he is an apostle to the Gentiles but that he has not given up on the Jews. "I speak to you Gentiles; inasmuch as I am an apostle to the Gentiles, I magnify my ministry, if by any means I may provoke to jealousy those who are my flesh and save some of them. For if their being cast away is the reconciling of the world, what will their acceptance be but life from the dead?" (11:13-15). Then he warns the Gentiles not to boast because they are like branches of a wild olive tree being grafted into a cultivated olive tree and are therefore supported by its trunk and root. "You will say then, 'Branches were broken off that I might be grafted in'" (11:19). They were broken off that you might be attached by faith and you must continue in faith otherwise you too will be cut off. And voicing hope again for his brethren of the flesh, the Jews, he says that "if they do not continue in unbelief, [they] will be grafted in, for God is able to graft them in again. For if you were cut out of the olive tree which is wild by nature, and were grafted contrary to nature into a good olive tree, how much more will these, who are the natural branches, be grafted into their own olive tree?" (11:23-24).

Paul's metaphor sheds light on the relationship of Judaism and Christianity, on the relationship of the Old Testament and the New. Is not Christianity grafted into the trunk of Judaism? Does not the New Testament grow out of the Old?

How Long Israel's Rejection?

Paul believed Israel's rejection of God's Son was temporary and happened so that the Gentiles might receive mercy: "that hardening in part has happened to Israel until the fullness of the Gentiles has come in" (11:25). Thus, eventually "all Israel will be saved, as it is written: 'The Deliverer will come out of Zion, / And He will turn away ungodliness from Jacob; / For this is My covenant with them, / When I take away their sins'" (11:26). Paradoxically, the Jews' rejection saves the Gentiles, but their election makes it possible in the first place, or as Paul says, "Concerning the gospel they [the Jews] are enemies for your sake [Gentiles], but concerning the election they [the Jews] are beloved for the sake of the fathers" (11:28). The Jews are the elected people, the chosen people, the covenant people and through the seed of Abraham came the Messiah as promised.

In a somewhat convoluted argument Paul says that as the Gentiles were once disobedient, but now obtained mercy through Jewish disobedience, so the Jews through the mercy shown the Gentiles may also obtain mercy. "For God has committed them all to disobedience, that He might have mercy on all" (11:32). Paul acknowledges his assessment is based heavily on hope saying, "For who has known the mind of the Lord?" (11:34). Yet he is consoled by faith: "For of Him and through Him and to Him are all things, to whom be glory forever. Amen" (11:36).

Application of Righteousness:

Yourself

Paul now turns to application exhorting his brothers in Christ to "present your bodies a living sacrifice, holy, acceptable to God, which is your reasonable service" (12:1). Do not be conformed by the world, but live in the world conformed by God. Ideally, in a righteous relationship with God, one's body becomes a temple of the Holy Spirit for transforming the world.

Your Gifts

Speaking directly to the church at Rome, Paul exhorts each believer not to think of himself too highly for "God has dealt each one a measure of faith" and different persons serve different purposes as the different members of one's body serves different purposes, but all for the good of the total body. So the body of Christ, the Church, has individual members serving different purposes depending on their individual gifts which differ "according to the grace that is given to us" (12:6). Therefore, it is important that our individual gifts be used in the service of the whole body, the body of Christ. If our gift is prophecy, we prophesy; if our gift is ministering, we minister; teaching, we teach; exhorting, we exhort. Thereby, each of us serves an essential role in the function of the church.

Your Attitudes and Actions

Be kind and affectionate to one another. Be diligent and longsuffering. Rejoice in hope, patient in tribulation; and always prayerful. Do not curse those who persecute you, but bless them. "Do not be wise in your own opinion" (12:1). Strive to live peacefully with all persons. Do not resort to vengeance, punishment belongs to God. In summary, "Do not be overcome by evil, but overcome evil with good" (12:21).

Attitude toward Government

Paul counsels submission to the civil governing authorities for he sees them as God's appointees. This is consistent with his view of God's sovereignty in all things. And believing thus would allow for seemingly evil government which could be God's will in the scheme of things. Think of Jeremiah counseling Judah to bear the yoke of Nebuchadnezzar for it was God's will. "For rulers are not a terror to good works, but to evil," says Paul (13:3). Therefore, give them their due: "taxes to whom taxes are due, customs to whom customs, fear to whom fear, honor to whom honor" (13:7).

Love Your Neighbor as Yourself

Paul gives further guidance by focusing on love. He says that the commandments governing human relationships are summed up in the saying, "You shall love your neighbor as yourself" (13:9). And to this he adds, "Let us walk properly, as in the day, not in revelry and drunkenness, not in licentiousness and lewdness, not in strife and envy, but put on the Lord Jesus Christ, and make no provision for the flesh, to fulfill its lusts" (13:13-14).

Romans Poetic Summary Three
Jew and Gentile, Salvation and Application

Though zealous in his role as apostle to the Gentiles, Paul grieves for his brethren of the flesh
The Jews who, beginning with the Sanhedrin, have generally rejected the story of the crèche
Yet Paul believes Jewish unbelief purpose driven, and in a peculiar way, driven by God's hand.
How could it be otherwise since these Israelites are God's adopted from all others of the land?
They live under promise, under covenant, under law; both Abraham and Moses they can claim.
Furthermore, is it not from their fathers, according to the flesh, that the promised Christ came?

So Paul lives in hope his brethren of the flesh, fellow Jews, will some day some way reprieve
Lamenting he would gladly take on their accursedness if doing so would their situation relieve.
Simultaneously though, Paul takes consolation that God's word has taken some effect even so
Saying "they are not all of Israel who are of Israel," meaning it is the unlikely ones who know,
Meaning those who are the children of the flesh, the circumcised, are not the children of God,
Meaning those who follow the promise, uncircumcised or circumcised, are the children of God.

Concerning Abraham's sons, Paul finds explanation in the sovereignty of God phenomenon

The apostle sees God's sovereignty implicit in the promise to
Abraham and his sons to come.
The problem came when later sons would lose the promise
while with the law preoccupied
Not noting that the promise came to Abraham centuries
before Moses was the law supplied
Not quite grasping that faith came first bringing
righteousness and the law later as the guide
Not remembering that God passed over Esau for Jacob, the
elder brother He would not abide.

Nor remembering that Pharaoh was told he had been raised
up to magnify the Lord worldwide.
"Thus," says Paul, "the Lord has mercy on whom He wills
and wills to harden those denied."
Since Creation is God's design is it not imperative that He
determine its purpose and its way?
May not God have hardened the hearts of the Jews their
having forgot the promise, their stay
And have shown mercy to the Gentiles, thus challenging the
chosen ones in their apostasy?
Does not the uncircumcised receiving righteousness mean to
magnify God in all His mercy?

Paul concludes that the Gentiles who did not pursue
righteousness have through faith attained it
Yet the sons of circumcision who insist righteousness comes
through the law have not attained it.
They stumbled at the stumbling stone and rock of offense
that lay in Zion as Scripture foretold
For seeking to establish their own righteousness they
removed themselves from the Lord's fold.
Stubbornly, they deny Christ and always declare the law,
their own, to be the rock of righteousness
And their denial accounts great grief to Paul who so saliently
searches the Scripture to disprove this.

Putting his grief on hold, Paul preached the means of
salvation to the Gentiles, and to them he said,
"Confess with your mouth Lord Jesus and believe in your
heart that God raised Him from the dead
And you will be saved: if your heart believes and your mouth
confesses, salvation is sure for you
For whoever calls upon the name of the Lord shall be saved,
forget the distinction, Gentile or Jew.
But ere long Paul is again agonizing over the Jews' ever
blindness to what seems so self-evident.

"All day long I have stretched My hands to a disobedient and
contrary people," the Lord bemoaned
And Isaiah recorded, but Paul refuses to believe that God
has given up on His people, despite wrong.
"I also am an Israelite, of the seed of Abraham, of the tribe
of Benjamin, so God has not cast all away
All His people whom He foreknew," reasons Paul as he
delves for answers to this agonizing mystery.
For solace he thinks of Elijah who tells God, "all altars
burned, all priests slain, I alone remain alive
In all of Israel, one righteous man," only to learn that God had
caused a significant number to survive.

God had saved seven-thousand for Himself, seven thousand
men who had not bended knee to Baal
So, Paul presumes, at the present time there is a remnant
according to the election of grace in Israel.
Though Israel has not it obtained, the elect have obtained,
and the rest were hardened in their unbelief.
But in it all there is surely a Providential plan, Israel's
stumble surely a sign for the dark world's relief?
To extend salvation to the Gentile and that in turn provoke
the Jew, out of jealousy, to seek grace too?
Will not their fall credit to them accrue, great gain going to
the Gentile, thus greater fullness to the Jew?

Paul could not fathom his brethren lacking rescue, certainly
not God's chosen and covenanted too!
Thus, his mind reasonably reconciled concerning the destiny
of the Jew, he focuses on Gentile review:
"I speak to you Gentiles; inasmuch as I am an apostle to the
Gentiles, I magnify my ministry true
If by any means I may provoke to jealousy those who are my
flesh and thus save some of them too.
For if their being cast away is the reconciling of the world,
what will their acceptance be? I say,
It will be but life from the dead!" Thus pacified, Paul prescribes
to the Gentiles their role to play:

"Take care, Gentiles, not to boast, for you are like branches
of the wild olive grafted in
Into the trunk of the cultivated tree and therefore supported
by its trunk and root then.
If you say that branches were broken off that you might be
grafted in, then well said
For because of unbelief they were broken off, and you stand
by faith, no longer dead
Yet be not haughty, humbly keep in mind that God the
natural branches did not spare!
Does this not speak of severity for disobedience? One thing
only—faith—can it impair."

"They were broken off that you might be attached by faith,
and in faith must continue you
Lest you are cut off too," Paul cautions the Gentile before
again turning to his brother Jew.
Voicing hope for his brethren of the flesh, he surmises that if
they do not in unbelief continue
They can be grafted in again, for God is able to graft them
in, and why would that He not do?
Were not the Gentiles, the wild olive branches, grafted
expertly into the cultivated tree, unnaturally?
Why can not then the Jews, the natural branches, be again
grafted into their own olive tree, naturally?

And does not Paul's tree grafting metaphor magnify what
the Judeo/Christian relationship is about?
Think of Christianity grafted into Judaism's trunk, and of
the Old trunk nourishing the New sprout.
Metaphor can imaginatively transform reams of theology
into one compact and graphic image
And magically make the abstract concrete, the abstruse clear,
and the bulging book into a page.
Yes, the remarkable apostle Paul, apostle to the Gentiles,
knew how to wield a figure of speech
Letter after letter reveals a master rhetorician using his gift to
bridge the ever occurring breach.

Sometimes it seems that Paul conjectures a little much
concerning the destiny of his flesh brethren
Though understandable his obsession since prior to
Damascus a persecuting Pharisee he had been
But after that eye-opening Light set his righteousness right,
an obsessed apostle he had become
Finding the Gentile generally receptive but his beloved
brethren of the flesh enemy number one.
Nevertheless, he preaches salvation to them endlessly never
failing to respect their customs true
And never slacking in his salient search for assurance that the
Jew will in the end find faith too.

Paul conjectures Israel's rejection of God's Son a temporary
thing that the Gentile might mercy gain
And that the hardening of Israel's heart has happened until
fullness of mercy the Gentile has attained.
Eventually "all Israel will be saved," says God, "when I take
away their sins their recovery ensues."
Paradoxically, Gentiles, once disobedient, have mercy
attained through the disobedience of the Jews
But God would not turn His face eternally from His elected
people, His chosen and covenanted ones
Concludes Paul, consoled by faith that through God salvation
to his brethren of the flesh surely comes.

Through conjecture convoluted, Paul concludes, as the
Gentiles, once disobedient, now mercy obtain
Through Jewish disobedience, so the Jews through the mercy
shown the Gentiles may also mercy gain
For God has committed them all to disobedience, that He
might have mercy on them all, all one accord.
Acknowledging this assessment a theology of hope, he says,
"For who has known the mind of the Lord?
For of Him and through Him and to Him are all things, to
whom be glory forever. Amen."
Thus, scouring Scripture of old, Paul finds hope, and in hope
faith, and is consoled again.

Consoled that his brothers of the flesh are redeemable, he
returns to his brothers in Christ for review
And exhorts them to righteousness: their bodies committed
as living sacrifices to God, service due.
They must not be conformed by the world, but live in the
world conformed by God: this, their venue.
Living righteously one's body becomes a temple of the Holy
Spirit for transforming the world anew.
And one does not live apart in righteousness, but functions
as part of a whole, as part of the one body.
Thus, of oneself no believer thinks too highly, for how could
the one part ever presume to be haughty?

So the body of Christ, the Church, has individual members
serving different purposes according to gift
Thus, individuals are given different gifts according to grace,
and according to grace work without rift.
If the gift be preaching, preach; if it be prophecy, prophesy; if
it be teaching, teach; thus, our lives.
Thereby, each gift an essential function serves in the body of
Christ, the Church, and so it thrives.
It thrives in affection to one another, in patience with
tribulation, and in a perpetual attitude of prayer.
And essential to remember is that retribution belongs to God,
for only God perceives the everywhere.

In civil government, Paul views ruling authorities to be God's
appointees, thus counsels submission.
Not surprising knowing the apostle's belief in God's
sovereignty in all things, in all things His vision.
And believing thus allows for evil government being God's
will in the scheme of things extended.
Think of Jeremiah as he counsels Judah to bear the yoke of
Nebuchadnezzar, for God so demanded.
"Rulers are not a terror to good works, but to evil," says Paul,
"so give them their due:
Taxes to whom taxes are due, fear to whom fear is due, and
honor to whom honor due."

But the most important ingredient of all is love cautions
Paul, for only love conquers all.
Thus, the commandment governing human relationships
can be summed up in one call,
"You shall love your neighbor as yourself." Still there are
specifics that concern Paul:
Avoid revelry and drunkenness and licentiousness and
lewdness, acts of the flesh all.
Believers must put on the Lord Jesus Christ, making no
provision for the flesh at all.
Love neighbor as self and shun the lusts of flesh sum up Paul's
prescribed protocol.

Romans Prose Summary Four
Ideal Relationships and Closing Remarks

Judge Not One Another

Paul, concerned about contention over debatable issues, counsels believers to exercise utmost discretion and compassion in their relationships with one another. One problem for Jews newly converted was the traditional dietary laws. The Jewish view and the Christian view about clean (pure) and unclean (impure) differed. Jesus seemingly laid the groundwork for setting aside the Leviticus tradition of clean and unclean food when responding to the Pharisee and scribe charge that His disciples had broken the tradition of the elders by not washing their hands before eating: "Listen and understand. What goes into a man's mouth does not make him unclean, but what comes out of his mouth, that is what makes him unclean" (Lev 11; Mat 15:10-11). Peter's housetop vision also seems to set aside the Leviticus tradition of clean and unclean animals. He sees heaven open and a large sheet being let down to earth containing "all kinds of four-footed animals, as well as reptiles of the earth and birds of the air." When a voice instructs him to kill and eat, he replies that he has never eaten anything "impure or unclean." The voice then rebukes him saying, "Do not call anything impure that God has made clean" (Acts 10:9-15).

Though the Gentile convert would be free of the Jewish dietary tradition, he too might feel strongly about eating meat that had been sacrificed to an idol. Thus, Paul's advice is for each believer to take great care not to offend another's belief about such debatable things. Christian fellowship does not depend on everyone's agreement on disputable matters such as dietary traditions, the keeping of the Sabbath, and other special days. Paul says a person is not to be judged and condemned on these debatable issues:

"Receive one who is weak in the faith, but not to disputes over doubtful things" (14:1). Presumably, Paul thinks of those who need certain rituals to bolster their faith as being weak in faith and counsels the strong in faith not to demean their weaker brethren or dispute with them. "Let not him who eats despise him who does not eat, and let not him who does not eat judge him who eats; for God has received him. Who are we to judge another's servant? To his own master he stands or falls. Indeed, he will be made to stand, for God is able to make him stand" (14:3-4).

Paul goes on to say that he who eats, eats to the Lord, for he gives thanks to the Lord, and that he who does not eat, to the Lord does not eat, and gives thanks to the Lord. Thus, who is one believer to judge and to show contempt toward another believer. "For we shall all stand before the judgment seat of Christ" (14:10).

Cause Not One Another to Stumble

Paul says we should neither judge nor put a stumbling block in our brother's way. "I know and am convinced that there is nothing unclean of itself, but to him who considers anything to be unclean, to him it is unclean," says Paul. "Yet if your brother is grieved because of your food, you are no longer walking in love. Do not destroy with your food the one for whom Christ died" (14:14-15). Though all things are pure, it is evil for a person who eats with offense. It is not good to eat meat or to drink wine or to do anything which causes a stumbling block for your brother. "Happy is he who does not condemn himself in what he approves," says Paul. The kingdom of God is not meat and drink and food, but "righteousness and peace and joy in the Holy Spirit" (14:17).

Imitate Christ

Each should consider the edification of his neighbor as opposed to pleasing self. "May the God of patience and comfort grant you to be like-minded toward one another, according to Christ Jesus," declares Paul (15:5). And as example, he notes "that Jesus Christ has become a servant to the circumcision for the truth of God, to confirm the promises made to the fathers, and that the Gentiles might glorify God for His mercy" (15:8-9).

Personal Messages to the Church in Rome

Paul tells them he is confident they are full of goodness and complete in knowledge and thus able to instruct one another, but that he has written to them quite boldly on some points so as to remind them "because of the grace God gave me to be a minister of Christ Jesus to the Gentiles with the priestly duty of proclaiming the gospel of God, so that the Gentiles might become an offering acceptable to God, sanctified by the Holy Spirit" (15:15-16).

Becoming more personal, Paul declares that he will not venture more than what Christ has accomplished through him in leading the Gentiles to God. He says that the Holy Spirit has led him from Jerusalem to Illyricum proclaiming the gospel of Christ, and adds that it has always been his desire to preach the gospel where it was not known so that he would not be building on a foundation laid by others.

Having awakened the eastern portion of the Roman Empire to the gospel of Jesus Christ, he now longs to awaken the western portion, wishing to travel to Spain to preach the gospel there. Furthermore, he hopes the church at Rome will serve as his operational base in his proposed ministry in Spain. He writes, "Now, no longer having a place in these parts [the eastern region], and having a great desire these many years to come to you, whenever I journey to Spain, I shall come to you. For I hope to see you on my journey, and to be helped on my way there by you, if first I may enjoy your company for a while" (15: 23-24).

But first, Paul tells them that he must go to Jerusalem to minister to the saints there, that he is carrying a contribution from Macedonia and Achaia for the poor among the saints in Jerusalem. Paul is very pleased about the contribution because of the spirit in which it was given. "It pleased them indeed and they are their debtors. For if the Gentiles have been partakers of their spiritual things, their duty is also to minister to them in material things," says Paul (15:27). Realizing the danger he faces in Jerusalem because of Jewish animosity toward him, Paul asks the church at Rome for their prayers "that I may be delivered from those in Judea who do not believe, and that my service for Jerusalem may be acceptable to the saints" (15:31). We know, of course, that Paul is arrested in Jerusalem and, to escape death at the hands of the Jews, appeals to Caesar and arrives at Rome in chains.

Personal Greetings

Paul first commends one named Phoebe, "a servant of the church in Cenchrea," and presumably the one delivering his letter to the church at Rome. Then he sends greetings to friends and relatives, twenty-four persons in all, eighteen men and six women, presumably all associated with the church there. Among these are the couple Priscilla and Aquila, fellow tent makers who had labored with Paul in Corinth.

Admonition and Benediction

Paul admonishes the brethren at Rome to beware of those who cause division and put obstacles in the way contrary to the doctrine which they have learned. Stay away from them, he says, for they are not serving our Lord Jesus Christ; they are serving themselves. Through smooth talk and flattery, they deceive the naïve. Everyone has heard of your obedience; "therefore, I am glad on your behalf; but I want you to be wise in what is good" (16:19).

Besides his own greetings to the church in Rome, Paul includes greetings from a few others: "Timothy, my fellow worker, and Lucius, Jason, and Sosipater, my kinsmen, greet you" (16:21).

And Tertius, Paul's stenographer, also sends greetings: "I, Tertius, who wrote down this epistle, greet you in the Lord" (16:22).

Paul ends the letter with the benediction: "To God, alone wise, be glory through Jesus Christ forever. Amen" (16:27).

Romans Poetic Summary Four Ideal Relationships and Closing Remarks

Fearing contention resulting from debatable issues, Paul
cautions believers exercise discretion
Compassion and concern for each other should always
triumph any prescribed dietary selection.
Such things as what to eat and what not to eat, what is clean
and what is not clean, leave unsaid.
All those traditional intricate distinctions the Lord Jesus
seems so solemnly to have put to bed
Saying, "*what goes into a man's mouth does not make him
unclean, it is that which comes out!*"
And is not the folly of trivial ritualistic quibbling mainly what
Peter's housetop vision is about?

Though free of Jewish dietary tradition, the Gentile might
be repelled by meat to an idol slain
And so, Paul advises each believer take great care not to
offend another over a debatable thing.
If one eats meat to please God, how can we say that God is
not pleased? Can we really know?
If one abstains from meat to please God, can we say God is
not pleased? Can we really know?
If we abuse him who eats meat because he eats meat, God
will not be pleased with us for sure.
And if we abuse him who abstains because he does so, God
will not be pleased with us for sure.

So, let us use discretion, let us always place compassion
ahead of debatable doctrinal actions

Christian fellowship is not synonymous with dietary
traditions or Sabbath keeping restrictions.
A person is not to be judged and condemned on such
debatable issues Paul will repeat,
"Who is one believer to judge another, for we shall all stand
before the Judgment seat."
Therefore, we should neither judge nor put a stumbling
block in our brother believer's way
Though we are convinced there is nothing unclean of itself, is
it imperative that we so say?

No, if it offends your brother who believes contrary to you:
that there are things unclean
And your eating certain foods gives him grief, for then where
is your love, can it be seen?
"It is not good to eat meat or to drink wine," says Paul, "or in
any way a stumbling block become.
Happy is he who does not condemn himself in what he approves;
happy the compassionate one."
God's kingdom is not meat and drink and food, but
righteousness and peace and joy in the Spirit.
It is not the pleasing of oneself but the compassion for one's
neighbor that elicits heavenly merit.
"Be like-minded to one another, according to Christ Jesus,
our Lord," says Paul, summarizing it.

Becoming personal, Paul assures his brethren at Rome that
he is confident of their goodness
Also that he is confident of their knowledge and ability to
instruct one another and to confess.
Yet he has written to them quite boldly on certain points so
as to remind them of his call
Through the grace of God he has been given the mission of
ministering to the Gentile, all.
He has been given the priestly duty of proclaiming God's
gospel to the Gentile host
That they might become an offering acceptable to God,
sanctified by the Holy Ghost.

Paul says that he traveled from Jerusalem to Illyricum as the
Holy Spirit led him to do
Adding that his own desire had been to preach the gospel in
places where it was new
For in doing so he could, guided by the Holy Spirit, lay a
foundation sound and true.
And having labored bountifully in the Empire east he now
longed to labor in its west
In the region Spain, and lest he preached the gospel there his
own spirit would not rest
Yet in this matter the church at Rome could assist, and thus
Paul puts forth his request:

"Now, no longer having a place in these parts, I turn to the
west to there a journey proclaim
And having a great desire these many years to come to you, I
shall do so on my way to Spain.
Not only do I hope to see you on my way to Spain but to be
helped on my way there by you
If first I may enjoy your company awhile," says Paul,
revealing truly what he desires to do.
But first he must go to Jerusalem to minister to the saints
there and to deliver a contribution
From Macedonia and Achaia lovingly sent, sent to the poor
among the saints for distribution.

Paul is most pleased about the contribution, the spirit in
which it was given, the retribution done.
Jerusalem sent them a spiritual gift, the Gentiles in loving
spirit returned to them a material one:
"Gentiles partakers of their spiritual things dutifully
minister to them in material things," says Paul.
But to many Jews, Paul's laboring to reconcile the Jew the
Gentile and the Way was labor to appall
And delivering the gift from Macedonia to the needy saints
in Jerusalem put Paul in dire jeopardy.
Attacked by Jewish mob and by the Sanhedrin charged, he is
forced to appeal to Caesar for safety.

And so he will eventually get to Rome, but not on his way to
Spain as had long been his plan
Nor will the church at Rome be able to assist him in
preaching the gospel to this western land.
While writing his letter to the Romans, Paul cannot know
what awaits him in Jewish Jerusalem
Yet before heading for Spain he must complete his promised
Jerusalem mission, a perilous one.
And perilous it is, sending Paul to Rome a prisoner rather
than free missionary headed for Spain
Yet this indomitable apostle persists in preaching the gospel
whether free or imprisoned by chain.

Though his visit to the church in Rome does not materialize,
his letter to them is eternalized
And, like Caesar Augustus' decree, goes out to all the world,
thereby the gospel recognized.
Perhaps it is not by chance that all roads led to Rome and
that Paul was led there to stay
Be that as it may, most of what Paul said to the Romans is
still pertinent to this very day.
Even the personal statements he includes as he brings his
letter to a close echo universally
Like warning his brethren beware of those who cause division
by deviating from the Way.

"Stay away from them, for rather than serving our Lord Jesus
Christ, themselves they serve.
Now, I have heard of your obedience and am glad; obedience
will always wisdom preserve."
And with that admonition Paul ends his letter to the
Romans except for a greeting addendum
Completing his reflective theological epistle designated to be
delivered by a commended one
A woman named Phoebe, "a servant of the church in
Cenchrea," and perhaps known in Rome.
Known or no, she carries a letter laden with theology and a
plethora of greetings for the known.

Greetings are sent to friends and relatives, twenty-four
persons total, six women and eighteen men.
Among familiar names are Priscilla and Aquila, fellow tent
makers, who in Corinth Paul befriend.
Besides his own greetings, Paul includes greetings from
others: Timothy, his fellow worker,
And Lucius, Jason, and Sosipater, his kinsmen, send
greetings, also Tertius, his stenographer.
Benediction follows greetings and renders Paul's letter to the
Romans ready for Phoebe's hand.
For closure, Paul prays, "To God, alone wise, be glory through
Jesus Christ forever. Amen."

I Corinthians Prose
Summary One
Divisions, Causes, Solutions

Difficulties in Reading the New Testament Letters

Reading the letters of the New Testament is a challenging exercise, for the reader is primarily privy to only one side of the communication thus often making it difficult to discern what precipitated the letter under consideration. For instance, as we read I Corinthians, we learn that Paul had written a letter to the Corinthians (5:9) previous to the I Corinthians letter which is a response to messengers from the household of Chloe (1:11) and to a letter sent him by the Church at Corinth (7:1). The "previous letter" is generally believed to be lost although some scholars believe the previous letter to be contained in II Corinthians (6:14-7:1). Whatever the case, Paul's response to the messengers from the household of Chloe and the letter from the Church at Corinth is called I Corinthians, a letter probably delivered by Timothy (4:17).

Apparently, the result of Paul's response, I Corinthians, was that things got worse thus prompting him to pay a personal visit (II Co 12:14). Presumably, the visit did not assuage matters and Paul then wrote a "severe letter" (II Co 2:4, 7:8). Some scholars believe the severe letter to be chapters 10-13 of II Corinthians.

Scholars defending their conjectures concerning the "previous letter" and the "severe letter" point out the difficulty of collecting and ordering the Corinthian letters because of the passage of time between their having been written and their collection and of their being on various scraps of papyrus making their exact order difficult to ascertain. Keep in mind that books of the bible being divided into chapters and verses is a much later development, not completed until the sixteenth century.

The City of Corinth

Located adjacent to the narrow Corinthian isthmus between the Aegean and the Adriatic Seas, the city of Corinth was a crossroads for trade and travel. To avoid the dangerous trip around the southern tip of Greece, ships going west from the Aegean or east from the Adriatic were hauled across the narrow isthmus. Corinth was known for its wealth, its diversity, and its immorality. Most notable perhaps was the Temple of Aphrodite, goddess of love, with its 1,000 sacred prostitutes.

Paul in Corinth

Arriving in Corinth on his second missionary journey, Paul remains some eighteen months, staying and working with Aquila and Priscilla, and preaching first in the synagogue. Being forced out of the synagogue, he moves next door to the house of Titus Justus and continues preaching, the result being the Church at Corinth. We know that Paul wrote I Corinthians (16:8) while in Ephesus, a city in which he labored some three years.

The Letter's Format

This letter follows the general format of Paul's letters: the salutation followed by a prayer of thanksgiving; then the special content of the letter, and ending with personal greetings and benediction.

The Salutation

"Paul, called to be an apostle of Jesus Christ through the will of God . . . to the Church of God which is at Corinth, to those who are sanctified in Christ Jesus, called to be saints, with all who in every place call on the name of Jesus Christ our Lord, both theirs and ours: Grace to you and peace from God our Father and the Lord Jesus Christ" (1:1-3).

The Prayer of Thanksgiving

"I thank my God always concerning you for the grace of God which was given to you by Christ Jesus, that you were enriched in everything by Him in all utterance and all knowledge . . . God is faithful, by whom you were called into the fellowship of His Son, Jesus Christ our Lord" (1:4-9).

Content Concerning Divisions

Paul pleads with his brethren at Corinth "that there be no divisions among you, but that you be perfectly joined together in the same mind and in the same judgment" (1:10), for he has been informed by "those of Chloe's household, that there are contentions among you" (1:11).

Divisions Concerning Allegiance

Paul learns that there are divisions according to misconceived allegiance. One may say "I am of Paul," another may say "I am of Apollos," another "I am of Cephas," or still another "I am of Christ" (1:12). Paul responds with rhetorical questions intended to reveal to them their misguided perceptions: "Is Christ divided? Was Paul crucified for you? Or were you baptized in the name of Paul" (1:13)? He follows up by saying that "Christ did not send me to baptize, but to preach the gospel, not with wisdom of words, lest the cross of Christ should be made of no effect" (1:17). Paul explains that it is not through wisdom that we come to know God, it is not through wisdom that we are saved, we are saved only through believing in Jesus Christ crucified. "Jews request a sign, and Greeks seek after wisdom; but we preach Christ crucified, to the Jews a stumbling block and to the Greeks foolishness, but to those who are called, both Jews and Greeks, Christ the power of God and the wisdom of God" (1:22-24).

In further explanation Paul says that "God has chosen the foolish things of the world to put to shame the wise and God has chosen the weak things of the world to put to shame the things which are mighty . . . and that no flesh should glory in His presence. But of Him you are in Christ Jesus, who became for us wisdom from God—and righteousness and sanctification and redemption—that as it is written, 'He who glories, let him glory in the Lord'" (1:27-31).

Paul Emphasizes Message over Medium

Paul explains that when he came to them he came not "with excellence of speech or of wisdom declaring to you the testimony of God. For I determined not to know anything among you except Jesus Christ and Him crucified . . . And my speech and my preaching were not with persuasive words of human wisdom, but in demonstration of the Spirit and of power, that your faith should not be in the wisdom of men but in the power of God" (2:1-5).

God's Wisdom Revealed through the Spirit

Paul makes it abundantly clear that the wisdom he speaks of is not the wisdom of the age, nor the wisdom of the rulers of this age, but "the wisdom of God in a mystery, the hidden wisdom which God ordained before the ages for our glory" (2:7). And that wisdom comes through the Spirit, for "no one knows the things of God except the Spirit of God" (2:11). And the natural man (the non-believer) "does not receive the things of the Spirit of God . . . because they are spiritually discerned" (2:14), but "we (the believer) have the mind of Christ" (2:16).

Spiritual Growth Stunted by Division

Through metaphor Paul assesses their situation saying that when he came to them he could not address them as spiritual ones but as carnal ones, as babes in Christ. He had to milk feed them, and sadly they are still carnal because of the envy, strife, and divisions among them. Paul asks, when one says "I am of Paul," and another says "I am of Apollos," are you not carnal? Who are Paul and Apollos but ministers through whom you believed? "I planted, Apollos watered, but God gave the increase" (3:7). Thus, neither he who plants nor he who waters is anything, but God who gives the increase. "He who plants and he who waters are one, and each one will receive his own reward according to his labor, for we are God's fellow workers; you are God's field, you are God's building" (3:8-9).

Loss and Rewards

Paul says that God's grace made him a wise master builder and no other foundation could anyone lay "than that which is laid, which is Jesus Christ" (3:11). Those who build on this foundation their works will be tested by fire and if one's work endures that one will be rewarded; if one's work is burned, that one will suffer loss, but will be saved. Salvation is a free gift but rewards for those who are saved are earned.

As a Temple of God, You are Sacred

"Do you not know," says Paul, "that you are the temple of God and that the Spirit of God dwells in you? If anyone defiles the temple of God, God will destroy him. For the temple of God is holy, which temple you are" (3:16-17).

True Wisdom Comes from God

Paul says "the wisdom of this world is foolishness with God. For it is written . . . 'The Lord knows the thoughts of the wise that they are futile.' Therefore let no one glory in men. For all things are yours: whether Paul or Apollos or Cephas, or the world or life or death, or things present or things to come—all are yours. And you are Christ's, and Christ is God's" (3:19-23).

Paul as Example

Paul cautions the Corinthians about being "puffed up on behalf of one against another. For what makes you differ from another? And what do you have that you did not receive" (4:6-7)? Then in barbed irony, he contrasts the imagined exaltation of the Corinthians with the degradation of the apostles. "We are fools for Christ's sake, but you are wise in Christ! We are weak, but you are strong! You are distinguished, but we are dishonored! Even to the present hour we both hunger and thirst, and we are poorly clothed, and beaten, and homeless. And we labor, working with our own hands. Being reviled, we bless; being persecuted, we endure it; being defamed we entreat. We have been made as the filth of the world, the offscouring of all things until now. I do not write these things to shame you, but as my beloved children I warn you" (4:10-14).

Next, Paul tells them that though they may have many instructors, they have only one spiritual father, himself. "For though you might have ten thousand instructors in Christ, yet you do not have many fathers; for in Christ Jesus I have begotten you through the gospel. Therefore, I urge you, imitate me" (4:15-16).

He further informs them that he is sending Timothy, his beloved and faithful son in the Lord to remind them of "my ways in Christ, as I teach everywhere in every church" (4:17). He also informs them that he will come soon himself if the Lord wills it, and asks, "Shall I come to you with a rod, or in love and a spirit of gentleness?" (4:21).

I Corinthians Poetic Summary One Divisions, Causes, Solutions

Paul to Corinth came on his missionary journey second, and eighteen months remained,
Remained in this ancient city, crossroads of trade and travel of acquired infamous name.
All the world knew of Aphrodite's temple and its thousand priestesses, each a prostitute
Helping foster immorality to the point that to be Corinthian became a mark of ill repute.
Here Paul preached, first in the synagogue and later in the house adjacent owned by Justus
Living and laboring with Aquila and Priscilla, he preached with persistence and great gust.

Leaving the infant church at Corinth, Paul moved on to Ephesus the gospel there to spread.
All too soon bad news comes from Corinth, messengers from Chloe's household, it's said.
And in a letter too comes more unwelcome news that spurs Paul's response: I Corinthians
Though not the first according to chapter five of verse nine of this so called I Corinthians
Where Paul mentions previously writing them about their sexually immoral associations.
But this letter, aside from sexual immorality, focuses on current contentions and divisions.

The salutation begins, "Paul, called to be an apostle of Jesus Christ through God's will

To the Church of God at Corinth, to those sanctified in
Christ Jesus and called saints still
And to those in every place who call on the name Jesus
Christ our Lord, theirs and ours:
Grace to you and peace from God our Father and the Lord
Jesus Christ, grace and power."
Next comes the prayer thanking God for grace given them
by Jesus Christ His Son,
Grace that enriches them in knowledge and in utterance, and
in everything, each one.

Then, like a loving father correcting his children, Paul pleads
that division among them end
That they be perfectly joined together in mind and judgment
same, all the Corinth brethren.
Factions saying "I am of Paul, or of Apollos, or of Cephas"
are factions sorely misguided.
"Was Paul or Apollos or Cephas crucified for you," asks
Paul? "And was Christ divided?"
"It is not through wisdom that we are saved," says Paul, "but
believing in Christ crucified.
The Jews request a sign and the Greeks seek after wisdom,
but we preach Christ crucified."

Christ crucified may be to the Jew a stumbling block and so
much foolishness to the Greek
But to those who are called, both Jew and Gentile, He is the
wisdom and power they seek.
God has chosen the foolish to confound the wise, and the
weak to put the strong to shame
For God's foolishness is wiser than the wise, and His power
greater than all worldly fame.
No flesh glories in His presence except through Christ Jesus;
glory comes through the Son
Through the Son come righteousness and sanctification and
redemption, offered everyone.

Paul professed declaring to them God's testimony, but doing
so in excellence he denied:
"In addressing you I claimed to know nothing more than
Jesus Christ and Him crucified.
My speech and my preaching were not with persuasive
words of human wisdom said
But by demonstration of Spirit, so presume not that your
faith by human wisdom led."
The wisdom Paul preaches is not the wisdom of the world;
it is not the wisdom of the ages;
It is the hidden wisdom that God ordained before the ages,
the glory that the Son presages.

Wisdom comes through the Spirit, for no one knows the
things of God except God's Spirit
And the natural man cannot receive the things of the Spirit,
only the believer can receive it.
Paul says that when he came to the Corinthians, he could
not address them as ones spiritual
Their being carnal he had to milk feed them as babes in
Christ, and sadly they are carnal still
For when they say "I am of Paul" or "I am of Apollos," envy,
strife and division they reveal.
That he and Apollos were mere ministers through whom they
believed, the apostle must instill.

"I planted and Apollos watered," says Paul, "but God gave
the increase and that's the crux
Neither he who plants nor he who waters is anything, but
He who gives the increase thus."
Paul continues saying metaphorically that he who plants and
he who waters awarded will be
For laboring as God's fellow workers true, "but you are God's
field, you are God's building."
Paul says that God's grace made him a wise master builder:
Jesus Christ the foundation he laid
And that the works of those who build on this foundation
will be tested by fire, yet be not afraid.

Those whose works endure will be rewarded; those whose
works burn suffer loss, but are saved
Though salvation is a free gift, rewards are earned but earned
only by the saved meetly behaved.
"Do you know," Paul asks, "that you are a temple of the Holy
Spirit a sacred place for It to dwell?
Knowing this, knowing you are a temple of God, how could
you ever allow defilement to prevail?"
Know that the wisdom of the world is foolishness to God,
and knowing glory not in men
Whether Paul, Apollo, Cephas, or any man; you are Christ's
and Christ's is God's. Amen.

That the contentious Corinthians are puffed up one against
the other Paul can readily perceive,
"What makes one different from another? What have any of
you that you did not freely receive?"
With barbed irony, he contrasts their imagined exaltation to
the degradation the apostles endure:
"We are fools for Christ's sake, but you are wise in Christ;
we are weak and you are strong sure.
You are distinguished, but we are dishonored! Even until
this hour we are hungry and thirsty
We are poorly clothed, we are beaten and homeless, and we
labor with our hands endlessly."

"Furthermore, being reviled, we bless, being persecuted, we
endure it; being defamed we entreat
We have been made as the filth of the world, the offscouring
of all things, the bottom of the heap.
I do not write these things to shame you, but as my beloved
children to warn you," explains Paul.
Continuing, he tells them that though they may have many
instructors, one spiritual father is all.
"For though you might have ten thousand instructors, yet
you do not multiple fathers see.
In Christ Jesus I have begotten you through the gospel;
therefore, I urge you, imitate me."

Tied to this exhortation is the information that he is sending his spiritual son Timothy there
To be his voice reminding them of "my ways in Christ, as I teach in churches everywhere."
Wishing to visit Corinth himself, Paul prays that his wish finds not the Lord's will amiss
And in directive asks, "Shall I come to you with a rod, or in love and a spirit of gentleness?"

I Corinthians Prose
Summary Two
Addressing More Church Disorders

Case of Incest: the Problem and the Prescription

Paul is shocked to hear of a case of incest and that no action has been taken. He notes that even the pagans do not tolerate incest—and in the Church at Corinth a man is cohabiting with his father's wife! And furthermore, "you are puffed up, and have not rather mourned, that he who has done this deed might be taken away from among you" (5:2).

That one of the Corinthian brethren is cohabiting with his step mother is bad enough but that the congregation is ignoring the act is even more appalling. Whether they are ignoring this immoral act because sexual immorality is a way of life in Corinth or whether they consider that grace gives them the liberty to do with their bodies as they please, or both, is not entirely clear. But Paul's response is clear. He insists that immediate action be taken and explains the reasons for doing so. He tells them that though absent in body he is present with them in spirit and has already judged the situation.

"Deliver such a one to Satan for the destruction of the flesh, that his spirit may be saved in the day of the Lord Jesus" (5:5). It is clear that disciplinary action is for the good of the violator as well as the Church. Satan's domain is the world and the flesh, and the violator's sexual immorality is of the flesh and of the world. God's domain is the Church and the spirit. This violator is to be excommunicated, to be put out of the Church as punishment for his immoral behavior. As Paul explains, delivering him to Satan—excommunicating him—is to punish the flesh that the spirit might be saved. There is no reason that repentance would not reinstate him into the church, his flesh chastened and his spirit lifted. Furthermore, excommunicating him is essential to the health of the Church as Paul explains metaphorically in which leaven stands for evil and Passover for Christ. "Purge out the old leaven, that you may be a new lump, since you truly are unleavened. For indeed Christ, our Passover, was sacrificed for us. Therefore let us keep the feast, not with old leaven, nor with the leaven of malice and wickedness, but with the unleavened bread of sincerity and truth" (5:7-8).

Further clarifying, Paul mentions a letter preceding the present one in which he cautioned them about keeping company with the sexually immoral (5:9). He explains that he "certainly did not mean with the sexually immoral people of this world or with the covetous, or extortioners, or idolaters, since then you would need to go out of the world" (5:10). What he meant then and means now in his present letter is not to keep company with a brother in the Church who indulges in immoral behavior. Paul writes, "For what have I to do with judging those also who are outside?" God judges those who are outside, but you judge those inside. Therefore, "put away from yourselves that wicked person" (5:12-13).

Problem of Litigation

That the brethren of the Church are bringing law suits against each other concerns Paul greatly, for they should be resolving their differences within the Church. "Dare any of you, having a matter against another, go to law before the unrighteous, and not before the saints [believers]. Do you not know that the saints will judge the world"(6:1-2)? Paul is grieved that they go to law against each other, and is shocked that "brother [in Christ] goes to law against brother, and that before unbelievers" (6:6)!

More Instruction on Moral Laxity

Paul has more to say about moral laxity and thus addresses his Corinthian brethren: "Do you not know that the unrighteous will not inherit the kingdom of God? Do not be deceived. Neither fornicators, nor idolaters, nor adulterers, nor homosexuals, nor sodomites, nor thieves, nor covetous, nor drunkards, nor revilers, nor extortioners will inherit the kingdom of God. And such were some of you. But you were washed, but you were sanctified, but you were justified in the name of the Lord Jesus and by the Spirit of God" (6:9-11). Now their bodies are for God and not for self-indulgence.

"Now the body is not for sexual immorality but for the Lord, and the Lord for the body" (6:13). Their bodies are now "members of Christ" and they must not make them "members of a harlot" (6:13). He exhorts them to flee sexual immorality again reminding them that the believer's body is "the temple of the Holy Spirit" (3:16; 6:19), and that the believer is "bought at a price; therefore glorify God in your body and in your spirit, which are God's" (6:20).

Concerning Marriage and Celibacy

Apparently some at Corinth believed it better not to be married and consulted Paul for verification. Though Paul believed that the unmarried person could better serve the Lord, he recognized the force of natural instincts and took a practical stance on marriage, a stance summed up in his famous line, "For it is better to marry than to burn with passion" (7:9). This precept is especially appropriate for those living in Corinth, a city where sexual immorality would be a constant temptation. And Paul addresses their inquiry thus, "Because of sexual immorality, let each man have his own wife, and let each woman have her own husband. The wife does not have authority over her own body, but the husband does. And likewise the husband does not have authority over his own body, but the wife does. Do not deprive one another except with consent for a time, that you may give yourselves to fasting and prayer; and come together again so that Satan does not tempt you because of your lack of self-control" (7:2-5). Paul makes it abundantly clear that each partner, the husband and the wife, have equal authority and equal responsibility concerning their sexual relationship.

Paul counsels those already married to remain with their spouses, women not to leave husbands and husbands not to divorce wives. Even in the case of one spouse a believer and the other a non-believer, "for the unbelieving husband is sanctified by the wife, and the unbelieving wife is sanctified by the husband" (7:14). Presumably, Paul means that the home, because of one believing spouse, is set apart by that spouse's Christian influence.

Concerning the Changing of Status

Paul says, "as the Lord has called each one, so let him walk" (7:17). If one was called uncircumcised, no need to be circumcised; if one was called while a slave, no need to be concerned for you are the Lord's freedman. "You were bought at a price; do not become slaves of men. Brethren, let each one remain with God in that calling in which he was called" (7:23-24). The important thing is to serve God, and believers can do that regardless of their social status: married or unmarried, circumcised or uncircumcised, slave or free.

Concerning Food Offered Idols

Addressing the question concerning whether believers should eat food that had been sacrificed to idols, Paul focuses on the responsibility of believers. Since an idol is of no consequence, the eating of food having been offered to one would be no problem for the mature believer. But for a new convert immature in the faith, the eating of food having been offered to an idol might be a stumbling block. And seeing mature believers eating such food might also be a stumbling block; therefore, whether the eating of such food becomes a stumbling block for others is the important thing. Your knowledge that gives you freedom to do so should not close your mind to your responsibility to a weak fellow believer. "Knowledge puffs up, but love edifies" (8:1), says Paul. Consequently, "if food makes my brother stumble, I will never again eat meat, lest I make my brother stumble" (8:13).

Concerning Personal Example

Paul continues to stress the principle that believers should be willing to give up certain freedoms and privileges out of love and consideration of others, and presents himself as example. First, he presents his credentials as an apostle: "Am I not an apostle? Have I not seen Jesus Christ our Lord? Are you not my work in the Lord" (9:1)? After establishing that he is an apostle he addresses an apostle's right to be supported by his congregation.

Making his case he notes that one who tends a vineyard eats of its fruit; he who tends a flock drinks of its milk; the law of Moses forbids the muzzling of an ox while it treads out the grain; and finally, "the Lord has commanded that those who preach the gospel should live from the gospel" (9:14). But

Paul does not take advantage of this privilege because he wants there to be no motivation to his preaching other than his commitment to the Lord. He wants his only reward to be conversion of souls. He phrases it thus, "What is my reward then? That when I preach the gospel, I may present the gospel of Christ without charge, and I may not abuse my authority in the gospel" (9:18). He goes on to say, "though I am free from all men, I have made myself a servant to all, that I might win the more" (9:19). To the Jews he is willing to be as a Jew so that he might win Jews; to the weak he is willing to become weak in order to win the weak: "I have become all things to all men, that I might by all means save some" (9:22). This he does for the sake of the gospel and for the sake of sharing it with others. And he does it with great discipline, like an athlete training to run for the prize. "I discipline my body and bring it into subjection, lest, when I have preached to others, I myself should become disqualified" (9:27).

Concerning Historical Example

Lest the Corinthian converts become too complacent in their conversion, thinking they had been united with Christ through baptism and had received Him into their bodies through the sacrament they were immune to temptation, Paul gives them a history lesson comparing them to the Israelites under Moses. "Our fathers . . . all were baptized into Moses in the cloud and in the sea, all ate the same spiritual food, and all drank the same spiritual drink. For they drank of that spiritual Rock that followed them, and that Rock was Christ. But with most of them God was not well pleased, for their bodies were scattered in the wilderness" (10:1-5). Extending the comparison, Paul cautions, "Therefore let him who thinks he stands take heed lest he fall" (10:12). But after cautioning, he consoles, "But God is faithful [and] will not allow you to be tempted beyond what you are able" (10:13).

Caution against Idolatry

Paul exhorts them to flee idolatry. As idolatry had been a great stumbling block for the Israelites, so it would be for them. Explaining, he notes that the breaking of the bread, Christ's body, and the drinking of the cup, Christ's blood, is communion with Christ. But things sacrificed to idols are sacrificed to demons, and "you cannot drink the cup of the Lord and the cup of demons, you cannot partake of the Lord's table and the table of demons" (10:21).

Personal Freedom versus Concern for Others

Still addressing the problem of eating or not eating meat that had been sacrificed to an idol, Paul says, "Let no one seek his own, but each one the other's well-being" (10:24). For example, if you eat meat that has been sacrificed to an idol knowing that it offends your brother then you not only violate the conscience of another, but you violate your own conscience. Though "the earth is the Lord's, and all its fullness" (10:26, 28), and you may have gotten beyond any feeling of association between the meat and a meaningless idol, your brother may not have. Thus, you should be more concerned about your bother's conscience than your freedom. Self-sacrifice out of love is edifying; self-indulgence is degrading. One's freedom does not take precedence over another's well-being.

Concerning Etiquette for Women and Etiquette for Men in Public Worship

Paul entreats the Corinthians to "keep the traditions as I delivered them to you" (11:2), and then focuses on head covering, its appropriateness or inappropriateness. Paul says that for the man to cover his head in public worship would be offensive; whereas, for the woman not to cover her head would be offensive. Paul reasons as follows: "I want you to know that the head of every man is Christ, the head of woman is man, and the head of Christ is God" (11:3). Thus reasoned, the order of creation is God, Christ, man, woman. To reflect this order the man does not cover his head in public worship "since he is the image and glory of God" (11:7), but the woman does cover her head since she "is the glory of man" (11:7). Yet neither man nor woman is independent of each other, "for as the woman was from the man, even so the man also is through the woman, but all things are from God" (11:11).

Concerning the Lord's Supper

Paul has received disturbing reports about their celebration of the Lord's Supper: "For in eating each one takes his own supper ahead of others, and one is hungry and another is drunk" (11:21). Such gross violation of the intent of the Lord's Supper is subject to judgment and damnation. Consequently, Paul instructs them again: "For I received from the Lord that which I also delivered to you: that the Lord Jesus on the same night in which he was betrayed took bread; and when He had given thanks, He broke it and said, '*Take, eat; this is My body which is broken for you; do this in remembrance of Me.'* In the same manner He also took the cup after supper, saying, '*This cup is the new covenant in My blood. This do, as often as you drink it, in remembrance of Me.*' For as often as you eat this bread and drink this cup, you proclaim the Lord's death till He comes. Therefore whoever eats this bread, or drinks this cup of the Lord in an unworthy manner will be guilty of the body and blood of the Lord. But let a man examine himself, and so let him eat of that bread and drink of that cup. For he who eats and drinks in an unworthy manner eats and drinks judgment to himself, not discerning the Lord's body" (11:23-29). Thus, Paul explains the sacredness of Holy Communion.

I Corinthians Poetic Summary Two Addressing More Church Disorders

The apostle Paul stands stunned hearing of incest
committed by one of the Corinthian brethren
Cohabiting with his father's wife while the Church stands
blindly by as if the odious act no sin.
What are they thinking to ignore what even pagans would
not tolerate, would soundly condemn?
Are they thinking that living under grace grants the license
to use their bodies as it pleases them?
Whatever their rationale, the apostle Paul sets them aright
by sending message abundantly clear:
Though not present with them in body he is present in spirit
and that spirit's urging they must hear.

"Deliver such a one to Satan for the destruction of the flesh,
that his spirit may be saved in that Day."
Saving the sinner, saving the Church, necessitates
disciplinary action now, lest sin conquer the Way.
This violator must be excommunicated, put out of the
Church, as punishment for his hideous sin
For delivered to Satan's domain he may awaken to the spirit
and through repentance return again.
Left within the Church, within God's domain, thus
condoning a sin so severe sends signal wrong
Harboring Satan's sons within God's domain damages the
spirit and destroys the Church ere long.

Or as Paul figuratively phrases it, "phase out the old leaven
that you may a new unleavened lump be
And in Christ, our Passover, our sacrifice, keep the feast with
unleavened bread of truth and sincerity."
In further clarification, Paul mentions a letter preceding the
present one addressing sexual immorality
And explains he did not mean then nor does he mean now
that you must judge those of the world
Those God will judge, but your brethren you judge now, "so
put away from you that wicked churl."

Aside from sexual immorality, the practice of litigation
between the brethren gave Paul great concern
Rather than resolve their differences within the Church
anon, they litigiously to the unrighteous turn.
"Do you not know that the saints will judge the world?" asks
Paul, grieved that brother distrusts brother
That brother brings law suit against brother before
unbelievers rather than investing trust in one another.
Lest his admonitions again go unheeded, the grieved apostle
saliently reiterates and further enumerates:
"Corinthians, be not mislead, the unrighteous will not inherit
the kingdom of heaven," he boldly states.

"Do not be deceived, for neither the fornicator, the idolater,
the adulterer, the homosexual, the sodomite,
The thief, the covetous, the drunkard, the reviler, nor the
extortionist will inherit the kingdom of Light.
And such were some of you, but you were washed, but you
were sanctified, but you were justified
In the name of Jesus Christ and by the Spirit of God, thus
self-indulgence must forever be denied.
Know that your body is not for sexual immorality but for
the Lord, and the Lord for the body true.
Your bodies are now members of Christ, thus you must never
make them members of a harlot too."

Exhorting the Corinthians to flee sexual immorality, he
repeats "your body is a temple of the Holy Spirit
Bought at great price, it is meet to glorify God, but to glorify
in body and spirit both you must not forget."
On the marriage subject the Church at Corinth came up
with conflicting views for the apostle to review.
He knew theoretically the unmarried person could better
serve the Lord, but also knew practicality too.
He knew the force of natural instinct in lax circumstances
could overwhelming be, even to the upright
And thus tailored counsel and circumstance fittingly: "Better
to marry than to burn with passion bright."

More specifically, Paul says, "because of sexual immorality, let
each man his own wife have
And let each woman her own husband have though neither
over their own bodies authority has
Authority over the wife's body the husband has, authority
over the husband's body the wife has
One does not deprive the other except with consent for a
time dedicated to fasting and prayer
Then come together again so that you can resist Satan's
temptations together, fortified, a pair.

Thus, Paul counsels those married to remain with their
spouses, think separation and divorce not,
Not even if one spouse a believer, the other not, for by the
believer the family is sanctified, the lot.
"As the Lord has called each one, so let him walk,"
circumcised or uncircumcised, slave or free
Let each one remain with God in that calling in which he
was called, serving God the necessity.
Addressing the eating of food sacrificed to idols, Paul
focuses not on food but on responsibility,
Responsibility concerning the conscience of those whose
sensibilities have not reached maturity.

Seeing a mature brethren eating idol sacrificed food could be
a stumbling block for a convert new
Consequently, whether the eating of this food offends your
brother determines what you must do.
Eating idol sacrificed food is of no consequence lest it
become a stumbling block to other than you
In which case your brother's conscience becomes the
consequence determining what you must do.
When maturation has set your conscience free, but your
brother's maturity has not come to pass
Let not your knowledge puff you up, rather show love for your
fledgling brother through the fast.

Continuing the motif of sacrificing freedom and privilege
out of love and consideration for others
Paul presents himself as example prime putting forth his
credentials: one of the apostolic brothers.
"Am I not an apostle? Have I not seen Jesus Christ our
Lord? And are you not my work in Him?"
Apostleship settled, he addresses the apostle's right to be
supported by his congregation, by them.
By example he makes his case: a vineyard keeper eats its
fruit; a flock's milk the herder drinks a bit
Even the ox treading the grain is not muzzled, thus those who
preach the gospel should live from it.

Yet himself this privilege he denies lest there be motivation
other than his commitment to the Lord.
By tent making he supports himself and by so doing keeps
his preaching and practice in one accord.
"And what is my reward? I preach the gospel without charge
that I may not abuse my authority.
Though I am free from all men, myself a servant to all I
make that I might win more in humility."
To Jews he is willing to be as a Jew, to the weak he is willing
to become weak, others number one.
Paul, being the Lord's servant, says, "I am all things to all men
that I might by all means save some."

The apostle does what he does for the sake of the gospel,
giving hope to the dead that they can arise
And with great discipline he does it, like an athlete, a
determined athlete in training to win the prize.
His body he disciplines lest when he preaches to others he
himself should become disqualified.
Thus, the apostle hopes his example of self-sacrifice and of
body discipline will serve as guide.
But to bolster his personal example, he turns to history
comparing Corinthian to Israelite
To illustrate memorably a lesson on the dire consequences of
presuming wrong to be right.

Perceiving the Corinthian converts too complacent in their
conversion, Paul a history lesson poses
Referencing the stiff-necked Israelites who insisted on
having their way despite warnings by Moses.
Corinthians thought themselves temptation immune
because they had Christ in baptism and sacrament.
Paul, perceiving a parallel, points the Corinthian converts to
the Israelites and to the wilderness event.
"Our fathers were baptized into Moses in the cloud and in
the sea, all ate the same spiritual food found
And all drank the same spiritual drink, for they drank of that
spiritual Rock that followed them around."

"Though that Rock that followed them was Christ, God was
not pleased with them at all
For their bodies were scattered wilderness wide. Hence, take
heed lest you likewise fall."
Paul tempers the warning with consolation saying, "God is
faithful and in all things fair
Temptations come, but God will not allow you to be
tempted beyond what you can bear."
And one great temptation is idolatry as becomes abundantly
clear reading Israelite history
Or hearing Paul exhort the complacent Corinthians saying,
"You must flee all idolatry."

The breaking of the bread and the drinking of the cup is
communion with Jesus the Lord
But things sacrificed to idols are sacrificed to demons and in
no way can there be accord.
You cannot drink of the cup of the Lord and the cup of
demons, such certainly cannot be.
Thus, if you wish to partake of the Lord's table, the demons'
table you must forever flee.
And celebration of the Lord's Supper is a special worship
that requires strict decorum too.
It is never a time to gorge and guzzle as some Corinthians had
reportedly been wont to do.

Thus, Paul lays out instructions following the example set by
Jesus on the night He was betrayed:
Breaking bread, He said, "*Take, eat; this is My body broken for
you; do this in remembrance of Me.*"
Taking the cup, He said, "*This cup is the new covenant in My
blood; drink in remembrance of Me.*"
Whoever partakes in an unworthy manner will be guilty of
profaning the body and blood of the Lord.
Therefore examine yourself prayerfully so that your heart and
the spirit of the Lord are of one accord.

Paul continues to exhort the Corinthians concerning Church
tradition right down to covering the head.
If you're a man do not cover your head when worshipping,
covering is reserved for a woman it's said.
Offensive it would be for man to cover his head; not to cover
her head would for woman an offense be
For man's head is Christ, woman's head is man, Christ's head
is God, and that's the reasoning, you see.
The order of creation being God, Christ, man, woman—and
head covering or no reflects that stand:
Man's uncovered head the image and glory of God, while
woman's head covered the glory of man.

Yet neither man nor woman is independent of each other,
first from Adam's rib, then from woman:
Though woman is from man, so man is also through the
woman, and all things are from God, amen.
If by chance you're a bit confused, peruse and ponder Paul's
musings in I Corinthians eleven
Even though inclined to doubt that covering or uncovering
one's head matters much to heaven.

I Corinthians Prose Summary Three Spiritual Gifts, Resurrection, Collections, Close

The Source and Variety of Spiritual Gifts

Chapter twelve is one of four chapters in I Corinthians beginning with the words "now concerning," the other three being chapters seven, eight, and sixteen. Each alerts the reader that the writer is about to address still another concern, another problem, and presumably one that has been referred to him either by letter (7:1), or by those from Chloe's household (1:11). The concern Paul addresses in chapter twelve is that of spiritual gifts. Though the Corinthian Church is said to have no shortage of spiritual gifts (1:7), there seems to be confusion concerning their source, their significance, and their use.

Concerning gifts, Paul says, "There are diversities of gifts, but the same Spirit; there are differences of ministries, but the same Lord. And there are diversities of activities, but it is the same God who works for all. But the manifestation of the Spirit is given to each one for the profit of all" (12:4-7). Those from a polytheistic pagan background may have been thinking that different gifts came from different sources and thereby required different allegiances. In clarifying, Paul makes three major points concerning spiritual gifts: (1) there are a variety of spiritual gifts; (2) all spiritual gifts are from God; and, (3) each spiritual gift is given to profit all, not just the person receiving it.

In addressing the variety of spiritual gifts, Paul names several saying one person may be given "the word of wisdom," another "the word of knowledge," another "faith," another "gifts of healing," another "the workings of miracles," another "prophecy," another "discerning of spirits," another "different kinds of tongues," and another "the interpretation of tongues" (12:8-10).

The Purpose of Spiritual Gifts: Unity in Variety

To help explain the purposeful function of spiritual gifts, Paul utilizes an extended metaphor in which the Church is seen as the body of Christ and each person of the Church is seen as a member of Christ's body. Extending the comparison, each person of the Church, like each member of the human body, has a special role in the functioning of the body. The head has its function, the eye has its function, the heart its function, the hand its function, and so on. Each member of the body must carry out its function, and out of this variety of functions comes the unity of the functioning body. Obviously, the body could not function properly should certain members be envious of others, the heart wanting to be the head, hands wanting to be eyes, feet wanting to be ears, and so on. Each member of the body has its special function and the health of the body depends upon the harmonious functioning of its composite members. Likewise, persons in the Church, the body of Christ, have special functions, special gifts to perform—being a prophet, being a teacher, being a healer, being a helper, being an administrator, being an interpreter—and the health of the Church depends upon all these persons, comprising the Church, the body of Christ, performing their special gifts harmoniously.

"Earnestly desire the best gifts," says Paul, "and yet I show you a more excellent way" (12:31). Paul concedes that one gift may be more desirable than another in terms of its contribution, yet each gift has its function and can be fully realized only when harmony among all prevails. And Paul is about to explain how this can happen, how this "more excellent way" can happen. If some are puffed up about their gifts, it cannot happen. If some are envious of others' gifts, it cannot happen. But it can happen, if an essential element prevails, and that element Paul reveals in chapter thirteen.

The Supremacy of Love

"Though I speak with the tongues of men and of angels, but have not love, I have become as sounding brass or a clanging cymbal. And though I have the gift of prophecy, and understand all mysteries and all knowledge, and though I have faith, so that I could remove mountains, but have not love, I am nothing. And though I bestow all my goods to feed the poor, and though I give my body to be burned, but have not love, it profits me nothing. Love suffers long and is kind; love does not envy; love does not parade itself, is not puffed up; does not behave rudely, does not seek its own, is not provoked, thinks no evil; does not rejoice in iniquity, but rejoices in the truth; bears all things, believes all things, hopes all things, endures all things. Love never fails. But where there are prophecies, they will fail; where there are tongues, they will cease; where there is knowledge, it will vanish away. For we know in part and prophesy in part.

But when that which is perfect has come, then that which is in part will be done away. When I was a child, I spoke as a child, I understood as a child, I thought as a child; but when I became a man, I put away childish things. For now we see in a mirror, dimly, but then face to face. Now I know in part, but then I shall know just as I also am known. And now abide faith, hope, love, these three; but the greatest of these is love" (13:1-13). Thus, one's gifts or actions or deeds are nothing without love. God is love, and only through love can we image God. Love is the essential element.

Prophecy versus Tongues

Presumably, the gift of speaking in tongues has taken on an aura of superiority in the Corinthian Church, for Paul singles it out to thoroughly analyze and juxtaposes it with prophecy to show its inherent dangers. Though no gift is of consequence without love, all gifts are for edification, for better understanding God. In the case of tongues, the speaker is speaking only to God, for those around him do not know what he is saying. In the case of prophecy, all know what is being said. Therefore, says Paul, "He who speaks in a tongue edifies himself, but he who prophesies edifies the church" (14:4). Thus, the gift of prophecy is being used "for the profit of all," the purpose of any particular gift, as Paul has stated earlier (12:7), and is now focusing on edification as the profiting of all. "Since you are zealous for spiritual gifts, let it be for the edification of the church that you seek to excel" (14:12).

Thus, Paul is not denying tongues as a gift, but using it as an example of a gift that readily lends itself to misuse. Further clarifying, he says, "let all things be done for the edification of the church. If anyone speaks in a tongue, let there be two or at the most three, each in turn, and let one interpret. But if there is no interpreter, let him keep silent in church, and let him speak to himself and to God" (14:26-28). Paul concludes his analysis saying, "Therefore, brethren, desire earnestly to prophesy, and do not forbid to speak with tongues [but], let all things be done decently and in order" (14:39-40).

The Case of Women

In name of order, Paul advises, "Let your women keep silent in the churches, for they are not permitted to speak; but they are to be submissive, as the law also says. And if they want to learn something, let them ask their own husbands at home, for it is shameful for women to speak in church" (14:34-35). Here Paul relies on both Jewish tradition and Greek tradition in placing women in a submissive role. Yet the passage is a bit troubling since in the section of the letter addressing the covering or uncovering of heads in church worship he mentions women praying and prophesying (11:5).

The Resurrection

Responding to those Corinthians who were expressing doubts about the resurrection of the body (15:12), Paul addresses the phenomenon in no uncertain terms. He calls their attention to the fact that he had preached the gospel to them as he had received it, passing it on as of first importance: "that Christ died for our sins according to the Scriptures (Isa 53:5-11); and that He was buried, and that He rose again the third day according to the Scriptures (Ps 16:8-11); and that he was seen by Cephas, then by the twelve" (15:3-5). And afterward He was seen by over five-hundred brethren, and then by James (the brother of Jesus) and by all the apostles, and finally by Paul himself. Paul is authenticating through Scripture and through eye-witness. Furthermore, he is giving evidence of his authority as an apostle called to witness to the gospel. With that established, he addresses the resurrection phenomenon telling the Corinthians that "if there is no resurrection of the dead, then Christ is not risen. And if Christ is not risen, then our preaching is vain and your faith is also vain" (15:13-14). There is no gospel without the resurrection.

Continuing, Paul says that if we had hope of Christ only in this life, we would be the most pitiable of persons, "but now Christ is risen from the dead, and has become the first fruits of those who have fallen asleep. For since by man came death, by Man also came the resurrection of the dead. For as in Adam all die, even so in Christ all shall be made alive" (15:19-22).

Finally, Paul addresses the question concerning the form in which the body will be resurrected. He says "that flesh and blood cannot inherit the kingdom of God, nor does corruption inherit incorruption . . . but we shall all be changed—in a moment, in the twinkling of an eye, at the last trumpet. For the trumpet will sound, and the dead will be raised incorruptible, and we shall be changed . . . So when this corruptible has put on incorruption, and this mortal has put on immortality, then shall be brought to pass the saying that is written [Hosea 13:14]: 'Death is swallowed up in victory. O Death where is your sting? O Hades where is your victory?'" (15:50-55).

Collection for the Saints in Jerusalem

From addressing the resurrection, Paul turns to collection: "now concerning the collection for the saints [in Jerusalem], as I have given orders to the churches of Galatia, so you must do also" (16:1). The saints in Jerusalem had become impoverished, possibly from famine as foretold by the prophet Agabus (Acts 11:28), as well as from persecution, and Paul believed it important that churches in other regions show their concern through love offerings. Jerusalem had shared the gospel with them, now they had an opportunity to share their substance with Jerusalem. Here, and in other letters, Paul demonstrates his dedication to this important mission and, in this letter particularly, he demonstrates how he had mastered practical procedures for carrying it out: "On the first day of the week let each one of you lay something aside, storing up as he may prosper, that there be no collections when I come. And when I come, whoever you approve by your letters I will send to bear your gift to Jerusalem. But if it is fitting that I go also, they will go with me" (16:2-4).

Remarkably, Paul could deal effectively with the most knotty theological problem, and then turn immediately to effectively work out an administrative problem.

Plans for Visiting Corinth

Paul is writing to the Corinthians from Ephesus (16:8), and telling them that he will come for a visit after going through Macedonia and hopefully will be able to stay awhile, perhaps spend the winter with them. In the meantime, Timothy may be visiting them, but not Apollos whom they had inquired about. He directs them to treat Timothy with respect and to send him on his journey in peace, for he will be waiting for Timothy.

Closing the Letter with Exhortations, Greetings, and Benediction

In closing, Paul exhorts the Corinthians to "watch, stand fast in the faith, be brave, be strong. *Let all that you do be done with love*" (16:14).

He sends greetings from the churches of Asia, and particularly from Aquila and Priscilla and the church in their house at Ephesus. And then adds, "All the brethren greet you. Greet one another with a holy kiss" (16:20)

He ends with the benediction, "The grace of our Lord Jesus Christ be with you. My love be with you all in Christ Jesus. Amen" (16:23-24).

I Corinthians Poetic Summary Three Spiritual Gifts, Resurrection, Collections, Close

Four chapters of I Corinthians begin with the words "now concerning," a transitional phrase
Signaling the reader a church practice is about to be addressed, maybe damned, maybe praised.
That phrase beginning chapter twelve concerns spiritual gifts, their source, significance, and use.
Though there was no shortage of these gifts at Corinth, there was misconception and thus abuse.
Their polytheistic pagan culture may have made it difficult to think of all gifts from one Lord
And even more difficult to think of each gift profiting all and all gifts performed as one accord.

These diverse gifts needed explanation: their from whence, their for why, their how to, their all.
Conceding such, the Corinthians consult their spiritual mentor, none other than the apostle Paul
For this missionary brother had no peer when it came to making muddied matters crystal clear.
Having been struck by the Almighty's Light, he never again to the Holy Spirit turned a deaf ear.
From Damascus to Rome the apostle made his way exhorting Jew and Gentile the gospel to hear
Anchoring churches where none were before, all requiring instruction by letter from far and near.

So it was in Corinth and so the apostle responding to their
plea penned letters to stay controversy
And in this particular one instructs the congregation
concerning spiritual gifts and their diversity.
There are gifts of wisdom, of knowledge, of healing, of
prophecy, of tongues, all by God given
And all gifts are given to profit all, and never for individual
gain, for they all come from heaven.
One may desire the higher gift but every gift serves its
purpose and diversity forms the whole.
Every gift performing harmoniously generates the perfect
whole, the Giver's designated goal.

Graphically describing their form and function, Paul
employs figurative language, metaphor clear.
Thus, the church is seen as Christ's body, and each person
therein a member of Christ's body dear.
All members of Christ's body, like all members of the human
body, perform their designated role
There cannot be a healthy body lest all its members function
harmoniously according to the scroll.
Each member carries out its function, and out of this variety
of functions comes unity of the whole.
Should some envy others thereby neglecting their own gifts,
think of the ensuing damage to unfold!

"Earnestly desire the best gifts," says the apostle Paul, "and
yet I show you a more excellent way."
And although one gift may be more desirable than another,
there is a mystery that brings harmony.
And the apostle reveals the mystery, I Corinthians thirteen,
as surely to him the Holy Spirit revealed:
"Though I speak with gifted tongue, but have not *love* I am
as sounding brass and clanging cymbal
Though I have gift of prophecy, with wisdom to understand
mysteries, but have not *love,* I am nothing
Though I have faith to move mountains, bestow my goods on
the poor, but have not *love,* I am nothing."

"*Love* does not envy, does not parade itself; is never puffed
up, is not rude, is not self-serving;
Love is never provoked, thinks no evil, rejoices not in
iniquity, but rejoices in truth unerring;
Love bears all things, believes all things, hopes all things,
endures all things. *Love* fails never.
But where there are prophecies, they will fail, and where
there are tongues they will cease ever.
Where there is knowledge, it will vanish away, for we know
in part and prophesy in part
But when that which is perfect has come, the part becomes
whole like circle from the arc."

"Now we see in a mirror, dimly, but then face to face. Then I
shall know just as I also am known.
And now abide faith, hope, *love*, these three; but the greatest
of these is *love*," for divine it lives on.
Thus, one's gifts or deeds are nothing without *love*, for God
is *love* and through *love* we image Him.
Love is the essential element; without it we can forget the
good deeds and faith and gifts, all of them.
The necessity of *love* established, Paul focuses on the gift of
tongues comparing it to that of prophecy
Presumably, of the several gifts practiced at Corinth that of
tongues was causing the most controversy.

Using edification as the touchstone, the apostle compares
speaking in tongues to that of plain prophecy
Asking who is edified by one speaking in tongues and
answering only the one speaking, "I" not "we."
If edification be the touchstone—a gift profits all, not just
the gifted—then the nod goes to prophecy
For the speaker in tongues is speaking only to God, and
those around him know not what the topic be
Consequently, the speaker in tongues edifies only himself
while the prophet edifies the church whole.
Only when there is an interpreter near should a speaker of
tongues unfold; otherwise, the tongue hold.

Next, Paul steps into a mine field on the matter of women
remaining in church services silent.
In its historical context his stance sounds relevant, but to the
modern ear an explosive incident.
Taking his cue from creation that woman was made from
man so always submissive she should be
And the man being the head, discourse becomes his purview
obligating him to instruct her orderly.
Should she desire doctrine further explained wait for the
husband at home to explain the same
Otherwise, let her in church keep the head covered and silent
there remain, lest she elicit shame.

To those expressing doubts about the resurrection of the
body, the apostle responded boldly
He notes that he had passed the gospel on to them as he had
received it, complete and holy:
Christ died for our sins, was buried and arose on the third
day, as prophesied in the Scriptures old.
The arisen Christ was seen by Cephas and the twelve, by
himself and others, five-hundred all told.
Thus, Paul authenticates by Scripture and by eye-witness
that Christ is risen, now all doubt gone
And that he has seen Him authenticates his own apostleship,
thereby giving him authority strong.

Then comes the conclusion strong, "If there is no
resurrection of the dead, then Christ is risen not
And if Christ is risen not, then our preaching is in vain, your
faith is in vain; we all, a hopeless lot."
Thus said, rhetorically and forcefully, there is no gospel
without the resurrection, it cannot be.
If we had hope of Christ only in this life, we would be the
most pitiable of persons most clearly
"But Christ is risen and has become the first fruits of those
who have fallen asleep awaiting Christ
Since by man came death, by Man also came resurrection of
the dead: death in Adam; life in Christ."

Resurrection of the body confirmed, the apostle then
addresses the question concerning its form.
Of course, "flesh and blood cannot inherit the kingdom of
God, for incorruption there is the norm.
Thus, we shall be changed—in the twinkling of an eye the
trumpet will sound and the dead arise
This corruptible becomes incorruptible, this mortal
immortal, and Hosea's prophecy we surmise:
"Death is swallowed up in victory—O Death where is your
sting? O Hades where is your victory?"
And thus we see the Spirit inspired apostle instructing
Christian novices in resurrection theology.

Paul moves from the ethereal to the mundane, from
resurrection theology to collection management
No matter preaching or teaching or administration, this apt
apostle's performance registers excellent.
He has ordered the churches in Galatia to take a collection
for the impoverished saints in Jerusalem
And now orders the Corinthians to take a collection too,
accordingly prescribing procedure to them.
"On the first day of the week let each one of you lay
something aside according to your prosperity,
And let it be completed before my coming; no collections
after I arrive, think only their adversity."

To stay suspicion, the apostle instructs the church to choose
its person to deliver the collection
And if need be he will accompany that approved person as a
matter of discretion and protection.
Though refusing church support for himself, Paul pushed
his churches to support the holy city.
Out of love Jerusalem sent the gospel to them; now their
collections elicited love in reciprocity.
After instructions concerning collection completed, the
apostle addresses his visitation plan:
From Ephesus he intends to journey through Macedonia and
on his return visit Corinth again.

In closing, the apostle includes one last exhortation: "Let all
that you do be done with *love.*"
Thus is the letter's message synthesized, a message from the
apostle from the Lord above.
No matter how good or gifted, how magnificent, how
gracious and poised
Done without love, your gifts and deeds become but
self-enhancing noise.

II Corinthians Prose
Summary Part One
Salutation, Explanation and Reconciliation

The Setting: Probable Scenario

Consider the following scenario as probable preamble to II Corinthians. Between the writing of I Corinthians and II Corinthians, Paul made a brief visit to the church at Corinth, but was not successful in resolving issues. Things having worsened, he then wrote a severe letter with "much anguish of heart" (2:4; 7:8). Titus either delivered the severe letter or followed up on it, or both, and witnessed a change of attitude at Corinth, a spirit of conciliation. He delivers the good news to Paul who anxiously awaits him in Macedonia, possibly Philippi. Paul's response is II Corinthians (2:13: 7:6-7).

Salutation

The salutation in this letter follows closely that of I Corinthians whereby Paul identifies himself as "an apostle of Jesus Christ by the will of God," addressing "the church of God at Corinth," and extending "grace . . . and peace from God our Father and the Lord Jesus Christ" (1:1-2). It may be noted that in the salutation, he includes Timothy and besides the church at Corinth he also addresses all the saints (believers) of Achaia.

Gratitude and Explanation

In a prayerful manner Paul expresses gratitude to God and to the Corinthians for helping him through a most difficult time: God for his goodness and the Corinthians for their prayers. "Blessed be the God and Father of our Lord Jesus Christ, the Father of mercies and God of all comfort, who comforts us in all our tribulation, that we may be able to comfort those who are in any trouble, with the comfort with which we ourselves are comforted by God . . . you also helping together in prayer for us, that thanks may be given by many persons on our behalf, for the gift granted to us through many" (1:3,4,11).

Besides an explanation of God's comforting goodness and the power of prayer, Paul is offering explanation of his desperate situation in Asia. Though he gives no details, he states that "we do not want you to be ignorant, brethren, of our trouble which came to us in Asia: that we were burdened beyond measure, above strength, so that we despaired even of life. Yes, we had the sentence of death in ourselves that we should not trust in ourselves but in God who raised the dead" (1:8-9). He is informing them of how much he is dependent on God for all things. This seems to be the beginning of a fuller explanation of his change of plans concerning two proposed visits. Presumably, some of his critics had pointed to this change of plans claiming it as evidence that Paul could not be trusted.

Explanation of Changed Plans

Despite what critics might have said, Paul assures the Corinthians that they are his boast as he is theirs: "we are your boast as you also are ours, in the day of the Lord Jesus" (1:14). Then explaining his earlier change of plans, he writes, "And in this confidence I intended to come to you before, that you might have a second benefit—to pass by way of you to Macedonia, to come again from Macedonia to you, and be helped by you on my way to Judea" (1:15-16). Because the Spirit of God moved his heart, he did not visit them on his way to Macedonia. Rather than go to them again and bring sorrow, he wrote them instead: "Out of much affliction and anguish of heart I wrote to you, with many tears, not that you should be grieved, but that you might know the love which I have so abundantly for you" (2:4). This letter is the letter written after I Corinthians and before II Corinthians, the so called severe letter. The letter was thought to have been lost although some scholars now think that chapters ten through thirteen of II Corinthians may actually be the letter or a portion of it. This conjecture is based on the change from conciliatory emphasis to corrective emphasis beginning with chapter ten; it sounds more like a letter of sorrow and tears, a severe letter, than a letter of conciliation. Especially note verses twenty and twenty-one of chapter twelve. Be that as it may, at this point in the II Corinthians letter

Paul is explaining why he changed his mind about his proposed visit: the Spirit of God moved his heart to do so. And he seems to be defending himself against critics who pointed to his not making the proposed visit as an example of his untrustworthiness.

On Punishment and Forgiveness

Without giving specifics, Paul mentions a person in the Corinthian Church who the majority has punished. It was probably someone who had opposed Paul and his teachings and may have been the leader of those opposing the apostle when he made his brief visit in an attempt to settle, in person, the contention within the congregation, but having been unsuccessful had written the tearful and severe letter. Whatever the specifics, Paul is now addressing the congregation's punishment of the individual and cautioning them not to take the punishment too far. It is now time for forgiveness: "This punishment which was inflicted by the majority is sufficient for such a man . . . you ought [now] to forgive and comfort him [and], whom you forgive anything, I also forgive. For if indeed I have forgiven anything, I have forgiven that one for your sakes in the presence of Christ, lest Satan should take advantage of us; for we are not ignorant of his devices" (2:6,7,10,11). Thus, Paul counsels them concerning the limits of punishment and the necessity of forgiveness lest punishment serve the wrong purpose. The punishment was to correct the rebel not to destroy him. If he is repentant, he should be welcomed back into the church and into Christian fellowship. This act of forgiving his enemy reveals Paul's sincerity and purity of purpose. His concern is for saving the rebel and the church not to revel in petty revenge. Paul not only teaches the gospel, but teaches by example.

Back to Explanation

After an interlude of instructing about punishment and forgiveness, Paul turns again to explanation, explanation of how concerned he had been about the Corinthians and how anxious he had been for news about them after his unsuccessful visit followed by his severe letter. So much so that when he goes from Ephesus up to Troas and Titus is not yet there, he departs for Macedonia (2:12-13). Presumably, Titus is traveling the reverse direction, coming from Corinth, and Paul expected to meet him in Troas. When Titus is not there, Paul is so anxious for news concerning Corinth that he travels on to Macedonia hoping to meet Titus, possibly in Philippi. We later learn that Paul does meet Titus (place not identified), and that

Titus brings good news from Corinth, news that gives great consolation to Paul (7:6-7). Relating this event reveals Paul's love and concern for the Corinthians among whom he has spent eighteen months nurturing into a church of great potential before stumbling into contention, contention aided and abetted by false teachers who descended upon the congregation in Paul's absence and began disparaging Paul and his teachings. But through it all, Paul's actions reveal his purity of purpose. "Now thanks be to God who always leads us in triumph in Christ, and through us diffuses the fragrance of His knowledge in every place," says Paul, "for we are not, as so many, peddling the word of God; but as of sincerity, but as from God, we speak in the sight of God and Christ" (2:14, 17).

Letters of Commendation

The ones coming to Corinth to challenge Paul's authority and teaching probably came with letters of recommendation, possibly letters from the Sanhedrin. It occurs to Paul that the explanation of his actions may sound as if he is presenting a letter of recommendation. Then he muses "do we need, as some others, epistles of commendation to you or letters of commendation from you? You are our epistle written in our hearts, known and read by all men" (3:1-2). Thus, the apostle's work and the work of the Corinthians serve as letters of commendation for each and they are from God, the Spirit of God manifested in the works of each.

Ministers of the New Covenant

"Not that we are sufficient of ourselves," says Paul, "not to think of anything as being from ourselves, but our sufficiency is from God, who also made us sufficient as *ministers of the new covenant,* not of the letter but of the Spirit; for the letter kills, but the Spirit gives life" (3:5-6). The apostle proceeds with an involved explanation comparing the new covenant with the old and extolling the enhanced glory of the new. If the "children of Israel could not look steadily on the face of Moses because of the glory of his countenance, which glory was passing away, how will the ministry of the Spirit not be more glorious? For if the ministry of condemnation had glory, the ministry of righteousness exceeds much more in glory" (3:7-9). The "ministry of condemnation" is a reference to the Law, particularly the Ten Commandments written on stone, which revealed to man his sinfulness but did not offer him a way of breaking out of sin. Following the letter of the Law was not sufficient, as is made clear in the Sermon on the Mount where Jesus dramatically contrasts the discrepancy of living by the letter as opposed to the spirit of the law. For example, He says, "You have heard that it was said to those of old, '*You shall not commit adultery.*' But I say to you that whoever looks at a woman to lust for her has already committed adultery with her in his heart" (Matt 5:27-28). He also says, "Do not think that I came to destroy the Law or the Prophets, I did not come to destroy but to fulfill" (Matt 5:17). Likewise, Paul explains to the Corinthians that the new covenant is a fulfillment and an enhancement. He writes, "You are manifestly an epistle of Christ, ministered by us, written not with ink but by the Spirit of the living God, not on tablets of stone but on tablets of flesh, that is, of the heart" (3:3). Paul's words echo Jeremiah's prophecy concerning the new covenant: "Behold the days are coming says the Lord, when I will make a new covenant with the house of Israel and the house of Judah—not according to the covenant that I made with their fathers in the day I brought them out of Egypt, My covenant which they broke, though I was a husband to them, says the Lord. But this is the covenant that I will make with the house of Israel: After those days, says the Lord, I will put My law in their minds, and write it on their hearts; and I will be their God, and they shall be My people" (Jer 31:31-33). This prophecy is fulfilled through the Son of God, Jesus Christ whose sacrifice on the cross, the ultimate act of love, puts the Spirit of the law in perspective and writes it on the hearts of all who believe. The law of the old covenant was in no way evil; it is the misdeeds of the people that bring on the condemnation, and the law written on stone cannot purge away sin. But under the new covenant, righteousness comes through the heart. "For if the ministry of condemnation had glory, the ministry of righteousness exceeds much more in glory . . . For if what is passing away is glorious what remains is much more glorious. Therefore, since we have such hope, we use great boldness of speech—unlike Moses, who put a veil over his face so that the children of Israel could not look steadily at the end of what was passing away. But their minds were hardened. For until this day the same veil remains in the reading of the Old Testament, because the veil is taken away in Christ. But even to this day when Moses is read, a veil lies on their heart. Nevertheless, when one turns to the Lord, the veil is taken away" (3:9-16). Only those who have through Christ removed the veil perceive how the new covenant transcends the old. The glory that shone on Moses' face was transient, but the glory that shines from the new convent is permanent for it brings pardon, and not condemnation, life and not death.

Presumably, Judaizers had been at work in the church at Corinth and Paul is responding with his explanation of the transcendence of the new covenant.

The Nature of the Ministry

Continuing with the veil metaphor, Paul stresses the validity of his ministry that claims no special knowledge, no craftiness in handling the word of God, but only the truth as manifested by the Spirit of the Lord. If it seems "our gospel is veiled," says Paul, "it is veiled to those who are perishing, whose minds the god of this age has blinded, who do not believe, lest the light of the gospel of the glory of Christ, who is the image of God, should shine on them. We do not preach ourselves, but Christ Jesus the Lord, and ourselves your servants for Jesus' sake. For it is the God who commanded light to shine out of darkness who has shone in our hearts to give light of the knowledge of the glory of God in the face of Jesus Christ" (4:3-6). With a second metaphor, Paul emphasizes the insignificancy of the messenger, the carrier of the gospel, and the super significance of the source of the gospel: "we have this treasure in earthen vessels, that the excellence of the power may be of God and not of us" (4:7). Thus, God is the treasure and we are the earthen vessel.

The Hardship of the Ministry

Paul's ministry, like that of all the apostles, subjected him to constant hardship. "We are hard pressed on every side, yet not crushed," he says; "we are perplexed, but not in despair; persecuted, but not forsaken; *struck down, but not destroyed*" (4:8-9). Not destroyed by the hardship suffered for Christ, for only through Christ comes transcendence of hardship, suffering and death. This message Paul both declares and demonstrates.

The Glory of the Ministry

And in this letter Paul emphasizes that he and they are inextricably bound together in Christ. Through his ministry they were led to Christ thus becoming his epistle. "You are our epistle written in our hearts, known and read by all men; you are manifestly an epistle of Christ, ministered by us, written not with ink but by the spirit of the living God, not on tablets of stone but on tablets of flesh, that is, of the heart" (3:2-3). Paul goes on to say, "we have the same spirit of faith, according to what is written, 'I believed and therefore I spoke,' we also believe and therefore speak, knowing that He who raised up the Lord Jesus will also raise us up with Jesus, and will present us with you . . . , therefore we do not lose heart. Even though our outward man is perishing, yet the inward man is being renewed day by day" (4:13-16). And the inward man is the focus, for if the "earthly house is destroyed, we have a building from God, a house not made with hands, eternal in the heavens" (5:1). This we know because "we walk by faith, not by sight" (5:7).

II Corinthians Poetic Summary Part One Salutation, Explanation and Reconciliation

Connecting I Corinthians and II Corinthians requires a bit of conjecture inferred from the latter
And so the following scenario inferred provides the most probable events relative to the matter:
After writing I Corinthians, Paul made visit brief, yet was unable to resolve issues contentious.
Vexed by failure of his visitation solicitous, he pens from "anguished heart" a severe letter thus.
Disciple Titus in delivering the letter severe, or in following up, discovers a mood of conciliation.
Happily, he informs Paul who awaits him in Macedonia, probably Philippi, in anxious anticipation.

Buoyed by the Church's conciliatory spirit, he pens from Macedonia epistle called II Corinthians
Expressing joy while reminding these reconciled of their offertory commitment to the Judeans
And while defending his apostolic authority, authentic, against the fulminating false infiltrator.
Echoing I Corinthians, Paul professes apostolic authority in the salutation of this letter, as before.
Declaring himself "an apostle of Jesus Christ by the will of God," he begins addressing believers,
Corinthian believers directly, but indirectly all saints, all believers, of Achaia being the receivers.

In prayerful manner, Paul expresses gratitude to God and to
the Corinthians, saviors twain:
God for his goodness and Corinthians for their prayers,
together assuaging his Asian pain.
From Corinth Paul had traveled to Asia where his
missionary zeal elicited little pleasure.
The specifics the apostle does not relate, only saying he was
"burdened beyond measure."
He mentions the ordeal to emphasize and clarify, to
emphasize his dependency on the Lord
And to clarify how this dependency changed his proposed
Corinthian visit, all of one accord.

Infiltrators false had presented Paul's visitation plan change
as evidence of his untrustworthiness
Causing the apostle to point to his Asian situation and his
dependence on God's guiding goodness.
Refuting his critics' false accusations, Paul reminds
Corinthians that each is the other's boast:
The apostle brought them the gospel and only through its
promise is Jesus Christ mutual host.
"My intent," says Paul, "was to pass by way of you both to
and from my journey to Macedonia
But because the Spirit of the Lord moved my heart I visited
you neither to nor from Macedonia."

Rather, he was moved to send the letter severe instead,
believing the letter Spirit directed clear
Go not to them again and bring sorrow, but write to them
with anguished heart a letter severe.
"Not that you should be grieved," says Paul, "but that you
should know my great love for you."
Verbal spanking was necessary to correct internal
contentiousness spurred by infiltrators untrue.
The content of the severe letter remains obscure, unless,
unless conjecture concerning the matter
Be believed that its content so constitutes chapters ten through
thirteen of Corinthians, the latter.

Chapters ten through thirteen, the reader may note, shifts
from tone conciliatory to tone forbidding
A tone, no doubt, so suitable for the severe letter, but for II
Corinthians, a tone seemingly unfitting.
Could scribes collating manuscripts, ancient and mangled,
have mistakenly merged the letters two?
Some scholars say yes, some say no; either way, Paul's
message comes through: hear the gospel true.
Explanation of his visitation change is implied message too:
it changed because the Lord said so.
When the Spirit moves, man must put aside his mundane
musings and let heavenly guidance flow.

And the spirit of conciliation that Titus had conveyed to
Paul after visiting the Church in Corinth
Paul applauds by example when counseling the Church
concerning a certain offender's punishment.
The offender, possibly leader of those opposing Paul on his
brief visit hoping to defuse contention,
Was now ostracized by the congregation, but Paul cautions
the congregation to show compassion.
"It is now time for forgiveness," he says, cautioning them
concerning the limits of punishment.
The apostle explains that punishment was not to destroy the
rebel, but to persuade him to repent.

"Being repentant," says Paul, "he ought to be forgiven and
welcomed back into the congregation.
Be assured, whom you forgive anything, I forgive also. Allow
not Satan to lure us into temptation.
Welcome the repentant rebel back into Church fellowship;
let not the Devil devious direct us wrong."
Does not the apostle's practice of patiently forgiving the
enemy reveal his purity of purpose strong?
Is Paul's concern not for saving the enemy rebel and the
Church rather than pursuing petty revenge?
Does not the apostle, in his selfless act of love, teach the gospel
both by word and by example keen?

After this interlude of instruction concerning punishment
    and forgiveness, Paul returns to explanation
Explanation of his anxiety following the failure of his brief
    visit to diffuse dissident bred contention
As well as his anguished concern while awaiting results of
    his severe letter so painfully penned.
When he journeys from Ephesus to Troas and Titus is not
    there, he hurries on to Macedonia then
Hoping to expedite receipt of the anxiously awaited news by
    the meeting of Titus, in Philippi possibly,
A town on the mapped Macedonian route that Titus would
    be taking from Corinth to Troas by the sea.

As the apostle had hoped he does indeed meet Titus in
    Macedonia and so expresses his delighted relief
Upon happily hearing consoling news from the Corinthian
    Church where contention had strained belief
But where Paul's severe letter, he learns, had transformed
    contention into corrective conciliation
For his teachings, once being disparaged and damaged by
    falsifiers, now enjoyed full restoration
Prompting Paul to exclaim, "Oh thanks be to God who
    always leads us through Christ to prevail
And through us diffuses the fragrance of His knowledge in
    every place, transforming all travail."

"We do not, like many, peddle the word of God for profit,"
    says Paul. "No, we speak in love,
We speak in Christ before God and speak with sincerity, for
    we are sent by the God above."
Hearing himself thus, Paul proceeds rhetorically asking is he
    not the self commending one
Then continues facetiously asking if letters of
    recommendations are needed, to and from?
And answering as is procedure when posing rhetorical
    questions says, "Our letter you are
Written in our hearts, known and read by all men; manifestly
    an epistle of Christ you are."

Thus, the apostle's acts and the acts of the Corinthians serve
as letters of commendation
Each for the other, and each from God, the Spirit of God
their manifested commendation.
The apostle professes that God made them sufficient as
ministers of the covenant new
For in the covenant old the letter of the Law kills but in the
new the Spirit gives life true.
Such the apostle proclaims comparing old and new for
extolling the new its glory galore
Saying if the ministry of condemnation had glory, the ministry
of righteousness has more.

The ministry of condemnation references the Law, especially
the portion written on Moses' stone
Revealing to man his sinfulness but not revealing the way for
breaking out as was done later on.
Following the letter of the Law was not sufficient as Jesus
makes clear in the Sermon on the Mount
By contrasting the discrepancy between living by the letter
of the Law and by its Spirit, its Fount.
Illustrating, Jesus says, "You have heard it said to those of
old, '*You shall not commit adultery*'
But I say to you whoever looks at a woman to lust has, in his
heart, committed adultery already."

Then He hastens to say, "Do not think I came to destroy the
Law, I came not to destroy but to fulfill."
So, the apostle explains to the Corinthians that the new
covenant is fulfillment, God enhancing still.
Further defining, Paul exclaims, "You are an epistle of Christ,
ministered by us, written not with ink
But by the Spirit of the living God, not on tablets of stone
but on tablets of flesh, of the heart, think."
And writing this the apostle must have recalled Jeremiah's
prophesy of what the Lord God would do:
The Lord would be replacing Isreal's broken covenant, that
covenant of old, replaced by covenant new.

Yes, the Lord says, "After those days, I will put My law in
their minds, and write it on their hearts see
And I will be their God and they will be My people," a
prophesy fulfilled by His Son on Calvary's tree.
This ultimate act of love puts the Spirit of the law in
perspective; on the hearts of believers it is written.
The law of the old covenant was in no way evil; the misdeeds
of the people bring on condemnation then
And the law written on stone cannot purge away sin, for
righteousness comes through the heart, amen!
And if the ministry of condemnation had glory, the ministry
of righteousness exceeds it mightily then.

"For if what is passing away is glorious, what remains is
more glorious," the apostle Paul hailed.
"Therefore, since we have such hope, we use great boldness
of speech—unlike Moses who veiled
Who veiled his face so that the children of Israel could not
look steadily at what was passing away
But their minds were hardened, and in the reading of the O.
T. the same veil remains until this day
Because the veil is taken away in Christ, yet to this day when
Moses is read, a veil on their heart lies.
Nevertheless, when one turns to the Lord, the veil is taken
away, and only then does the truth arise."

Only those having through Christ removed the veil perceive
how old covenant the new transcends:
The glory shown on Moses' face transient, but the shinning
glory of new covenant knows no ends
The new covenant being permanent brings pardon and not
condemnation, brings life and not death.
Presumably, to thwart jawing Judaizers Paul felt compelled
to explicate the new covenant in breadth.
Using the veil metaphor again, Paul stresses the validity of
his ministry, no special knowledge it
No craftiness implicit in his delivery, only the truth, the truth
as manifested by the Lord's Spirit.

"If it seems our gospel is veiled," says the apostle, "it is veiled
to those who are perishing
Whose minds the god of this age has blinded, who do not
believe lest gospel glory shine,
Lest the light of the gospel of the glory of Christ, the image
of God, should shine on them.
We do not preach ourselves, but Christ Jesus the Lord, and
ourselves your servants for Him
For it is the God who commanded light to shine out of
darkness who has shone in our hearts true
Shone giving light of knowledge of the glory of God in the
face of Jesus Christ, and so in ours too."

Paul's ministry, whether at Corinth or elsewhere, subjected
him to constant hardship crush
Prompting him to say to the Corinthians, "We are hard
pressed on every side, yet not hushed.
We are perplexed, but not in despair; persecuted, but not
forsaken; struck down but not destroyed."
Not destroyed because through Christ comes transcendence:
hardship, suffering and death all void.
Such is the apostle's message to the Corinthians as epistle
written and as personally demonstrated
And he insisted that the two of them, church and apostle, are
inextricably bound, forever mated.

"We have the same spirit of faith, according to what is
written, 'I believed and therefore I spoke.'
We believe and we speak knowing that He who raised up
Jesus will also raise up us, that we note."
Furthermore, says the apostle, "We do not lose heart though
our outward self is perishing each day
For the inward self is being renewed each day while our
earthly house destructs, destined for decay.
Yes, we have a building from God, a house not made with
hands, eternal in heaven's eternal light
And when asked how we know this, we say 'we know because
we walk by faith and not by sight.'"

II Corinthians Prose
Summary Two
Ministry, Puzzling Exhortations, Joy, Giving

The Ministry

Having expounded metaphorically on the difference between the person of the flesh and the person of the spirit, Paul says, "Therefore, if anyone is in Christ, he is a new creation, old things have passed away, behold all things have become new. Now all things are of God, who has reconciled us to Himself through Jesus Christ and has given us the ministry of reconciliation, that is, that God was in Christ reconciling the world to Himself . . . Therefore, we are ambassadors for Christ, as though God were pleading through us . . . For He [God] made Him [Jesus] who knew no sin to be sin for us, that we might become the righteousness of God in Him" (5:17-21).

Scripturally authenticating his claim, the apostle cites Isaiah (49:8): "In an acceptable time I have heard you, /And in the day of salvation I have helped you." Then he says, "Behold, *now* is the accepted time; behold, *now* is the day of salvation" (6:2). Old Testament references may not have been so important to the Gentile Corinthians, but Paul is also defending his ministry against Judaizers who are trying to destroy it.

Emphasizing the authenticity of his ministry in practice, Paul says, "In all things we commend ourselves as ministers of God: in much patience, in tribulations, in needs, in distresses . . . in labors . . . in fasting . . . [and] by knowledge and longsuffering, by the Holy Spirit, by sincere love . . . [and] as unknown and yet well known; as dying, and behold we live . . . as sorrowful, yet always rejoicing; as poor, yet making many rich; as having nothing, and yet possessing all things" (6:4-10). Thus, Paul sums up his ministry and Christian ministry in general.

Puzzling Exhortations

Note that 6:14-7:1 contains exhortations concerning the Corinthian congregation being yoked with unbelievers and the yoking of Christ with Satan, material that seems extraneous to this context, for Paul in verses 6:11-13 is reminding the Corinthians that he has opened up his heart to them by revealing his love for them and his pride in them and then invites them to open their hearts to him. Abruptly, verse 14 begins the seemingly intrusive exhortations that continue through verse 7:1. Then verse 7:2 picks up the openness theme again as if there were nothing between it and verse 6:13. To highlight this puzzling phenomenon, let us examine the three verses preceding verse 6:14, and the two verses following verse 7:1: "O Corinthians! We have spoken openly to you, our heart is wide open. You are not restricted by us, but you are restricted by your own affections. Now in return for the same . . . you also be open" (6:11-13). "Open your hearts to us. We have wronged no one, we have corrupted no one, we have defrauded not one. I do not say this to condemn; for I have said before that you are in our hearts, to die together and to live together. Great is my boldness of speech toward you, great is my boasting on your behalf. I am filled with comfort. I am exceedingly joyful in all our tribulation" (7:2-4). Note the seamless transition between verses 6:13 and 7:2 and then note the seemingly extraneousness material comprising the intervening verses 6:14 through 7:1, a list of exhortations beginning, "Do not be unequally yoked together with unbelievers. For what fellowship has righteousness with lawlessness? And what communion has light with darkness? And what accord has Christ with Belial [Satan]?" (6:14-15).

Some scholars believe, and I'm inclined to agree, that these seemingly extraneous verses (6:14-7:1) belong to the so called "previous letter" referenced by Paul in I Corinthians: "I wrote to you in my epistle not to keep company with sexually immoral people" (5:9).

Scholars also make a strong case that chapters ten through thirteen in II Corinthians actually belong to the so called "severe letter" that Paul references (2:4, 7:8). If these scholars are correct, the previous letter and the severe letter are not totally lost, but survive, at least portions thereof. It seems reasonable that copyists in ancient times may have unwittingly woven portions of the previous letter and the severe letter into II Corinthians.

Joy in Corinthian Repentance

Tribulation plagued Paul previous to his meeting Titus in Macedonia: he was "burdened beyond measure" by conflicts in Asia and "anguished of heart" over the Corinthian situation, a situation he had addressed in the severe letter. As prearranged, Paul goes to Troas to await Titus who had followed up on the letter and who would be traveling to Troas to join the apostle. When Paul reaches Troas and Titus has not arrived, the apostle, anxious to hear news concerning the Corinthians, travels on to Macedonia, the route which Titus would be taking to reach Troas. Recalling the experience, the apostle says, "For indeed when we came to Macedonia, our flesh had no rest, but we were troubled on every side. Outside were conflicts, inside were fears. Nevertheless God, who comforts the downcast, comforted us by the coming of Titus, and not only by his coming, but also by the consolation with which he was comforted in you, when he told us of your earnest desire, your mourning, your zeal for me, so that I rejoiced even more." (7:5-6).

Paul rejoices because his severe letter which he wrote with anguished heart had served its purpose well. Though the Corinthians were made sorry by it, the sorrow led to repentance and in their repentance the apostle rejoices. "For observe this very thing," says Paul, "that you sorrowed in a godly manner: What diligence it produced in you, what clearing of yourselves, what indignation, what fear, what vehement desire, what zeal, what vindication! In all things you proved yourselves to be clear in this matter. Therefore, although I wrote to you, I did not do it for the sake of him who had done the wrong, nor for the sake of him who suffered wrong, but that our care for you in sight of God might appear to you. Therefore we have been comforted in your comfort. And we rejoiced exceedingly more for the joy of Titus, because his spirit has been refreshed by you all. For if in anything I have boasted to him about you, I am not ashamed. But as we spoke all things to you in truth, even so our boasting to Titus was found true. And his affections are greater for you as he remembers the obedience of you all, how with fear and trembling you received him. Therefore I rejoice that I have confidence in you in everything" (7:11-16).

After expressing his joy over the repentance and reconciliation of the Corinthians, Paul turns to the topic of giving and specifically to a pledge the Corinthians had made a year earlier.

Collection for the Jerusalem Church, the Mother Church

Rejoicing that the Corinthians were back on track, having repented and reconciled, Paul remembers a financial pledge they had made previous to their troubled phase, and now sees fit to remind them of this pledge. The apostle saw giving an act of grace and placed great importance on it, believing it to be an emulation of the prime Giver, God the Father, who gave his only begotten Son, and the Son who freely gave up the riches of heaven for poverty on earth and death on a cross, all to benefit humanity. In the Christian context these acts are the supreme acts of grace, grace being to give where undeserved and without expectation of return. In this scenario, grace and love are inextricably bound, for the highest form of love is love that expects nothing in return.

One of Paul's pet projects was collecting monies to give to the Church at Jerusalem, the Mother Church, whose congregation (saints) had because of drought and famine and persecution become impoverished. Apostles and disciples from this Mother Church had carried the gospel far beyond the Holy City and thereby spiritually enriched the lives of many, both Gentile and Jew. Now the Mother Church was in need of fiscal support and Paul was determined to include this support as part of his ministry by encouraging the new churches on his missionary routes to send donations. Such a gift was a dual blessing, a blessing to the receiver and a blessing to the giver.

Paul wanted to be sure that the Corinthian congregation, now on track again, did not forget their previous pledge of generosity and lose their blessing through non compliance. To the congregation, the apostle writes, "But as you abound in everything—in faith, in speech, in knowledge, in all diligence, and in your love for us—see that you abound in this grace also. I speak not by commandment, but I am testing the sincerity of your love by the diligence of your love . . . For you know the grace of our Lord Jesus Christ, that though He was rich, yet for our sakes He became poor, that you through His poverty might become rich. And in this I give my advice: It is to your advantage not only to be doing what you began and were desiring to do a year ago; but now you also must complete the doing of it; that as there was readiness to desire it, so there also may be a completion out of what you have. For if there is a willing mind, it is accepted according to what one has, and not according to what he does not have" (8:7-12). In God's eyes it is not the actual amount given that counts, but the generosity according to one's ability to give.

Though this lesson on giving is directed to the Corinthian congregation, it is a lesson that will well serve any congregation of saints (believers) at any place and at any time.

Need for Propriety in Giving

Paul explains and demonstrates the special attention necessary in maintaining the integrity of giving. Having praised the Corinthians for their commitment to join other missionary churches in helping the Mother Church in Jerusalem, Paul explains the importance of taking great care to avoid any claim or even any suspicion concerning the propriety of the gift being collected for the Church at Jerusalem. He explains that his trusted partner Titus whom they know and love, will be coming to them to help in collecting the monetary gift for the saints at Jerusalem and that two other brethren will accompany him. These two brethren are also persons of impeccable integrity, one of whom has been praised by all the churches and has been chosen to represent them in delivering the gift.

The special care taken in collecting and delivering this lavish gift is imperative, Paul says, in "providing honorable things, not only in the sight of the Lord, but also in the sight of men" (8:21). Thus, through example and explanation, the apostle emphasizes the importance of taking great care to avoid even the appearance of impropriety in giving.

The Importance of Giving

Concerning giving, Paul tells the Corinthians that "he who sows sparingly will also reap sparingly, and he who sows bountifully will also reap bountifully. So let each one give as he purposes in his heart, not grudgingly or of necessity; *for God loves a cheerful giver*. And God is able to make all grace abound toward you, that you, always having all sufficiency in all things, have an abundance for every good work" (9:6-80). Giving is an expression of love, God having furnished the example in the giving of His Son.

Paul prepares the Corinthians by referring to their generous pledge to the Jerusalem Church and by reminding them that he will soon be collecting the gift for transporting to Jerusalem. Furthermore, he reminds them of the importance of their generosity and adds that he has boasted of them to the Macedonians who in turn were inspired by the zeal of the Corinthians. As further preparation, the apostle mentions that should some Macedonians come with him he would be shamed (as well as they) should they not be ready with their pledged gift. Thus, Paul explains his reason for sending ahead Titus and the other two trusted brethren. With advanced notice and assurance of propriety, the Corinthians can be fully prepared, be ready with their bountiful gift, previously promised, and also "be ready as a matter of generosity and not as a grudging obligation" (9:5).

In further praise and explanation, the apostle says, "you are enriched in everything for all liberality, which causes thanksgiving through us to God. For the administration of this service not only supplies the needs of the saints, but also is abounding through many thanksgivings to God" (9:12). In giving to the needy, one is giving to God; in giving to the needy one is worshiping God. "Inasmuch as you did it to one of the least of these [needy ones] . . . you did it to Me," says Jesus (Matt 25:40).

II Corinthians Poetic Summary Two Ministry, Puzzling Exhortations, Joy, Giving

Rejoicing over the Corinthians' reconciliation, reconciliation re-embracing his ministry
Paul not only praises their action but extemporizes on that ministry and its true identity.
After differentiating between the person of flesh and the person of spirit, he goes on to say,
"Therefore, if anyone is in Christ he is a new creation, in him old things have passed away
All things have become new. Now all things are of God who has reconciled us to Himself
Through Jesus Christ, has given us the ministry of reconciliation: in Christ God Himself."

"Therefore, we are ambassadors for Christ as though God were pleading through our ministry
For God made Jesus who knew no sin to be our sin, providing righteousness for you and me."
Not only does Paul extemporize the gospel but calling on Scripture quotes prophet Isaiah too:
"In an acceptable time says God I have heard you and in the day of salvation have helped you."
Interpreting, Paul declares, "Behold, *now* is the accepted time; *now* is the day of salvation."
No doubt Paul's Scriptural interpretation serves to counteract hostile Jewish condemnation.

As Paul preaches so he practices, maintaining his ministry
through tribulation, need and distress
Making the many rich though being poor himself, having
nothing yet possessing all things best.
Paul makes clear his ministry is not of himself but of God,
he being ambassador only
Yes, ambassador for Christ the apostle insists: what else
could Christian ministry be?
Thus, Paul explains his ministry, how he lives as ambassador
for Christ he wishes to relate
Pouring out his heart to his beloved, reformed Corinthians
and asking that they reciprocate.

Then Paul's letter takes a puzzling turn: talking exhortation
rather than reconciliation embraced
A subject suddenly broached that seems unrelated in tone
and theme, and thereby truly misplaced:
Note 6:14 through 7:1 are verses that talk of not yoking
with unbelievers nor Christ with Satan
All well and good, but seemingly off topic, for note 7:2
resumes the talk of reconciliation again.
Thus, when alert readers take note of the seamless transition
between 6:13 and 7:2
They may ponder the extraneous exhortations between and
wonder if there is issue.

Bible scholars offer explanation reasonable saying it may
belong to the so called letter previous
Saying, like the lost severe letter, was not totally lost, but
woven into II Corinthians mysterious.
Perhaps ancient copyists unwittingly weaved portions of the
two into Corinthians Two
Here a portion of the previous letter and later a sizeable
portion of the severe letter too.
Needless to say, such conjecture in no way questions divine
inspiration in the writing thereof
God's word has always worked its way in mysterious ways:
that we have it is sanction enough.

And so we read that tribulation had plagued Paul previous
to his meeting Titus in Macedonia
Burdened "beyond measure" by conflicts in Asia and
"anguished of heart" by Corinth's mania.
Reaching Troas before Titus, Paul cannot sit still without
knowing the news Titus will bring
So he travels on tracking the Macedonia route in reverse to
expedite the meeting of the twain.
Somewhere on the Macedonia track, possibly Philippi, the
two join hands much to Paul's relief
Who later recounts the bittersweet event remembering his
agitated state but savoring his belief.

"For when indeed we came to Macedonia, our flesh had no
rest, and on all sides troubled thus
Outside were conflicts, inside were fears. Yet God, who
comforts the downcast, comforted us
Comforted us by the coming of Titus, and not only by his
coming, but by his consolation shown
And by his telling us of your earnest desire, your mourning,
your zeal for me, for which I longed."
Learning of Corinthian reconciliation releases a heavy
burden and allows the apostle to rejoice
He can rejoice that his severe letter served its purpose despite
not having been written by choice.

Yes, the letter severe written with "anguished heart" had
gratefully served the apostle's purpose well
Though it had made the Corinthians sorry, the sorrow led
them to repentance; the epistle did not fail.
Rejoicing, Paul says, "Observe that you sorrowed in godly
manner: what diligence it produced in you
What clearing of yourselves, what indignation, what fear,
what desire, what zeal, what vindication too!
In all things you proved yourselves to be clear in this matter.
Yes, I wrote but for special sake known
Not for the sake of him who had done the wrong, and not
for the sake of him who had suffered wrong

But that our care for you in the sight of God might appear to
you, insight needed to bring you along."

"Therefore," Paul continues, "we have been comforted in
your comfort and in the joy of Titus too
Whose spirit has been refreshed after visiting and having
seen confirmed my boasts concerning you
Of which I am not ashamed, for as we spoke all things to
you in truth so our boasting was found true
And his affections are greater for you as he remembers your
obedience, how with fear and trembling
You all received him when he came. Therefore, I rejoice that
I have confidence in you in everything.
After expressing his joy over their repentance and
reconciliation, the apostle turns the topic to giving.

Paul, remembering a financial pledge the Corinthians had
made previous to their troubled phase,
Sees fit to remind the congregation of their pledge lest the
due date arrive and money yet to raise.
The apostle believed giving an act of grace, an act grounded
in the gift prime, God giving his Son
And the Son freely giving up the riches of Heaven for earth's
poverty and death on a cross anon.
Thusly viewed, grace is giving where undeserved and giving
without expectation of return.
Thusly viewed, grace and love are inextricably bound, giving
without expectation of return.

If Paul had a pet project, it was collecting monies for the
Mother Church, the Church at Jerusalem
Drought and famine and persecution had brought poverty to
this congregation of saints, all of them.
These same saints had spread the gospel far beyond
Jerusalem's wall thereby enriching many a soul
Both Jew and Gentile, but now the Mother Church needed
enrichment to assuage its poverty untold.

Perceiving the fiscal need of the Jerusalem saints a call to ministry, the apostle answers the call
Exhorting new churches on his missionary routes to send donations to the Mother Church of all.

Giving to the Mother Church was blessing dual, a blessing to the receiver and a blessing to the giver
And Paul not wanting the now contrite Corinthian congregation forget their previous pledge to deliver
Says to them, "As you abound in faith, in speech, in diligence, see that you abound in this grace too
I speak not to command you but to test the sincerity of your love by the excellence of what you do.
For you know the grace of our Lord Jesus Christ: though He was rich, He for our sakes became poor
That we through His poverty might become rich. Let that be our guide for grace now and evermore."

Continuing, Paul says, "And in this I give my advice: It is to your advantage not only to be doing
What you began doing and were doing a year ago; but now it is meet that you complete its doing.
As there was readiness to desire it, so is there need of readiness to complete it, out of your ability
For if there is a willing mind, it is accepted according to what one has, without willingness futility."
And so the apostle confirms criteria for giving: willingness according to ability comprises this grace.
And as he confirms the criteria of giving for the Corinthians so he confirms it for any time or place.

Besides its importance and its nature, Paul addresses maintaining integrity of the giving process.
Praising the Corinthians' commitment to aid the Jerusalem church, he discusses procedure best.
To protect the integrity of giver, carrier, and recipient, the apostle presents plan practical and sound

Responsibility for collecting and carrying must be given to
only the known and most trusted found.
The known must be widely known, for many churches on
Paul's vast circuit were giving graciously
Thus, great care must be taken to avoid claim or even suspicion
concerning any kind of impropriety.

Paul's trusted partner Titus would be coming to the
Corinthians to assist in their monetary collection
For the saints at Jerusalem, and with him two other trusted
brethren, one by all churches the selection.
The special care taken in collecting and carrying this lavish
gift is imperative in the mind of Paul
For such special care maintains integrity of giving in the
sight of the Lord and in the sight of all.
After extended explanation concerning the necessity for
maintaining an honorable giving process
The apostle returns to his earlier focus on the giver, on the
why of giving, and what giving is best.

"He who sows sparingly will reap sparingly, and he who sows
bountifully will reap bountifully,"
Says the apostle, "So let every one give as he purposes in his
heart, not grudgingly or of necessity
For God loves a cheerful giver. And God is able to make all
grace abound toward you, that you
Always having all sufficiency in all things, have an abundance
for every good work that you do."
Giving is an expression of love, and God furnished us the
example, both the Father and the Son.
When we give willingly, it is an act of love and grace, for we are
following the exemplary One.

Again Paul seeks to prepare the Corinthians by referencing
their generous pledge to Jerusalem
And by reminding them that he will ere long be collecting
the gift and transporting it for them.

Again he reminds them of the importance of their generosity
which had paid blessed dividends
He had boasted to the Macedonians who in turn were
inspired by the zeal of the Corinthians
And should some Macedonians come with him he would be
shamed should Corinthians not deliver.
Thereby, Paul instructs the Corinthians concerning both the
commitment and completion of the giver.

The apostle intends the Corinthians to be well prepared
having sent instructions and the brethren.
Possessing advanced notice and propriety assurance, how
could preparation for them be problem?
Paul expects readiness, but readiness "as a matter of
generosity and not as a grudging obligation."
Ever the teacher and exhorter, he says, "You are enriched in
everything for all liberality shown
And this gift not only supplies the needs of the saints, but it
abounds through thanksgivings to God."
Giving to the needy is giving to God, giving to the needy is
worshipping God, so said the Son of God.

II CORINTHIANS PROSE
SUMMARY THREE
THE APOSTLE'S DEFENSE

Change of Tone and Focus

Chapter ten ushers in a different tone and focus. The tone of celebrated reconciliation resulting from the effect of the severe letter so prominent in the preceding nine chapters is no longer present. The focus is now defense, Paul defending his acts and actions as if reconciliation had not taken place. And most likely it had not when chapters ten through thirteen were written, for they are probably a portion of the severe letter mistakenly tacked on to II Corinthians by copyists piecing together the letter from scraps of ancient manuscript. Be that as it may, the chapters are informative and instructive, for in defending his apostolic authority Paul defines true discipleship. And that these three chapters may belong to a separate letter, as some scholars presume, does not diminish their authenticity as divinely inspired.

Apostolic Authority Challenged

We can infer from Paul's defense that his authority has not only been challenged but even ridiculed. The apostle quotes a charge hurled against him: "For his letters . . . are weighty and powerful, but his bodily presence is weak, and his speech contemptible" (10:10). Presumably, false teachers have infiltrated the Corinthian Church with the intent of discrediting both Paul and the gospel he preached. The above charge implies that though Paul may write a strong letter, in person his physical presence is less than impressive and his oratorical skills are less than effective. Of course, the apostle is being attacked for deficiency of physical attributes rather than deficiency of spiritual attributes, and it is on this misconception that Paul bases his defense.

Apostolic Authority Defended

Paul asks, "Do you look at things according to the outward appearance" (10:7)? Then he answers, "If anyone is convinced in himself that he is Christ's, let him again consider this in himself, that just as he is Christ's, even so we are Christ's" (10:7). The apostle goes on to say, "For we dare not class ourselves or compare ourselves with those who commend themselves, for they, measuring themselves by themselves, and comparing themselves among themselves, are not wise" (10:12). Then, taking a line from Isaiah, says, "'He who glories, let him glory in the Lord,' for not he who commends himself is approved, but whom the Lord commends" (10:17-18). The true apostle gets his authority only from the Lord and his approval comes only from the Lord. The apostle must not be judged by what men say about him or what he says about himself, but by how well his actions exemplify the teaching and example of the Lord. And on this basis, Paul defends his apostolic authority.

Assessing the Situation

Paul believed himself a true apostle carrying out the great commission of Jesus Christ: to go into all the world and preach the gospel to all. And having been the founder of the church in Corinth, he feels fatherly affection for it and its well being as evidenced in his figurative explanation of what has caused confusion and contention. He says, "For I am jealous for you with godly jealousy, for I have betrothed you to one husband, that I may present you as a chaste virgin to Christ. But I fear, lest somehow, as the serpent deceived Eve by his craftiness, so your minds may be corrupted from the simplicity that is in Christ" (11:2-3). More specifically, Paul notes that opponents have come to the Corinthian Church preaching "another Jesus" and "a different spirit" and "a different gospel." Asserting his own authority, Paul declares, "I consider that I am not at all inferior to the most eminent apostles" (11:5).

To support his assertion, Paul reviews his actions. He recognizes that he is untrained in speech meaning he is no trained orator, yet he knows that he is not deficient in knowledge of the gospel which he has manifested to them and he has done so without pay. Presumably, he has been demeaned by detractors saying his preaching was too poor to warrant remuneration. Paul points out that his refusing remuneration was done to ensure the purity of his mission. His focus was strictly on spreading the gospel and not on selling the gospel. His emphasis was glorifying Christ and not himself. He asks, "Did I commit sin in abasing myself that you might be exalted, because I preached the gospel of God to you free of charge" (11:7)? Those condemning Paul were doing so to elevate themselves; whereas Paul was self-effacing they were self-exalting. "But such are false apostles," says Paul, "deceitful workers, transforming themselves into apostles of Christ. And no wonder! For Satan himself transforms himself into an angel of light. Therefore, it is not surprising that his ministers also transform themselves into ministers of righteousness, whose end will be according to their works" (11:13-15). Paul proceeds to assess his own works thereby implicitly exposing his detractors' deceitfulness.

Boasting for Christ

Since imposters had boasted of their eminence at Paul's expense, the apostle indulges in a bit of ironic boasting. Having been accused of being weak, Paul decides to capitalize on the accusation by revealing how his perceived weakness was actually his strength. Was the Son of God not weak in His suffering and in dying on the cross? And yet did this very weakness not conform to the Father's plan? And did the Son not receive the power of the Father through His suffering? This is the point Paul drives home in his ironic boasting.

"Seeing that many boast according to the flesh, I also will boast," says Paul, "for you put up with fools gladly, since yourselves are wise" (11:18-19)! He immediately disarms the Corinthians with his verbal irony: "since yourselves are wise!" Obviously, they are not wise having been taken in by the imposters and Paul inserts a barbed rebuke by saying one thing and meaning the opposite. This fits his ironic boasting format, for normally weakness would not be something to boast about, but in this case it is. For his perceived weakness is suffering for the sake of Christ, for sake of the gospel.

Like the imposters, Paul is a Hebrew, an Israelite, the seed of Abraham, and as a minister of Christ he is much more than they. He is much more in the things that count. "I am more," says Paul: "in labors more abundant, in stripes above measure, in prisons more frequently, in deaths often. From the Jews five times I received forty stripes minus one. Three times I was beaten with rods; once I was stoned; three times I was shipwrecked; a night and a day I have been in the deep; in journeys often, in perils of waters, in perils of robbers, in perils of my own countrymen, in perils of the Gentiles, in perils in the city, in perils in the sea, in perils among false brethren, in weariness and toil, in sleeplessness often, in hunger and thirst, in fasting often, in cold nakedness—besides what comes upon me daily: my deep concern for all the churches" (11:23-28). Besides all the physical hardships endured in founding numerous churches in hostile environments, there is the constant mental anguish over their continued welfare.

Assuming that this is a portion of the severe letter, it is no wonder that the contentious Corinthians had a change of heart after weighing Paul's horrendous hardship and anguish and suffering against his detractors' charges, one being a deficiency in physical appearance and oratorical skill. And ironically the severe suffering he encountered and endured, like that of Jesus Christ, was a manifestation of strength in carrying out God's plan of spreading the gospel. Though it might be seen as weakness by the world, suffering for Christ's sake is anything but weakness as Paul so aptly illustrates.

Vision, Revelation, Thorn, and Paradox

Following the mention of his miraculous escape from the authorities in Damascus after his conversion, his being lowered down the wall in a basket, Paul relates an even more miraculous event: his heavenly ascension. To gain distance in relating it, he speaks of himself in third person saying, "I know a man in Christ who fourteen years ago—whether in the body I do not know, or whether out of the body I do not know, God knows . . . how he was caught up into Paradise and heard inexpressible words, which it is not lawful for a man to utter. Of such a one I will boast; yet of myself I will not boast, except of my infirmities . . . . Lest I should be exalted above measure by the abundance of the revelations, a thorn in the flesh was given me, a messenger of Satan to buffet me, lest I be exalted above measure. Concerning this thing, I pleaded with the Lord three times that it might depart from me. And He said to me, *"My grace is sufficient for you, for My strength is made perfect in weakness."* Therefore most gladly I will rather boast in my infirmities, that the power of Christ may rest upon me. Therefore I take pleasure in infirmities, in reproaches, in needs, in persecutions, in distresses, for Christ's sake. *For when I am weak, then I am strong*" (12:2-10).

With this paradoxical statement, Paul underscores the import of his ironic boasting. At the center of irony is discrepancy and at the center of Paul's boasting is the discrepancy between heaven's view and the world's view of weakness. Paul presents his worldly perceived weaknesses which are in effect heavenly perceived strengths. And Paul dramatizes his point by punctuating it with paradox. Paradox grabs the audience's attention because of its seeming contradiction which on closer examination proves to be no contradiction at all, thus dramatizing its point. In saying "when I am weak, then I am strong" Paul dramatizes his point: it is Christ whom the true apostle seeks to glorify, not himself; it is the gospel that the true apostle seeks to perpetuate, not himself. When the apostle puts Christ first, he is the most Christ-like and thereby the strongest in Christ.

Scolding

Paul scolds the Corinthians telling them they have compelled him to "become a fool in boasting." Rather than being compelled to defend himself, he says, "I ought to have been commended by you, for in nothing was I behind the most eminent apostles, though I am nothing" (12:11). His list of physical suffering and mental anguish in spreading the gospel by establishing numerous churches is second to no other apostle. And the Corinthians had witnessed his apostleship close up since he had labored among them some eighteen months. "Truly," he says, "the signs of an apostle were accomplished among you with all perseverance, in signs and wonders and mighty deeds. For what is it in which you were inferior to other churches, except that I myself was not burdensome to you? Forgive me this wrong!" (12:12-13). Again Paul is scolding them for not seeing through the superficiality and pettiness of his detractors after having witnessed the work of the Holy Spirit in the founding and growth of the Corinthian Church in its hostile environment. He cannot resist the ironic barb about not being burdensome to them, referring to the fact that he accepted no remuneration for his labors, a fact that his detractors sought to exploit. Of course, it was in reality Paul sacrificing for Christ's sake.

The apostle informs them that he is ready to come to them a third time and again he will not be burdensome, "for the children ought not to lay up for the parents, but the parents for the children" (12:14). Furthermore, he says, "I will very gladly spend and be spent for your souls; though the more abundantly I love you, the less I am loved," (12:15), again scolding them for not recognizing true apostleship. Then he chastises them for giving credence to the false charge that being crafty he had caught them by guile, an insinuation that his motive for securing collections for the impoverished Jerusalem Church was to line his own pockets. Again he directs them to his actions while among them and the acts of his associates such as Titus who were sent by him. Had he or they ever taken advantage of them? Of course, the answer to his rhetorical question is that neither he nor his associates have ever taken advantage. To the contrary, they have only sacrificed for them. Paul is scolding the Corinthians for not listening to his actions rather than be led astray by listening to the frivolous and false accusations of his detractors, the false apostles.

Appeal and Warning

From scolding Paul moves to appeal telling the Corinthians that he is not defending his actions for any personal prestige, but he is standing before God in Christ speaking the truth and doing so for their edification. He hopes that this edification will lead them to repentance, though he fears it will not. And if not, he warns them he will take quick and strong action when he comes to them. He tells them, "This will be the third time I am coming to you. By the mouth of two or three witnesses every word shall be established. I have told you before, and foretell as if I were present . . . that if I come again I will not spare—since you seek a proof of Christ speaking in me, who is not weak toward you but mighty in you. For though He was crucified in weakness, yet He lives by the power of God. For we also are weak in Him, but we shall live with Him by the power of God toward you" (13:1-4).

In a final appeal, Paul urges them to examine themselves to determine if they are in the faith. Thus, they should know whether or not they are in Christ, unless they fail the examination. Furthermore, he trusts they will learn that he has not failed the examination: "I trust that you will know that we are not disqualified" (13:6). Completing his appeal, Paul says, "Now I pray to God that you do no evil, not that we should appear approved, but that you should do what is honorable, though we may seem disqualified. For we can do nothing against the truth, but for the truth. For we are glad when we are weak and you are strong. And this also we pray, that you may be made complete" (13:7-9).

Closing the Letter

In closing, the apostle calls for unity and peace and the love of God; urges the greeting of one another with a holy kiss; sends greetings from all the saints; and, ends with a benediction: "The grace of the Lord Jesus Christ, and the love of God, and the communion of the Holy Spirit be with you all. Amen" (13:14).

II Corinthians Poetic Summary Three The Apostle's Defense

The reconciliation tone of II Corinthians seems to end
beginning with chapter ten
The letter's celebratory focus turns defensive as if
reconciliation had never been
As if the severe letter had never been delivered and Titus
had never reported its success
As if this chapter and the following two do not belong, do
not fall in focus with the rest.
Some scholars say there is good reason for such, and argue
thus: the chapters do not belong
For they are the severe letter so long thought lost but all the
while to II Corinthians tacked on.

Copyists piecing together the letter from scraps of ancient
manuscripts could have erred
Scraps of papyrus without chapter or verse somewhat
scrambled and diverse and blurred
Two letters or portions thereof could have been pieced
together thinking the two were one.
Whatever the case, divine inspiration was not lost and the
pieces serve posterity on and on.
Whether these three chapters—ten through
thirteen—belong to letter severe or Corinthians Two
In them Paul defines his apostolic authority and in so doing
defines for everyone discipleship true.

From Paul's defense we infer not only his authority
challenged but his person brutally ridiculed:

Slanders seem to say his letters askew; his bodily presence
weak; his speech a contemptible tool.
False apostles have come to the Corinthian Church
intending to discredit Paul and his preaching
But responding ironically he proves his perceived weaknesses
to be true apostleship far reaching.
The true apostle gets his authority from the Lord; his
approval comes only from the Lord' read.
His authenticity is proven not by what is said about him but
how well he follows the Lord's lead.

"We dare not compare ourselves to those who measure
themselves by themselves; they are unwise
As Isaiah says 'He who glories, let him glory in the Lord'; it
is the Lord who commends or denies."
Paul proved himself the true apostle as he went into the
world preaching the gospel everywhere
Enduring all hardships and suffering all indignities that Jew
and Gentile might the gospel hear.
Churches he founded far and wide but not one dearer to his
heart than the one at Corinth
Where long labor rendered results miraculous, till false
apostles came with different intent.

Paul's fatherly affection for the Corinthians is reflected in his
figurative explanation
"I am jealous for you with godly jealousy, for I have
betrothed you to one husband
That I may present you as a chaste virgin to Christ, lest
somehow, as the crafty serpent old
Deceived Eve so your minds may be corrupted, no longer
attuned to Christ's simplicity bold."
Paul's opponents have come to Corinth preaching another
Jesus, another gospel and spirit
Prompting the apostle to declare, "I am not inferior to the
most eminent apostles, far from it."

To support his declaration, Paul reviews his apostolic labors
in light of critical accusation:
Readily he recognizes his deficiency of speech should the
criteria be oratorical perfection.
In knowledge of the gospel, however, he is not deficient and
has dispensed it to them without pay
And his refusal of remuneration was to ensure purity of
motive, regardless of what his critics say.
He sought to spread the gospel not to sell it; he sought to
glorify the Lord not to exalt himself.
"Did I sin in abasing myself that you might be exalted?" Paul
asks. "Should my aim be wealth?"

Those who had condemned Paul did so to elevate
themselves, but the apostle turned the tables keen
He boasted ironically of his perceived weakness proving it to
be the epitome of the Christian scene.
Was not the Son of God weak in His suffering and dying on
the cross asks the apostle patently?
Yet did not the Son clearly receive the power of the Father
through His suffering and humility?
"Seeing that many boast according to the flesh, I also will
boast, for you gladly put up with fools,
Since yourselves are wise," says Paul, disarming the Corinthians
with irony and sarcasm as tools.

Obviously, they are not wise having been taken in by the
imposters, thus Paul's barbed rebuke
His verbal irony compliments his strategy of ironically
boasting weakness to be his strong suit.
The apostle parades his perceived weaknesses proving them
to be sufferings for Christ's sake
Being a Hebrew, an Israelite, the seed of Abraham says the
apostle does not salvation make
He is much more in the things that count: in labors more
abundant, in stripes above measure
Five times from Jews, three times from Gentiles, in prisons
more frequently, often life unsure.

Once he was stoned and three times he was shipwrecked, in
journeys often, in perils of the sea
In perils of his own countrymen, in perils of the Gentiles, in
perils of robbers, in perils of the city
In peril among false brethren, in weariness and toil, in
sleeplessness often, in hunger and thirst
In fasting often, in cold nakedness, in constant physical peril,
yet daily mental anguish the worst
In his deep concern for the churches all, physical suffering in
the founding of the churches all
Mental anguish in shepherding all, Paul ever vigilant lest
contention cause one of them to fall.

Assuming this a portion of the letter severe, would one
wonder that the Corinthians reconciled?
Weigh Paul's horrendous hardships and anguish against the
petty charges by his detractors vile.
Deficiency of physical presence and oratory skill sound
somewhat hollow with full evidence in.
Was the apostle's severe suffering in spreading the gospel not
done to save the world from sin?
Ironically, the suffering Paul endured, like that of Jesus, was a
manifestation of strength manifold
What the world saw as weakness was in fact God's plan for
taking the gospel to every household.

Knowing he is a major actor in this plan the apostle Paul
pushes the Corinthians to take a stand.
Shifting to third person he tells them of his heavenly
ascension as if it were that of another man:
"I know a man in Christ who fourteen years ago, whether in
or out of the body he cannot say
But God knows how he was caught up into Paradise and
heard inexpressible words that day
Of such a one I will boast; yet of myself I will not boast,
except of my infirmities resounding.
Lest I should be exalted above measure, a thorn in my side
was given me thereby grounding."

"Three times I went to the Lord to plead that the thorn be removed, that it depart hence.
He replied, '*My grace is sufficient for you, for My strength is made perfect in weakness.*'
Thus, most gladly I will rather boast in my infirmities, that the power of Christ infuse me
Thus, I take pleasure in infirmities, in reproaches, in needs, in distresses, for Christ's sake
For when I am weak, then I am strong." Paul's paradox surely explodes his detractors' case.
They focused on appearance; Paul focused on faith that brought Christ up close, face to face.

Climatic paradox punctuates Paul's ironic boasting thereby enhancing its potency
At the center of irony is discrepancy, at the center of Paul's boasting is discrepancy
His ironic boasting juxtaposes the world's and heaven's view of weakness, at length
A contrast revealing that what the world views as weakness heaven views as strength
And then cinches his point with the paradox, "For when I am weak, then I am strong."
Paul's perceived weakness is truly his strength, he is right on, his detractors wrong.

Still scolding, Paul tells the Corinthians they have compelled him to become a fool in boasting
Rather than defending himself, he says, "I should have been commended by you, for in nothing
In nothing was I behind the most eminent apostles, though I am nothing," paradox again.
In suffering for the gospel, in establishing new churches, Paul was second to no brethren
And the Corinthians had witnessed his apostleship while he ministered to them an extended time
For eighteen months they witnessed his work up close as he labored to bring their church on line.

"Truly," says Paul, "the signs of an apostle were accomplished among you with all perseverance
In signs and wonders and mighty deeds, for what is it in which you were inferior to other churches
Except that I myself was not burdensome to you? Forgive me this wrong!" Again he scolds them
He scolds them for not having seen through the superficiality of his detractors' charges against him
Having witnessed the work of the Holy Spirit in the founding and growth of the church at Corinth
And he cannot resist the ironic barb concerning his refusal of remuneration, its misconstrued intent.

He informs them that he is ready to come to them again, but again will not burden them financially
"For the children should not lay up for the parents, but the parents lay up for the children, naturally."
Furthermore, he says, "I will very gladly spend and be spent for your souls though it proves true
The more abundantly I love you, the less I am loved," scolding them for apostleship misconstrued.
And not only apostleship but fellowship too: declaring his Jerusalem collection a calculated deception
Not a love offering going to the Mother Church, but a scheme to line his own pockets the intention.

Again he points to his actions while laboring among them and to the actions of his associates sent
Had he or they ever taken advantage of them? No, they had all been straight, never had one bent.
Paul scolds the Corinthians for not listening to his actions rather than be led astray by his detractors
Doing so they could readily discern between acts of the apostle true and acts of the deceitful actors.
From scolding Paul shifts to appeal cautioning that he defends his actions not for any personal gain
But that he is standing before God in Christ speaking the truth for their edification and good name.

He hopes the edification will lead them to repentance,
though he fears that may not be the case
And so he warns that if not he will take strong action when
he stands before them face to face.
"If I must come to you again I will not spare, for you seek a
proof of Christ speaking in me
Who is not weak toward you but mighty in you, for though
He was crucified in weakness
Yet He lives by the power of God, for we also are weak in
Him, but we shall live with Him
By the power of God toward you," says Paul, warning and
instructing as he appeals to them.

On the matter of faith, Paul, making a final appeal, counsels
self examination on their part
Thus, they would know whether they are in Christ, that is, if
they truly examine the heart.
And he trusts that they will learn he has done the self
examination and has not failed
Furthermore, he trusts that what he has done and what he
has written will lift the veil
"For we can do nothing against the truth, but for the truth,
from truth there is no retreat
We are glad when we are weak and you are strong; we pray
you may be made compete."

Thus, Paul has made his case concerning weakness as
strength and strength as weakness
Weakness for Christ is the greatest strength for God's
strength is made perfect in weakness
So Paul can boast, "For when I am weak, then I am strong"
meaning weak for Christ's sake
And in so doing hope that this paradox enlightens the
Corinthians concerning what's at stake.

Galatians Prose Summary
Paul's Apostleship and Gospel Challenged

Possibly One of Paul's Earliest Letters

At the time that Paul was writing his epistles, Galatia was a Roman province in Asia Minor. And in Acts we learn that the apostle, on his first missionary journey, established churches in the southern portion of the province, namely the cities Iconium, Lystra and Derbe; therefore, one is inclined to believe that this letter addressed "to the Churches of Galatia" is a letter written to these churches. Of course, it is possible that Paul established churches in the northern portion of Galatia at a later time as some scholars speculate. If, however, the letter were written to the Galatian churches established on the first missionary journey, as is reasonable to believe, and was written from Antioch in Syria where Paul stayed for "a long time" following the first missionary journey (Acts 14:28), the letter would be one of Paul's earliest.

The Salutation

The salutation is short and begins with defensive tone. Paul declares himself an apostle "not from men nor through man, but through Jesus Christ and God the Father who raised Him from the dead" (1:1). It soon becomes clear that Paul's apostleship and his gospel have been attacked, hence his defensive beginning.

Defending the Gospel and His Apostleship

That the Galatian churches are so soon turning away from the gospel disturbs and provokes Paul: "I marvel that you are turning away so soon from Him who called you in the grace of Christ to a different gospel" (1:6). He goes on to say that there is only one gospel—the one that he preached—and "if anyone preaches any other gospel to you than what you have received [from Paul], let him be accursed" (1:9). In defense of both his apostleship and the gospel, Paul says, "I make known to you, brethren, that the gospel which was preached by me is not according to man. For I neither received it from man, nor was I taught it, but it came through the revelation of Jesus Christ" (1:11-12). Paul is referring to his Damascus experience in which he was struck down by a light from heaven and then spoken to by a voice from heaven calling him to witness for Jesus Christ and not against Him. Therefore, he knows that what he preached to the Galatians was the true gospel revealed by the Lord Himself.

Relationship with the Twelve

Paul emphasizes the authenticity of his apostleship by explaining that though his call came after the resurrection, it came, like that of the Twelve, from Jesus Christ and that he received instruction, though his instruction came through revelation. He says that it is three years before he goes to Jerusalem and spends time with Peter. Paul places himself on the same level as the original Twelve because of his special call and special revelation. It may be said that Paul sees himself as the thirteenth apostle with the special mission of carrying the gospel to the Gentiles.

Relationship with the Jerusalem Church

Paul says that after fourteen years he again went to Jerusalem, this time accompanied by Barnabas and a Greek convert named Titus. He says he went because of revelation to communicate "to them that gospel which I preach among the Gentiles, but privately to those who were of reputation, lest by any means I might run, or had run, in vain" (2:2). Though Paul has established his independence as an apostle, he wants the blessing of the Jerusalem Church and its leaders—"James, Cephas, and John"—and the best way for that is to present his case first hand. He brings the uncircumcised Titus with him as a test case and is pleased that even though a certain faction argued for the necessity of the Gentile's circumcision the leaders of the Church did not go along. "But on the contrary, when they saw that gospel for the uncircumcised had been committed to me, as the gospel for the circumcised was to Peter (for He who worked effectively in Peter for the apostleship to the circumcised also worked effectively in me toward the Gentiles), and when James, Cephas, and John, who perceived the grace that had been given to me, they gave me and Barnabas the right hand of fellowship, that we should go to the Gentiles and they to the circumcised. They desired only that we should remember the poor, the very thing which I also was eager to do" (2:7-10).

With this background information, Paul is building his case against circumcision and the law versus grace and faith. If the Mother Church at Jerusalem does not require circumcision for Gentile converts then the Judaizers challenging Paul in Galatia have no apostolic authority for their insistence on circumcision.

Rebuke of Peter

To further build his case and support his authority, Paul relates an incident in which he rebukes Peter for not consistently practicing the gospel of grace. In Jerusalem, Peter had supported Paul in his gospel of grace that denied the necessity of circumcision and the law as requisites for salvation (Acts 15). And when Peter came to Antioch he would eat with the Gentiles, but when certain Jerusalem brethren came Peter no longer ate with the Gentiles, but "separated himself, fearing those who were of the circumcision" (2:12). And when Peter separated himself so did the other Jews and even Barnabas joined in their hypocrisy. At this point Paul rebukes Peter saying, "If you being a Jew, live in the manner of Gentiles and not as the Jews, why do you compel Gentiles to live as Jews?" (2:14). Exposing this hypocrisy, Paul says, "We who are Jews by nature, and not sinners of the Gentiles, know that a man is not justified by the works of the law but by faith in Jesus Christ, even we have believed in Christ Jesus, that we might be justified by faith in Christ and not by the works of the law, for by the works of the law no flesh shall be justified" (2:15). And to underscore his point, Paul says, "if righteousness comes through the law, then Christ died in vain" (2:21).

Rebuke of the Galatians

Paul rebukes the Galatians calling them foolish and asking who has bewitched them not to obey the truth after Jesus Christ crucified had been preached to them. Continuing, he asks (3:2), "Did you receive the Spirit by the works of the law, or by the hearing of faith?" Could they be so foolish he asks as to think that having begun in the Spirit they could now be made perfect by the flesh, that is to say by the law?

The Faith of Abraham

The Spirit comes through faith, witness Abraham who "'believed God and it was accounted to him for righteousness'" (3:6). And Paul adds, "Therefore know that only those who are of faith are sons of Abraham. And the Scripture, foreseeing that God would justify the nations by faith, preached the gospel to Abraham beforehand, saying, 'In you all the nations shall be blessed'" (3:7-8). The apostle makes it clear that those of the faith, not of the law, are the true sons of Abraham, that it is faith, not the law, that justifies, and that through the same faith as that of Abraham all nations, all persons, Jew or Gentile, can be justified. (See Genesis 15:6 and 12:3 for Paul's quotations concerning Abraham.)

The Law Curses but Faith Justifies

Paul says that those under the law are cursed and quotes Deuteronomy as confirmation: "Cursed is everyone who does not continue in all things which are written in the book of the law, to do them" (27:26). The apostle reiterates that no one is justified by the law and quotes Habakkuk as evidence: "The just shall live by faith" (2:4). And the good news, says Paul, is that "Christ has redeemed us from the curse of the law, having become a curse for us . . . that we might receive the promise of the Spirit through faith" (3:13-14).

The promise was made to Abraham and his Seed, and Paul believes "his Seed" to mean Christ, for Christ took the curse upon Himself "that the blessing of Abraham might come upon the Gentiles" (3:14). Paul goes on to say that "the law which was four hundred and thirty years later [time frame between the covenant with Abraham and the law given to Moses at Sinai] cannot annul the covenant that was confirmed before by God in Christ, that it should make the promise of no effect" (3:17). In explaining the purpose of the law, Paul says it was added because of transgression and became "our tutor to bring us to Christ, that we might be justified by faith. But after faith has come, we are no longer under a tutor, for you are all sons of God through faith in Christ Jesus" (3:24-26). And all baptized in Christ put on Christ so that "there is neither Jew nor Gentile, there is neither slave nor free, there is neither male nor female; for you are all one in Christ Jesus. And if you are Christ's, then you are Abraham's seed, and heirs according to the promise" (3:28-29).

Sons and Heirs of Abraham and the Promise

Paul expands the heir/son analogy by adding the child/slave factor. When the heir/son is a child, he is in a sense like a slave, for he lives under guardians and stewards, "even so we, when we were children, were in bondage under the elements of the world. But when the fullness of the time had come, God sent forth His Son, born of a woman, born under the law, to redeem those who were under the law, that we might receive the adoption as sons. And because you are sons, God has sent forth the Spirit of His Son into your hearts, crying out, Abba, Father" (4:3-9). The apostle makes it clear that though the Jews were tutored under the law to become heirs, only through faith can they become heirs, the same faith in Christ that makes heirs of Gentiles. The law directs; faith saves.

Appalled that the Galatians Turn

Paul wants to know how they who have known God or who were known by God could turn away. "I am afraid," he says, "lest I have labored for you in vain" (4:11). He recalls that it was because of illness that he first preached the gospel to them and that even though his illness was a trial to them they did not resent him; they welcomed him as if he were an angel or Jesus Christ himself. In fact, he believes they would have gladly torn out their eyes and given them to him, but now they have turned away from the gospel he preached. He asks, ironically, if he has become their enemy because he told them the truth.

Allegorical Explanation

Paul turns to allegory hoping it will help convince the Galatians that they have made a wrong turn. Using Abraham again he notes that the patriarch had two sons, one by a bondwoman and one by a freewoman, the one born to the bondwoman being born of the flesh and the one born to the freewoman being born of the promise. He views these two births as symbolic ones: "For these are the two covenants: the one from Mount Sinai which gives birth to bondage, which is Hagar—for this Hagar is Mount Sinai in Arabia, and corresponds to Jerusalem which now is, and is in bondage with her children—but Jerusalem above is free, which is the mother of us all . . . Now we, brethren, as Isaac was, are children of promise" (4:25-28). Continuing the allegory, Paul says "he who was born according to the flesh then persecuted him who was born according to the Spirit, even so it is now. Nevertheless what does the Scripture say? 'Cast out the bondwoman and her son for the son of the bondwoman shall not be heir with the son of the freewoman.'" (4:29-30). Obviously, Paul uses the allegory to illustrate to the Galatians that if they side with the Judaizers concerning circumcision and the law, they become children of the bondwoman to be cast out. To be children of the freewoman and free of bondage, they must be children of faith. They must hold to the gospel of Jesus Christ that Paul preached to them.

Justification by Faith

Paul again urges the Galatians not to become entangled with a yoke of bondage, for "I testify again to every man who becomes a circumcised man that he is a debtor to keep the whole law. You have become estranged from Christ, you who attempt to be justified by law; you have fallen from grace" (5:3-4). Paul makes it abundantly clear that justification comes through faith not the law, and if they accept circumcision they embrace the law and give up faith. "For we through the Spirit eagerly wait for the hope of righteousness by faith. For in Christ Jesus neither circumcision nor uncircumcision avails anything, but faith working through love" (5:5-6).

Paul expresses his confidence in their rejecting the Judaizers and trusts that judgment will fall on these troublemakers. Then he vents his ire toward the circumcision troublemakers saying, "I could wish that these who trouble you would go the whole way and emasculate themselves" (5:12).

Love Must Guide Liberty

Paul cautions the Galatians concerning the liberty to which they have been called. Their liberty is not liberty of the flesh, for they must serve one another through love. The law he tells them is fulfilled through this one principle: "You shall love your neighbor as yourself" (5:14).

The Spirit and the Flesh

The Galatians are instructed to walk in the Spirit and not the flesh, for the works of the flesh include "adultery, fornication, uncleanness, licentiousness, idolatry, sorcery, hatred, contentions, jealousies, outbursts of wrath, selfish ambitions, dissensions, heresies, envy, murders, drunkenness, revelries, and the like" (5:19-21). And Paul assures them that those who practice these works of the flesh will not inherit the kingdom of God. On the other hand, the fruit of the Spirit includes "love, joy, peace, longsuffering, kindness, goodness, faithfulness, gentleness, self-control, and against such there is no law. And those who are Christ's have crucified the flesh with its passions and desires" (5:22-14).

Those of the Spirit must keep these contraries in mind and walk in the Spirit. "Do not be deceived, God is not mocked, for whatever a man sows, that he will also reap. For he who sows to his flesh will of the flesh reap corruption, but he who sows to the spirit will of the Spirit reap everlasting life" (6:7-8).

Conclusion

Passionately, Paul takes the pen from his scribe and writes the conclusion to his letter: "See with what large letters I have written to you with my own hand" (6:11). The large letters could be the result of weak eyesight or lack of penmanship skill, but more than likely their largeness is for emphasis, and certainly taking the pen into his own hand is prompted by the desire to personalize his message. In his own hand he summarizes the preceding counsel given the Galatians. He writes that those trying to compel them to embrace circumcision and the law as opposed to faith do so that they may not suffer persecution for the cross of Christ (presumably from neither the Jews nor the Romans). Furthermore, even though they do not keep the law "they would have you circumcised that they might glory in your flesh" (6:13). Paul declares that, unlike his own motives, the Judaizers' motives are selfish ones. "God forbid that I should glory except in the cross of our Lord Jesus Christ, by whom the world has been crucified to me, and I to the world" (6:14). And to substantiate his claim he has body scars that testify to his sufferings for Christ's sake. Like the slave whose body carries the mark of his master, so Paul can say, "I bear in my body the marks of the Lord Jesus" (6:17). Thus, the apostle concludes his recap written in his own hand and in large script. To the recap he adds the benediction: "Brethren, the grace of our Lord Jesus Christ be with your spirit. Amen" (6:18). We do not know the Galatians' response to Paul's letter, but his passionate recap and benediction bid well for a positive response.

Galatians Poetic Summary Paul's Apostleship and Gospel Challenged

The letter to the churches of Galatia may well be among
Paul's earliest epistles, if not the first
For on his first missionary journey through this Roman
province in Asia Minor he did traverse
Spawning churches in the cities of Iconium, Lystra, Derbe,
and others scattered along the way
Before returning to his home base at Antioch of Syria where
he settled in for quite a long stay
And since it is uncertain just when or where the letter was
transcribed, conjecture must suffice
Therefore our surmise says he sent the letter from Antioch,
thus beginning his epistolary advice.

The letter's short salutation and defensive tone immediately
reveal something gone wrong
Both Paul's apostleship and gospel preached are being
challenged we soon learn reading on.
But the apostle wastes no time informing the Galatians that
he and what he preached were true:
"What I preached came straight to me, revelation from the
Lord," he says, "and straight to you."
Paul's apostleship begins at Damascus where light from
heaven struck him blind but made him see:
Jesus Christ the Lord through revelation called, forever
changing this Christian persecuting Pharisee.

Paul defends the authenticity of his apostleship even though
his call came after the resurrection.

His call came, like that of the Twelve, from Jesus Christ, and
like them he received instruction
He received instruction through revelation and a special call
to carry the gospel to the Gentile.
He spends three years absorbing his call before going to
Jerusalem to visit Peter a little while
Thus, making clear that he is an apostle on the same level as
the Twelve and with special call
And surely seeing himself as the Thirteenth apostle equally
elevated in rank to Peter and all.

Sometimes this writer wonders if Paul might not be the
replacement authentic for Judas Iscariot!
Yes, I know that led by Peter the Eleven choose a
replacement named Matthias, choosing by lot
Yet, it is the Church persecuting Pharisee Paul, chosen by
the Lord, who becomes apostle supreme,
Grasping the gospel and taking it into the world, traveling
Rome's eternal roads the lost to redeem.
But let us not quibble over whether Paul is apostle thirteen
or replacement for Judas the betrayer:
By leg and by letter he traversed the Roman world nurturing
churches, this great gospel conveyor.

Though establishing his independence as apostle, he reveres
the Mother Church in Jerusalem:
He desires its leaders' blessing on his ministry and is
steadfast in collecting offerings for them.
Paul cites a visit to Jerusalem occasioned by revelation
fourteen years following the first one
Accompanied by Barnabas and convert Titus he meets
privately with the leaders of reputation
To test the tides concerning circumcision for the Gentile
convert, Titus being example at hand.
Paul is more than pleased when leaders of reputation—James,
Cephas, John—back him to a man.

The gospel for the uncircumcised they saw to be Paul's
purview, Peter's purview the circumcised.
"He who worked effectively in Peter for apostleship to the
circumcised so worked for me likewise,
Likewise worked for me toward the Gentiles, and when
James, Cephas, and John perceived such,
They gave me and Barnabas the right hand of fellowship to
go to the Gentiles, pleasing us much.
They desired only that we should remember the poor, the
very thing which I also was eager to do."
And we know Paul did his utmost always to aid his Jerusalem
brethren, to collect and deliver too.

The apostle uses background information concerning
circumcision to begin building his case
Against the Judaizers who had invaded the Galatian
churches Paul and the gospel to debase.
To further build his case and defend his authority, he relates
an incident of rebuking Peter.
He rebukes him for inconsistency concerning circumcision
and the law, this apostolic leader.
In Antioch, Peter dines with the Gentiles until those of the
circumcision arrived from Jerusalem.
Almost immediately he separates himself from them
prompting Barnabas and others to join him.

Paul points out Peter's hypocrisy asking how he can expect
the Gentile to do what he cannot do
He well knows that only by faith in Jesus Christ can one be
justified, the law will never save you.
Had not the apostles learned and affirmed that faith not law
justifies, else why did the Savior die?
"If righteousness comes through the law, then Christ died in
vain," Paul rebukes Peter eye to eye.
His authority and theology thus supported, Paul begins
rebuking the Galatians taking them to task
Boldly asking who bewitched them so that they not obey the
gospel of Jesus Christ crucified, alas!

"Did you receive the Spirit by works of the law, or by the
hearing of the faith," Paul's question?
"Do you foolishly think that having begun by the Spirit you
can now turn to the law for perfection?
Oh deluded Galatians, Abraham believed God and it was
accounted to him for righteousness.
Therefore know," continues Paul, "that only those of faith are
the sons of Abraham, no less.
The Scripture foresaw that God would justify the nations by
faith, and through Abraham addressed.
To Abraham the gospel was given beforehand: 'In you all the
nations of the world will be blessed.'"

The apostle makes the case that through faith, not the law,
we become heirs of Abraham
It is faith, and not the law, that justifies one, male and female,
Jew and Gentile, all of them.
Those under the law are cursed as Deuteronomy confirms:
Cursed is everyone who does not continue
Does not continue in all things that are written in the book
of the law, yet the law does not save you
For the Scripture through the prophet Habakkuk declares
emphatically, "The just shall live by faith."
And be assured, says the apostle, "Christ redeemed us from
the curse of the law," lifted the weight.

Turning again to Abraham and the covenant the apostle
finds special meaning in the word "seed"
In the promise to Abraham and his seed, Paul sees Seed
capitalized for it prophesies Christ's deed
Christ took the curse upon Himself "that the blessing of
Abraham might come upon the Gentiles"
Noting that the covenant preceded the law four-hundred
and thirty years, witness the biblical files.
And how could the law annul the covenant Paul asks, it
having been added because of transgression?
The law became "our tutor to bring us to Christ, that we might
be justified by faith," is his impression.

And after faith has come we are no longer under a tutor, for
we are then sons of God through faith
Through faith we become sons of God being baptized in
Christ thereby putting on Christ by faith
So that "there is neither Jew nor Gentile, there is neither
slave nor free, neither male nor female
For if you are all one in Christ Jesus, and if you are Christ's,
then you are Abraham's seed real
And heirs according to the promise," claims Paul,
counteracting the contentious Judaizers
Who are causing consternation insisting the Galatians become
circumcision sympathizers.

Incrementally, Paul makes his case: that though the Jews
were tutored under the law to become heirs
Only through *faith* can they actually become heirs, the same
faith in Christ that makes Gentiles heirs.
Then how could the Galatians who have known God
through faith turn away he wants to know:
"I am afraid lest I have labored for you in vain," laments the
apostle observing the present woe.
In nostalgic mode he recalls that his illness was tolerated
most gracefully when preaching to them
That they welcomed him as if he were an angel or Jesus Christ
himself the way they embraced him.

He believes then they would have torn out their eyes for
him, but now reject the gospel he preached.
Have they become his enemy because he told them the truth,
ironically is that what caused the breach?
Putting sarcasm aside, Paul turns to allegory to convince the
Galatians they are making a wrong turn:
Note Abraham's two sons, one by a bondwoman and one by
a freewoman, acts of symbolic concern
The one born of the bondwoman being born of the flesh, the
freewoman's being born of the promise
The two sons are the two covenants, one being the son of
bondage and one being the son of promise.

The one from Mount Sinai, the birth of bondage, is Hagar which "corresponds to Jerusalem now
And is in bondage," but Jerusalem above is free, and thereby the mother of us all, thus we now
As Isaac was, are children of promise," the apostle says, "but the one born according to the flesh
Persecuted him who was born according to the Spirit, even so it is now, Spirit persecuted by flesh
Nevertheless, the Scripture says 'cast out the bondwoman and her son for he shall not be the heir
He shall not be the heir with the son of the freewoman,'" and so faith, not law, becomes the heir.

Thus, Paul illustrates through Scriptural allegory that if the Galatians listen to the Judaizers bold
They become children of the bondwoman to be cast out, for they stand in the circumcision fold.
To be children of the freewoman and free of bondage, they must be children of faith as foresaid
They must hold to the gospel of Jesus Christ that Paul preached, for only faith can free the dead.
So again the apostle pleads with the Galatians not to put on the yoke of bondage, that action dire
"For I testify again, everyman who becomes circumcised becomes a debtor to keep the law entire."

"Taking on circumcision you have become estranged from Christ, for the law can never justify
You have fallen from grace," says Paul, again emphasizing that to give up faith for law is to die
"For we through the Spirit eagerly wait for the hope of righteousness from God above
In Christ it is neither circumcision nor uncircumcision, but faith working through love."
Then expressing confidence that the Galatians will reject the Judaizers seeing what's at stake
Paul cries out in righteous ire, "I could wish these circumcisers might themselves emasculate."

Next, he cautions the Galatians that the liberty to which
they are called is not liberty of the flesh
That they must serve one another through love, for in loving
neighbor as self faith and law mesh.
Then he instructs them to walk in the Spirit and not the
flesh, for the works of the flesh debauch
Like adultery, drunkenness, dissensions, idolatry, jealousy,
envy, hate, selfish ambition and such
And those who walk in works of the flesh can be assured
that the kingdom they will not inherit.
The kingdom welcomes those who walk in love, joy and
goodness, and in all fruits of the Spirit.

Against the fruits of the Spirit there is no law, for those who
are Christ's have the flesh crucified
Believers must always keep the contraries in mind and walk
in the Spirit, works of flesh denied.
"Do not be deceived, God is not mocked, for whatever a man
sows he reaps that thing
If he sows of the flesh he reaps destruction, if he sows of the
Spirit it is life everlasting."
To conclude the epistle, Paul passionately takes the pen from
the hand of his scribe into his own
And calling attention to the large letters in his own handwriting
makes his deep feelings known.

Whether the large letters are due to poor eyesight or
penmanship, or for emphasis, who can say?
But that he feels compelled to write the conclusion in his
own hand is as clear as the light of day.
He feels strongly about the subject matter and more strongly
about the Galatians going astray
And in this personal way takes these converts into his
confidence lest they be stolen away.
The Judaizers he says "would have you circumcised that *they*
might glory in your flesh, selfishly
But God forbid that *I, Paul,* should glory except in the cross
of our Lord Jesus Christ, unselfishly."

And to substantiate his claim, Paul has body scars that
testify to his sufferings for Christ's name
As the slave whose body carries the mark of his master so
the apostle can passionately proclaim:
"I bear in my body the marks of the Lord Jesus," writing it
large in the hearts of the Galatians.
And concluding the epistle on this personal and impassionate
note must surely reclaim relations.

EPHESIANS PROSE SUMMARY
FROM DISUNITY TO UNITY THROUGH CHRIST

Originally Addressed to Whom?

The so called Letter to the Ephesians may not have been originally addressed to the Ephesians. Scholars, for several reasons, argue pretty convincingly that the letter is circular in intent and not addressed to a single church. First, the earliest manuscripts make no mention of the Ephesians. Second, Paul's statement in verse fifteen of chapter one—"after I heard of your faith in the Lord Jesus and your love for all the saints"—sounds incongruous for one having labored three years nurturing the church at Ephesus. Third, unlike a letter addressing particular problems in a particular church, this letter is more general in nature. It addresses bedrock theology concerning unity through Jesus Christ, how unity in the universe can be achieved only through Jesus Christ because that is God the Father's plan. Consequently, it seems to be a letter of general instruction, a circular letter.

God's Blessed Plan

Paul declares that God has blessed us with every spiritual blessing through Christ, "that He chose us in Him before the foundation of the world, that we should be holy and without blame before Him in love, having predestined us to adoption as sons by Jesus Christ to Himself" (1:3-5). We have redemption through Christ's blood in accordance with God's grace lovingly offered everyone that He might bring all things in heaven and earth together under one head, that being Jesus Christ the Son.

In saying "we who first trusted in Christ," Paul must be referring to himself and other Jews who became believers before the Gentiles, for he goes on to say "in Him you also trusted after you heard the word of truth, the gospel . . . and having believed were sealed with the Holy Spirit of promise" (1:12-13). He is presumably addressing new Gentile converts judging from this statement and the following statement, "after I heard of your faith in the Lord Jesus and your love for all the saints" (1:15).

Paul Imprisoned in Rome

Paul at the time of writing this letter is distanced from Ephesus and the other Asian churches that he had founded or nurtured or both. He is imprisoned in Rome and refers to himself as "the prisoner of Jesus Christ for you Gentiles" (3:1), and having heard of their growing numbers in the faith wishes by letter to keep them theologically grounded.

Paul's Instructive Prayer

Paul prays "that the God of our Lord Jesus Christ, the Father of glory, may give you the spirit of wisdom and revelation in the knowledge of Him, the eyes of your understanding being enlightened; that you may know what is the hope of His calling, what are the riches of the glory of His inheritance in the saints, and what is the exceeding greatness of His power toward us who believe according to the working of His mighty power which He worked in Christ when He raised Him from the dead and seated Him at His right hand . . . and put all things under His feet, and gave Him to be head over all things to the church which is His body, the fullness of Him who fills all in all" (1:17-23).

Paul prays for their enlightenment; he prays that the eyes of their heart may be enlightened so that they may know the hope and the riches of their inheritance through Jesus Christ and the incomparably great power for the saints (believers). That power he says is like the mighty strength exhibited by God in raising His Son from the dead and seating Him at His right hand at the zenith of heaven where He places all things under Him and appoints Him to be head of everything for the Church, which is His body, the fullness of Him who fulfills all.

Unity through Christ

Continuing, Paul says "you He made alive, who were dead in trespasses and sins in which you once walked according to the course of this world . . . among whom also we all once conducted ourselves in the lusts of our flesh . . . But God, who is rich in mercy, because of His great love with which He loved us, even when we were dead in trespasses, made us alive together with Christ (by grace you have been saved) and raised us up together and made us sit together in the heavenly places in Christ Jesus" (2:1-6). Paul emphasizes that unity comes through Christ: since all, Jew and Gentile, are saved by grace through faith, faith in Jesus Christ. He reminds them that they were once Gentiles in the flesh called the uncircumcised by those who called themselves of the circumcision, that they were separated from Christ and excluded from membership in Israel and foreigners to covenants of promise, without hope and without God. But now in Christ Jesus they "who once were far off have been made near by the blood of Christ" (2:13). Consequently, "you are no longer strangers and foreigners, but fellow citizens with the saints and members of the household of God, having been built on the foundation of the apostles and prophets, Jesus Christ Himself being the chief cornerstone, in whom the whole building, being joined together, grows into a holy temple in the Lord, in whom you also are being built together for a habitation of God in the Spirit" (2:19-22). Through Jesus Christ, Jew and Gentile are united becoming the building stones of the Church where God dwells in Spirit.

Paul's Special Dispensation

Paul, calling himself the prisoner of Jesus Christ for the Gentiles, addresses his special dispensation, how by revelation God had made known to him the mystery "which in other ages was not made known to the sons of men, as it has now been revealed by the Spirit to His holy apostles and prophets: that the Gentiles should be fellow heirs, of the same body, and partakers of His promise in Christ through the gospel, of which I became a minister according to the gift of the grace of God given me by the effective working of His power. To me, who am less than the least of all the saints, this grace was given, that I should preach among the Gentiles the unsearchable riches of Christ" (3:1-6). The apostle implores them not to lose heart because of his present tribulations, his imprisonment, for he is on his knees praying "that Christ may dwell in your hearts through faith; that you, being rooted and grounded in love, may be able to comprehend with all the saints" the width and length and depth of the love of Christ which passes all knowledge "that you may be filled with the fullness of God" (3:17-19).

Walking in Unity

Having thus informed and assured the Gentile believers, Paul exhorts them to "have a walk worthy of the calling with which you are called, with all lowliness and gentleness, with longsuffering, bearing with one another in love, endeavoring to keep the unity of the Spirit in the bond of peace, [for] there is one body and one Spirit . . . one Lord, one faith, one baptism; one god and Father of all, who is above all, and through all, and in you all" (3:1-6).

Practicing Spiritual Gifts

The apostle says that to each believer grace is given according to the measure of Christ's gift: "some to be apostles, some prophets, some evangelists, and some pastors and teachers, for the equipping of the saints [believers] for the work of ministry, for the edifying of the body of Christ, till we all come to the unity of the faith and the knowledge of the Son of God" (4:11-13). Thus, believers will "no longer be children tossed to and fro and carried about with every wind of doctrine . . . but speaking the truth in love, may grow up in all things into Him who is the head—Christ—from whom the whole body, joined and knit together by what every joint supplies, according to the effective working by which every part does its share, causes growth of the body for the edifying of itself in love" 4:14-16). This description of believers exercising their spiritual gifts in truth and love frames a picture of the church as it should be.

Putting off the Old

No longer would they be walking as the rest of the Gentiles walk, for they would have put off their former conduct, the old person growing more and more corrupt in deceitful lusts, "for this you know, that no fornicator, unclean person, covetous person, nor idolater, has any inheritance in the kingdom of Christ and God" (5:5). They are now new persons, and though once they were darkness, they are now light in the Lord and walk as children of light and, as such, they are exhorted to be guided by the words of the enlightening hymn: "Awake, you who sleep, / Arise from the dead, / And Christ will give you light" (5:14).

Be Lead by the Holy Spirit

Be not drunk with wine but be filled with the Holy Spirit, "speaking to one another in psalms and hymns and spiritual songs, singing and making melody in your heart to the Lord, giving thanks always for all things to God the Father in the name of our Lord Jesus Christ, submitting to one another in reverence for God" (5:18-21).

Husband and Wife Relationship

Wives are to submit to their husbands, for the husband is head of the family as Christ is head of the Church. Husbands are to love their wives just as Christ loved the Church and gave Himself for it "that He might present it to Himself a glorious church, not having spot or wrinkle or any such thing, but that it should be holy and without blemish. So husbands ought to love their own wives as their own bodies; he who loves his wife loves himself. For no one ever hated his own flesh, but nourishes and cherishes it, just as the Lord does the church" (5:26-29). In this sense the husband and wife become one flesh in loving relationship so that the husband loves his wife as himself and the wife loves and respects the husband.

Parents and Children Relationship

Drawing on the fifth commandment, Paul declares, "Children obey your parents in the Lord, for this is right. 'Honor your father and mother' which is the first commandment with promise: 'that it may be well with you and you may live long on the earth'" (6:1-3). Then he directs the father not to provoke his children to wrath, but "bring them up in the training and admonition of the Lord" (6:4). Again, this seems to imply that the father as head of the house should follow the lead of Christ as head of the Church in making his family as perfect as possible through love and instruction and example. And since husband and wife become one flesh and since the fifth commandment says that children should obey their "parents," presumably this directive to the father concerning the children also includes the wife. Thus, the ideal family lives in love and reverence: parents to children, children to parents, and parents and children to the Lord.

No Slaves and Masters

Paul advises servants to be obedient to their masters and masters to be considerate and kind to their servants, reminding both that in God's eyes servants and masters are equal, for "whatever good anyone does, he will receive the same from the Lord, whether he is slave or free" (6:8).

Protection for Believers

Believers must be strong in the Lord in order to stand up against the evil forces of the world ruled by Satan. "Therefore," says Paul, "take up the whole armor of God, that you may be able to withstand in the evil day . . . having girded your waist with truth, having put on the breastplate of righteousness, and having shod your feet with the preparation of the gospel of peace, [and] above all, taking the shield of faith with which you will be able to quench all the fiery darts of the wicked one. And take the helmet of salvation and the sword of the Spirit, which is the word of God; praying always with all prayer and supplication in the Spirit, being watchful to this end with all perseverance and supplication for the saints [believers]" (6:13-18).

Prayer for Paul, Ambassador in Chains

Paul asks for their prayers that he may continue to carry out his mission: "that utterance may be given to me, that I may open my mouth boldly to make known the mystery of the gospel, for which I am an ambassador in chains; that in it I may speak boldly, as I ought to speak" (6:19-20).

EPHESIANS POETIC SUMMARY FROM DISUNITY TO UNITY THROUGH CHRIST

Scholars argue pretty convincingly that the so called
Ephesian epistle is circular in intent:
That earliest manuscripts make no mention of the Ephesians
suggests no single recipient
And Paul saying in 1:15 that he has *heard* of their faith in
the Lord and love for the saints
Rings incongruous for one having labored long in Ephesus
acquiring numerous acquaints
So most likely Ephesians entered later manuscript as Paul's
letters were in Ephesus collected
But let us not continue to conjecture about its circulation
leaving its classic content neglected.

Unlike the typical Pauline epistle addressed to a particular
church concerning particular problems
This epistle addresses inspired theological insight the apostle
wishes to reach the farthest realms
For it is theology explaining the role of Jesus Christ and the
Church in God's creation planning
It is theology explaining that God in the fullness of time sent
his Son to bring unity to humanity
It is theology explaining that disunity of the universe can
through Jesus Christ become unity again
It is theology explaining that the Church is the body of Christ
the earthly force against divisive sin.

"Praise be to God the Father of our Lord Jesus Christ, who
has blessed us in the heavenly domains

With every spiritual blessing in Christ," cries the apostle
Paul tracing the Creator's purposed aims.
"He chose us in Him before the creation of the world to be
holy and blameless in His eternal sight
In love He predestined us to be His adopted children
through Jesus Christ in the fullness of time right.
We have redemption through His blood in accordance with
God's grace lovingly offered everyone
That He might bring all things in heaven and earth together
under one head, Jesus Christ the Son."

"In Jesus Christ, as predestined, we trusted first and in Him
you also trusted after hearing hence
And you were instilled, as were we, with the Holy Spirit of
promise, the seal of our inheritance."
Obviously, the epistle is addressed to converted Gentiles, the
focus of Paul's predestined ministry
And after hearing of their faith and love for all the saints, he
has been giving thanks unceasingly.
Paul is imprisoned in Rome and thus distanced from
Ephesus and other of the Asian churches founded
But hearing of their growing numbers in the faith wishes by
letter to keep them theologically grounded.

"Oh, may the God of our Lord Jesus Christ, the Father of all
glory, give you the spirit of wisdom
And revelation in the knowledge of Him, and with
enlightening your eyes of understanding done
May you then know the hope of His calling as well as the
glory of His inheritance in the saints
And the exceeding greatness of His power toward us who
believe wholeheartedly sans restraints
In His mighty power which He worked in Christ when He
raised Him from the dead
And seated Him at His right hand in heaven's zenith," prays
Paul with bowed head.

"And put all things under His feet, and gave Him to be head over all things to the Church
Which is His body, the fullness of Him who fills all in all," the apostle masterfully asserts.
Continuing his theological course, he asserts that though the Gentile was dead in trespasses
God made it possible for him to come alive through Christ, thus both Jew and Gentile, alas
Through faith could be raised up together and sit together with Him at heaven's highest zone
Thereby, revealing forever the inimitable riches of God's grace in the kindness to us shown.

Paul points out that their salvation is a gift from God, for all are saved by grace through faith, all of us
And not by works less anyone should boast, we are God's workmanship created through Christ Jesus
For good works, which God prepared beforehand that we should walk in them as heavenly prescribed.
"Remember," says the apostle, "that formerly you who are Gentiles by birth and called uncircumcised
By those who call themselves 'of the circumcision,' were at the time separate from Christ,
Excluded from citizenship of Israel, and thus foreigners to covenants of the promise fast."

"But now you who once were far off are through the blood of Lord Jesus Christ brought near
Through His blood both Jew and Gentile have access by one Spirit to the Father we revere
Therefore, you are no longer aliens and foreigners, but fellow members of God's household own
Built on the foundation of the apostles and prophets with Christ Jesus himself as the cornerstone
And in Him the whole building is joined together and grows into a holy temple in the Lord.
In Him you also are being built together becoming a dwelling for God in the Spirit, in accord."

Calling himself a prisoner of Jesus Christ for the Gentiles,
Paul explains his special dispensation
That by the grace of God he had been chosen and through
revelation instructed of his mission
That he had been given knowledge in the mystery of Jesus
Christ not previously known
As now made known by the Spirit to God's holy apostles
and prophets, not on their own
That the Gentiles should be fellow heirs, fellow heirs with
the Jews in the covenant promise
That they become partakers of the promise in Christ as
revealed in the gospel Paul dispenses.

And he says though he is the least of all the saints God
called him a minister to the Gentiles be
To preach to them the inimitable riches of Christ so they
rooted and grounded in love could see
And comprehend with all the saints the width and length
and depth and height of Christ's love
Love that passes all knowledge, and filled with that love
experience the fullness of God above.
Thus, this prisoner of the Lord beseeches these converted
Gentiles to walk according to their call
To be humble and gentle and longsuffering, always walking
with one another in love, one to all.

They should make every effort to maintain unity of the
Spirit in the bond of peace, one and all
For there is one body, one Spirit, one Lord, one faith, one
baptism, one God and Father of all
And to each of us a gift has been given, according to our bent
Christ apportioned us as servers
He gave some to be apostles, some prophets, some
evangelists, and some pastors and teachers
Thus, the saints are equipped for the work of ministry in
edifying the body of Christ until
Until we all reach unity in the faith and the knowledge of the
Son of God, in maturity real.

No longer then are we infants blown about with every wind
of doctrine, but enveloped in truth's seal
We grow up in all things into Him who is the Head, that is
Christ, and thereby fulfill the Father's will.
Indeed, if you know Christ, you put off your former conduct,
you put off that person corrupt in lust
For you know that no fornicator, no idolater, no unclean
person enters the kingdom, repent you must
This you know: you were once darkness, but now are light in
the Lord walking as children of light.
Listen to the old song: "Awake, you who sleep, arise from the
dead, and Christ will give you light."

Walk in the light of Christ speaking to each other in psalms
and hymns and songs, earnestly done
Singing and making melody in your heart to the Lord giving
thanks to the Father through the Son.
Promote harmony in the home, husbands and wives and
children living in hierarchal bond
The husband, head of the family, as Christ is head of the
Church, binds together everyone
Wives submit to your husbands, husbands love your wives
willingly submitting to self sacrifice
Thereby, husband and wife become one flesh in loving bond,
God's will for husband and wife.

Children obey your parents in the Lord; know obedience
holds promise of reward of great worth:
"Honor your father and mother that it may be well with you
and you may live long on the earth."
The family, as conceived by the Father above, much like
Christ's Church serves His cohesive plan
It furnishes the framework for living in sync with the great
design, the one created by God not man.
And whether one is master or slave, in the great design both
must be servants of Christ, no matter
It is the good one does that pleases the Lord, rank or title
mean no more than meaningless chatter.

Finally, Paul cautions the brethren he is addressing to be strong in the Lord, never shirking
Put on the whole armor of God in order to stand against the wiles of the devil, ever lurking.
Gird your waist with truth, strap on the breastplate of righteousness, shod your feet with gospel
Put on the helmet of salvation, and armed with the sword of the Spirit, the word of God, set sail
Praying unceasingly for the preservation of the saints says Paul and for him, ambassador in chains
That utterance be given him to make known the mystery of the gospel he courageously proclaims.

Philippians Prose Summary The Sad Sweet Thank You Letter

The Sad and the Sweet

It is sad that Paul is imprisoned at Rome, yet it is sweet that he continues his ministry by converting those attending him ("All the saints greet you, but especially those who are of Caesar's household" (4:22), and by continuing to write nurturing letters to the various churches he had either founded or labored in or both.

Philippi, a Special Case

The Philippians hold a special place in Paul's heart because they have from the beginning been supportive of the apostle, quick to discern his needs and quick to act upon that discernment. They sent him financial help when he was ministering in other churches in other areas. Now, while Paul is imprisoned in Rome, they have not only sent him material support but have also sent him one of their own, Epaphroditus, to attend his needs while imprisoned. Though the apostle says he has learned to live within his circumstances, whether abased or abounded, he is grateful for the support from the Philippians nevertheless. He is grateful not merely for their love and care for him, but even more so because their action exhibits the fruits of their faith. He takes pride in their charity which reflects the fruits of the gospel that he has taught them. Their fruits are his fruits, thus his greater joy.

Thank God for the Philippians

"I thank my God," writes Paul, "upon every remembrance of you, always in every prayer of mine making request for you all with joy, for your fellowship in the gospel from the first day until now" (1:3-5). We know from reading Acts that the church at Philippi was the first church Paul founded in Europe. At a certain point in his second missionary journey, the Holy Spirit forbids him "to preach the word in Asia," and a person appears to him in a vision pleading, "Come over to Macedonia and help us" (Acts 16:6-9). The apostle answers the call and with the conversion of Lydia, a merchant who offers her home as a meeting place, the church at Philippi begins and presumably, judging from Paul's praise, excelled in producing fruits of the Spirit.

Bound in chains in Rome, the apostle writes to them, "For God is my witness, how greatly I long for you all with the affection of Jesus Christ, and this I pray, that your love may abound still more and more in knowledge and all discernment, that you may approve the things that are excellent, that you may be sincere and without offense till the day of Christ, being filled with the fruits of righteousness which are by Jesus Christ, to the glory and praise of God" (1:9-11).

Assurance Concerning His Imprisonment

Paul assures the Philippians that his imprisonment has "turned out for the furtherance of the gospel, so that it has become evident to the whole palace guard and to all the rest, that my chains are in Christ, and most of the brethren in the Lord, having become confident by my chains, are much more bold to speak the word without fear" (1:12-14). Some are speaking boldly out of envy hoping to gain eminence at Paul's expense, while others are speaking boldly out of good will. But the apostle exclaims, "whether in pretense or in truth, Christ is preached, and in this I rejoice" (1:18).

Paul writes, "For to me, to live is Christ, and to die is gain" (1:21), and that he is hard pressed between the two. To depart this life and live with Christ would be far better for him, but to remain in the flesh would be better for them. This he realizes, and expresses confidence that he will remain and will be able to return to them before long. But either way, he exhorts them to continue their fruitful ways: "Let your conduct be worthy of the gospel of Christ, so that whether I come and see you or am absent, I may hear of your affairs, that you stand fast in one spirit, with one mind striving together for the faith of the gospel" (1:27).

Necessity of Unity in Humility

The apostle cautions the Philippians concerning humility. Consolation in Christ comes through humility: "Let nothing be done through selfish ambition or conceit, but in lowliness of mind let each esteem others better than himself; let each of you look out not only for his own interests, but also for the interests of others" (2:3-4).

Christ the Epitome of Humility

"Let the mind be in you which was also in Christ Jesus," writes the apostle (2:5), for He being divine did not hesitate to take on servant status and come in the form of man. "He humbled Himself and became obedient to the point of death, even the death of the cross," and God exalted Him "above every name that at the name of Jesus every knee should bow, of those in heaven, and of those on earth, and of those under the earth" (2:8-10). The life of Jesus Christ defines humility.

Practicing Humility

Pointing to Christ as the example, Paul exhorts the Philippians to continue in their good work. Whether the apostle is present or absent, they must work out their own salvation in fear and trembling. They must continue to work in humility doing "all things without murmuring and disputing" (2:14).

Preparing the Philippians for Epaphroditus' Return

After thanking the Philippians for their concern and support, informing them of his present condition, and exhorting them to continue in their fruitful ways, Paul prepares them for the return of Epaphroditus, their person sent to attend him.

Seemingly concerned that Epaphroditus' return might be viewed as failure, Paul spends time justifying why his return is better for all concerned: Epaphroditus, himself, and them. Believing his imprisonment will soon end, Paul plans to send Timothy to them shortly, thinking that he himself, before long, would be able to come to them also. In the meantime, he has returned Epaphroditus. "I considered it necessary to send you Epaphroditus, my brother, fellow worker, and fellow soldier, but your messenger and the one who ministered to my need; since he was longing for you all, and was distressed because you had heard that he was sick. For indeed he was sick almost unto death; but God had mercy on him, and not only on him but on me also, lest I should have sorrow upon sorrow. Therefore, I sent him the more eagerly, that when you see him again you may rejoice, and I may be less sorrowful. Receive him therefore in the Lord with all gladness, and hold such men in esteem; because for the work of Christ he came close to death, not regarding his life, to supply what was lacking in your service toward me" (2:25-30). Paul seems to want to make sure that the return of Epaphroditus is not seen as failure, but as triumph on the part of everyone involved: Epaphroditus has served humbly and well; the Philippians have given graciously and generously by sending him; and, Paul, though greatly appreciative, no longer sees a need for his services.

Warning against Judaizers

Wanting his beloved Philippians to be ever alert against a common threat, that posed by the Judaizers, Paul admonishes them: "Beware of dogs, beware of evil workers, beware of the mutilation! For we are the circumcision, who worship God in the Spirit, rejoice in Christ Jesus, and have no confidence in the flesh" (3:2). He presents himself as a testimony saying that if anyone might have confidence in the flesh he would have greater cause having been "circumcised the eighth day, of the stock of Israel of the tribe of Benjamin, a Hebrew of the Hebrews; concerning the law, a Pharisee; concerning zeal, persecuting the church; concerning the righteousness which is in the law, blameless. But what things were gain to me, these I have counted loss for Christ" (3:5-7). Thus, Paul presents himself as prime witness that righteousness comes not from the law but from faith in Jesus Christ.

In Jesus Christ Is Our Peace:

Peace comes through Jesus Christ he reminds the Philippians; "therefore, my beloved and longed for brethren, my joy and crown, so stand fast in the Lord, beloved" (4:1).

Peace with Others

And on this note he implores two revered members of the congregation, Euodia and Syntyche, who had labored with him in the gospel, "to be of the same mind in the Lord" (4:3). And to the rest of his fellow workers there, he implores them to also help in the reconciliation, reminding them that through Christ comes reconciliation for those who believe. And he trusts they will all rejoice together in the Lord.

Peace with Self
Be anxious for nothing; in everything seek guidance through prayer and supplication and thanksgiving, "and the peace of God, which surpasses all understanding, will guard your hearts and minds through Christ Jesus" (4:6-7). Focus on the good: "Whatever things are true, whatever things are noble, whatever things are just, whatever things are pure, whatever things are lovely, whatever things are of good report, if there is any virtue and if there is anything praiseworthy—meditate on these things"(4:8).

Will not Paul's advice to the Philippians to focus on the good also well serve the Christian in today's world of twenty-four hour cable T.V. and ubiquitous internet both filled with endless images of questionable human behavior?

Peace with Circumstances
The apostle writes, "I have learned in whatever state I am, to be content . . . [for] I can do all things through Christ who strengthens me" (4:11, 13). And he has so demonstrated in his imprisonment that one of faith can continue to minister whatever the circumstances.

Why So Thankful
So that his theology of finding peace through Christ regardless of circumstances does not seem to imply a lack of appreciation for the concern and care rendered him by the Philippians, Paul quickly qualifies his "peace in all circumstances" statement by adding, "Nevertheless, you have done well that you shared in my distress. Now you Philippians know also that in the beginning of the gospel, when I departed from Macedonia, no church shared with me concerning giving and receiving but you only. For even in Thessalonica you sent aid once and again for my necessities. Not that I seek the gift, but I seek the fruit that abounds to your account" (4:14-17). Again Paul makes it clear that he appreciates their attention to his fiscal and physical needs, which they have done more than any other church, and they have done so without being asked, which gets to the heart of the matter. What gives him the greatest joy is that their actions evidence the fruit of the gospel that he has preached to them and which they have ingested as their charitable acts so graciously demonstrate.

It is an understatement to say that Paul is overjoyed with the Philippians.

Philippians Poetic Summary
The Sad Sweet Thank You Letter

Paul sends greetings to his beloved Philippians from himself
and all the saints in Rome
Especially he says those who are from Caesar's household,
presently the apostle's home.
Though imprisoned there alternately shackled to imperial
guards, from Paul not a whine
While awaiting his trial this indomitable apostle continues
to convert, one guard at a time
This thirteenth apostle who the gospel to the Gentile world
was predestined to take
And now in the capital of the known world chained but
witnessing for Christ's sake.

Paul's intent had long been to visit Rome and establish a
base for a foray into Spain
But circumstance altered his plan: the Sanhedrin hatched a
scheme to have him slain
Forcing the harassed apostle to play his trump card, the one
that read Roman citizen
Allowing Paul to appeal to Caesar and thereby travel to
Rome a protected denizen.
But arriving there he is no longer free to travel the empire
planting churches more
He is confined to converting guards and posting letters to
churches planted before.

Yet despite Paul's somewhat sad circumstance, sweetness
pervades the Philippi letter
Of all churches by the apostle planted, no matter their
means, none treated him better.

Never did he seek support from any church desiring not to
burden it or to seem self serving
Nevertheless, the Philippians take the initiative supporting
Paul seeing his work so deserving.
"I thank my God," writes Paul, "upon every remembrance of
you from the first day till now
Endlessly and joyfully I pray for all of you, your steadfast
fellowship in the gospel I avow."

That the Philippians have always seen to his needs he avows
but there is more to appreciate:
He receives great joy knowing that their charity to him
exhibits the fruits of their true faith
A faith having grown out of the gospel he taught them, thus
their fruits are also his fruits
And the fruits continue in Epaphroditus' prison visit lovingly
sent by these early recruits
Sent to attend the needs of the apostle, their benefactor,
while imprisoned far away in Rome
Though having learned to live within his circumstances, he
joys in the charity from Macedon.

No doubt the apostle remembers the vision and the call,
"come over to Macedonia and help us"
On that second missionary journey focused on Asia only
until the Holy Spirit intervened thus
So that he traveled on to Europe and at Philippi converted
Lydia and there a church began
For benevolence a church that had no peer always exemplary
in extending a helping hand
Moving Paul to say, "How greatly I long for you all, and this I
pray that your love may abound
Til the day of Christ, always filled with the fruits of
righteousness given by His example sound."

Paul assures the Philippians that his imprisonment has
turned out for the furtherance of the Way

That his chains are in Christ is evident to the whole palace
guard and to all the rest, thus they say
And most of the brethren gaining confidence from his
chains preach more boldly, even shrill
Though some speak hoping to gain eminence at Paul's
expense, others speak out of good will
"But whether in pretense or in truth," exclaims the apostle,
"Christ is preached, in this I rejoice
For to me, to live is Christ, and to die is gain, and I would be
hard pressed if given the choice."

To depart this life for a heavenly one might be preferable for
him, but would not be so for them
As a faithful follower of Christ, he knows he must pray for
what is preferable for them, not him
And thus expresses confidence he will remain and will, ere
long, return to them again
But return or no, he exhorts them to continue their fruitful
ways always among all men.
And above all revel in humility, for consolation in Christ
through humility comes, as is known.
Guard against selfish ambition or conceit putting the best
interests of others ahead of your own.

Let the mind be in you which was also in Christ Jesus, for
He though divine a servant became
Hesitating not to take on servant status in human form and
to die on a cross for a world profane
Prompting God to proclaim his glory so that in heaven and
earth knees should bend at His name
Humility is heaven's highest honor despite Satan and the
world's diametric and dinning dissent
So says the apostle exhorting the Philippians to always stay
focused on Jesus whatever the event.
May they be as charitable in all things as in their ministering
to his distresses, past and present.

After thanking the Philippians for their caring and support,
informing them of his current status
Paul exhorts them continue their charitable ways and
prepares them for the return of Epaphroditus.
Thinking Epaphroditus' return might be perceived as failure,
the apostle writes out a brief for him
Explaining why the return is better for all concerned: for
Epaphroditus, for himself, and for them.
"I consider it necessary to send you Epaphroditus, my
brother, fellow worker, and fellow soldier
But your messenger, and the messenger who came to minister
to my need while imprisoned here."

"Since he was longing for you, and was distressed because
you had heard that he was ill
Ill almost unto death, but God had mercy on him, and not
only on him but on me as well
Lest I should have sorrow upon sorrow; therefore, I send
him more eagerly so you may rejoice
And that I being less sorrowful may also rejoice, so receive
him in the Lord as a person choice
Hold this man in high esteem because for the work of Christ
he came close to death for thee
He regarded not his own life exerting every effort to supply
your desired service toward me."

Thus, the apostle sets the stage for Epaphroditus' return, a
return not of failure but of triumph
All involved have served well and have been well served;
Paul's Philippians remain his trump.
And being so he wishes to include an admonition against the
common threat: the Judaizers.
Since the Church's early expansion, Peter and Paul had done
battle against the circumcisers.
"Beware of dogs, beware of evil workers, beware of the
mutilation," the apostle exclaims
"We are the circumcision, who worship God in the spirit,
worship in Christ Jesus' name."

The apostle discounts any confidence in the flesh for if true
he would be example prime
Having been circumcised the eighth day of the stock of
Israel, the tribe of Benjamin fine
A Hebrew of the Hebrews; concerning the law, a Pharisee;
concerning zeal, church persecutor
Concerning the righteousness which is the law, blameless;
yet gain to him, loss to Christ savior
Thus, Paul presents himself as prime witness: righteousness
comes not from law but from faith
Circumcision of the heart is the circumcision that counts, for
it is of the spirit and carries weight.

Paul reminds the Philippians again that peace comes
through Jesus Christ, peace and accord
"Therefore, my beloved and longed for brethren, my joy and
crown, stand fast in our Lord."
And on this note the apostle implores two revered members
of the congregation take heed
Euodia and Syntyche, who had labored with him, be of the
same mind in the Lord, indeed.
And the rest of his fellow workers there help in the
reconciliation, for in Christ it can come
And the apostle trusts that through Jesus Christ it will come
and they will rejoice, everyone.

Paul makes plea to his beloved Philippians they ever excel in
peace and righteousness too:
"Be anxious for nothing; in everything seek guidance
through prayer and supplication true
And the peace of God, which surpasses all understanding,
will guard your minds and hearts
Guard them through Jesus Christ, thus focus on the good,
for in such focus uplifting starts
Whatever things are true, whatever things are pure, whatever
things are noble and august
If there is any virtue and if there is anything praiseworthy,
meditate on these, you must!"

Would not the apostle's plea to his beloved Philippians be
equally appropriate to you and me?
Is it not necessary to focus on the good in our world of
ubiquitous internet and 24/7 cable T.V.
Flooded with endless images of unsavory human behavior
invading most everything we see?
Excuse the intrusion so didactically done, but sometimes
spontaneous pedantry takes hold of me.
Now back to Paul in first century Rome dictating directives
lovingly to his beloved Philippians
He gives them more good advice, again advice applicable to
our own century and social situations.

"I have learned in whatever state I am, to be content, for I
can do all things through Christ Jesus
Who constantly strengthens me," says Paul, primarily to the
Philippians, secondarily to all of us.
And the apostle not only says such but demonstrates such as
he witnesses imprisoned in Rome
But so that his applied theology of finding peace through
Christ regardless is not taken wrong
Paul hastily qualifies his "peace in all circumstances"
statement by thoughtfully adding, *nevertheless*
"Nevertheless, you have done well sharing my distress; your
sharing certainly assuaged the anguish."

Paul cannot close his letter without indulging his beloved
Philippians in a bit more praiseworthiness
The apostle can never forget that this congregation, of his
many ones, excels in acts of charitableness.
Even when he left Macedonia, the Philippians continued to
send support ever sensitive to his need
"Not that I seek the gift," says Paul, "but I seek the fruit that
abounds from your charitable deed."
Thus, the apostle praises his beloved Philippians who have,
without nudging, done the right thing
And having done so bring great joy to their gospel benefactor
though he be imprisoned and in chain.

Colossians Prose Summary
Addressing Heresy

The Setting

Epaphras, who presumably knew Paul at Ephesus and carried the gospel to Colosse, has come to Rome to seek out the imprisoned apostle for purposes of alerting him to the heresy problem in the Colossian church. Apostolic authority is needed to counter the false teachings. Paul, in chains, composes a letter to the Colossians countering the false teachings and exhorting the congregation to hold fast to the gospel as originally preached to them. Judging from Paul's response, and that is all we have to go on, the problem at Colosse is a kind of syncretism in which groups are trying to inject elements of Greek philosophy, Judaism, and Gnosticism into the gospel at the expense of Jesus Christ.

The Approach

The apostle opens the letter by identifying himself, "Paul, and apostle of Jesus Christ by the will of God . . . to the saints and faithful brethren in Christ who are in Colosse" (1:1). After the greeting, he makes known his prayerful concerns for them since first learning of their faith in Christ. In reviewing his prayerful concern, he implicitly conveys what it means to be one of faith, and from there he focuses on the preeminence of Christ in God's plan of reconciliation. This he does before mentioning false teachings, and when he does mention them, rather than a frontal attack he focuses on their inadequacies in a way that exalts the preeminence of Christ. This indirect approach allows Paul to discount the false teachings with less likelihood of offending those who may have been entertaining them, thereby enhancing the effectiveness of his letter.

His Prayerful Concerns

Paul tells the Colossians that he had thanked God upon first hearing of their faith and had continued to pray for them always "because of the hope which is laid up for you in heaven, of which you heard before in the word of the truth of the gospel, which has come to you, as it has also in all the world, and is bringing forth fruit, as it is also among you since the day you heard and knew the grace of God in truth" (1:5-6). It is interesting to note that Paul points out to the Colossians that the gospel preached to them is the same gospel preached to the rest of the world, and it is "bringing forth fruit" to all the world. Indirectly, he is emphasizing the sufficiency and universality of the gospel. The gospel they heard from Epaphras, "faithful minister of Christ" on their behalf, is the same gospel preached everywhere; it is faith in Christ and it is the faith that bears fruit.

Paul further informs the Colossians that since first hearing of their faith he has not ceased praying that "you may be filled with the knowledge of God's will in all wisdom and spiritual understanding, that you may have a walk worthy of the Lord, fully pleasing Him, being fruitful in every good work and increasing in the knowledge of God . . . who has delivered us from the power of darkness and translated us into the kingdom of the Son of His love, in whom we have redemption through His blood, the forgiveness of sins" (1:9-14). Next, Paul characterizes Christ emphasizing His preeminence in God's plan of salvation.

Characterizing Christ

Paul's characterizing Christ at this point in the letter is his way of indirectly diminishing the heretical teachings invading the Colossian church before making specific mention to them. He makes clear that for the believer, faith in Christ is an absolute necessity for He is the way, the light, and the truth as Paul emphasizes in his characterization. "Christ is the image of the invisible God, the firstborn over all creation, for by Him all things were created that are in heaven and that are on earth, visible and invisible, whether thrones or dominions or principalities or powers. All things were created through Him and for Him, and He is before all things, and in Him all things consist. And He is the head of the body, the church, who is the beginning, the firstborn from the dead, that in all things He may have the preeminence, *for it pleased the Father that in Him all the fullness should dwell, and by Him to reconcile all things to Himself, by Him, whether things on earth or things in heaven, having made peace through the blood of His cross.* And you, who once were alienated and enemies in your mind by wicked works, yet now He [Christ] has reconciled in the body of His flesh through death to present you holy, and blameless, and irreproachable in God's sight—if indeed you continue in the faith, grounded and steadfast, and are not moved away from the hope of the gospel which you heard, which was preached to every creature under heaven, of which I, Paul, became a minister" (1:15-23).

Paul Defines His Commission

Paul informs the Colossians that he rejoices in his suffering for them explaining that he is helping finish Christ's suffering for the Church of which he, Paul, is an apostle called by God to spread the gospel, to the Gentile especially, to make known God's word whose mystery though hidden from earlier generations has now been revealed, the mystery "which is Christ in you, the hope and the glory. Him we preach, warning everyone and teaching everyone in all wisdom, that we may present everyone perfect in Christ Jesus. To this end . . . I labor, striving according to His working which works in me mightily" (1:27-29).

Paul wants them to know, those at Colosse, at Laodicea and other places, that though they may not have seen him in the flesh he struggles for them "that their hearts may be encouraged, being knit together in love, and attaining to all riches of the full assurance of understanding, to the knowledge of the mystery of God, *both of the Father and of Christ, in whom are hidden all the treasures of wisdom and knowledge*. Now this I say lest anyone should deceive you with persuasive words" (2:2-4).

Now that Paul has defined his authority as a called apostle whose mission it is to define and distribute the gospel mystery, and has made clear that the treasures of this mystery lie with God who makes them available only through His Son, Jesus Christ, he is ready to address heretical suppositions that are challenging the gospel.

Philosophical Supposition Discounted

"Beware lest anyone cheat you through philosophy and empty deceit, according to the tradition of men, according to the basic principles of the world and not according to Christ" (2:8). Presumably, there were those at Colosse and Laodicea (Paul asks that the Colossians share this letter with the church at Laodicea) arguing that faith in Christ was not enough that certain philosophical principles were essential, and others of the Gnostic bent arguing that esoteric knowledge possessed by only a special few was essential, and that Jesus could not have been divine since all matter (flesh) is evil, and so and so on. Paul discounts philosophical supposition saying, "As you have received Christ Jesus the Lord, so walk in Him . . . For in Him dwells all the fullness of the Godhead bodily; and you are complete in Him, who is the head of all principality and power" (2:6, 9-10). Believe in the gospel of Jesus Christ; faith, not philosophy, saves you.

Legalistic Supposition Discounted

"In Him you were also circumcised with the circumcision made without hands, by putting off the body of the sins of the flesh, by the circumcision of Christ, buried with Him in baptism, which you also were raised with Him through faith in the working of God, who raised Him from the dead" (2:11-12). Through Christ we are delivered from legalistic requirements such as circumcision and dietary laws of the Mosaic tradition. "The handwriting of requirements that was against us [the Mosaic law that put us in debt to God] Jesus Christ took away by nailing it to the cross . . . Therefore let no one judge you in food or in drink, or regarding a festival or a new moon or Sabbaths, which are a shadow of things to come, but the substance is of Christ" (2:14,16-17). Faith in Jesus Christ saves you, not laws and rituals.

Mystical Supposition Discounted

"Let no one defraud you of reward taking delight in false humility and worship of angels, which he has not seen, vainly puffed up by his fleshly mind, and not holding fast to the Head [Christ as head of the Church] from whom all the body, nourished and knit together by joints and ligaments, grows with the increase which is from God" (2:18-10). Do not let mystics whose visions give them illusions of special insight detach you from the true source of salvation, the true source of insight for spiritual growth: Jesus Christ.

Ascetic Supposition Discounted

"If you died with Christ from the basic principles of the world, why, as though living in the world, do you subject yourselves to regulation: 'do not touch, do not taste, do not handle.' These are all destined to perish because they are based on the commandments and doctrines of men" (2:20-23). This self-imposed harsh treatment of the body is of no value in restraining sensual indulgence. Salvation comes from above; it comes through faith in Jesus Christ.

The One Certainty Confirmed—If

"If then you are raised with Christ [a believer in Christ], seek those things which are above, where Christ is, sitting at the right hand of God. Set you mind on things above, not on things of the earth, for you died, and your life is hidden with Christ in God. So when Christ who is our life appears, then you also will appear with Him in glory" (3:1-4). If we believe in Jesus Christ, then we die with Him and are raised with Him.

Transformation in Christ

You are a different person in Christ; therefore, look above and put to death those things that belong to our earthly nature: "fornication, uncleanness, lust, evil desire, and covetousness, which is idolatry. Because of these things the wrath of God is coming upon the sons of disobedience, in which you also once walked when you lived in them. But now you must also put off all these: anger, wrath, malice, blasphemy, *filthy language out of your mouth*" (3:5-8).

Do not lie to one another now that you have put off the old person and put on the new person with renewed knowledge of the image of our Creator, for we can only know our intended image through Jesus Christ who exemplified it, and in that image "there is neither Greek nor Jew, circumcised nor uncircumcised . . . slave nor free, but Christ is all and in all. Therefore, as the elect of God holy and beloved, put on tender mercies, kindness, humbleness of mind, meekness, longsuffering; bearing with one another and forgiving one another . . . *but above all these things put on love which is the bond of perfection*" (3:14).

"Let the peace of God rule in your hearts . . . Let the word of Christ dwell in you richly in all wisdom, teaching and admonishing one another in psalms and hymns and spiritual songs, singing with grace in your hearts to the Lord. And whatever you do in word or deed, do all in the name of the Lord Jesus, giving thanks to God the Father through Him" (3:15-17).

Family Relationships

"Wives, submit to your own husbands, as is fitting in the Lord. Husbands, love your wives and do not be harsh with them. Children, obey your parents in all things, for this is well pleasing to the Lord. Fathers, do not provoke your children, lest they become discouraged" (3:18-21).

Slave/Master Relationships

In Christ, there is no slave/master relationship, but in the world class distinction is prevalent and even more so in Paul's time when slavery was universally accepted. And Paul addressed the problem instructing servants to obey their masters in earthly matters not simply giving eye service but with sincerity of heart and reverence for the Lord. Work heartily as for the Lord "knowing that from the Lord you will receive the reward of the inheritance for you serve the Lord Christ. But he who does wrong will be repaid for the wrong which he has done, and there is no partiality. Masters give your servants what is just and fair, knowing that you also have a Master in heaven" (3:24-26). Paul's treatment of the slave/master relationship is most appropriate here since Onesimus will be delivering the letter with Tychicus: both the slave Onesimus and his master Philemon are Colossians.

Continue in Prayer and Thanksgiving and Witnessing

Paul counsels the Colossians to continue earnestly in prayer and thanksgiving and to remember him in their prayers that God might open more doors for him "to speak the mystery of Christ, for which I am also in chains" (4:3). He also counsels them to "walk in wisdom toward those who are outside . . . [and] let your speech always be with grace seasoned with salt, that you may know how you ought to answer them"(4:5-6).

Closing Personal Remarks

Tychicus, a beloved and faithful minister, will be delivering the letter and giving them news about the apostle's present situation. He is being sent that he may know their circumstances and give comfort to them. Accompanying him will be Onesimus, a faithful and beloved brethren and one of them. Sending greetings are associates Mark, cousin of Barnabas; Luke, the beloved physician; Epaphras, one of them; and Aristarchus, fellow prisoner.

"Now when this epistle is read among you, see that it is read also in the church of the Laodiceans, and that you likewise read the epistle from Laodicea" (4:16). The apostle closes the epistle saying, "This salutation by my own hand—Paul [verifying authorship]. Remember my chains. Grace be with you. Amen" (4:18).

Colossians Poetic Summary
Addressing Heresy

Epaphras to Rome came seeking Paul concerning heresy in
the church at Colosse
Apostolic authority was needed to stem a rising tide that
threatened authenticity
Little is known about the so called Colossian heresy except
what can be inferred
Typical fare for Paul's epistles where only one side of the
dialogue can be heard
Epaphras, probably converted at Ephesus, carried the gospel
to Colosse and vicinity
And presided there bishop-like till heresy arrived challenging
the gospel's simplicity.

Seemingly, some concerned about the gospel's lack of ritual
and sophistication
Offered pieces of philosophy, of Gnosticism and Judaism as
way of adjudication
An insidious development that Epaphras recognized to be a
budding abomination
Sensing such he makes his way to Rome to alert apostle Paul
what was being done
For he knew the apostle's calling and reputation, knew to
Ephesus and Asia he had come
He knew the apostle to the Gentiles the appropriate authority
for he was God's called one.

Though in chains Paul is free to speak and speak he does
through the transcribed word
Prayerfully preparing epistle to the Colossians after digesting
facts from Epaphras heard

Identifying himself as the apostle of Jesus Christ by the will
of God he salutes them
These saints in Christ at Colosse whose circumstances have
been made known to him
The apostle next informs the Colossians of his continuing
thanks to God for them
Thanks beginning when first hearing of their faith and their
love for all the brethren.

"Thanks because of the hope laid up for you in heaven of
which you learned the truth
Learned the gospel truth which came to you, as it also came
to all the world forsooth
And is bringing forth fruit as it is among you since the day
you heard its very truth."
The apostle relates the Colossians to the world, for the
gospel they heard is universal
The gospel they learned from their own Epaphras is gospel
true, is gospel universal
On this point Paul proceeds to dwell: that Jesus Christ is
preeminent and universal.

"He is the image of God invisible and by Him all things
were created, above and below
Whether visible or invisible, whether thrones or dominions
or principalities or powers so
All things were created through Him and for Him, in Him
all things exist, He is the head
He is the head of the body, the church, He is the beginning
and first born among the dead
For it pleased the Father that in Him all the fullness should
dwell and by Him to reconcile
Reconcile all things to Himself, by Him: through the blood of
His cross all things reconcile."

"And you, who were once enemies in your mind by wicked
works, yet now He has reconciled

In the body of His flesh through death, to present you holy and blameless in His sight undefiled
If, if indeed you continue in the faith steadfastly, adhering to the gospel first preached to you
The same gospel preached universally, the gospel of which I, Paul, was called to minister true."
And thus the apostle approaches the heresy gently and indirectly, admonition without accusation
Giving apostolic assurance that the gospel heard from Epaphras needed no addition or alteration.

Paul says he rejoices to be suffering servant of the Church with commission great
Commission given by God to present to the world His word in its fullness straight
The mystery that had been kept hidden for ages, but now disclosed to the saints
To them God has chosen to make known to all the world its riches, no restraints
To reveal the riches of this mystery: which is Christ in you, the hope and the glory.
"To this end I labor striving with all my God-given strength to proclaim the story."

Paul wants those at Colosse and the adjacent Laodicea to know his struggles for them
Though they may not know him in the flesh, he prays that in the spirit they know him
That they may be encouraged in heart and united in love and have understanding real
That they may know the mystery of God, namely Christ in whom the Father is revealed
"In Christ are hidden all the treasures of wisdom and knowledge; He is the light and the way.
Lest anyone should think to deceive you with persuasive words, steadfastly hold to this I say."

Allow no one take you captive through hollow and deceptive
philosophy humanly grounded
You have received Christ Jesus the Lord, so walk in Him, be
not misguided or dumbfounded
For in Him dwells all the fullness of the Godhead and in
Him you are complete
In Him you are circumcised not of the foreskin but of the
heart, Spirit's holy seat
And you are buried with Him in baptism and raised with
Him through faith alone
All the trespasses billed against us from Adam on, now nailed
to the Cross: gone.

Therefore let no one judge you by what you eat or drink or
by religious festival done
Nor new moons or Sabbath days, all of which are shadows
of things thought to come
Ignore shadows and trust in substance which is Jesus Christ
the giver of life eternal
Be not deceived by those who worship angels and such in
puffed up minds corporeal.
Since you died with Christ to the world, why do you want to
submit to their rules obtuse:
Do not touch, do not taste, do not handle, which all concern
things that perish with use.

These things do indeed have the appearance of wisdom in
religion self-imposed
But this false humility and neglect of the body does not our
sensual nature depose.
Since you have been raised with Christ, set you hearts on
things above where Christ is seated
Seated at the right hand of God; set not your hearts on
things of the earth, on things unweeded
For you died and your life is now hidden with Christ in God
so that when Christ, our life sure
Appears, you also will appear with Him in glory; why not
then put to death your erring nature.

"Put to death fornication, uncleanness, lust, evil desire, and covetousness which is idolatry
Because of these the wrath of God is coming, and in these you once walked wholeheartedly
But now must put these things off: anger, wrath, and malice, no filthy language spew
And lie not to one another for you have put off the old self to wisely take on the new
The new self is taking on knowledge in the image of its Creator where frivolous distinctions die
Where there is neither Gentile nor Jew, circumcised or uncircumcised, slave or free, low or high."

"Therefore, as the elect of God, holy and beloved, put on tender mercies, kindness, humility
Meekness, longsuffering, always bearing with one another, forgiving one another faithfully
Let the word of Christ dwell in you richly as you teach and admonish one another wisely
In psalms, hymns and songs spiritual, singing with God's grace in your hearts advisedly.
If any has a complaint against another; even as Christ forgave you so you must also do
But above all else this admonition hear: put on love for it is the bond that perfects you."

Turning to family relationships, Paul prescribes for household accord
For wives, husbands, and children what he perceives fitting to the Lord:
"Wives, submit to your husbands ever respectful before them
Husbands, love your wives and do not be harsh toward them
Children, obey your parents in all things, be obedient to them
Fathers, do not provoke your children lest you alienate them."

Also, for the slave/master relationship, a fact of his day, Paul
had plenty to say
And appropriately said here for at Colosse the Onesimus/
Philemon conflict lay:
"Slaves obey your earthly masters not merely in eye service
to win their favor
But do it in sincerity of heart and reverence for the Lord,
honesty truly savor
Know that you are working for the Lord, not men, the Lord
is ultimate reality
Whoever does wrong receives his just deserts, for the Lord
shows no partiality
So masters to your slaves be fair forgetting not the Master of
all sees impartially."

Paul exhorts the Colossians to devote themselves earnestly
and ever to prayer
And to include himself as one who constantly seeks to speak
the gospel clear
Be wise in actions toward outsiders never allowing an
opportunity to pass
Let your conversation be full of grace and always seasoned
with salt, alas!
Thus ends Paul's admonitions and exhortations to his
Colossian brethren dear
Then comes personal information concerning his brethren
assisting him here.

Tychicus will deliver the letter and further inform them of
the apostle's situation
And knowing their circumstances seek to comfort their
hearts with loving affection
With Tychicus is Onesimus, one of their own, and subject of
the epistle to Philemon
Paul also names Aristarchus and Mark who send their
gracious greetings to everyone
Epaphras sends greetings fervently praying for the Colosse,
Laodicea, Hierapolis vicinity

And before greetings end, Luke the beloved physician and
Demas add theirs respectfully.

Lastly, the apostle requests that this epistle also be read in
the church at Laodicea
Likewise then the Colossians should read the Laodicea
letter, whatever that may be
Then calling attention to the salutation written in his own
hand asks one last thing
That his brethren remember him in prayer, especially so
since he ministers in chain.
How can the Colossians hear this epistle from the apostle
Paul and in confusion remain?
How can anyone peruse this epistle from the apostle Paul and
still in confusion remain?

I Thessalonians Prose Summary
Staying the Course

Background

We learn in Acts that Paul, on his second missionary journey, receives his call to Macedonia where he establishes the first churches in Europe. After establishing a church at Philippi, Paul and his companions, Silas and Timothy, move on to Thessalonica where they find a synagogue and where Paul "for three Sabbaths reasoned to them from the Scriptures" (Acts 17:2). Though he convinced only a few of the Jews that Jesus was the Messiah, "a great multitude of the devout Greeks, and not a few of the leading women, joined Paul and Silas" (Acts 17:4). Soon, however, the unconvinced Jews become envious of Paul and caused him to be driven from the city. After arriving in Athens, Paul, concerned about the infant congregation at Thessalonica left without experienced leadership, sends Timothy to check on their situation. Completing his mission, Timothy joins Paul at Corinth, and his report occasions Paul's first letter to the Thessalonians (3:1-6).

Conjecture Concerning Timothy's Report

We can conjecture from Paul's letter that Timothy found the church at Thessalonica thriving despite its infancy and adverse circumstances including Jewish opposition, tempting pagan practices, and theological confusion, especially the Parousia or Second Coming. The apostle, delighted that the new church has maintained its fidelity in the face of strong opposition, first commends the Thessalonians for their exemplary behavior and then offers counsel for their continued spiritual growth.

The Salutation

The epistle begins with the apostle identifying himself, his associates, and his affiliation: "Paul, Silvanus [Silas], and Timothy, to the church of the Thessalonians in God the Father and the Lord Jesus Christ" (1:1).

Commendations

After informing the Thessalonians that they are always in his prayers, the apostle commends them saying, "our gospel did not come to you in word only, but also in power, and in the Holy Spirit and in much assurance, as you know what kind of men we were among you for your sake, and you became followers of us and of the Lord, having received the word in much affliction, with joy of the Holy Spirit, so that you became examples to all in Macedonia and Achaia who believe" (1:5-7). Continuing the commendation, Paul says, "your faith has gone out, so that we do not need to say anything, for they themselves declare concerning us what manner of entry we had to you, and how you turned to God from idols to serve the living and true God and wait for His Son from heaven whom He raised from the dead, even Jesus who delivers us form the wrath to come" (1:8-10). Much to Paul's delight, the Thessalonians are exhibiting steadfastness in their newly found faith under trying circumstances and need only to maintain their steadfastness as they mature in faith. And he intends to support them in their maturation by offering up prayers and sending instruction, the purpose of the present epistle which, incidentally, is one of the earliest (about 50 A.D.), if not the earliest of Paul's epistles as well as one of the earliest written of the New Testament books.

Defense of His Character and Conduct

Presumably, Timothy reports that the Jews who drove Paul out of Thessalonica continue to discredit him, for the apostle dedicates a portion of his letter to defending his character and conduct. He says that though spitefully treated at Philippi, we dared bring the gospel to Thessalonica boldly preaching the truth despite opposition there also: "We were bold . . . to speak to you the gospel of God in much conflict . . . [for] we have been approved by God to be entrusted with the gospel even so we speak not as pleasing men, but God who tests our hearts" (2:2, 4). Paul and his associates were selfless and nurturing: "We were gentle among you, just as a nursing mother cherishes her own children . . . we were pleased to impart to you not only the gospel of God, but also our lives because you had become dear to us" (2:7-8) Furthermore, we neither demanded nor requested financial support though we might have done so as apostles of Christ: "You remember, brethren, our labor and toil; for laboring night and day, that we might not be a burden to any of you, [while] we preached to you the gospel of God" (2:9). We cannot be rightfully charged with any wrongdoing: "You are witnesses, and God also, how devoutly and justly and blamelessly we behaved ourselves among you who believe, as you know how we exhorted, and comforted, and charged every one of you, as a father does his own children, that you would have a walk worthy of God who calls you into His own kingdom and glory" (2:10-12).

Enumerating His Concern for Their Sufferings

Continuing, Paul commends the Thessalonians while voicing his concern for their sufferings saying that when they heard the gospel they welcomed it, received it, and reflected it in their lives. "You, brethren, became imitators of the churches of God which are in Judea in Christ Jesus, for you suffered the same things from your own countrymen just as they did from the Jews who killed both the Lord Jesus and their own prophets, and have persecuted us . . . forbidding us to speak to the Gentiles that they may be saved" (2:14-16). Paul knows from his own experience, being both perpetrator and victim, of the hostility against believers of the gospel, and Thessalonica is no exception for Jews there instigated mob action that forced him to leave the city charged as one of those "who has turned the world upside down" (Acts 17:6). Not only is Paul commiserating with the sufferings of the Thessalonians but, no doubt, also responding to a false charge that his premature departure proved his lack of concern. Thus, he emphasizes his concern saying though forced to leave Thessalonica, he was only away in presence and not in heart, always wishing to return but always by Satan hindered. When he could stand it no longer, he sent Timothy, "our brother and minister of God, and our fellow laborer in the gospel of Christ to establish you and encourage you concerning your faith . . . [and] now that Timothy has come to us from you, and brought us good news of your faith and love, and that you always have good remembrance of us, greatly desiring to see us, we also to see you—therefore, brethren, in all our affliction and distress we were comforted concerning you by your faith, for now we live, if you stand fast in the Lord" (3:2-8).

The apostle informs the Thessalonians that he rejoices and gives thanks to God for their faith, "night and day praying exceedingly that we may see your face and perfect what is lacking in your faith" (3:10). He prays that God will direct him to them and also direct them that they may "increase and abound in love to one another and to all, just as we do to you, so that He may establish your hearts blameless in holiness before our God and Father at the coming of our Lord Jesus Christ with all His saints" (3:12-13).

Instruction and Exhortation

In regard to sexual immorality

"You know," says Paul, "what commandments we gave you through the Lord Jesus, for this is the will of God, your sanctification: that you should abstain from sexual immorality that each of you should know how to possess his own vessel in sanctification and honor, not in passion of lust . . . for God did not call us to uncleanness, but in holiness" (4:2-7).

In regard to brotherly love and orderly living

As you know you are taught by God to love one another and you have demonstrated your love toward the brethren in all of Macedonia, "but we urge you, brethren, that you increase more and more; that you also aspire to lead a quiet life, to mind your own business, and to work with your own hands, as we commanded you, that you may walk properly toward those who are outside, and that you may lack nothing" (4:10-12). Paul is exhorting them toward maturity in their faith. One way they could increase their love for one another was to avoid idleness, live quietly, and earn their own bread. Supposedly, some of the Thessalonians were idle and living off others, their justification being belief in the imminent return of Christ and in the Greek belief that manual labor was demeaning. Paul set the example of the Christian work ethic in his tent making that allowed him to earn his own bread. In doing so he avoided being a financial burden to those to whom he preached and also avoided the appearance of compromising belief for bread. No doubt, there is some truth in the adage: Tell me where you get your bread and I will tell you where you get your opinions.

In regard to the resurrection of the dead

Presumably, there was concern among the Thessalonians about dying before Christ returned. Paul put their minds at ease by assuring them that those of the faith who fell asleep (died) before Christ's return would be the first to rise to meet Him in the clouds. "The Lord Himself will descend from heaven with a shout, with the voice of an archangel, and with the trumpet of God, and the dead in Christ will rise first. Then we who are alive and remain shall be caught up together with them in the clouds to meet the Lord in the air. And thus we shall always be with the Lord" (4:16-17).

In regard to the time of the Second Coming

Paul relates Christ's return to the Day of the Lord referred to by the Old Testament prophets, a day in which God would correct a wayward world by destroying it along with the unrighteous while redeeming the righteous. In doing so he emphasizes that, as Jesus had informed His disciples, no one but God knew the day nor the hour when the Day would come. Paul counsels the Thessalonians to concentrate on preparation rather speculate on the time, and all would be well. "For you yourselves, know perfectly that the day of the Lord so comes as a thief in the night . . . but you, brethren, are not in darkness, so that this Day should overtake you as a thief. You are all sons of light and sons of the day. We are of the light . . . therefore let us not sleep as others do, but let us watch and be sober" (5:2-6) Paul emphasizes that preparation relieves worry, "for God did not appoint us to wrath, but to obtain salvation through our Lord Jesus Christ, who died for us that whether we wake or sleep, we should live together with Him. Therefore comfort each other and edify one another, just as you also are doing" (5:9-11).

In regard to certain duties

Paul counsels them to live responsibly respecting their leaders, "those who labor among you, and are over you in the Lord and admonish you, and esteem them very highly in love for their work's sake" (5:12-13). And he exhorts them to take individual responsibility in warning those who are unruly, in comforting those who are fainthearted, in upholding those who are weak, and in having patience with all. Never render evil for evil, but pursue what is good for others as well as yourself, "pray without ceasing, in everything give thanks; for this is the will of God in Christ Jesus for you" (5:17-18). In all things exercise wise judgment: "*Test all things; hold fast to what is good*" (5:21).

In Closing

The apostle closes with a benediction and a charge that the epistle be read to the entire congregation.

I Thessalonians Poetic Summary
Staying the Course

On the second missionary journey, Asia and Bithynia were scratched from Paul's plans
Not by the apostle but by the Holy Spirit who sternly steered him between the two lands
For this trip Europe was to take precedent, as the Macedonian call soon revealed:
Come over and help he plead, enshrined in vision divinely sanctioned and sealed.
So to Troas Paul and party trudged before setting sail for the seaport Neapolis
Then went overland to Philippi where the apostle begins his European witness.

Leaving converts in Philippi, Paul travels the Egnatian Way to Thessalonica, the capital city
Where he finds a synagogue and for three Sabbaths scours Scripture postulating Christianity.
Though only few Jews are convinced, a multitude of the synagogue's devout Greeks believe
So many so the unconvinced Jews, becoming envious, a heinous plot against Paul conceive.
They engage rowdies to riot against the house of Jason where Paul and party are staying
Causing believers, concerned for his safety, send him down to Berea, thus harm delaying.

When the Bereans embrace Paul's preaching, the jealous Jews from Thessalonica react
Straightway streaming down to incite crowds against the gospel, and its proponent attack

Again causing concerned believers to rush to the apostle's protection by spiriting him away
This time putting him on a boat bound for Athens where Paul, undaunted, continues his say
Most famously said on Mars Hill, the Areopagus, where he addresses many a learned Greek
Telling them he has solved their "unknown god" mystery: it is the Lord Jesus Christ they seek.

Yet all the while Paul harbors huge concern over how the infant church at Thessalonica fares
How these babes in Christ cope with the hostile unconvinced Jews and the pagan practitioners
So he sends Timothy to survey the situation while he sets sail for Corinth, his next undertaking.
There he reasons in synagogue on Sabbaths while on weekdays working his craft of tent making.
The Thessalonica survey completed, Timothy joins Paul in Corinth, to report on mission sent
A report occasioning the apostle's epistle I Thessalonians, as recorded in the New Testament.

We can infer from this letter that Timothy found the infant church faring remarkably well
That despite external challenge and certain theological confusion, in behavior they excel
For Paul commends the congregation for its fidelity before offering counsel of any kind.
Beyond doubt Timothy found much to praise and thereby had much relieved Paul's mind.
And thus relieved the apostle composes what may be his first epistle to a church he planted
First of many shedding much needed light for those early converts as well as today, granted.

Paul, as is usually the case, begins by identifying himself and associates and their affiliation:

He, Silas, and Timothy hail the church at Thessalonica in
the name of the Father and the Son.
After informing the Thessalonians they are always in his
prayers, the apostle commends
Saying "our gospel did not come to you in word only, but also
in power the Spirit sends
We were among you for your sakes and you became
followers, followers of the Lord
And despite affliction you became examples to all Macedonia
and Achaia, one accord."

The commendation continues: "Your faith has gone out, so
we need not say anything
For they themselves declare readily what kind of reception
you gave us when we came
How you turned from idols to serve the living and true God
and wait for His Son
Whom He raised from the dead and Who will deliver us
from the wrath to come."
Paul could hardly be more delighted than to hear his
Thessalonians lived exemplary
And to know his infant church although facing trying
circumstances fared faithfully.

Paul is delighted knowing they need only maintain their
steadfastness as they in faith mature
And he intends to support that maturation by offering up
prayers and sending instruction sure.
Through messenger and epistle the apostle took on the task
of nurturing his churches numerous
And First Thessalonians may well be the first of the epistles
and Timothy first of the messengers.
Epistle and messenger kept Paul in touch with his
established churches while establishing more
Through epistle and messenger Paul commended, consoled
and cajoled, congregations to shore.

First Thessalonians implies Timothy reported the Jews who outed Paul still disparage him
For a portion of the epistle defends the apostle's character and conduct as if refuting them.
The apostle writes, "We dared bring the gospel to Thessalonica boldly preaching the truth
Preaching the gospel of God despite deadly defiance, for we follow our Lord's will forsooth.
Entrusted with the gospel we speak not to please men but God; only He our hidden hearts tests.
What we say and what we do we do to glorify the Lord our God, for therein righteousness rests."

In defensive mode the apostle says, "we neither demanded nor requested financial support, none
Though as apostles of Christ we could have done so rather than supporting ourselves, every one.
You remember, brethren, our labor and our toil laboring night and day so as not to burden you.
It is plain as day we cannot be charged with any wrongdoing; you are witnesses, and God too!
And you know how we exhorted, and comforted, and charged each of you as a father would do
That you would walk with God who calls into His own kingdom and glory every one of you."

Continuing, Paul both commends and commiserates in noting their suffering brought on by belief:
"Hearing the gospel, brethren, you became imitators of the churches of Judea, believers' early fief
And you suffered the same things from your own countrymen we apostles suffer from the Jews
Who crucified Jesus and abuse His apostles even when it is conversion of Gentiles they choose.
How well Paul can relate being both perpetrator and victim of hostility toward the gospel true
Did not the Jews in Thessalonica instigate action forcing him from that Gentile city, déjà vu?

Paul's commiseration with their suffering challenges charges
concerning his premature departure.
Though forced to leave Thessalonica, he was only away in
presence; in heart there was no rupture.
Always longing to return, but by Satan hindered, he sent
Timothy, "our fellow minister of God."
A capable and faithful messenger he proved instructing and
encouraging, faith and love his rod.
Encouraging news he brings Paul harbored in Corinth:
"Thessalonica remembers you lovingly."
Knowing the Thessalonians stand fast in faith further inspires
the apostle to labor unceasingly.

The apostle thus informed and inspired rejoices giving God
thanks for Thessalonian backing
And prays "night and day exceedingly that we may see your
face and perfect what is lacking."
He prays that God will direct him to them and also direct
them that they may abound in love
"That they may increase and abound in love to one another
and to all," glorifying God above.
Paul prays that their hearts be blameless in holiness before
God the Father, love without restraints
In the Lord Jesus Christ their hearts are blameless and at His
coming will join Him with His saints.

After commendations and consolations come the apostle's
instructions and exhortations
Presumably, responses to areas of concern voiced in
messenger Timothy's observations.
Regarding sexual immorality, Paul reminds them they have a
special obligation, a special trust:
"God did not call us to uncleanness, one's vessel is to be
possessed in sanctification, not in lust."
Regarding brotherly love, they could increase their love for
one another by avoiding idleness
By quietly living, by minding their business own, by never
exploiting a neighbor's goodness.

Presumably, some of the Thessalonians were idle and living
off their neighbors without concern
Their justification, more a rationalization: "the return of
Christ being imminent no need to earn."
But had not Paul belied such thinking when ministering to
them while pursuing tent making?
And earning his own bread also belied any insinuation the
apostle exploited his undertaking.
Whether it took the form of idleness or some other, the
Second Coming proved a preoccupation.
Even though believing that Christ's coming was imminent,
there was still certain consternation:

"What if the believer died before Christ came, would he be
left behind, left forever in his grave?"
Among some, perhaps many, this seemed to be topic of
much concern, would He the dead save?
To relieve Thessalonian thinking along this line, Paul
proclaimed assurance, not surmise
Saying, "those of faith who fall asleep before Christ's return
they will be the first to rise.
The Lord Himself will descend from heaven and the dead in
Christ will rise up first and away
Then we who are alive will join them in the clouds and with
the Lord we all will forever stay."

Paul relates Christ's return to the Day of the Lord testified
to by prophets of the Old Testament
On that Day, God would destroy the wayward world though
redeeming the righteous His intent.
Paul proposes they concentrate on preparation rather than
speculate on the time it takes place.
Knowing He will come like a thief in the night, vigilance and
preparation become our solace.
The apostle points out that preparation relieves worry, for
God did not appoint us to wrath
He appointed us to seek our Lord Jesus Christ, for everyone
who finds Him salvation hath.

In closing, Paul counsels them to live responsibly to respect
their leaders admonishing grave
And exhorts them to take individual responsibility in
warning the unruly who play the knave
To uphold those who are weak and to exercise patience with
all, never return evil for evil
But pursue what is good for others as well as self, and pray
unceasingly that good prevail.
In all things give thanks to God above through His beloved
Son who in our stead stood
Live responsibly exercising judgment wise: test all things
holding fast to what is good.

II Thessalonians Prose Summary
Called to Service

Need for a Second Letter

Not long after sending his first epistle to the Thessalonians, Paul saw need to send a second. As in the first letter, the apostle begins the second by commending the congregation before addressing the present problem, confusion concerning the Day of the Lord. Some of the congregation insists that the Day of the Lord had already begun as evidenced by the persecution taking place. Apparently, the congregation is being persecuted by both Jews and pagans and certain members believe this is happening because the Day of the Lord has begun. Yet they recall Paul saying that because of their being believers, being righteous ones, they would be exempt from punishment when the Day came. The result is confusion. Has the day of the Lord begun? If it has why are we believers being punished?

Causing further confusion is an element in the congregation who believe the coming of the Lord is imminent and thereby see no need to work and have become idle busybodies living off the bread of others.

Paul addresses the confusion, but first commends the congregation for the good work they are doing.

Commendation and Encouragement

The apostle tells the congregation that he thanks God always for them, "as is fitting, because your faith grows exceedingly, and the love of every one of you all abounds toward each other, so that we ourselves boast of you among the churches of God for your patience and faith in all persecutions and tribulations that you endure" (1:3-4). All this is evidence, he assures them, that God's judgment is right and that as a result they will be worthy of the kingdom of God for which they are suffering. God is just and He will bring tribulation to those who are troubling them and they will receive rest along with all the other saints (gospel believers) "when the Lord Jesus is revealed from heaven with His mighty angels in flaming fire taking vengeance on those who do not know God, and on those who do not obey the gospel of our Lord Jesus Christ. These shall be punished with everlasting destruction from the presence of the Lord and from the glory of His power, when He comes, in that Day, to be glorified in His saints and to be admired among all those who believe because our testimony among you was believed" (1:7-10). Therefore, the apostle prays always that God will count them worthy of their calling and "that the name of our Lord Jesus Christ may be glorified in you, and you in Him, according to the grace of our God and the Lord Jesus Christ" (1:12).

Addressing the Confusion Concerning the Day of the Lord

After commending and encouraging the congregation in the work of the gospel, Paul turns to the Day of the Lord confusion telling the congregation not to be troubled or shaken "either by spirit or by word or by letter as if from us [Paul] as though the day of Christ had come. Let no one deceive you by any means *for that Day will not come* unless the falling away comes first, and the man of sin is revealed, the son of perdition, who opposes and exalts himself above all that is called God or that is worshiped, so that he sits as God in the temple of God, showing himself that he is God" (2:2-4). Paul asks if they do not remember his telling them *this* [the falling away comes first]. Paul does not reveal how he knows about "the falling away" and "the son of perdition" coming first, but asserts his apostolic authority in revealing it.

Yet his revelation dispels the rumor that the Day of the Lord has begun. That Day can not begin previous to "the falling away" at which time a Satan sponsored lawlessness takes over in the form of "the son of perdition." This lawlessness is not happening because it is being restrained. Paul does not explain how it is being restrained, whether it is by the Holy Spirit working through the Church or whether it is by human government (at the time Rome), but it is being restrained until the designated time known by God only. It will, however, be released for it is the lie that the unrighteous have pursued and it is the delusion that will destroy them because they "did not believe the truth but had pleasure in unrighteousness" (2:12).

The Thessalonians Chosen Ones

In assuring the Thessalonians the apostle reminds them they are special for they are "beloved by the Lord, because God from the beginning chose you for salvation through sanctification by the Spirit and belief in truth, to which He called you by our gospel, for the obtaining of the glory of our Lord Jesus Christ. Therefore, brethren, stand fast and hold the traditions which you were taught, whether by word or our epistle" (2:13-15).

This statement falls into what might be called the election motif sounded from time to time in Paul's epistles. In the case of the Thessalonians, it is easy to see why Paul views them as specially called elect, for he was led by the Holy Spirit to bypass Asia and Bithynia and by a vision to cross over into Macedonia (see Acts 16:6-10) and on to Thessalonica, the capital city of Macedonia located on the Egnatian Way, a Roman thoroughfare. And though he was able to minister in the synagogue there only three weeks, many were converted and were remaining faithful to the gospel despite stiff persecution. Thus, circumstances seem to favor election over coincidence.

John Calvin is the best known proponent of election theology which surely he carried too far. Calvin viewed all mankind as being born totally depraved because of the fall of Adam who broke the original covenant [read contract] thereby forever dooming man to depravity. Because of the fall, God has no obligation to redeem a single person, but being a merciful God has chosen to elect certain ones through irresistible grace.

Considering his Damascus experience, Paul's election theology is not surprising, but it stops short of that of Calvin. In the Thessalonian example, Paul seems to be thinking more along the lines of a special call much like Abraham's call in which God's intent was to choose a single person whose faithful commitment would lead not only to his salvation but to the potential salvation of the whole world as the last portion of the Abrahamic covenant declares: "And in you [Abraham] all the families of the earth shall be blessed" (Gen 12:3). Abraham was called, not coerced; he could have resisted God's grace, as could have the Thessalonians. Note that Paul says they were chosen "for salvation through sanctification by the Spirit and belief in truth" (2:13). They could have rejected the Spirit, but chose to be chosen like Abraham and, according to Paul, became living examples for others considering salvation.

Prayer and Confidence

Paul asks that the Thessalonians pray for his ministry, pray that he will be delivered from the "unreasonable and wicked men" (3:2), for he has confidence in the Lord concerning them. The apostle assures them that he believes they will do the things he commands them and prays that the Lord will direct their hearts "into the love of God and into the patience of Christ" (3:5).

The Apostle's Commands

Having prepared them through exhortation and commendation, Paul now sets forth commands to guide them in their challenging role. They must, in the name of the Lord Jesus Christ, dissociate themselves from "every brother who walks disorderly and not according to the tradition which he received from us [Paul]" (3:6). The apostle has not only preached the truth but has set example while among them. He did not walk disorderly; he did not eat anyone's bread free of charge, but toiled night and day in order not to be a burden to them. He reminds them of the command he gave while among them: "If anyone will not work, neither shall he eat" (3:10).

They must not grow weary of striving for the good. "If anyone does not obey our word in this epistle, note that person and do not keep company with him, that he may be ashamed. Yet do not count him as an enemy, but admonish him as a brother" (3:14). Discipline must be maintained; the church must be exemplary, but the discipline must be maintained in a charitable manner.

II Thessalonians Poetic Summary
Called to Service

Paul presumably received troubling news from Thessalonica
not long after sending epistle one
For soon he sends epistle two addressing eschatology, to the
Thessalonians subject troublesome.
But as in epistle one, the apostle first compliments the
congregation for their achievements
For their abiding and abounding faith he thanks God always
and boasts of them at all events.
And now he consoles them concerning their suffering, saying
reward awaits them at the end
God being just, tribulation will come to those who trouble
them while they to Christ ascend.

Thus, the apostle approaches rumor of major concern: "The
Day of the Lord had already begun."
Rumor asserting Paul had preached such roamed the
congregation causing consternation for some.
Their present and persistent suffering, supposedly from
pagans and Jews alike, seemed to verify
But learning of the hearsay situation the apostle readily
released epistle two, this rumor to deny.
"My brethren," writes Paul, "concerning the coming of the
Lord Jesus Christ, let us reason some:
Be not mislead by spirit, by word, or letter *as if by us* in
erroneously thinking that Day has come."

"Let no one deceive you by any means; that Day will not
come until the falling away comes first
Revealing the man of sin, the son of perdition, who exalts
himself above God in one great burst

So that he sits in God's temple and proclaims himself to be
God, demanding all submit to his will."
Paul then asks if they do not remember his explaining all
these things when he was with them still.
No doubt the apostle intends to turn them away from rumor
and direct them to the record real:
Nothing has changed, the gospel is the same, the Parousia will
come but the time is under seal.

Apparently Paul's Parousia explanation, in person and in
epistle, to some has become a blur
In epistle one he stressed the time factor, but in epistle two
he stresses what must first occur
Paul had echoed Jesus saying since no man knew the day or
hour all must prepare and watch
Unfortunately, "prepare and watch" was by some conveniently
misconstrued creating botch.
Wanting to believe the time near they elected not to work
but to watch, eating others' bread.
Add to the idle watchers those listening to rumor: the Day of
the Lord already here and dread.

To stem the tide of idleness and rumor concerning the
Parousia, Paul put pen to papyrus stern
Interpreting the Day of the Lord of O. T. prophecy and the
gospel's account of Christ's return
He assures the Thessalonians that the Day has not come and
will not until perdition's son appears.
Rumor to the contrary circulating through their
congregation is distortion writ large, utter arrears.
"The lawless one now restrained, as I told you when there,
remains so until the restraint is undone
Restraint removed and the lawless one revealed, all this must
happen before our Lord will come."

In summary, the apostle says, "the coming of the lawless one
is according to the working of Satan

Who with power and with lying wonders the unrighteous
deceives purposely bringing destruction.
Since they chose not to receive the love of truth that they
might be saved, God sends them delusion
That they should believe the lie and be condemned having
spurned truth to revel in self indulgence."
After putting to rest the rumor concerning "that Day" the
apostle conjures up peace and consolation
He reviews the true Thessalonian situation thereby assuring
them all they are chosen for salvation.

From time to time Paul leans heavily toward election, a
theological bent manifested here surely
Saying, "we are bound to give thanks to God always for you,
brethren beloved by the Lord truly
Because God from the beginning chose you for salvation
through the Spirit and belief in truth
And He called you by our gospel, for obtaining the glory of
our Lord Jesus Christ forsooth."
Would it not seem so since the Holy Spirit directed Paul to
Macedonia passing Asia by?
Would it not seem so since Paul's preaching lasted a few weeks
only in Thessalonica?

Defining election can become a knotty theological thing as
John Calvin's definition became.
And concerning definition, what Paul perceived and what
Calvin perceived are not the same:
Calvin reasoned that since Adam's fall fell all, God could
justly elect whomever He pleased
How could fallen man still hold any right to paradise, how
could he possibly expect reprieve?
That God chose to elect any was a show of mercy
undeserved, for obligation He had none
But such a legalistic take leaves most believers cold, for they
see God's mercy in His Son.

Let us conjecture that Paul's election take presumes a
different covenant test:
God definitely chooses but He chooses to take in more not
to exclude the rest.
Abraham was chosen, yes, but chosen to lead others to God
not to exclude them?
"And through you all the families of the world shall be
blessed," God said to him.
Paul felt led to the city of Thessalonica on the Egnatian Way,
a Roman thoroughfare
Where, in short order, pagans grasped the gospel and speedily
spread it far and near.

Thus, Paul sees election as inclusive not exclusive: to be
chosen is responsibility plus
Think of Abraham, Moses, and most of all Jesus, chosen to
pave the way for all of us
And that is his message to the Thessalonians: they are
chosen, thus they are models to be.
So far they have met expectations admirably and the apostle
prays they do so continually
Yet they cannot allow the loafers and alarmists misconstrue
the Parousia that Paul preached
The gospel he had preached while with them and later by
letter shored must not be breached.

"Therefore, brethren, stand fast and hold the tradition you
were taught by word and by epistle
And may God our Father and Jesus Christ our Lord comfort
you and cleanse any heart fickle."
Not only does the apostle pray for the Thessalonians but
asks that they pray for him in return
Pray that the word of the Lord, that His message, will
spread though by the wicked spurned.
Paul assures them that the Lord is always faithful and will
guide and guard them
For he is confident they do and will continue to do the things
commanded by him.

And with this thought the apostle begins, in the name of the
Lord, instructive commands thus:
Withdraw from every brother who walks disorderly, not
according to tradition received from us
For you know yourselves how you ought to follow us who
were not disorderly when among you
We ate no one's bread but our own and worked night and
day that we in no way burdened you.
This we did not because we do not have authority, but to
establish example for you to repeat
Recall that when among you we commanded: "If anyone will
not work, neither shall he eat."

The apostle recalled this command because of having heard
there were those work refusing
Though idle busybodies they always cited the imminent
Parousia, thus themselves excusing.
These idlers the apostle commands through the Lord Jesus
Christ to cease their disorderliness
They must work in quietness and provide their own bread;
to labor for the Lord is blessedness.
Paul exhorts the brethren not grow weary in doing good; do
not the epistle's commands disdain
Duly note anyone not obeying these commands and then
shun that person making him ashamed.

Yet take care not to treat the wayward one as an enemy, take
care to admonish him as a brother
Never unnecessarily drive a wayward one from the
congregation, love and respect one another.
The apostle commands through the Lord Jesus Christ the
measure for the Thessalonians thus
And the New Testament canonizing of this epistle thereby
commands the same measure for us.

I Timothy Prose Summary
The Pastoral Letter

Introduction

Because First and Second Timothy and Titus are addressed to pastor associates of Paul they are generally referred to as the pastoral letters. With the exception of the three pastoral letters and Philemon, Paul's other letters—Romans, First and Second Corinthians, Galatians, Ephesians, Philippians, Colossians, First and Second Thessalonians—are addressed to churches rather than individuals.

The pastoral letters appear to have been written after Paul completes the three missionary journeys chronicled in the Book of Acts, for a number of references in the pastoral letters do not fit within the framework of those journeys. The last chapter of Acts, chapter 28, leaves Paul imprisoned in Rome. He is imprisoned because after having completed three missionary journeys he felt compelled to exercise his Roman citizenship and appeal to Caesar in order to escape death at the hands of Jewish authorities in Jerusalem who resented his declaring Jesus the Son of God and preaching the gospel. As the Book of Acts ends, Paul is awaiting trial while under house arrest where imperial guards monitor him. Nevertheless, he is able to continue his missionary work by witnessing (even to the imperial guards) as well as by communicating with associates in person or by letter. But whether Paul made a fourth missionary journey the Book of Acts does not tell us; that is left to conjecture.

One can surmise from certain comments in the pastoral letters (e.g., I Tim 1:3; Titus 1:5, 3:12) and comments by early writings about the Church (e. g., Eusebius, early Church historian) that Paul must have been released from the imprisonment recorded in Acts and thereafter embarked on a fourth missionary journey as certain biblical scholars contend. We know from his letter to the Romans that he wanted to take the gospel to Spain and requested their support in doing so (Rom 15:23-29). Though there is no hard evidence that he ever went to Spain, he may have done so between his first imprisonment, presumably ending around A.D. 63, and a presumed second imprisonment at Rome. Tradition places Paul's death in Rome around A.D. 67, victim of Emperor Nero. Tradition also holds that both Peter and Paul were executed in Rome, that Peter was crucified, but that Paul, because of his Roman citizenship, was beheaded.

Though the pastoral letters say nothing about Paul's having visited Spain, they do seem to furnish evidence that he embarked on a fourth missionary journey. For example, in I Timothy we read that he instructs Timothy to stay in Ephesus while he visits Macedonia (1:3), and in Titus we read that he leaves Titus in Crete (1:5). Neither of these events fit into the framework of the three missionary journeys chronicled in Acts and thereby lends credence to the supposition that Paul embarked on a fourth missionary journey.

Authorship of the Pastoral Letters Questioned

There is some controversy about the pastoral letters having been written by Paul. Two particular phenomena bother certain scholars: a considerable portion of the vocabulary of the pastoral letters not having been used in Paul's earlier letters and the structural level of church organization discussed in these letters seemingly too developed for Paul's time. It is conjectured that someone writing at a later time may have used Paul's name and prestige for purposes of redressing church problems. Yet early tradition ascribes the pastoral letters to Paul and, despite an element of dissent, contemporary scholarship leans toward Paul's authorship. So let us assume Paul the author of the pastoral letters as we explore them beginning with I Timothy.

Paul Sends a Letter to Timothy in Ephesus

Paul, presumably from Macedonia, writes to Timothy in Ephesus saying, "As I urged you when I went to Macedonia: remain in Ephesus that you may charge some that they teach no other doctrine, nor give heed to fables and endless genealogies, which cause disputes rather than godly edification which is in faith. Now the purpose of this command is love from a pure heart, from a good conscience, and from sincere faith, from which some, having strayed, have turned aside to idle talk" (1:3-6). One may infer from this directive that Timothy had expressed a desire to leave Ephesus.

Perhaps he wanted to be with Paul or suffers from lack of confidence or both. Whatever the case, Paul in this epistle directs Timothy to stay in Ephesus and gives him instructions for coping with the problems there. No doubt this letter from Paul, his mentor, calling him "my true son in the faith" bolsters Timothy's spirit and confidence.

The Paul and Timothy Relationship

That Paul trusts Timothy with such major responsibility reveals the apostle's high regard for his associate. We know from Paul's refusal to allow John Mark to accompany him on the second missionary journey that the apostle expected a high level of performance from his associates (see Acts 15:36-40). Although John Mark later redeemed himself, Timothy appears to have been an exemplary associate from the beginning. Early in the second missionary journey, at a place called Lystra, Paul took special note of Timothy, son of a devout Jewish mother and a Greek father. The apostle was so pleased with Timothy that he chose the young disciple to accompany and assist him (see Acts 16:1-3). And judging from the numerous references to Timothy in Acts and in Paul's letters Timothy remained a beloved, trusted, and able assistant throughout the remaining years of the apostle's life accompanying and assisting him in taking the gospel to such places as Philippi, Thessalonica, Corinth, and Ephesus, at times becoming messenger and monitor as in the case of Thessalonica, and never shirking his prescribed duties as witnessed in his loyal and unwavering service to the imprisoned apostle in Rome.

Timothy at Ephesus

One may conjecture that Paul was released from his first Roman imprisonment around A.D. 63, and thereafter embarked on a fourth missionary journey. There is little evidence that this journey took him to Spain in the western portion of the Empire other than the intent voiced in Romans, but there is considerable evidence in the pastoral letters that Paul again visits and revisits eastern portions of the Empire: Crete, Ephesus, and Macedonia in particular. The first pastoral letter reveals that he and Timothy returned to Ephesus, a city where they had spent three years, more or less, on the third missionary journey and where they had made great progress spreading the gospel in the city and surrounding area. Ephesus, located in Asia Minor, was one of the major cities in the Roman Empire. Further, the letter reveals present problems of false teachings at Ephesus, probably the reason Paul and Timothy had returned. But for some unexplained reason

Paul leaves Timothy in Ephesus and goes to Macedonia; from there he sends a letter to Timothy directing him to stand firm in dealing with the Ephesus church problems, and proceeds to give him instructions on how best to deal with them.

Paul's Strong Sense of Apostolic Responsibility

Though this is Paul's fourth missionary journey and almost three decades following his conversion, this thirteenth apostle (called by the Lord after his ascension) still hears his calling clearly and urgently: "a chosen vessel of Mine to bear My name before Gentiles, kings, and the children of Israel" (Acts 9:15). Hearing, the apostle urges Timothy, "my true son in the faith," to remain in Ephesus to see that sound doctrine is taught, "sound doctrine, according to the glorious gospel of the blessed God which was committed *to my trust*" (1:10-11). Our hearing Paul alerts us to the apostle's resounding sense of responsibility. One can imagine the burden that Paul shoulders trying to carry out his apostolic calling of spreading the gospel to both Jew and Gentile throughout the Roman Empire, of establishing churches far and wide, and then of nurturing them indirectly through associates, most not as dedicated and competent as Timothy, and directly through personal visitations and letters. Ephesus is the church where Paul had labored the longest, some three years, and the church through which he had spread the gospel to much of Asia Minor. Ephesus, a major city and seaport, furnished great opportunity for spreading the gospel and Paul was anxious that the church located in this strategic city continue to flourish and to flourish in teaching sound doctrine that he had taught them.

Concerning Fables and Endless Genealogies

Paul first mentions to Timothy that some persons were focusing on "fables and endless genealogies" at the expense of sound doctrine and thereby causing disputes rather than bolstering the gospel (1:4). We can only surmise what the apostle meant by "fables" and "endless genealogies," but we know that there are a number of genealogies in the Scriptures serving to link a person to a particular tribe or family such as connecting a priest to the Levite tribe and specifically the family of Aaron. In Ezra, genealogy is utilized in determining the pure Jewish blood line of those returning to Jerusalem after the Captivity. And Matthew opens his gospel with a genealogy tracing the human line of Jesus to David and on to Abraham. Furthermore, tracing a person's lineage, especially a hero, to some god was a common practice in the ancient pagan world. And creating fables around famous persons and heroes was common in both the Jewish and Gentile world. Therefore, either Jew or Gentile teachers may have been attempting to pitch certain fables and genealogies as important or essential to salvation, but Paul is commanding Timothy to allow only the teaching of sound doctrine: salvation based on faith in Jesus Christ.

Concerning the Teaching of the Law

Paul says some have strayed and turned to idle talk "desiring to be teachers of the law, understanding neither what they say nor the things which they affirm" (1:7). The law, he points out, is good in that it identifies sin: murder, fornication, sodomy, lying, perjury and "any other thing that is contrary to sound doctrine" (1:9-10). But law is not made for the righteous; it is made for the lawless and the ungodly. Knowledge of the law is not the key to salvation or righteousness; faith in Jesus Christ is the key to salvation, and living that faith is the key to righteousness.

Concerning Grace through Faith

The apostle testifies to God's grace through faith in his own life: "I thank Christ Jesus our Lord who has enabled me, because He counted me faithful, putting me into the ministry, although I was formerly a blasphemer, a persecutor, and an insolent man; but I obtained mercy because I did it ignorantly in unbelief. And the grace of our Lord was exceedingly abundant, with faith and love which are in Christ Jesus. This is a faithful saying and worthy of all acceptance, that Christ Jesus came into the world to save sinners, of which I am chief" (1:12-15).

The Charge to Timothy

Recalling previous prophecies made concerning Timothy's destined role in ministering (presumably, prophecies made at his ordination), Paul hands him a tough assignment. Confirming his associate as one "having faith and good conscience" (1:19), the apostle charges him to keep the church at Ephesus on course, noting that some there have rejected the faith and suffered shipwreck, two of whom he names, "Hymenaeus and Alexander, whom I delivered to Satan that they may learn not to blaspheme" (1:20), meaning he has excluded them from the church in order to discipline them.

Pray for the Authorities; Pray for All

The apostle instructs Timothy to pray, to make intercessions, and to give thanksgiving for all men, "for kings and all who are in authority, that we may lead a quiet and peaceable life in all godliness and reverence, for this is good and acceptable in the sight of God our Savior, who desires all men to be saved and to come to the knowledge of the truth" (2:1-4). Praying for those in authority is not only praying for their salvation and righteousness but also for a stable society without which the church could not flourish. And it is necessary to pray for all men Paul says because "there is one God and one Mediator between God and men, the Man Christ Jesus, who gave Himself a ransom for all, to be testified in due time," and who Paul proudly declares appointed him "a preacher and an apostle . . . a teacher of Gentiles in faith and truth" (2:5-7). And as the Lord's appointed apostle, Paul desires that men everywhere pray "lifting up holy hands, without wrath and doubting" (2:8).

Instructions Concerning Women

Women, Paul says, should dress modestly without adornment, dress appropriately as one would professing godliness. Also, "let a woman learn in silence with all submission, [for] I do not permit a woman to teach or to have authority over a man, but to be in silence. For Adam was formed first, then Eve. And Adam was not deceived, but the woman" (2:11-14). Dressing for reverence and not for personal show seems as relevant today as in Paul's day, but relegating the woman to silence in a present day democratic society with equal education and equal opportunity raises questions. It doesn't change the Adam and Eve situation, but it does raise the woman's level of education to that of the man's, which was not the case in Paul's day.

Concerning Bishops

The clause "This is a faithful saying" appears a number of times in the pastoral letters to introduce what the writer considers a truism. (See I Tim 1:15, 3:1, 4:9; II Tim 2:11; Titus 3:8.) It is used here concerning bishops. "This is a faithful saying: If a man desires the position of a bishop, he desires a good work. A bishop then must be blameless, the husband of one wife, temperate, sober-minded, of good behavior, hospitable, able to teach; not given to wine, not violent, not greedy for money, but gentle, not quarrelsome, not covetous; one who rules his own house well, having his children in submission with all reverence . . . not a novice, lest being puffed up with pride he fall into the same condemnation as the devil. Moreover, he must have a good testimony among those who are outside, lest he fall into reproach and the snare of the devil" (3:1-7). In short, he must be a seasoned believer exemplary in all avenues of life. In the New Testament, the word "bishop" is sometimes used interchangeably with "overseer" and "elder." Basically, it involved the overseeing of a church.

Concerning Deacons

The word "deacon" means minister or servant and in New Testament church practice was one who helped the bishop (elder, overseer). As one would assume and as Paul prescribes, the qualifications for deacons are very similar to those for bishops. "Deacons must be reverent, not double-tongued, not given to much wine, not greedy for money, holding the mystery of the faith with pure conscience" and whose wives "must be reverent, not slanderers, temperate, faithful in all things." Furthermore, deacons should "be the husbands of one wife, ruling their children and their own houses well" (3:8-12). As the man who desires to be a bishop desires a good work, the same is so for the deacon. The deacon who serves well obtains for himself "a good standing and great boldness in the faith which is in Christ Jesus" (3:13).

Stated Purpose of the Letter

At this point in the letter Paul tells Timothy that he hopes to come to Ephesus shortly, but that he might be delayed. Therefore, "I write so that you may know how you ought to conduct yourself in the house of God, which is the church of the living God, the pillar and ground of truth" (3:15). And as if to further ground Timothy in sound doctrine the apostle includes in poetic form what appears to be a doctrinal creed, one that could be recited in unison or sung: "God was manifested in the flesh / Justified in the Spirit / Seen by angels, / Preached among the Gentiles, / Believed on in the world, / Received up in glory" (3:16).

Returns to His Attack on Heresy

As if nudged by the Holy Spirit, Paul returns to his attack on heresy (false teachings) that he mentioned in the opening of the letter, the "fables and endless genealogies" (1:4). "Now the Spirit expressly says that in latter times some will depart from the faith, giving heed to deceiving spirits and doctrines of demons, speaking lies in hypocrisy, having their own conscience seared with a hot iron, forbidding to marry, and commanding to abstain from foods which God created to be received with thanksgiving by those who believe and know the truth. Every creature of God is good, and nothing is to be refused if it is received with thanksgiving; for it is sanctified by the word of God and prayer" (4:1-5). Gnosticism, a heresy that plagued early Christianity, appears to be at work in the Ephesus church. The fables and genealogies mentioned earlier in the letter, now the mentioned doctrines of demons and food abstention may very well have been elements of Gnosticism. For example, the asceticism mentioned here (the forbidding marriage and the food abstention) may have been the work of Gnostics claiming the material world to be evil. And the reference to doctrines of demons may have been a reference to Gnostics claiming certain esoteric knowledge essential to salvation.

A Note on Gnosticism [from Greek *gnosis* meaning knowledge]

The major precept of Gnosticism being that spirit is good and that matter is evil seriously questioned incarnation thereby casting doubt on Jesus' divinity, a Gnostic heresy addressed by the apostle John in his gospel. A basic Gnostic principle held that God being all spirit and therefore all good could not have created the world because it was matter and thereby evil. Therefore, it was surmised that God sent out a number of emanations until an emanation far removed from God, and able to touch matter, created the world. From this premise theories evolved concerning how man being matter could connect with God. The Gnostics, unable to accept Jesus as both human and divine, sought to know God through knowledge rather than faith. For them salvation was a matter of attaining special knowledge and they pursued circuitous and esoteric paths such as creating genealogies and myths around the emanations sent out by God as a way of connecting with God. Thus, touting knowledge over faith as the route to salvation, Gnosticism became a thorn in the flesh of early Christianity and remained so through at least the second century.

Defense against the Heresies

The apostle counsels Timothy to stay alert rejecting the various heresies and countering them with the sound doctrine that he knows and has followed. "Reject profane and old wives' fables, and exercise yourself rather in godliness. For bodily exercise profits a little, but godliness is profitable for all things, having promise of the life that now is and of that which is to come" (4:7-8). Then for emphasis comes the refrain: "This is a faithful saying and worthy of all acceptance: we both labor and suffer reproach because we trust in the living God who is the Savior of all" (4:9-10).

Things for Timothy to Command and Teach

Do not be anxious because of your youth the apostle instructs Timothy: "be an example to the believers in word, in conduct, in love, in spirit, in faith, in purity" (4:12). Set such high example that your youth will not be noticed Paul instructs his young associate. Timothy is probably in his mid thirties at this time and may look even younger. To further strengthen Timothy's hand, Paul commands him to "give attention to reading, to exhortation, to doctrine" (4:13). And seemingly to bolster his young associate's confidence, the apostle reminds him of his God given gift: "Do not neglect the gift that is in you, which was given to you by prophecy with the laying on of the hands of the presbytery [body of elders, presumably at his ordination]. Meditate on these things; give yourself entirely to them, that your progress may be evident to all" (4:14-15). Busy yourself faithfully and prayerfully with your duties and all will be well Paul seems to say.

Specific Instructions Concerning Certain Duties:

In several areas, Paul provides Timothy specific instructions for carrying out his duties.

The Older and the Younger

"Do not rebuke an older man, but exhort him as a father, the younger men as brothers, the older women as mothers, the younger as sisters, with all purity" (5:1-2).

Widows

Since widows ordinarily had no means of support, the church was obligated to take care of them, but only the "really widows," meaning those widows without children and grandchildren, the wife of one man, a reputation for good works, and over sixty years of age. Younger widows were not to come under the care of the church since their sexual desires were likely to become stronger than their dedication to Christ, thus bringing "condemnation because they have cast off their first faith" (5:12). Furthermore, they were likely to become idle, "wandering about from house to house, and not only idle but also gossips and busybodies . . . therefore, I [Paul] desire that the younger widows marry, bear children, and manage the house"(5:13-14), thereby giving the adversary less opportunity to lure them away.

It should be noted that the apostle makes it abundantly clear that the first responsibility in caring for the widow belongs to her family: "If anyone does not provide for his own, and especially for those of his household, he has denied the faith and is worse than an unbeliever" (5:8).

Elders

Paul says that elders are to be honored for their labors and those who excel are to be doubly honored. And judging from the supporting examples, that of not muzzling the ox treading the grain and that of "the laborer being worthy of his wages" (5:18), the honor would include financial compensation.

Receive no accusation against an elder without two or three witnesses, but when it is certain that an elder has transgressed he should be rebuked in front of the congregation so that all may fear. He has dishonored himself and his office.

Above all, Timothy is to monitor the congregation with total impartially and with studied judgment: "Do not lay hands on [ordain] anyone hastily, nor share in other people's sins; keep yourself pure" (5:22). Probably thinking of Timothy's health, Paul, in an aside, charges him to no longer drink only water, but to drink wine moderately "for your stomach's sake and your frequent infirmities" (5:23).

Masters and Slaves

The master/slave relationship is one that Paul addresses in several of his letters, the most notable example being Philemon which is addressed to a slave master. Here the instruction to Timothy concerns primarily the slave who as believer must still honor his master, perhaps even more so lest he cause adverse criticism of the church: "Let as many servants as are under the yoke count their own masters worthy of all honor, so that the name of God and His doctrine may not be blasphemed" (6:1). If the slave's master is a non-Christian, he is not to feel superior to him and show less respect, and if his master is Christian, he is not to expect special treatment. It has been said that New Testament writers did not question the institution of slavery but tried to mitigate it through promoting better attitudes of both slaves and masters. References to the institution of slavery in Paul's letters would confirm such.

Money

Paul relates false teaching to the desire for monetary gain saying that if anyone teaches false doctrines not agreeing with the sound instructions "of our Lord Jesus Christ and the doctrine which is according to godliness, he is proud knowing nothing, but is obsessed with disputes and arguments over words, from which come envy, strife, reviling, evil suspicions, useless wranglings of men of corrupt minds and destitute of the truth, who suppose that godliness is a means of gain" (6:3-5). The apostle sees these false teachers as ones preoccupied with self-exaltation and economic gain: "For the love of money is a root of all kinds of evil, for which some have strayed from the faith in their greediness" (6:10). The apostle is not condemning money per se, but the preoccupation with money, allowing it to become a person's major motivation. Later, he instructs Timothy to "command those who are rich in this present world not to be haughty, nor to trust in uncertain riches but in the living God, who gives us richly all things to enjoy. Let them do good that they be rich in good works, ready to give, willing to share, storing up for themselves a good foundation for the time to come, that they may lay hold on eternal life" (6:17-19).

Summarizing the Charge to Timothy

Near the letter's close, the apostle summarizes his charge to Timothy thus: "But you, man of God, flee these things [the false teachings and other enumerated ungodly actions], and pursue righteousness, godliness, faith, love, patience, gentleness. Fight the good fight of the faith, lay hold on eternal life, to which you were also called and have confessed the good confession in the presence of many witnesses" (6:11-12). As he closes the letter, the apostle exhorts his "true son of the faith" to hold firm in the faith: "O Timothy! Guard what was committed to your trust, avoiding the profane and vain babblings and contradictions of what is falsely called knowledge" (6:20). Faith and commitment, not esoteric knowledge touted by the Gnostics and others, is the salvation that leads to eternal life.

I Timothy Poetic Summary
The Pastoral Letter

Timothy and Titus each receive official communiqué from a
mentor, the apostle Paul
Timothy receives two and Titus one, the composite being the
pastoral letters so called
The epistles pastoral and Philemon and Paul's other epistles
total exactly thirteen in all
The pastoral three and Philemon sharing a commonality,
each penned for personal ear
The other epistles nine also commonality share, their being
penned for churches to hear.
Like the gospels, Paul's letters do not fall in chronological
place, but otherwise appear.

In sequence they stand: Romans, I and II Corinthians,
Galatians, Ephesians, Philippians,
Then Colossians, I and II Thessalonians, I and II Timothy,
Titus, Philemon, and thereby they end.
Acts sheds much helpful light on Paul's epistles, three of his
journeys having been recorded there.
Yes, Luke, the Church's first historian, notes journeys one
through three validating how things fare
Unfortunately, his Book of Acts ends with the apostle under
house arrest in Rome awaiting trial
And without Luke's elucidating pen what happens next is left
to letters and tradition to reconcile.

Into this time frame the pastoral letters seem to fall,
following Paul's journeys one through three.
Thus, historian Luke's silence sends scholars to the pastoral
letters seeking clues to the mystery

Such as Paul telling Timothy to remain in Ephesus and take
charge while he in Macedonia traveled
Or instructing Titus, left in Crete, to set things in order and
to appoint elders so nothing unraveled.
Since such sayings seem not to fit into the time frame of the
first three journeys, by Luke validated
Reasonable conjecture conceives Paul set free and embarking
on a fourth journey, as hereby stated.

Just where this presumed fourth journey led the apostle
cannot be fully fleshed for lack of evidence:
That he traveled to Spain in the Empire's west, as some
scholars contend, holds very little credence
In the Roman epistle, Paul did say he wanted to take the
gospel to Spain and requested they assist
But simply to cite as evidence the fact he wished to carry the
gospel west seems somewhat remiss
That he traveled the Empire's eastern region again epistles to
Timothy and Titus seem to verify
Though the time frame is less than clear, tradition and
conjecture aptly furnishes something nigh.

If Rome freed Paul from house arrest around A. D. 63, he
had time for another missionary spree
For tradition holds that both he and Peter were executed
there around A. D. 67, by Nero's decree:
Peter crucified, by choice upside down, while Paul, a Roman
citizen rated beheading, no less.
Whether Paul traveled west to Spain remains a mystery,
some scholars saying no, others yes
But again, the pastoral letters place Paul in the Empire's east
between his house arrest and death
Nurturing churches planted previously, dutifully doing all
things possible prior to his last breath.

To avoid a charge of ignorance, let us note that some scholars
say the pastoral letters, not Paul:

Much of their vocabulary is foreign to that of his other
letters, enough some scholars to appall
Whether one reads Greek or no, the wording and style is
noticeable, that one can hardly overlook
But their pattern and frame sounds so Pauline, and early
tradition places them patently in his nook.
Also, one common critique more: the church organization
discussed seems a bit developed for then
Yet despite these two critiques that certain scholars submit, it
is generally thought their case too thin.

So let us assume Paul author of the pastoral letters and with
that bent begin our study of I Timothy.
Why the letter anyway, had the mentor sensed hint of panic
in a disciple facing huge responsibility?
Knowing Ephesus the apostle's longest stay and his ministry
in that city a series of miraculous results
The Ephesus church proselytizing the mainland connected
to this ancient city of commerce and cults
This venerable ministry suddenly entrusted to him,
Timothy, stalwart associate but timid as head,
May have signaled the apostle a need for guidance, or voiced a
preference to be with him instead.

Whatever the case, Timothy faces a difficult situation at
Ephesus for heresy is on the horizon
And the apostle's authority and wisdom are needed to boost
the confidence of his spiritual son
That he may counter those focusing on fables and
genealogies rather than on the gospel true.
Paul, preoccupied in Macedonia, relies on epistle to instruct
his "son of the faith" what to do
That he left Timothy in charge reveals his high regard for
this youthful but devoted stalwart
Especially recalling how he refused to suffer Mark a second
journey after a first false start.

Though John Mark later redeemed himself, Timothy proved
exemplary from the beginning.
Having discovered him at Lystra early in his second journey,
Paul praised him non-ending.
This son of a Jewish mother and a Greek father became the
apostle's staunchest companion
Accompanying and assisting his mentor in carrying the
gospel to every available dominion
Laboring in Philippi, Thessalonica, Corinth, Ephesus, filling
offices known and unknown
Messenger and monitor in Macedonia, overseer at Ephesus,
Paul's steadfast son in Rome.

Now with Paul on his fourth journey, the one following his
first imprisonment in Rome
Timothy is left in Ephesus to counter contrary doctrines
while Paul labored in Macedon.
Poor Paul, the thirteenth apostle so called, specially called by
the Lord after His ascension
Called "a chosen vessel to preach the gospel to the Gentiles,"
hardly old Saul's intention.
Yet after the Lord's call just as zealous promoting the gospel
as before in preventing its spread
Then, the apostle is so hounded by the Sanhedrin only an
appeal to Caesar could save his head.

Though confronted by hostile opposition, the apostle Paul
labors on, ever faithful to his call
Never forgetting that heavenly light he saw and voice he
heard on Damascus' road reveals all.
And it echoes in his words to Timothy, "remain in Ephesus
to see that sound doctrine is taught
Sound doctrine, according to the glorious gospel committed
to my trust," though then unsought
Unsought, but embraced and carried world wide, that clarion
call being ever present and revered
No matter the circumstances, no matter how drear, in the
glorious gospel he always found cheer.

And this perception the apostle passes on to Timothy, his son in the faith and paragon protégé
Exhorting him to steadfast stand in Ephesus, strategic city for anchoring the gospel of the Way
As Ephesus went so likely went the Asia of that day, for it was the region's purveyor pertinent
False doctrine flowing from the Ephesus church would mean more than one church's detriment.
Thus, in this context the apostle Paul takes up pen and in prayerful thought I Timothy begins
He addresses several subjects but develops one major motif: see that false teaching there ends.

See that those focusing on "fables and endless genealogies" are set straight or disenfranchised
Those who fail to put faith in the Lord first and foremost for salvation have the gospel revised.
One can only conjecture the nature of the fables and endless genealogies so disturbing to Paul
Some, Jews or Gentiles, may have promoted genealogy as a means for validating wherewithal
Jews scouring Scripture and Gnostics producing esoteric explanations of God's master plan.
Perhaps both cited fables of some divine or demiurge whose story claimed sole truth for man.
Seeing the gospel pushed aside, Paul perceives heresy and charges Timothy take a firm stand.

Also, some were presenting themselves teachers of the law, but unable to understand its intent
Law identifies sin—"murder, fornication, lying,"—but as means to salvation it was never meant
Knowledge of the law is not the key to salvation; the key to salvation is faith, always and ever
Faith in Jesus Christ is salvation and living it is righteousness, but knowledge of the law never.
Should we then toss law aside? Certainly not, it is our moral compass at Sinai codified

And on another Mount, discrepancy between its letter and its
spirit God's Son clarified.

Continuing, the apostle personally testifies to the fact of
grace through faith in his own life:
"I thank Christ Jesus Lord who granted grace to me, once
blasphemer and persecutor rife
Yet He poured out His grace on me abundantly, thus
verifying the very reason He came
He came into the world to save sinners, of which I am chief
having been called by name."
Then the apostle calls Timothy to task reminding him of
prophecy concerning his destiny
Presumably, prophecy voiced at his ordination and concerning
his leadership role to be.

With further confidence bolstering words, Paul confirms his
associate as one to be trusted
As one "having faith and good conscience" and nothing like
shipwrecked ones now busted
Two specifically named, Hymenaeus and Alexander, who
have been handed over to Satan
Meaning from church excluded for disciplinary purposes,
God's house must be kept clean.
Thus, by personal witnessing, by theological tutoring, by
recalling destiny to fulfill
By commendation fervid, and by example specific Paul
prepares Timothy for ordeal.

Addressing the dimension of prayer, Paul directs Timothy
not only to pray, but pray for all
Pray and give thanksgiving for everyone, for kings and all in
authority, pray they chaos stall
That we may lead a quiet and peaceable life, stability through
authority, heavenly blessed
For our Lord desires all persons to be saved and to come to
the knowledge of truth, no less.

Paul, living in the Roman Empire during the period of Pax
Romana, sensed stability a godsend
Its law had saved his life; its order was allowing him to travel
its extensive regions to their end.

Praying for those in authority is prayer dual: for their
salvation and for a stable society
The Church could only flourish in a stable society, a
prerequisite for promoting piety.
Necessity for praying for all persons is clear, for there is only
one God and one Mediator
Only one God and one Mediator between God and
humanity: Lord Jesus Christ, our Savior
Who gave Himself a ransom for all, and who called Paul to
minister to the world Gentile.
Paul, ministering, exhorted persons everywhere pray: hands
uplifted; hearts free of guile.

Next comes Paul's counsel concerning appropriate behavior
within ecclesia for women
Counsel to offend lest we keep in mind the universal bent
concerning gender roles then.
Women should dress without adornment, shunning all
baubles in the interest of godliness
And let women learn in silence, for speech and office belong
to men, this divine holiness
For Adam was formed first, then Eve, and Adam was not
deceived, but Eve, the woman
So we see the design in the beginning set, the mantle of
authority rightfully falls to man.

Dressing for reverence and not for personal show seems as
relevant today as Paul's day
But silencing women in a present day democratic society
would be something given stay.
Adam and Eve remain the same but woman's learning now
equals man's, unlike Paul's day

The supposition being, were Paul here today would he see
gender relationship the same way?
This question rhetorically is not, the writer thinking wiser
the answer left for the reader's say
Thinking wiser that the reader ponder and pray, thinking
wiser to invoke the democratic way.

The next topic of pastoral concern is that of overseer, here
called bishop, leader of the flock
To qualify for such authority he must first exemplary be,
totally so, having nothing in hock
He must be blameless, the husband of one wife, temperate,
sober minded, and hospitable so
One of good behavior, able to teach, not given to wine, not
violent, not greedy for money no
Not quarrelsome, not covetous; one who governs his own
house well, have children who obey
Not a novice, lest being puffed with pride he fall into
condemnation as did the devil, same way.

Moreover, the bishop must have a good reputation among
those outside avoiding Satan's snare
In short, he must be a seasoned disciple exemplary in all
avenues of life, proficient everywhere
"This is a faithful saying," says Paul, "If a man desires the
position of bishop, good he so desires."
Ideally then, whether the office is called overseer, elder, or
bishop, its holder to godliness aspires.
And under the overseer, elder, or bishop served the deacon, a
helper to the higher order he became
Deacon means he who serves and serving under the bishop
requires qualifications mostly the same.

A deacon must be reverent, not double tongued, not given to
excessive wine, not greedy for gain
But a man of faith and of conscience pure, and whose wife is
of the faith, reverent and restrained

Furthermore, he must be the husband of one wife and able
ruler of their children and household.
Thus, the deacon who serves well obtains good standing for
his steadfastness and example bold.
Can we think of deacons in the New Testament mold,
without thinking of bold Philip and Stephen?
They among those first seven servers, chosen as helpers to the
apostles, the church overseers then.

Before forging ahead with instruction, Paul pauses telling
Timothy he hopes to be in Ephesus shortly
But fearing unavoidable delay, "I write so that you may know
how to conduct yourself appropriately
Appropriately in the house of God, that is the church of the
living God, the pillar and ground of truth."
Then the apostle expresses for his helper in poetic form
what seems to be a creed doctrinaire forsooth:
"God was manifested in the flesh / Justified in the Spirit /
Seen by angels, / Preached among Gentiles /
Believed on in the world, / Received up in glory," sung or
recited in unison God and gospel reconciles.

As if nudged by the Holy Spirit, Paul returns to his attack
on heresy, "the fables and genealogies"
The troubling disturbances referenced earlier, probably
disturbances fueled by Gnostic ideologies.
He says, "Now the Holy Spirit expressly says that in latter
times some will depart from the faith true
Giving heed to deceiving spirits and doctrines of demons,
speaking lies in hypocrisy, dissembling too
Their own conscience seared by iron hot, forbidding to
marry, and to the eating of foods forsooth
Foods that God created to be received with thanksgiving by
those who believe and know the truth."

Gnosticism, a heresy that plagued early Christianity, seems
to be at work in the Ephesus congregation

The fables and genealogies earlier mentioned and now the
doctrines of demons and of foods abstention
Distortions declaring the material world evil and claiming
esoteric knowledge the essential to salvation.
A major precept of Gnostic ideology declaring spirit good
and matter evil challenged the incarnation
Thus casting doubt on the divinity of Jesus, a heresy
implicitly refuted in one gospel, John's the latter.
A basic Gnostic principle held that God being all spirit and
therefore all good could not create matter.

God could not create the world for it was matter and thereby
evil, therefore creation was otherwise
God sent out emanations until one far removed and able to
touch matter created it, Gnostic surmise
From this premise theories evolved concerning how man
being matter could connect with God divine.
Rejecting Jesus as both human and divine, Gnostics sought
to know God through knowledge sublime
Salvation becomes a matter of attaining special knowledge so
they pursued a circuitous, esoteric route
Creating genealogies and myths around the supposed
emanations sent out by God, and these they tout.
Gnostics claimed knowledge, not faith, their salvation route, a
heresy through the second century stout.

So Paul commands Timothy to stay alert rejecting heresy
and countering it with doctrine sound
Expound the doctrine you know true and "reject profane and
old wives' fables" wherever found.
"Exercise yourself in godliness for it gives promise to life that
is now and that which is to come,"
Counsels the apostle, communicating confidence his faithful
protégé will see the job well done.
And then for emphasis he sounds the refrain, "this is a
faithful saying and worthy of recall:
We both labor and suffer reproach because we trust in the
living God who is Savior of all."

Aware of Timothy's self-consciousness concerning his youth,
Paul proffers surety:
"Be an example to believers in word, in conduct, in love, in
spirit, in faith, in purity"
That is to say, set such high example that your youth goes
unnoticed in notability.
Supposedly, Timothy was in his mid thirties at the time, but
may have younger looked
Yet the apostle Paul knew his many strengths and lack of
confidence would not brook.
He reminds him of his God given gift given him by prophesy
with laying on of hands
The hands laid on at his ordination back in Lystra before they
set out for foreign lands.

"Meditate on these things; give yourself entirely to them,
that your progress may be evident to all"
Busy yourself faithfully and prayerfully with your duties and
all will be well, advises apostle Paul
And to insure that all goes well Paul sees need to address
certain duties with specific instruction
There is instruction concerning the older man the younger
one, the older woman the younger one:
"Do not rebuke an older man, but exhort him as a father, the
younger men as brothers,
Exhort the older women as mothers, and with all purity the
younger women as sisters."

Widows were a special case and warranted special
consideration and careful scrutiny
Often widows had no means of support thereby relegating
them a church responsibility
Yet only those known as "really widows" was the church
obligated to take under wing
Meaning those without children or grandchildren, wife of
one man, of good works seen
And one more thing, having reached the age of sixty for
widows younger were problem prone

Sexual desire overriding dedication to Christ or idleness
breeding gossips, as was well known.

It was the apostle's desire that the younger widows marry,
bear children and manage their homes
And in all cases, as Paul makes abundantly clear,
responsibility for widow care to family belongs
"Anyone who does not provide for his own has denied the
faith and is worse than the unbeliever."
Widows are family responsibility first, only in the case of
"really widows" is church the receiver.
As for elders, honor them for their labors and those who
excel see they are honored all the more
And never presume to accept accusation against an elder
without two or three witnesses before.

But if certain the elder has transgressed, rebuke him before
the congregation that all may hear
For hearing they should fear knowing the elder has both
dishonored himself and his office dear.
Above all, Timothy must monitor the congregation in total
impartiality and judgment sure
"Do not ordain anyone hastily nor share in other people's
sins, always keep yourself pure."
Thus reminded of Timothy's health, Paul charges him drink
not water only, please
But drink wine moderately for the sake of his stomach and his
frequent infirmities.

The master/slave relationship Paul addresses in several
letters most notably being Philemon
There addressing how believer slave to master is known,
here how master to believer known.
Slave believer must honor his master still, even more so lest
the church receive criticism adverse
Servants who are under the yoke must count their masters
worthy of honor, never objects of curse.

If the slave's master is non-Christian he is not to feel
superior to him and thereby less respect show
If the slave's master is Christian he is not to expect special
treatment but to revere him even more so.

It is said New Testament writers did not question the
institution of slavery, but sought to mitigate
Like Paul, by promoting better attitudes between master and
servant and thereby improve its state.
Lastly, the apostle addresses money relating it to false
teaching, its gain being a motivator thereof
He sees false teachers as creatures obsessed with
self-exaltation and financial gain, corrupting stuff
"For the love of money is a root of all kinds of evil, causing
some to lose their faith in greediness
And to teach doctrines contrary to those voiced by our Lord
Jesus Christ who taught us godliness."

Think not the apostle is condemning money per se, but
obsessive preoccupation with financial gain
For he instructs Timothy "to command those who are rich
avoid haughtiness and humility maintain
Never trust in uncertain riches but in the living God who
gives us richly all things to enjoy
Rather do good that they be rich in good works, ready to
give, willing to share, love employ
Laying a foundation for the time to come, preparing beyond
this life, preparing for the eternal one."
Thus, having instructed his protégé in church décor and much
more Paul proceeds to total the sum.

Summarizing his charge to Timothy, the apostle says, "but
you, man of God, flee false teaching
Pursue righteousness, godliness, faith, love, patience, and
fight the good fight of faith reaching
Ever reaching to lay hold on eternal life, to which you were
also called and have confessed

And having confessed the good confession in the presence of
many witnesses you are blessed."
The apostle closes the epistle exhorting his "true son of the
faith" to hold firm in his belief
To remain in Ephesus overseeing the church heeding his
charges and instructions as briefed.

Paul tells Timothy guard that committed to your trust, flee
that falsely called knowledge or erudition
For esoteric Gnostic knowledge cannot lead to life eternal,
only faith committed fills the prescription.

II Timothy Prose Summary
Paul Awaits Execution

The Second Imprisonment at Rome

Because the Sanhedrin was plotting to end Paul's life, he appealed to Caesar from Caesarea where he was being held prisoner by Festus, the Roman curator of Judea (Acts 24:27). He made the appeal around A.D. 61 and was taken to Rome and placed under house arrest where he remained until released around A.D.63, at which time he embarked on a fourth missionary journey taking him back to the eastern portion of the Empire, the area targeted in his first three journeys. Though information about the fourth journey is sketchy, we know he left Timothy in Ephesus (I Ti 1:3) and Titus in Crete (1:5). We learn from this second letter to Timothy, that he is again imprisoned in Rome (1:8; 2:8), and this time not under house arrest but seemingly dungeon confined with no hope of being freed.

Paul's Call to Timothy

In a past tense mode, Paul tells Timothy, "I have fought the good fight, I have finished the race, I have kept the faith" (4:7), leaving little doubt that he has any hope of being released. This letter is a call to his spiritual son to put aside timidity, to take heart from the exemplary life of his apostle mentor [Paul], to continue in his ministry in the manner prescribed by his mentor, and to come post haste to Rome to attend his mentor whose life is "already being poured out like a drink offering" (4:6).

Testimony and Concern

Addressing Timothy as his "beloved son," Paul says, "I remember you in my prayers night and day, greatly desiring to see you, being mindful of your tears, that I may be filled with joy, when I call to remembrance the genuine faith that is in you, which dwelt first in your grandmother Lois and your mother Eunice, and I am persuaded is in you also" (1:3-5). Then as if to bolster Timothy's courage says, "I remind you to stir up the gift of God which is in you through the laying on of my hands, for God has not given us a spirit of fear, but of power and of love and of a sound mind" (1:6-7). Seemingly Paul, like a father who knows his son well, knows that though Timothy has been nurtured in faith and has demonstrated faithfulness he has a tendency toward timidity and the apostle wants to bolster his courage. Certainly, Paul dearly loves Timothy and wants him nearby for personal comfort but also to better prepare him for future ministry. As his exemplary ministry ends, he wants his spiritual son to emulate him so that he may also be able to say at the end of his own ministry, "I have fought the good fight, I have kept the faith, I have finished the course."

Perhaps Paul fears that Timothy, now serving at Ephesus, might lose the courage to face present challenges as some had already done: "This you know, that all those in Asia have turned away from me, among whom are Phygellus and Hermogenes" (1:15). Presumably, Paul and other Christian leaders became victims of Nero who needed a scapegoat to divert suspicion from himself for the flames that, in A.D. 64, devoured a large portion of the city of Rome. He blamed the Christians and had many arrested and put to death. No doubt, fear ran rampant throughout the Christian community.

Take Courage

The apostle exhorts Timothy to take courage, "do not be ashamed of the testimony of our Lord, nor of me His prisoner, but share with me in the sufferings for the gospel according to the power of God, who has saved us and called us . . . according to His own purpose and grace which was given to us in Christ Jesus before time began, but has now been revealed by the appearing of our Savior Jesus Christ, who has abolished death and brought life and immortality to light through the gospel, *to which I was appointed a preacher, an apostle, and a teacher of Gentiles. For this reason I also suffer these things; nevertheless I am not ashamed, for I know whom I have believed and am persuaded that He is able to keep what I have committed to Him until that Day" (1:8-12).* Timothy is to take courage from his faith as has his mentor.

Hold Fast to Faith and Example

"Hold fast the pattern of sound words which you have heard from me," exhorts Paul, "in faith and love which are in Christ" (1:13). Guard the good thing, meaning the gospel, that was committed to you; guard it with the help of the Holy Spirit. Remember Onesiphorus who came to Rome and diligently sought me out, "and often refreshed me and was not ashamed of my chain. Surely he will find mercy from the Lord in that Day" (1:16-18).

Pass It On

Paul charges his "beloved son" to be strong in grace and faith and pass it on: "And the things that you have heard from me among many witnesses, commit these to faithful men who will be able to teach others also" (2:2).

Hardship and Commitment Prerequisites to Triumph

A good soldier of Jesus Christ cannot avoid hardship Paul reminds Timothy noting that he now suffers chains because of his commitment to the gospel, but that "I endure all things for the sake of the elect, that they also may obtain the salvation which is in Christ Jesus with eternal glory" (2:10). Though he suffers chains, the word of God is not chained Paul notes. And to further enhance his point he quotes what he calls a faithful saying which could be lines from a hymn: "If we died with Him / We shall also live with Him / If we endure, / We shall also reign with Him. / If we deny Him, / He also will deny us. / If we are faithless, / He remains faithful; / He cannot deny Himself" (2:11-13).

Avoid Babblings and Foolish Disputes

"Shun profane and vain babblings, for they will increase to more ungodliness [and] their message will spread like cancer," warns the apostle as he gives two examples of this sort: Hymenaeus and Philetus (2:16-17). Stay focused on sound doctrine avoiding "foolish and ignorant disputes, knowing that they generate strife" (2:23). Keep in mind that "the solid foundation of God stands, having this seal: 'The Lord knows those who are His,' and, 'Let everyone who names the name of Christ depart from iniquity'" (2:19).

Correct in Humility

The servant of the Lord must not quarrel but exercise patience and gentleness in teaching, always in humility correcting those who are in opposition in the hope that God will grant them repentance so they may know the truth.

Perilous Times in the Last Days

"But know this," warns Paul, "that in the last days perilous times will come: For men will be lovers of themselves, lovers of money, boasters, proud, blasphemers, disobedient to parents, unthankful, unholy, unloving, unforgiving, slanderers, without self-control, brutal, despisers of good, traitors, headstrong, haughty, lovers of pleasure rather than lovers of God, having a form of godliness but denying its power. And from such people turn away!" (3:1-5). This warning suggests that things on earth will continue to deteriorate; despite the believer's efforts only a remnant will be saved. Yet the believer is not to despair, for at some point when things become hopelessly evil, the Lord will return and set things right. Paul, experiencing Nero's Rome, may have thought the last days near.

Keep the Faith and Know the Scriptures

Paul has kept the faith and now he exhorts Timothy to do likewise, believing that he will because of his calling and because of the example the apostle has set for him. "You have carefully followed my doctrine, manner of life, purpose, faith, longsuffering, love, perseverance, persecutions, afflictions which have happened to me . . . and out of them all the Lord has delivered me" (3:10-11). Thus, Timothy is to take note of this example and "continue in the things which you have learned and been assured of, knowing from whom you have learned them, and that from childhood you have known the Holy Scriptures, which are able to make you wise for salvation through faith which is in Christ Jesus. *All Scripture is given by inspiration of God, and is profitable for doctrine, for reproof, for correction, for instruction in righteousness, that the man of God may be complete, thoroughly equipped for every good work" (3:14-17).*

Keep the Faith and Fight the Good Fight

Paul charges Timothy "to preach the word, to be ready in season and out of season . . . [though] the time will come when they [the hearers] will not endure sound doctrine . . . and they will turn their ears away from the truth, and be turned aside to fables. But you be watchful in all things, endure afflictions, do the work of an evangelist, fulfill your ministry, *for I am already being poured out like a drink offering, and the time of my departure is at hand. I have fought the good fight, I have finished the race, I have kept the faith" (4:2-7).* Obviously, Paul greatly desires that his spiritual son carry on the good fight and at the end of his life also be able to say, "I have fought the good fight, I have finished the race, I have kept the faith."

Paul sees his life and ministry coming to an end but takes comfort in knowing that he has served the Lord faithfully and that "there is laid up for me the crown of righteousness, which the Lord, the righteous Judge, will give me on that Day, and not to me only but also to all who have loved His appearing" (4:8).

He takes further comfort knowing that his spiritual son will soon be at his side, for he has charged him, "Be diligent to come to me quickly . . . for only Luke is with me" (4:9,11). And not only is Timothy to come quickly, but he is to bring the apostle's scrolls and parchments that he had left in Troas. Though he is "being poured out like a drink offering," he intends to continue working until his last breath, for not only does he ask for his scrolls and parchments but that Timothy bring with him Mark, "for he is useful to me for ministry" (4:11). When Timothy arrives with Mark, the apostle will have at his side three beloved comforters and able associates. We can only hope that Timothy and Mark arrived before Nero's death sentence.

II Timothy Poetic Summary
Paul Awaits Execution

Imprisoned in Rome for the second and final time, and
awaiting execution nigh
Paul summons Timothy savoring the hope of having his
"beloved son" nearby
Remembering that the gift of God flowed through his own
hands to this spiritual son
First nurtured in faith by his mother Eunice and
grandmother Lois, each a devoted one
Remembering young Timothy, his spiritual son and
co-worker, since missionary journey two
Who was wont to shed tears when circumstances dictated
separate ministries each must pursue.

His life being poured out like a drink offering, Paul
summons Timothy to his prison cell
Desiring the presence of his surrogate son that both may
witness faith over death prevail.
"I have fought the good fight, I have finished the race, I have
kept the faith," Paul proclaimed
Like a humbly proud athlete never to have transgressed the
rules, always temptation disdained.
Now the race honorably completed and heaven's crown
awaiting, what matters prison chains
What matters the apostle slain a scapegoat for mad Nero's
nefarious scheme: Rome in flames.

"For God did not give us a spirit of timidity, but a spirit of
power, of love and self-discipline"
Writes the apostle to remind the sometimes timid Timothy
that the Holy Spirit is power divine

Be not ashamed of my chains but join me in suffering for the
gospel, thanking God for His grace
Thanking the Lord Jesus for calling us to a holy life, but for
Him eternity for us a different place.
Paul thus exhorts his surrogate son and closest associate to
rely on the power of spirit limitless,
The power witnessed in the faith of his mother and
grandmother, and in his mentor matchless.

Unlike the liquid house arrest of his first Rome
imprisonment, Paul is now prison-wall confined
Chained like a common criminal in dungeon dark and cold,
without hope of just release any time.
From Caesarea Paul appealed to Caesar to escape death at
Sanhedrin behest, in A.D. 61 or before
A house arrest ending in acquittal circa A.D. 63, allowed the
apostle one missionary journey more
Yet sometime during the fourth journey he was again
imprisoned in Rome, this time not of his call
But supposedly Nero's call accusing Christians of setting the
fires that enflamed the city, almost all.

In turn Paul calls Timothy telling him that though he is
chained God's word is not chained, therefore
He endures everything for the sake of the elect that they too
may obtain salvation in Christ evermore.
The apostle intends to indelibly instill in Timothy that
suffering for Christ will inevitably glory bring
And to enhance this motif quotes some verses from a hymn,
supposedly, he had heard churches sing:
"If we die with Him we will also live with Him; if we endure
with Him we will with Him reign
If we deny Him He denies us; when we are faithless He
remains faithful, steadfastly the same."

Grace was given us in Christ Jesus before the beginning of
time and now in His appearing to reveal:

Foremost, in appearing He has destroyed death and brought
life and immortality to light, the gospel
"And of this gospel," says Paul, "I was appointed herald,
apostle, and teacher, the reason I suffer so
Yet I am not ashamed believing and knowing He is able to
guard what I have entrusted from all foe.
Dear Timothy, what you heard from me keep as the pattern
of sound teaching with faith and love
Guard the good deposit that was entrusted to you—guard it
with the help of the Spirit from above."

As Paul's life is being poured out like a libation, Timothy
must shoulder a heavier gospel load
For his mentor—the herald, apostle, and teacher—now
speaks of himself in a past tense mode
"I have fought the good fight, I have finished the race, I have
kept the faith," says the sage
So now it is time his protégé, his trusted companion, his
beloved son in spirit, come of age
And the fatherly mentor wants his spiritual son with him
when libation ends and majority begins:
"You know everyone in the province of Asia has deserted me,
only Luke remains, the physician."

Do your utmost to come before winter and pick up my cloak
left with Carpus in Troas, says Paul
And my scrolls, especially my parchments, thinking of
warmth of study of bequest, surely of all
Perhaps he must prepare a second defense judging from
stated circumstances concerning the first
That everyone deserted him—may they be forgiven—but
the Lord stood by him in that time worst.
That a second official defense is scheduled can only
speculation be, but defense to Timothy, yes
The apostle presents himself as exhibit A in his defense of
exemplary ministry, best for bequest:

The things that you have heard from me, words and deeds,
commit to the faithful to teach others
Accept that hardship accompanies the good soldier of Jesus
Christ, hardship and soldier brothers
The soldier and the athlete must stay focused and follow the
rules lest their prize go unrealized
"For preaching my gospel—Jesus Christ was raised form the
dead—I am chained, criminalized
Therefore I endure all things for the sake of the elect that
they may obtain salvation and glory"
For the good soldier of Jesus Christ knows no victory but
total commitment to telling the story.

And the good soldier serving as pastor anticipates multiple
conflicts developing simultaneously
Requiring diligence and unceasing vigilance lest attacked
unaware and unprepared disgracefully
It is imperative to present oneself approved before God
having followed the word of truth
Having shunned profane and vain babblings and thus having
avoided ungodliness forsooth.
Paul cites Hymenaeus and Philetus prime examples of
persons indulging speculation too much
Both probably persons of Gnostic bent conjecturing about
the divinity of Jesus Christ and such.

Though babbling speculators lead many astray, the solid
foundation of God stands with this seal:
"The Lord knows who are His, and those who call Christ
Savior strive to shun iniquity's appeal."
The servant of the Lord must not quarrel but be gentle to
all, patient and humble in correction
Considering that God will grant misguided ones repentance
that they discern truth over fiction
But beware, warns the apostle, in the last days expect times
perilous and perversely painted
Men will be lovers of themselves and of money, boastful and
proud and unholy and tainted.

The apostle has confidence though that Timothy will
continue to follow his mentor's lead
A life of faith and longsuffering, of love and perseverance, a
life open for anyone to read
Witness the persecution and affliction suffered in Pisidian
Antioch, Iconium, and Lystra too
Timothy's home region, and Lystra his home town where
Paul was stoned but lived through
Lived through to enlist Timothy on his second missionary
journey that traversed there anew
He braved persecution in the knowledge that those who
follow the Lord have suffering to do.

Yes, evil men and impostors will grow worse and worse,
deceiving and being deceived too
But you my son Timothy continue in the things you have
learned, knowing it learning true
From childhood you have known the Holy Scriptures which
are able to make you salvation wise
Wise for salvation through faith which is in Christ Jesus,
this is truth forsooth, this is not surmise.
*"All Scripture is given by inspiration of God, and is profitable for
doctrine, reproof and correction*
*It is instruction in righteousness to equip the people of God for
good work and for holy discretion."*

Thus, my dear son, "in the presence of God and Christ Jesus,
who will judge the living and the dead
And in view of His appearing and His kingdom, I give you
this charge: preach the Word as so lead
Be prepared in season and out of season; correct, rebuke and
encourage patiently and instructively
Though others may turn away from truth, you remain the
evangelist of truth, ministering dutifully"
[And indirectly implies] "so that when the end comes for
you, you can claim with me, can repeat,
*'I have fought the good fight, I have finished the race, I have kept
the faith, life is now complete.'"*

Titus Prose Summary
Organizing the Churches in Crete

Identifying Titus

Titus was one of Paul's close associates who probably preceded his beloved Timothy, for Timothy joins Paul at Lystra on his second missionary journey, but Titus is reported being with the apostle soon after his first missionary journey. This is assuming that Paul's mention in Galatians (2:1) of taking Titus, an uncircumcised believer, with him to Jerusalem as a test case concerning the matter of Gentile believers and liberty from the law is the same instance as the Jerusalem Council on this subject recorded in Acts 15. We know that Timothy came from Lystra, but can only conjecture that Titus is from Antioch, Paul's home base for the first three missionary journeys. We do know that Titus was most helpful to Paul in dealing with problems in the church at Corinth (II Cor 7:6; 8:16, 23).

Time Frame for the Letter to Titus

Two of the three pastoral letters, I Timothy and Titus, were written during Paul's fourth missionary journey; the third pastoral letter, II Timothy, was written a little later during the apostle's second imprisonment in Rome. He probably wrote I Timothy while in Macedonia and Titus while in Greece. Paul's fourth missionary journey is not recorded in Acts, but is a journey presumed from his pastoral letters and from tradition. During this journey, Paul leaves Timothy in Ephesus and Titus in Crete (I Ti 1:3; Tit 1:5); then after himself traveling to Macedonia, and presumably Greece, sends each a letter of instruction concerning respective assignments.

Paul's fourth missionary journey takes place between his first imprisonment at Rome and his second imprisonment there: sometime between A.D. 63 and A. D. 67.

The Island of Crete

Crete, a major island located in the eastern Mediterranean, has the distinction of producing the ancient Minoan civilization, Europe's earliest. Though the Minoan civilization with the legendary Knossos as its capital city flourished for centuries, the island eventually fell under the power of Greece and later Rome. Apparently, the island attracted Jews, for Luke tells us that Cretans were among the Jews from various lands in Jerusalem for the Day of Pentecost when Peter and the other disciples were filled by the Holy Spirit and thus able to speak in tongues that those from other lands could understand (Acts 2:1-41). It is conjectured that some of the Cretan Jews may have been converted by Peter's preaching and in turn carried Christianity back to Crete. If this conjecture is true, Paul and Titus may have visited Crete to shore up existing churches as well as establish new ones.

The Cretans of the first century had a reputation for untruthfulness and immorality. Paul, calling the sixth century BC Cretan poet Epimenides a prophet, quotes a hyperbolic line from him saying, "Cretans are always liars, evil beasts, lazy gluttons" (1:12). No doubt, Paul is reminding Titus of the necessity of carefully choosing exemplary elders to lead the churches in this difficult environment.

Titus Left in Crete

For whatever unknown reason, Paul moves on to other regions before completing the mission in Crete and leaves Titus in charge. Sometime later he sends a letter to Titus saying, "For this reason I left you in Crete, that you should set in order the things that are lacking, and appoint elders in every city as I commanded you" (1:5).

Nature of the Letter to Titus

Though more brief than I Timothy, the Titus epistle is similar in that it addresses sound doctrine, false teaching, qualifications of church leaders, and appropriate conduct of believers. Like Timothy in Ephesus, Titus in Crete is to see that the churches there are properly organized and staffed so that sound doctrine is confirmed and taught, false teaching condemned, and the congregations instructed in proper conduct. The epistle gives Titus written authority to do his job along with instruction and encouragement for doing so.

As usual, Paul states his apostolic authority in the letter's salutation declaring himself "a servant of God and an apostle of Jesus Christ" (1:1), called to manifest His word through preaching. As an apostle he speaks with authority and in this case he is speaking "to Titus, my true son in our common faith" (1:4).

Qualifications for Elders (Also called Bishops, 1:7)

The elder must be "the husband of one wife, having faithful children not accused of dissipation or insubordination. For a bishop must be blameless, as a steward of God, not self-willed, not quick-tempered, not given to wine, not violent, not greedy for money, but hospitable, a lover of what is good, sober-minded, just, holy, self-controlled, holding fast the faithful word as he has been taught, that he may be able, by sound doctrine, both to exhort and convict those who contradict" (1:6-9). Obviously, the elder/bishop is to teach by exemplary living as well as by expounding sound doctrine and correcting false teaching.

Warnings Concerning Offenders

The apostle warns of rampant insubordination, of idle talkers and deceivers, especially those of the circumcision, presumably those espousing Jewish ceremonial law a perquisite for salvation. These idle talkers and false teachers, some teaching merely for gain, must be stopped says the apostle: "Rebuke them sharply, that they may be sound in the faith not giving heed to Jewish fables and commandments of men who turn from the truth." Sound doctrine must be taught and followed.

Maintaining Sound Doctrine

A disciplined congregation is necessary for maintaining sound doctrine. Titus is to "speak the things which are proper for sound doctrine: that the older men be sober, reverent, temperate, sound in faith, in love, in patience; the older women likewise, that they be reverent in behavior, not slanderers, not given to much wine, teachers of good things" (2:1-3). The older men and women of the congregation are to set the example and then to admonish their younger counterparts, the older women admonishing "the younger women to love their husbands, to love their children, to be discreet, chaste, homemakers, good, obedient to their own husbands" and the older men "exhort the young men to be sober-minded," and all the while themselves, the older men and women, exercising "a pattern of good works; in doctrine showing integrity, reverence, incorruptibility, sound speech that cannot be condemned, that one who is an opponent may be ashamed, having nothing evil to say of you" (2:4-10).

The Grace of God for All

Exhort slaves to try to be pleasing to their masters in all ways, not talking back to them, not stealing from them, but showing them they can be fully trusted so that they "may adorn the doctrine of God our Savior in all things," says Paul, "for the grace of God that brings salvation has appeared to all men" (2:10-11). And that grace teaches us to deny worldly lusts, to live godly lives in the present world while we wait for that glorious and blessed hope, "our great God and Savior Jesus Christ, who gave Himself for us that He might redeem us from every lawless deed and purify for Himself His own special people, zealous for good works" (2:13-14).

To Live Peacefully

Congregations are to be reminded to subject themselves to rulers and authorities, to obey, and to be ready for good work, speaking evil of no one, practicing peacefulness and gentleness, showing humility to all, demonstrating the kindness and love that God has shown us and remembering that "according to His mercy He saved us, through the washing of regeneration and renewing of the Holy Spirit, whom He poured out on us abundantly through Jesus Christ our Savior" (3:5-6). In His will, our peace.

The Faithful Saying Refrain

Throughout the pastoral letters Paul uses the refrain "this is a faithful [trustworthy] saying" to introduce certain profound perceptions that he wishes to give special emphasis (e.g., I Ti 1:15, 4:9; II Ti 2:11; Tit 3:8). Following his instructions concerning peaceful living, the apostle writes, "This is a faithful [trustworthy] saying, and these things I want you to affirm constantly, that those who have believed in God should be careful to maintain good works" (3:8). In doing so everyone profits. We are saved by grace through faith, but good works should follow.

Concerning Disputation and Divisiveness

Avoid foolish disputes such as genealogies and strivings about the law for this is unprofitable says the apostle. Reject a divisive person after a second admonition, for "such a person is warped and sinning, being self-condemned" (3:11). In closing, Paul informs Titus that he plans to winter at Nicopolis, a city in Greece. When he sends either Artemas or Tychicus to Crete, Titus is to join him at Nicopolis.

Titus Poetic Summary Organizing the Churches in Crete

Sometime during his missionary journey four, Paul leaves Titus on the island of Crete
For some unspecified reason the apostle suddenly feels compelled to make hasty retreat
Yet, from some unspecified place, probably somewhere in Greece, instructs by missive
Sending his faithful associate a letter laden with wise counsel, succinct but expressive.
Titus was a veteran of trust having been a circumcision test case at Jerusalem Council One
Having taken the severe letter to the Corinthians, and having collected a sizable charity sum.

Though Paul not at his side, Titus has missive in hand heralding apostolic authority to act
The salutation so specifies, "Paul, a servant of God and apostle of Jesus Christ," to be exact.
Titus' task is stated succinctly and clear, "I left you in Crete to set in order the things lacking
And to appoint elders in each city," Paul repeats, reminding his associate what he is backing.
As to when the churches on the island began and how, the apostle's brief epistle remains mum
Was it by Paul and Titus or by Jewish Cretans possibly converted by Peter's Pentecost sermon?

Founding aside, Paul perceived major mending needed on this island of legendary notoriety

Witness a Cretan poet dubbing his people "a pack of liars, a
beastly, lazy, gluttonous society."
Despite circumstances, Paul had faith that the gospel would
prevail and planned pragmatically
To cleanse every church of false teaching, to shore doctrine
sound, to install elders exemplary
And to get this done the apostle assigns one of his true sons
of the faith, revered veteran Titus
Test case at Jerusalem, messenger/ mediator at Corinth,
missions accomplished: grade, A-plus.

Perusing Paul's epistle, Titus finds the directives he needs for
completing the Cretan mission
And to each exhortation/explanation, to each charge and
command he pays reverent attention.
"An elder must be blameless, the husband of one wife, having
faithful children obedient sure
A steward of God, not self-willed, not quick-tempered, not
given to wine, not greedy for lucre
Not violent, but hospitable, a lover of what is good,
sober-minded, just, holy, self-controlled
Holding fast to doctrine true, always ready to exhort the
faithful and refute the opposing bold."

Whether called elder or bishop the qualifications are the
same, exemplary and without blame
As church leader, he sets example strong and sees that the
congregation follows in the main.
Paul knows leadership exemplary and strong essential to
counter the rampant insubordination:
Idle talkers and deceivers, especially those of the
circumcision espousing Jewish ritualization
These idle talkers and false teachers, many teaching for
financial gain, must be stopped anon
"Rebuke them sharply that they may be sound of faith turning
from Jewish fables and so on."

Exemplary elders in place, sound doctrine espoused and false
teaching rebuked, what next?
A committed congregation self-disciplined and active, all
members following the same text
The older men and women set the example, then admonish
their younger counterparts hear
The older women admonish the younger women to love
their husbands and their children dear
To be discreet, to be homemakers chaste, obedient to their
husbands and doers of good works
The older men admonish the younger to be sober minded,
shunning all falsifiers and perverts.

Thus, the older of the congregation admonishing the
younger while themselves exemplary
In exercising a pattern of good works, in supporting doctrine
sound with utmost integrity
In showing sound speech that cannot be condemned that
those who oppose do so in shame
And one thing more, exhort slaves to strive to please their
masters doing so in God's name
Not stealing from them nor talking back to them but
exemplifying the Savior in everything
For the grace of God bringing salvation has appeared to all
men, master and slave the same.

Living in the time of Pax Romana, Paul could fully
appreciate Roman law and order priorities
And consequently counseled congregations subject
themselves to their bona fide authorities
Thinking this the providential plan that if obeyed would
lead to universal peace ultimately
So speak evil of no one, practice gentleness and show
humility, as would Jesus definitely
"Remembering that according to His mercy He saved us
through the washing of regeneration
And renewing of the Holy Spirit, whom He poured out
abundantly, sanctifying our salvation."

At times in the pastoral letters, Paul pinpoints through the
refrain, "this is a trustworthy saying"
Thus, introducing some profundity that the apostle in his
wisdom sees worthy of special relaying
And so Titus hears, "this is a trustworthy saying, and these
things I want you to affirm constantly
*That those who have believed in God take care to maintain good
works,"* from Paul passionately
Having recalled Crete the island of liars and beastly gluttons
wishes good works to emphasize
For if saved by grace through faith but lack good works, what
do unbelievers naturally surmise?

A couple things more, avoid foolish disputes over genealogies
and fine points of law and such
Shun a divisive person after a second admonition, for he
self-condemns exalting self so much.
Now, allow me a worthy saying essay, *believe in the Lord Jesus
Christ emulating him every day*
*Good works then follow naturally and disputes disintegrate since
the Holy Spirit guides the way.*

PHILEMON PROSE SUMMARY
EQUAL IN CHRIST

Background

Paul writes the letter to Philemon, whom he calls a dear friend and fellow worker, during his first imprisonment at Rome around A.D. 60. Actually, greetings are addressed to Philemon first, but include Apphia (probably the wife), Archippus (probably the son), and "to the church which meets in your house" (v. 2). The topic of the letter is Onesimus, Philemon's runaway slave who somehow made his way to Rome and to Paul who converted him while in prison. Following the conversion, Paul and Onesimus become close and Paul comes to depend on Onesimus' assistance, yet he feels it imperative that Onesimus return to Philemon his master who lives in Colosse and writes the letter for Onesimus to take with him. Accompanying Onesimus is Tychicus who carries a letter to the Colossian church.

In the letter, Paul does not explicitly condone or condemn slavery, rather he gives the converted slave Onesimus the opportunity to rectify his wrong to his master Philemon, and gives Philemon the opportunity to forgive his slave Onesimus and to accept him as an equal in Christ. The apostle exercises wisdom in appealing to Philemon's good heart rather than exercising his authority as an apostle to command him to receive the converted Onesimus. Paul realizes that the gospel works through a person's heart and not through authoritative directives. He knows a change of heart is necessary to dissolve the chains of slavery.

Praise for Philemon

Paul praises Philemon for his faith in the Lord and his love for the saints. Presumably, Philemon is a dedicated and generous person as indicated in making his house a place for the church to meet. Paul reveals that when he thanks God, he always makes mention of Philemon "for we have great joy and consolation in your love, because the hearts of the saints have been refreshed by you, brother" (v. 7).

Plea for Onesimus

Paul notes that he might have been bold in Christ and commanded what would be fitting, "yet for love's sake I rather appeal to you—being such a one as Paul, the aged, and now also a prisoner of Jesus Christ" (v. 9). It should be noted that Paul opens the letter with the words, "Paul, a prisoner of Christ" (v. 1), rather than his usual opening, "Paul, an apostle of Jesus Christ." He does not want to use his authority as an apostle to force Philemon to do the right thing and thereby risk resentment; rather he wants to appeal to his goodness as a brother in Christ to take the initiative in doing the right thing: forgiving his runaway slave and accepting him as a brother.

"I appeal to you," writes Paul, "for my son Onesimus, whom I have begotten while in my chains, who once was *unprofitable* to you, but now is *profitable* to you and me" (vv. 10-11). Note that Paul puns on the name Onesimus (meaning profitable or useful) presumably to lighten the tone and thereby support his intent of appealing rather than prescribing.

Implicit Persuasion or Persuasion by Indirection

Paul writes, "I am sending him back. You therefore receive him, that is, my own heart, whom I wished to keep with me, that on your behalf he might minister to me in my chains for the gospel. But without your consent I wanted to do nothing, that your good deed might not be by compulsion, as it were, but voluntary" (vv. 12-14). Paul's plea is well constructed to achieve its purpose: Paul implies and Philemon infers that Onesimus is dear to Paul, that he is a valuable helper to the imprisoned apostle, that if there helping the apostle he would be doing so on behalf of his master, and that the master is free to say yes or no. Thus, implicitness fits Paul's purpose. He wants Philemon's response to be a voluntary one, not one of compulsion. To achieve his purpose he is indirect simply implying what he would like, thus leaving the response a voluntary matter.

Adding a more indirect persuasiveness, Paul writes, "perhaps he departed for a while for this *purpose*, that you might receive him forever, no longer as a slave but more than slave, as a beloved brother, especially to me but how much more to you, both in the flesh and in the Lord" (vv. 15-16). Indirectly, Paul suggests that Onesimus' running away may have been a providential thing benefiting all three: Philemon, Paul, and Onesimus.

Next, Paul adds the clincher, "If then you count me as a partner, receive him as you would me" (v. 17). The implication: If you count me a brother in Christ, you must also count him a brother in Christ.

The Economic Factor

Presumably, Onesimus took from his master in order to make his way to Rome, for Paul pledges to pay anything he might owe, and then to seal his pledge says, "I, Paul, am writing with my own hand. I will repay" (v. 19). Then he adds, somewhat facetiously, "—not to mention to you that you owe me even your own self besides" (v. 19). As with the pun earlier, Paul seems to be deliberately keeping the tone light so as not to sound authoritative. Even so, the apostle does not want the monetary factor to be a stumbling block for Philemon. And juxtaposing a monetary debt with a spiritual debt dramatizes the inequity: how important is the material compared to the spiritual, the former ephemeral, the latter everlasting.

Indirect Directive

Paul continues to make his case through indirect directive. "Yes, brother, let me have joy from you in the Lord; refresh my heart in the Lord" (v. 20). Implication: My heart will be refreshed by your carrying out the Lord's will. "Having confidence in your obedience, I write to you, knowing that you will do even more than I say" (v. 21). Implication: I know you will live up to your generous reputation. "But meanwhile, also prepare a guest room for me, for I trust that through your prayers I shall be granted to you" (v. 22). Implication: Not only is the welfare of Onesimus in your hands but also that of the apostle Paul. Thus, if Philemon refuses to respond positively, he fails to carry out the will of the Lord, he disappoints the great apostle Paul, and he shatters his own revered image.

Conjectured Epilogue

How Philemon receives Onesimus is left to conjecture, so let us conjecture. Could Philemon have resisted Paul's ingeniously persuasive appeal? Would he have wanted his revered image shattered in the eyes of the great apostle Paul? I think not! Furthermore, had he not honored Paul's request would he not have destroyed the letter? I think so. The fact that it survived, the only personal letter of Paul's to do so, gives further credence to the belief that Philemon received Onesimus, and may have done more than merely receive him. Knowing how much Paul wanted and needed him in Rome, Philemon may well have given Onesimus his freedom allowing him to return to the apostle.

Some scholars believe this Onesimus to be the same person as Onesimus, bishop of Ephesus, mentioned by Ignatius early in the second century. This is possible since Paul wrote the Philemon letter around A.D. 60, and Ignatius identifies an Onesimus as bishop of Ephesus around A.D. 110. Conjecturing that bishop Onesimus is the Onesimus of Paul's letter possibly furnishes further explanation of why the letter survived. It is believed that Paul's letters were first collected at Ephesus sometime near the beginning of the second century. Could Onesimus as bishop of Ephesus have been responsible for including the Philemon epistle? It is possible.

PHILEMON POETIC SUMMARY
EQUAL IN CHRIST

Between master and slave, Philemon and Onesimus, Paul
plays arbiter sublime
Between runaway slave, his converted son, and slave's master,
his friend divine
While a prisoner of Christ in Rome, Paul converts
Onesimus who from Colosse had run
The how or why to Rome he had come, Paul simply says he
will pay for any wrong done
And yet returning him to Colosse is thought painful, for the
two of them are like one heart
He needs Onesimus to minister to him while in chains for the
gospel, not from him depart.

Philemon the slave master is Paul's friend, Onesimus the
runaway slave is his friend too
The problem poses a dilemma for the apostle who must
decide the appropriate thing to do
And in so deciding must not assault the centuries old secular
laws concerning the slave
For the gospel works through each person's heart for change,
not through political rave
This Paul knew and practiced too as his epistle to Philemon
illustrates most convincingly
His prudent action allowed the gospel to work in the heart of
master and slave judiciously.

With Paul's epistle in hand, Onesimus returns to Colosse his
master Philemon's home
And beside him is Tychicus carrying epistle Colossians, so
Onesimus returns not alone

No doubt Tychicus lends moral support to Onesimus who must face master and confess
Of wrongdoing under the law, presumably stealing, and certainly running away at best
For which the law allowed severe punishment including death should the master decide
Yet the apostle trusts friend Philemon to forgive the converted slave returned to his side.

As Paul points out, apostolic authority allows him to command that Onesimus be forgiven
But that authority he chooses not assert, wanting Philemon's forgiveness to be heart driven.
Rather than authority the apostle engages praise, plea, and pledge as the pegs of persuasion
Commending his brother in Christ for furnishing others much joy occasion after occasion
Acknowledging every good thing in him through Jesus Christ of which he shares readily
He refreshes the souls of numerous saints who take consolation in his love and hospitality.

Not by bold authority but for love's sake Paul appeals to Philemon concerning Onesimus
Runaway slave but also the apostle's son, begotten while in chains, both in bondage thus.
Yet, Philemon must make the call, for it can only be a heart felt call if done voluntary all
Consider, counsels Paul, if it were meant that he depart a while to be forever at your call
No longer as a slave but more than a slave, as a beloved brother in Christ Jesus the Lord
If you count me as a partner, then receive him as you would me, brothers of one accord.

Knowing the name Onesimus means profitable, Paul takes license to pun for the sake of Jesus

By pointing out to Philemon that one once unprofitable to
you is now profitable to both of us.
Paul also pledges to repay any wrong or debt owed by
Onesimus, let no such thing be a thorn
Hoping to assuage any reluctance Philemon might still
harbor in receiving his servant reborn.
Presuming great confidence in his friend's obedient bent,
little doubt in Paul's heart remains
He requests a guest bed reservation at friend Philemon's when
prayers unlock his own chains.

And here the letter ends and so the story, the reader left to
conjecture Philemon's response:
Could he have resisted the apostle's gifted persuasive
nudging for taking action righteous?
Would this generous hearted man of God who made his
home a church have said no to Paul
With moral burden on his shoulders and the Lord's apostle
and the Lord monitoring his call?
I think not, knowing what we know of Philemon and
knowing Paul's laser sharp perception
More likely Philemon forgave Onesimus, accepted a brother
and extended him manumission.

Had he done otherwise, would the letter not have been
destroyed denying history its due?
Yet history has its letter, believers their inspiration, but
conjecture still more work to do.
Fast forward fifty years and church father Ignatius tells us
bishop Onesimus at Ephesus reigned
Could bishop Onesimus have been the same Onesimus of
Paul's letter as some have maintained?
A real possibility since Paul's letters were first collected
about this time in the city of Ephesus
Did bishop Onesimus include this one and only personal, but
inspiring, letter for the rest of us?

Believe what you will of the above conjectured epilogue, but
lose not sight of the letter per se
Is not Paul's plea to Philemon to search his heart before
decision made, always the gospel way?
The apostle perceived change of heart the one way open to
change entrenched slavery
And may we not perceive change of heart the one way open to
change evils of our day?

HEBREWS PROSE SUMMARY ONE
CHRIST SUPERIOR AS PERSON

Letter from Whom to Whom for What Purpose

The author of Hebrews identifies neither himself, his place of composition, or the intended destination of his composition. Two things, however, are obvious: it is a letter, and it addresses Hebrews. Furthermore, we can infer from its content that the Hebrews addressed are Jewish Christians who are having second thoughts about Christianity, and the writer of the letter poses persuasive arguments to convince them that the new covenant supersedes the old and that Christ, the High Priest of the new covenant, is not only superior to what has preceded Him but that He is the only hope for salvation.

Two conjectures concerning the author of the letter are noteworthy. Barnabas, a noted Christian Jew, a member of the priestly tribe of Levi, and a companion of Paul in missionary work could conceivably have authored the letter. A second plausible possibility is the Alexandrian Jew Apollos, an elegant rhetorician and master of the Scriptures, who after being schooled in the gospel by Aquila and Pricilla at Ephesus went to Achaia where "he vigorously refuted the Jews publicly, showing from Scripture that Jesus is the Christ" (Acts 18:24-28). Yet the identity of the author of this letter must be left to conjecture for no one has been able to convincingly establish its authorship.

Time Frame

The letter was surely written before A.D. 70, the date of the destruction of the Temple, for it talks of animal sacrifice there in the present tense. What then is the probable date of the letter? Since persecution is mentioned in the letter, two possible dates come to mind. First, Emperor Claudius expelled a number of Jews from Rome around A.D. 49 because of a religious conflict within the group causing disturbances in the city. Second, Emperor Nero began a severe persecution of Christians around A.D. 64 blaming them for the great fire that destroyed a large portion of the city. The disturbances at the time of Claudius were probably conflicts between Jews who embraced Jesus and those who rejected him. The Nero persecution was carried out to transfer suspicion of the cause of the fire from the Emperor to the Christians. Jewish Christians would have been subjected to persecution in both instances, but the Nero persecution seems the more probable date of the letter since Jewish Christians may have been tempted to return to the safety of the synagogue and Judaism.

Superiority of the Son

The letter opens with a reminder to the Hebrews that in the past God has spoken to their fathers in different ways and at different times, but this time He has spoken through the Son who is much superior to any previous spokesman, including angels: "God, who at various times and in different ways spoke in time past to the fathers by the prophets, has in these last days spoken to us by His Son, whom He has appointed heir of all things through whom also He made the worlds; who being the brightness of His glory and the express image of His person, and upholding all things by the word of His power, when He had by Himself purged our sins, sat down at the right hand of the Majesty on high, having become so much better than the angels, as He has by inheritance obtained a more excellent name than they" (1:1-4).

In the past God has spoken through different mediums, namely prophets and angels, but now during the last days He has spoken through the Son, the image of the Father's power and glory, who has completed the process by Himself purging our sins and then taking His place at the right hand of the Father where there is none other above Him. The implication of these assertions: Jesus Christ is the Son of God; He ushered in the new covenant by offering himself as the perfect sacrifice thus becoming the High Priest for forgiveness of sin; the old covenant has been superseded by the Son's sacrifice and only through the Son is salvation possible. That Christ is superior as person, as priest, and in power is the primary thesis of this letter to the Hebrews.

The Son Compared to Angels

Angels were highly revered by the Jews especially since they were involved with the giving of the law at Sinai (See Deut 33:2 and Acts 7:38, 53). But the author of Hebrews quotes several passages of Scripture to exemplify Christ's superiority over angels and to verify Him as the Son of God and being God, yet distinguished from the Father. He writes (1:5), "To which angel did God ever say 'You are My Son, / Today I have begotten You'" (Ps 2:7)? Then he follows up with the messianic quote: "I will be to Him a Father, / And He shall be to Me a Son" (II Sam 7:14).

To further show the superiority over angels (1:6), he writes that God says of His Son, "Let all the angels of God worship Him" (See Ps 89:27 and I Pet 3:22). He finds validation in Psalms that Christ is the creator of all things and is never changing in the midst of change: "You Lord, in the beginning laid the foundation of the earth, / And the heavens are the work of Your hands; / They will perish, but You remain; / And they will all grow old like a garment; / Like a cloak You will fold them up, / And they will be changed. / But You are the same, / And your years will not fail" (Ps 102:25-27). In closing the comparison showing the superiority of Christ over angels (1:13), he utilizes the following clincher. "But to which of the angels has He [God the Father] ever said: 'Sit at My right hand, / Till I make Your enemies Your footstool'" (Ps 110:1)? Angles, he declares, are ministering spirits sent to serve those who receive salvation, but Christ is the Savior.

Heads Up Concerning Salvation

Taking an admonishing stance that includes himself, he declares "we must give more earnest heed to the things we have heard, lest we drift away" (2:1). If the word spoken through the angels was steadfast with any disobedience receiving just punishment, how shall we escape if we ignore such great salvation first spoken by the Lord and confirmed to us by those who heard him? Not only was it confirmed by those who heard Him, but also by God through miracles and through gifts of the Holy Spirit.

God has not subjected the world to come to the angels; it is not angels who will provide the way for man to be what he was intended to be. Let us review from Scripture: "What is man that You are mindful of him, / Or the son of man that You take care of him? / You made him a little lower than the angels; / You crowned him with glory and honor, / And set him over the works of Your hands. / You have put all things in subjection under his feet" (Ps 8:4-6). Because of sin, we presently do not see everything subject to man, "but we see Jesus, who was made a little lower than the angels, now crowned with glory and honor because He suffered death, so that by God's grace He might taste death for everyone" (2:9).

It is Christ, assuming the form of man and giving Himself as sacrifice, who redeems fallen man. Thus, "the One who makes men holy and those who are made holy are of the same family" (2:11). And to support this point, the writer quotes a messianic passage from Psalms: "I [Christ] will declare Your name [God] to my brethren; in the presence of the congregation I will sing Your praises" (22:22). For further support he also quotes a pertinent passage from Isaiah: "Here am I [Christ] and the children [the redeemed] God has given Me" (8:18).

Christ had to be made "like His brethren that He might be a merciful and faithful High Priest in service to God, and that he might make atonement for the sins of the people" (2:17).

Christ Superior to Moses

The writer exhorts his "holy brethren," let us fix our thoughts "on Jesus, the apostle and the High Priest whom we confess" (3:1), for Jesus has been found worthy of greater honor than Moses. Though Moses was a faithful servant in God's house, "Christ is faithful as a Son over God's house. And we are His house, if we hold on to our courage and the hope of which we boast" (3:6). Again, the writer of Hebrews cautions his brethren there is only one way and that way is forward with Christ and the new covenant; there is no going back. Believe in the Christ.

Consequences of Unbelief

He enlists example from early Israelite history in warning his brethren never to turn away from the living God: "'Today, if you will hear His voice, do not harden your hearts as you did in the rebellion' (Ps 95:8), but encourage one another daily, as long as it is called Today, so that none of you may be hardened by sin's deceitfulness" (3:13). Milking his allusion, he poses several revealing rhetorical questions: Who were they who heard and rebelled? Were they not those led by Moses? With whom was God angry for forty years? Was it not those who disobeyed and whose bodies fell in the wilderness? Were those who fell not the ones God had sworn would never enter His rest? "So we see they were never able to enter because of their unbelief" (3:19).

Entering God's Rest

The writer of Hebrews assures his audience that the promise of entering God's rest still stands and exhorts them not to fall short of it as did the Israelites in the wilderness. "For indeed the gospel was preached to us as well as to them; but the word which they heard did not profit them because those who heard it did not combine it with faith" (4:2). Continuing, he says, "let us therefore be diligent to enter that rest [which comes only through faith], lest anyone fall after the same example of disobedience" (4:11). Having "a great High Priest who has passed through the heavens, Jesus the Son of God," and who can sympathize with our weaknesses having been tempted as we, "let us therefore come boldly to the throne of grace, that we may obtain mercy and find grace in our time of need" (4:14-

Hebrews Poetic Summary One
Christ Superior as Person

He who authored Hebrews identifies neither himself nor the
destination of his letter luminous
Yet Jewish Christians of the Empire he counsels well,
ingeniously tutoring them as well as us
A master rhetorician he argues his case: the superiority of
Christ in person, priest, and power
Think not angels or Moses or covenant old; think Son and
covenant new, and Scripture scour.
The case and not its advocate should the focus be, yet a
couple of conjectures seem noteworthy
Barnabas the exalted missionary or Apollos the rhetorician
plus, either Christian Jew it could be.

The letter's time frame is also mystery shrouded but
historical conjecture can approximate
Because of Chrestus conflict Emperor Claudius expelled
Jews from Rome around A.D. 48.
Emperor Nero began severely persecuting Christians around
A.D. 64, diversion his game
Highly suspected of burning Rome, the Emperor found it
convenient the Christians blame.
Since the letter speaks of animal sacrifice in the Temple and
uses the present tense consistently
Reason dictates either date a possibility since the Temple was
not destroyed until A.D. seventy.

Yet the impetus for the letter seems to have been
encouragement for Christian Jews to stand firm
And think not of returning to the synagogue and Judaism
hoping there escape persecution concern

Presuming this assumption true, the latter date of the Nero
persecution would fittingly be
Date aside, the author of Hebrews scours Scripture finding
evidence of Christ's superiority
Opening the letter with reminders that God had spoken to
their fathers in different times and ways
But in these last days He has spoken through the Son, a more
superior One than any of earlier days.

And "He appointed Him heir of all things for through Him
was the universe created true
The Son being the radiance of God's glory and the exact
representation of His being too
Upholding all things by the power of His word and
providing purification for our sin
Sat down at the right hand of the Majesty of heaven having
surpassed all angels then
As He has by inheritance obtained a more excellent name,
Son, and thus the superior one.
To which of the angels did God ever say, 'You are My Son,
today your Father I become?'"

So the author of Hebrews argues thus: Jesus Christ, the Son
of God, the new covenant ushered in
By offering Himself as sacrifice perfect and thus becoming
the High Priest for forgiveness of sin
The old covenant was superseded by the Son's sacrifice and
only through Him can salvation come
Christ superior in person, priest, and power forms the thesis
of Hebrews: Christ, the anointed One.
Though angels were involved in the giving of the law at
Sinai, what is that to sacrifice of the Son?
The messianic "I will be to Him a Father, And He shall be to
Me a Son" heralds Him number One.

Scouring the Scriptures the author of Hebrews finds a
preponderance of messianic evidence

Using it liberally to substantiate Christ's superiority for
those who might yet be on the fence
What Christ Himself said was "confirmed to us by those
who heard Him," says this counselor bold
As he supports his case through careful scrutiny of ancient
scroll and contemporary confession told.
Armed with scriptural evidence and rhetoric rare, he builds a
compelling case, jury Jew or Gentile
Whether heard by those scripture savvy or no, this cogent
case for Christ closes the doors of denial.

Taking admonishing stance, he declares, "we must give
earnest heed to the things we have heard
Lest we drift away," keeping in mind that what was spoken to
the angels was truly steadfast word
Brooking no disobedience without punishment, then how
can we escape if we the Lord ignore
Ignore such great salvation first spoken by Him and
confirmed by those who heard Him implore?
Not only was it confirmed by those who heard Him but by
God through gifts of the Holy Spirit
It is a new day when God speaks not through angels but
through His Son: dare we not listen to it?

God has not subjected the world to come to the angels; it is
not angels who will provide the way
Provide the way for man to be what he was intended to be;
listen to what the Scripture has to say:
"What is man that You are mindful of him or the son of
man that of him You take care?
You made him a little lower than angels, You crowned him
with glory and honor dear
And set him over the works of Your hands, putting all things
in subjection under his feet"
Because of sin we at present do not see everything subject to
man, but we think not defeat.

For "we see One who was made a little lower than the angels now crowned with glory, the Son
Crowned because He suffered death so that by God's grace He might taste death for every one"
It is Christ assuming the form of man and giving Himself as sacrifice who redeems fallen man
Thus, the One who makes men holy and those who are made holy are of the same family: man.
So reveals the Psalmist, "I [Christ] will declare Your name [God] to my brethren," Isaiah also
"Here am I [Christ] and the children [the redeemed] God has given Me," messianic we know.

Christ had to be made like His brethren that He might be a merciful, faithful High Priest
In service to God, and that He might make atonement for the sin of man, even to the least
"So let us fix our thoughts on Jesus, the apostle and the High Priest whom we confess,"
Exhorts the counselor, "for Jesus has been found worthy of greater honor than Moses."
Moses was a faithful servant in God's house, but Christ is over God's house as faithful Son
And we are His house, if we hold fast our courage and the hope of which we boast, each one.

There is no turning back, the way is forward with Christ and the new covenant, he insists
Today, if you will hear His voice, do not harden your hearts as they did in the wilderness
Today, let us encourage one another praying that none is hardened by sin's deceitfulness
Adding rhetorical question to allusion he shores his point, "Who were they who rebelled?
Were they not those led by Moses? With whom was God angry for forty years, the failed?
Was it not those who disobeyed whose bodies fell in the wilderness, those who rebelled?"

Were those who fell not the ones God had sworn would
never enter His rest?
Do we not see they were never to enter because their
rebellion put God to test?
He assures them the promise of entering God's rest still
stands and faith the way
Then exhorts them not lose faith as did the wilderness
Israelites of Moses' day.
The gospel has been preached to us as well as them, but it
profited them not
For those who heard it did not combine it with faith and died
a rebellious lot.

Therefore let us be diligent in keeping faith, he exhorts, lest
we too fall by example same
Should we through disobedience fall, we need look no
further than ourselves for all blame
We have a great High Priest who has passed through the
heavens, Christ the Son of God
Who can sympathize with our weaknesses having been
tempted as we by Satan's façade
So let us come to the throne of grace there to find mercy from
our Savior the Son of God.

Hebrews Prose Summary Two
Christ Superior as High Priest

Priesthood Designated not Assumed

The writer spends more than a third of the letter explaining Christ as High Priest and its significance. He begins by saying that every high priest is taken from among men and appointed for them in things pertaining to God, particularly the offering of gifts and sacrifices. He can have compassion on those who are ignorant and going astray because being man he also is beset by weakness. And since he is weak he has to offer gifts and sacrifices for himself as well as for others.

The writer also points out that no man can truly take priesthood upon himself; he must be called by God just as was Aaron. "So also Christ did not glorify Himself to become High Priest, but it was God who said to Him: (Ps 2:7) 'You are My Son, / Today I have begotten You,' and in another place says, (Ps 110:4) 'You are a priest forever / According to the order of Melchizedek'" (5:5-6). During the days of Christ on earth, his time in the flesh, He offered up prayers and supplications with pleading cries and tears to the One able to save Him from death and was heard. Although a Son he learned obedience through suffering, and "having been perfected, He became the author of eternal salvation to all who obey Him and was designated High Priest 'according to the order of Melchizedek'" (5:9-10).

Recipients Scolded and Warned

The writer says he has much to say about this, about Christ as High Priest, but that it is hard to explain because they have become dull of hearing. He tells them they should by this time have become teachers, yet they need someone to teach them. They are more like babes needing to be milk fed in learning elementary truths. Presumably, he is shaming them a bit as a means of motivating them to listen more carefully to what he will be saying, for a little later he says, "let us leave the elementary teachings about Christ and go on to maturity" (6:1). Before going on however, he adds a strong warning: "It is impossible for those who have once been enlightened, and have tasted the heavenly gift, and have shared in the Holy Spirit, and have tasted the goodness of the word of God and the powers of the coming age, *if they fall away*, to renew them to repentance, since they crucify again for themselves the Son of God, and put Him to an open shame" (6:4-6).

Encouraged to Stay the Course

Now calling his recipients beloved, he tells them he has confidence they will not fall away but will stay the course. He assures them that God will not forget the work and labor of love they have shown Him in ministering to the saints. He encourages them to not become sluggish but to imitate those who have through faith and patience inherited the promise. He reminds them of the surety of the promise noting that when God made a promise to Abraham He sealed it with an oath, and after Abraham faithfully and patiently endured he received what was promised. Actually, there is double surety: God's promise being absolutely trustworthy, and God's oath confirming the promise. Anyone looking for refuge can lay hold of this hope so furnished, "this hope we have as an anchor of the soul, both sure and steadfast, and which enters the Presence behind the veil, where Jesus, who went before us, has entered on our behalf having become High Priest forever according to the order of Melchizedek" (6:19-20).

Significance of the Melchizedek/Abraham Event

First, the writer describes Melchizedek saying that he was the king of Salem and priest of the Most High God who met Abraham returning from defeating several kings and blessed him. Abraham in turn gave Melchizedek a tenth of everything. Commenting on the significance of the event, he notes that the name Melchizedek means "king of righteousness," and that king of Salem means "king of peace," and "without father or mother, without genealogy, without beginning of days or end of life, like the Son of God he remains a priest forever" (7:2-3). Then the writer comments on the importance of the event. "Just think how great this Melchizedek was that even the patriarch Abraham gave him a tenth of the spoils! Now the law requires that descendants of Levi who become priests to collect a tenth from the people—that is their brothers—even though their brothers are descended from Abraham. This man did not trace his descent from Abraham and blessed him who had the promises. And without doubt the lesser person is blessed by the greater" (7:4-7).

It begins to become clear where the writer is going with his argument; he is making the case for the inadequacy of the law and the Levitical priesthood. He concludes, "If perfection could have been attained through the Levitical priesthood (for on the basis of it the law was given to the people), why was there still need for another priest to come—one in the order of Melchizedek, not in the order of Aaron? For when there is a change of priesthood, there must also be a change of the law. He of whom these things are said belonged to a different tribe, and no one from that tribe has ever served at the altar. For it is clear that our Lord descended from Judah, and in regard to that tribe Moses said nothing about priests. And what we have said is even more clear if another priest like Melchizedek appears, someone who has become a priest not on the basis of regulation as to his ancestry but on the basis of the power of an indestructible life. For it is declared: 'You are a priest forever, in the order of Melchizedek.' The former regulation is set aside because it was weak and useless (for the law made nothing perfect), and a better hope is introduced by which we draw near to God" (7:11-18). Thus, the better hope by which we draw near to God is Jesus Christ, the Son of God and High Priest forever according to the order of Melchizedek.

Jesus Priest Forever

Sounding the oath theme again, the writer says this hope is not without oath. Others became priests without any oath, but not the Christ. When He became a priest, God said to Him: (Ps 110:4) "The Lord has sworn and will not change His mind: / 'You are a priest forever.' Because of this oath, Jesus has become the guarantee of a better covenant" (7:21-22). There have been many priests because death prevented them for continuing in office, but since Jesus lives forever, His is a permanent priesthood. And being so, He is able to save completely those who come to Him because he is always there to receive them and to intercede for them. "Such a High Priest meets our needs," says the writer, "One who is holy, blameless, pure, set apart from sinners, exalted above the heavens" (7:26). Other high priests had to offer sacrifices day after day, first for their own sins and then for the sins of the people, but Jesus sacrificed for all our sins when He sacrificed himself. "The law appoints as high priests men who are weak; but the oath, which came after the law, appointed the Son, who has been made perfect forever" (7:28).

The High Priest and the New Covenant

The writer says the point he is making is that we have a High Priest who sits at the right hand of the Majesty in heaven and who serves in the sanctuary there, the true tabernacle, set up by God, not man. Every high priest is appointed to serve both gifts and sacrifice so it was necessary that this High Priest also have something to offer. If He were on earth He would not be priest because there are already men who offer gifts prescribed by the law, but they serve in a sanctuary that is only a shadow of the heavenly sanctuary. This is why Moses, instructed to build the tabernacle, was told to build it according to the instructions given at Sinai. "But the ministry Jesus has received is as superior to theirs as the covenant of which He is mediator is superior to the old one, and it is founded on better promises, for if there had been nothing wrong with the first covenant, no place would have been sought for another" (8:6-7).

But God did desire another, argues the writer, and revealed such through the prophet Jeremiah (31:31-34): "Behold, the days are coming, declares the Lord, when I will make a new covenant with the house of Israel and with the house of Judah. It will not be like the covenant I made with their fathers when I took them by the hand to lead them out of the land of Egypt because they did not remain faithful to My covenant, and I turned away from them, declares the Lord. This is the covenant I will make with the house of Israel after that time, declares the Lord. I will put My laws in their minds and write them on their hearts. I will be their God, and they will be My people . . . they will all know Me, from the least of them to the greatest. For I will forgive their wickedness and will remember their sins no more." The writer then argues that by calling the covenant "new" He made the first one obsolete, and "what is obsolete and aging will soon disappear" (8:13). Thus, they must hold fast to Jesus Christ, High Priest of the new covenant and mediator of salvation.

Superiority of Christ's Priesthood

Priesthood under Old Covenant

The writer reviews the first covenant's regulations for worship in the earthly tabernacle. In the outer room of the tabernacle were the lamp stand, the table and the show bread. This first room was called the Holy Place. Behind the second curtain was the Most Holy Place fronted by the golden altar of incense, and within the Most Holy Place was the ark of the covenant overlaid with gold and containing the golden pot of manna, Aaron's rod that had budded, and the tablets of the covenant. Above the ark of the covenant were the cherubim of glory overshadowing the mercy seat. The priests regularly enter the outer room to carry out their duties, but only the high priest enters the inner room, the Most Holy Place (the Holy of Holies), and then only once a year, and never without blood which he offered for himself and for the people's sins committed in ignorance. "The Holy Spirit was showing by this," says the writer, "that the way into the Most Holy Place had not yet been disclosed as long as the first tabernacle was still standing. It was symbolic for the present time in which both gifts and sacrifices are offered but which are not able to clear the conscience of the worshiper. They are only a matter of food and drink and various ceremonial washings—external regulations applying until the time of the new order" (9:8-10).

Priesthood under New Covenant

But Christ's priesthood is superior, for He "came as High Priest of the good things to come, with the greater and more perfect tabernacle not made with hands, that is, not of this creation. Not with the blood of goats and calves, but with His own blood He entered the Most Holy Place once and for all, having obtained eternal redemption" (9:11-12). If the blood of bulls and goats suffices for purifying the flesh, asks the writer, "how much more shall the blood of Christ, who through the eternal Spirit offered Himself without spot to God, purge your conscience from dead works to serve the living God? And for that reason He is the Mediator of the new covenant, that those who are called may receive the promised eternal inheritance now that He has died a ransom to set them free from the sins committed under the first covenant" (9:14-15).

The Law only a Shadow

The writer says the law is only the shadow of the good things that are coming not the realities themselves; therefore, it cannot by the same sacrifices repeated endlessly year after year make perfect the worshiper. The sacrifices are an annual reminder of sins because it is impossible for the blood of animals to take away sins. That was left for Christ, who said, (Ps 40:6-8) "Sacrifice and offering You did not desire, but a body You prepared for Me . . . with burnt offerings and sin offerings You were not pleased . . . [thus] I have come to do Your will." The writer explains, "He sets aside the first to establish the second [first covenant to establish the second], and we have been made holy through the sacrifice of the body of Jesus Christ once and for all" (10:10).

Let Us not Shrink Back

"Therefore, brothers," says the writer, "since we have confidence to enter the Most Holy Place by the blood of Jesus, by a new and living way opened for us through the curtain, that is, His body, and since we have a great priest over the house of God, let us draw near to God with a sincere heart in full assurance of faith, having our hearts sprinkled to cleanse us from a guilty conscience and having our bodies washed with pure water. Let us hold unswervingly to the hope we profess, for He who promised is faithful" (10:19-23). For whatever reason, persecution or otherwise, the "brothers" he addresses are losing their initial zeal, for he alludes to "earlier days" when they "stood their ground in a great contest in the face of suffering" (10:32). He mentions how they sympathized with those in prison and how they accepted confiscation of their own property because they knew they had better possessions awaiting them, and he exhorts them now not to throw away their confidence. As way of warning, he references a bit of pertinent prophetic Scripture (from Habakkuk 2:3-4): "He who is coming will come and will not delay. But the righteous will live by faith. And if they shrink back, I will not be pleased with them." As way of exhorting, he declares, "But we are not of those who shrink back and are destroyed, but of those who believe and are saved" (10:39).

Hebrews Poetic Summary Two
Christ Superior as High Priest

A third or more of Hebrews focuses on Christ as the High
Priest and His superiority thereof
Contrasting essential differences between earthly high
priests and the one High Priest above
Noting all high priests are taken from among men and
appointed, for men, special things to do
Things pertaining to God, regularly offering gifts and
sacrifices, and showing compassion too
For being man and also by weakness beset must for himself
so offer gifts and sacrifices anon
Knowing that no man takes upon himself priesthood but
must be called by God as was Aaron.

So also Christ did not take priesthood upon himself, He was
called by God just as was Aaron
Neither did Christ glorify Himself High Priest to become,
rather God said "You are My Son
Today I have begotten You," then, "You are a priest forever in
the tradition of Melchizedek."
During His time in flesh, He offered up prayers and
supplications as cries, His body wrecked
Pleading to the One who could save Him from death and
was heard, a Son obedience learned
Becoming the mediator of eternal salvation, the Son designated
High Priest and so confirmed.

The recipients of the letter hear reproof firm from its author
telling them they are of hearing dull
For at a time when they should be teachers, they seem not
the truth to know nor toward it pulled

Perhaps he overstates hoping to provoke them to listen
carefully to what further he has to say
By making it abundantly clear they are falling away from
their commitment of an earlier day.
It is impossible asserts the author for those who have been
enlightened and tasted the heavenly gift
If they fall away, to renew them to repentance for they crucify
again God's Son, an irreparable rift.

Then calling his recipients beloved he offers complimentary
and encouraging words of confidence
Confidence that they will not fall away recalling how they
had in the past ministered to the saints
And encouraging them to imitate those who through faith
and patience have the promise inherited
Assuring them of the surety of the promise, God being
trustworthy, and the promise oath merited
Did not Abraham, man of faith and patience, receive the
promise, covenant and oath fulfilled?
Anyone looking for refuge finds it here and may lay hold this
hope, God given and oath sealed.

This hope anchors our soul, sure and steadfast, for it enters
the Presence behind the veil, alack!
Where Jesus entered on our behalf having become High
Priest forever, the order of Melchizedek
The Melchizedek of Genesis, the king of Salem, and priest
of the God Most High we know him
How he met Abraham coming from kings defeated and
blessed him, there honored both of them
Melchizedek as king of Salem king of peace, as priest king of
righteousness, without genealogy
No beginning, no ending, like the Son of God, he remains a
priest forever, without chronology.

Where the author of the letter is going with his Melchizedek
narrative we do not yet perceive

Though sensing something about inadequacy of the law and
Levitical priesthood, we believe
He comments on how great this Melchizedek was that the
patriarch Abraham gave tithe to him
For the law requires descendants of Levi tithe collect, yet
here tithe goes to the king of Salem
Though not tracing his descent from Abraham, does so bless
him who had the promises best
Thus suggesting to author of Hebrews that the lesser person
by the greater is hereby blessed

That he is making his case for the inadequacy of the
Levitical priesthood, our suspicion:
"If perfection could have been attained through it why need
for another priest to come?"
Asks the Hebrews author, "one in the order of Melchizedek,
not in the order of Aaron
For when there is a change of priesthood there must also be
a change of law, and anon
And He of whom these things messianic are said belonged
to a different tribe forsooth
A tribe who never at the altar served; as well known, our Lord
descended from Judah."

"And in regard to that tribe Moses said nothing about
priests, so He did not regulation fit
But in the order of Melchizedek came, not on the basis of
regulation, ever much above it
Not on the basis of regulation as to ancestry but on the basis
of the power of life indestructible
The former regulation is set aside because it was weak, the
law made nothing perfect, admittedly
And a better hope is introduced by which we draw near to
God, and that hope His select:
Jesus Christ, His own Son and High Priest forever, according
to the order of Melchizedek."

Others he notes became priests without oath, but Jesus
Christ had the Father's oath sublime
Upon becoming priest, God said to Him, "the Lord has
sworn and will not change His mind"
And because of this oath, says the author, Jesus has become a
guarantee of a better covenant
Previous priests were subject to death; He lives forever, His a
permanent priesthood adamant.
He is able to save completely for he is always there for those
who come and can intercede
He is living and blameless and holy and heaven exalted, such
a High Priest meets our need.

Other priests had to sacrifice day after day, but Jesus
sacrificed once for all time, and rearranged
The law appoints as high priests men, thus weak, but the
oath coming after the law sought change
And change came in the self-sacrifice of Jesus Christ, the
appointed High Priest forever for us
The High Priest sitting at the right hand of the Majesty in
heaven there to direct our true focus
If He were on earth He would not priest be; priests there
already offer that prescribed by law
But they serve in a sanctuary that is only shadow of the
heavenly sanctuary, shadow and flaw.

Though Moses followed faithfully the instructions for
building the tabernacle in every detail
Its construction and ministry with its priests and its curtains
and Holy of Holies, shadow still
But the ministry Jesus has received is as superior to theirs as
the covenant He is mediator of
Had there been nothing wrong with the first covenant, no
need for intervention from above
But God above did desire another, we know, and revealed
such through the prophet Jeremiah
Saying, "Behold the days are coming when I will make a *new*
covenant with Israel and Judah."

"It will not be like the covenant I made with their fathers
when I led them out of Egypt's snares
They did not remain faithful to My covenant and I turned
away from them," the Lord declares.
In covenant new He will put His laws in their minds and
write them in their hearts, truly stated
He will be their God and they will be His people; they will
know Him, the lowest to the greatest.
Thus, the author argues, by calling the covenant new God
made the first one obsolete for sure
And what is obsolete and aging will soon disappear, thus it is
in Jesus Christ we remain secure.

Let us review the priesthood under the first covenant's
regulation for the earthly tabernacle space:
There was outer room, containing the lamp stand, the table
and show bread, called the Holy Place
Behind the second curtain the Most Holy Place, Holy of
Holies, fronted by the gold altar of incense
The ark of the covenant overlaid in gold, and within it a pot
of manna, miracle from the wilderness
Aaron's rod that budded, and the tablets of the covenant,
above the ark the cherubim face to face
Wings spread over the mercy seat; this Holy of Holies the
high priest only can enter in this space.

The outer room, the priests enter regularly duties to
perform, but behind inner room curtain never go
The high priest only enters once a year with blood to offer
for himself and for the people's sins also.
"Now," says Hebrews, "the Holy Spirit was showing by this
that the way to the Most Holy Place
Had not yet been disclosed as long as the first tabernacle was
still standing, filling symbolic space
It was symbolic for the present time in which both gifts and
sacrifices are offered but clear cannot
Conscience they cannot clear their being merely food and
drink and ceremonial washings, the lot.

They are external regulations applying until the time of the
new order, time the old order forgot."

For Christ's priesthood superior is: "He came as High Priest
of the good things to come
The greater and more perfect tabernacle the one not made
with hands, not of this creation
Not with the blood of goats and calves but with His own
blood He entered the Most Holy Place
He entered once and for all having obtained eternal
redemption, redemption through God's grace.
If the blood of bulls and goats sufficed for purification, how
much more the blood of Jesus Christ
Who offered Himself spotless to purge your conscience of
dead works and to serve the Highest?"

"And for that reason He is the Mediator of the new
covenant, that those who believe may receive
They may receive the promised eternal inheritance now that
He has died: ransom to set them free
To set them free from the sins committed under the first
covenant that points the way
The law is only the shadow of the good things that are
coming, not the realities per se
It cannot by sacrifices repeated year by year make perfect the
worshipper, it only makes amends
The sacrifices being annual reminders of sins since animal
blood could never take away the sins."

That was left for Christ who said, "sacrifice and offering You
desired not, but a body You prepared for Me
With burnt offerings and sin offerings You were not pleased,
therefore I come to do Your will completely."
Hebrews explains, "thus, God sets aside the first covenant to
establish the new, and we are truly blessed.
We have been made holy through the body of Christ
sacrificed, once and for all in Him we find our rest;

Therefore, since we have confidence to enter the Most Holy
Place through the blood of Christ Jesus,
Since we have a new and living way opened for us through
the curtain, that is, His body sacrificed for us
Let us draw near to God with sincere heart in full assurance
of faith, our conscience cleansed forever thus."

Whether from persecution or otherwise, the Hebrews'
author sees his brethren losing their early zeal
When they stood their ground in the face of suffering, of
accepting confiscation of their property real
As he boldly argued his case for Christ and the covenant
new so with warning and exhortation teased:
"God through Habakkuk says the righteous live by faith and
if they shrink back He is never pleased
But we are not of those who shrink back and are destroyed,
but of those who believe and are saved"
Says the Hebrews' author, both warning and exhorting his
brethren to take action on this matter grave.

HEBREWS PROSE SUMMARY THREE
CHRIST SUPERIOR IN POWER

The Power of Faith

Giving a memorable definition of faith, the author says, "faith is the substance of things hoped for, the evidence of things not seen" (11:1), meaning faith is being sure of things hoped for, and certain of things we have not seen. Following the definition he lists numerous examples of faith from the Scripture beginning at the beginning. By faith we understand that the universe was created by the word of God and not made from things visible. By faith Abel offered a better sacrifice than Cain and was commended by God. By faith Enoch was taken without experiencing death for he had pleased God. By faith Noah built the ark thereby saving his family and becoming the heir of righteousness. By faith Abraham went to a land unknown to him obeying God's call. By faith he lived in that land in tents as did Isaac and Jacob looking forward to the city with foundations built by God [the heavenly Jerusalem]. By faith Abraham and Sarah, both past the age, were enabled and from them came descendants numerous as the stars and countless as sand of the seashore. "These all died in faith, not having received the promises but having seen them afar off were assured of them, embraced them, and confessed that they were strangers and pilgrims on the earth" (11:13).

The author emphasizes that these people of faith were looking forward, looking for a better country, a heavenly one and that God, who is not ashamed to be called their God, has prepared a city for them. And then as way of justification, he recounts more instances of their undying faith as well as that of succeeding ones. By faith Abraham when tested prepared to offer up Isaac even though the promise was to be delivered through him. By faith Joseph on his death bed spoke of exodus from Egypt and gave instructions concerning the transporting of his bones. By faith Moses' parents hid him, braving Pharaoh's edict, for they recognized that he was special. By faith Moses, coming of age, refused to be called son of Pharaoh's daughter but threw his lot with his people, the people of God, "regarding the disgrace for the sake of Christ of greater value than the treasures of Egypt" (11:26). By faith Moses endured seeing Him who is invisible and kept the Passover sprinkling the doorposts with blood lest the first born of his people be destroyed. By faith the people passed through the Red Sea while their Egyptian pursuers were drowned. By faith the walls of Jericho tumbled after being encircled seven days. By faith the prostitute Rahab welcomed the spies and did not perish.

The author says he would like to go on with examples but time does not allow him "to tell of Gideon and Barak and Samson and Jephthah, also of David and Samuel and the prophets: who through faith subdued kingdoms, worked righteousness, obtained promises, stopped the mouths of lions. Quenched the violence of fire, escaped the edge of the sword, out of weakness were made strong, becoming valiant in battle . . . . Still others had trial of mockings and scourgings, yes, and of chains and imprisonment. They were stoned, were sawn in two, were tempted and slain with the sword . . . . And all these, having obtained a good testimony through faith, did not receive the promise, God having provided something better for us that they should not be made perfect apart from us" (11:32-40).

All these of faith who came before, says the author, did not receive the promise because the fulfillment for them is the same as with us, through Jesus Christ who, to use John's words, "is the resurrection and the life." Those of faith who came before focused their faith on God and His promises which have come to be fulfilled in Jesus Christ and their redemption is complete through Him as is our own, argues the author of Hebrews.

The Need for Discipline

In a figurative vein, the author exhorts his recipients to run the good race. Surrounded by those heroes of faith who came before as witnesses, "let us lay aside every weight, and the sin which so easily ensnares us, and let us run with endurance the race that is set before us, looking unto Jesus, the author and finisher of our faith, who for the joy that was set before Him endured the cross, despising the shame, and has sat down at the right of the throne of God" (12:1-2). With these witnesses to the power of faith and Christ the example and the goal of the race, how could they not be inspired to put aside all hindrances to finish the course that is marked out for them? He cautions them to keep their eye on Jesus and His example lest they become weary and lose heart reminding them they have not yet resisted to the point of bloodshed. He also calls their attention to counsel from Proverbs concerning suffering (3:11-12): My son do not despise the chastening of the Lord, / Nor be discouraged when you are rebuked by Him; / For whom the Lord loves He chastens, / And scourges every son whom He receives." Endure hardship as discipline. God is treating you as sons and correcting you as a father would. Undisciplined you would be as illegitimate children rather than true sons. "Our fathers disciplined us for a time as they thought best, but God disciplines us for our good, that we may share in His holiness" (12:10). Though discipline is painful at the time, in the long run it produces the fruit of righteousness for those trained by it.

Warning against Refusing God

The author warns the recipients to walk upright, "make straight paths for your feet, so that what is lame may not be dislocated, but healed. Pursue peace with all men, and holiness, without which no man will see the Lord" (12:13-14). Holiness must be discerned and pursued, "lest anyone fall short of the grace of God, lest any root of bitterness springing up cause trouble, and by this many become defiled; lest there be any fornicator or profane person like Esau who for one morsel of food sold his birthright" (12:15-16). Afterward, the author points out, Esau wished to inherit the blessing but found no place for repentance though he sought it with tears.

Continuing with his instructive warning, the author spotlights Sinai at the time the law was given and the terrifying conditions surrounding the occasion, the mountain that burned with fire, a place of blackness and darkness and tempest, "and the sound of a trumpet and the voice of words, so that those who heard it begged that the word should not be spoken to them anymore" (12:18-19). The author is recalling the tangibles of the old covenant—the mountain, the ordinances, the terrifying warnings, and the severe penalties—in order to contrast this with the new covenant which is much less threatening. In reference to Sinai he mentions that should even a beast touch the mountain it must be stoned, and that the whole experience was so terrifying that Moses himself cried out saying, "I am exceedingly afraid and trembling" (12:21). Then, in contrast, the author moves to the new covenant saying, "But you have come to Mount Zion and to the city of the living God, the heavenly Jerusalem, to an innumerable company of angels, to the general assembly and church of the firstborn who are registered in heaven, to God the Judge of all, to the spirits of just men made perfect, to Jesus the Mediator of the new covenant, and the blood of sprinkling that speaks better things than that of Abel" (12:22-24). Note the clincher comparing Abel's blood that cried out for justice and retribution to that Jesus shed on the cross crying out for forgiveness and reconciliation.

Thus, in contrasting the old and the new covenants the author has laid the groundwork for another warning against the thought of returning to Judaism: "See that you do not reject Him who speaks, for if they did not escape whom refused Him who spoke on earth [at Sinai], much less shall we escape if we turn away from Him [Christ] who speaks from heaven" (12:25).

Exhortations More

The author exhorts them concerning the power of love, the love of God and the love of neighbor. They should continue in brotherly love, not forgetting strangers, but recalling that strangers could be angels, remembering those in prison as if there with them, remembering all those suffering as if suffering with them. Honor marriage and keep the marriage bed pure, for God will judge the adulterer and all the sexually immoral. Live lives free from the love of money, and be content remembering God's promise (Deut 31:6), "Never will I leave you nor forsake you." Remember your leaders, the blessed outcome of their lives, and "imitate their faith, [for] Jesus Christ is the same yesterday, today, and forever" (13:7-8).

Do not be led astray by strange teachings. Our hearts are strengthened by grace not ceremonial foods "which have no value for those who eat them. We have a bar from which those who minister at the tabernacle have no right to eat" (13:9-10). Presumably, the author is again declaring that the order of the old covenant no longer suffices, for the new covenant furnishes a new order in which the Aaron priesthood is obsolete, ending at the cross, and is replaced, in the order of Melchizedek, by Christ the unique high priest forever.

As the high priests carries the blood of animals into the Most Holy Place, but burns the bodies outside the camp "so Jesus also suffered outside the city gate to make the people holy through His own blood. Let us, then, go to Him outside the camp, bearing the disgrace He bore. For here we do not have an enduring city, but are looking for the city that is to come" (13:12-14). As Jesus died in disgrace outside the city, so should they be willing to turn, unequivocally, from Judaism to Christ thereby readying themselves for the perfect city to come.

Hebrews Poetic Summary Three
Christ Superior in Power

Whether Day of the Lord of the O. T. or Second Coming of
the N. T., judgment day is yet to come
Life between present day and judgment day is lived by faith,
assuming righteousness saves one
For does not Genesis say that Abraham believed and God
accredited it to him as righteousness?
From the first patriarch, faith furnished the means for fallen
humanity to regain heavenly bliss.
The author of Hebrews in exploring faith prefaces Abraham
beginning with the creation scene
But first provides definition, a most helpful one, and like all
else in the letter, superb not mean.

"Faith is the substance of things hoped for, the evidence of
things not seen," yet known
And from definition flows a preponderance of evidence
exemplary, all Scripture drawn:
By faith we understand the universe was created by word of
God not made from visible things
By faith Abel offers a better sacrifice than that of Cain and
from God commendation brings
By faith Enoch does not experience death, for having walked
with God he pleased all Highness
By faith Noah builds the ark thereby saving his family and
becoming the heir of righteousness.

By faith Abraham abandons his native land venturing to one
unnamed, obeying God's call
By faith Abraham and Sarah, past age, produce descendants
numerous as sands and stars all.

These and others all died in faith not receiving the promises
but having seen them from afar
And doing so embraced them confessing that on this earth
strangers and pilgrims they are.
The author of Hebrews emphasizes the people of faith look
forward, looking for a better place
A heavenly city, and that God, not ashamed to be called their
God, will truly provide such place.

As way of justification he recounts more instances of heroes
of faith, a goodly number of them:
By faith Abraham prepares to offer up Isaac though the
promise was to be delivered through him
By faith the dying Joseph speaks of exodus and of the
carrying out of Egypt his bones interred
By faith the parents of Moses recognize the child special and
hide him as if edict never occurred
By faith Moses threw his lot with his subjected people
rejecting the role of Egyptian royalty
By faith Moses believing I AM keeps the Passover, doorpost
blood sprinkled, first born free.

By faith the people pass through the Red Sea on dry ground
while the pursuing Egyptians drown
By faith Joshua and the people encircle the city seven days
and the walls of Jericho tumble down.
The author says he wishes to go on with examples, but time
does not allow him "to tell of Barak
And Samson, and Jephthah, also of David and Samuel and
the prophets who through faith, alack!
Subdued kingdoms, worked righteousness, obtained
promises, stopped the mouths of lions bold
Quenched the violence of fire, out of weakness were made
strong, becoming valiant in battle old."

"Yet these of old having obtained testimony good through
faith did not the promise receive thus

God having provided something better for us that they
should not be made perfect apart from us"
Those of faith who came before us focusing their being on
God and His promises, now known,
Are to be fulfilled in Jesus Christ, their redemption being
complete through Him as is our own.

"Surrounded by these heroes of faith who came before as
witnesses, let us run the good race
Let us lay aside every weight, and the sin which so easily
ensnares us, let us set steady pace
And run with endurance the race that is set before us,
looking unto Jesus, the author and finisher
The author and finisher of our faith, who for the joy that
was set before Him prayerfully endured
Endured the cross, despising the shame, and has sat down at
the right hand of God's throne
Let us finish the race while these witnesses to the power of
faith, and Christ above, look on."

With metaphor athletic he exhorts his cohorts to keep the
faith, to recall the faith heroes of old
To keep their eye on Jesus, to finish the course marked out
for them pacing onward ever bold
Reminding them they have not yet resisted to the point of
bloodshed, and even should it come
Hear Proverbs saying, "despise not chastening from the Lord,
for whom He loves He chastens"
Endure hardship as discipline, for God is treating you as
sons correcting you as a father would
Like a father, God disciplines us for our good that we may
share in His holiness as we should.

Discipline though painful at the time produces fruit of
righteousness for those trained by it
Insists the author, compelled to exhort and warn and
instruct his cohorts hopefully to profit:

"Make straight paths for your feet, so that what is lame may
not be dislocated but healed
Pursue peace with all men, and holiness, without which to
no man is the Lord revealed
See to it that no one misses the grace of God or no root of
bitterness grows up to defile despite
See to it that no one is sexually immoral or godless like Esau
who for morsel sold his birthright."

The Esau allusion triggers instruction by way of contrast
between old covenant and new
It is Sinai at the time the law was given and the terrifying
conditions there, he first turns to
To the reality of the mountain that burned with fire, to
darkness and tempest and trumpet din
To the voice of words that those who heard begged that the
word not be spoken to them again
Focus is on the tangibles of the covenant old, the mountain
and the terrifying warnings not a few
The ordinances and the penalties severe, all in contrast to the
much less threatening covenant new.

In reference to Sinai, he says even Moses terrified cries out,
"I am sorely afraid and I tremble"
Emphasizing that circumstance of the new covenant and
circumstance at Sinai little resemble
"For you have come to Mount Zion and the city of the living
God, the heavenly Jerusalem
To an innumerable company of angels, to the general
assembly and church of the firstborn
Who are registered in heaven, to God the Judge of all, to the
spirits of just men made perfect
To Jesus Mediator of covenant new whose sprinkled blood to
those of faith will always elect."

As way of clincher the author alludes to Abel's blood which
cried out for justice and retribution

In contrast to the blood of Jesus shed on the cross crying out
for forgiveness and reconciliation.
Through contrasting the old and new covenants he has laid
the groundwork for warning more
Same warning given before: do not think of returning to
Judaism—warning at the letter's core
"See that you do not reject Him who speaks, for if they did
not escape Him who spoke on earth
Much less shall we escape if we turn away from Him who
speaks from heaven, promise birthed."

Before closing the author has a few exhortations more
especially concerning the power of love
The love of God and brotherly love continue, not forgetting
strangers who could be from above
Remember those in prison as if imprisoned with them, those
suffering as if you suffer with them
Honor marriage and keep the marriage bed pure, the
sexually immoral God will always condemn
Love not money, be content remembering God's promise,
"Never will I leave you nor you forsake
Remember your leaders, the blessed outcome of their lives,
lives dedicated in faith, them imitate,
Imitate those of faith, for Jesus Christ is the same yesterday,
today, and forever," Him celebrate.

JAMES PROSE SUMMARY
FAITH WITHOUT WORKS

Possible Author

Which James is the author of the James epistle? To a reader of the New Testament the name "James" would, no doubt, bring to mind particularly James the apostle and James the brother of Jesus. James the apostle is, of course, linked with his brother John, both sons of Zebedee, and both within the inner circle of the apostles closest to Jesus: Peter, James, and John. James the brother of Jesus, to whom Jesus appeared after His resurrection (I Cor. 15:7), became leader of the Jerusalem church. Either of these, James the apostle or James the brother of Jesus and leader of the Jerusalem church, can certainly be viewed as knowledgeable persons of authority and capable of writing a letter to believers "scattered abroad."

However, since James the apostle was executed early on by King Herod Agrippa, it is less likely that he is the author of the James epistle. Furthermore, it can be argued there is a resemblance of style between this James epistle and a speech given by James the brother of Jesus at the Jerusalem Council and a letter that follows, both of which are recorded in Acts fifteen. Thus, conjecturing between the two, James the brother of Jesus seems to have the stronger claim as author of the James epistle.

Possible Recipients

James, calling himself "a servant of God and of the Lord Jesus Christ," sends greetings "to the twelve tribes which are scattered abroad" (1:1). Presumably, the twelve tribes scattered abroad are Jewish Christians and if the letter is of an early date as seems to be the case it could possibly be directed to believers who fled the Jerusalem church after the stoning of Stephen and the execution of the apostle James. The content of the letter seems to point to an early period when the church was primarily Jewish, for there is no mention of the circumcision controversy that later developed with the entry of Gentiles into the church. It was the primary topic of the Jerusalem Council which took place following Paul's first missionary journey around A.D. 49. See Acts, chapter fifteen.

Profit from Trials

James counsels his brethren to count trials a joy, "knowing that the testing of your faith produces patience. But let patience have its perfect work, that you may be perfect and complete lacking nothing" (1:2-3). If you lack wisdom ask God to give you wisdom and if done in faith you can be assured that God will give liberally. "Blessed is the man who endures temptation; for when he has been proved, he will receive the crown of life which the Lord has promised to those who love Him" (1:12).

Know the Source of Temptation

Do not say that you are tempted by God, for God does not tempt anyone. A person is tempted when drawn away by his own desires. "Then, when desire has conceived, it gives birth to sin; and sin, when it is full-grown brings forth death" (1:15). Know the source of temptation; know the consequences of sin. Do not be deceived.

Early Believers the First Fruits

Every good gift, every perfect gift comes from above, "from the Father of lights, with whom there is no variation or shadowing of turning." And it is this Father of lights "who brought us forth by the word of truth, that we may be a kind of firstfruits of His creatures" (1:17-18). James sees these early believers, these early Jewish Christians as the firstfruits promising a fuller harvest to come.

Be Wise Doers of the Word

Be swift to hear but slow to speak and slow to wrath. Lay aside wickedness "and receive with meekness the implanted word, which is able to save your souls, but be doers of the word and not hearers only, deceiving yourselves" (1:21-22). A person who is a hearer and not a doer is like the person who looks into the mirror and then goes away and forgets what he is like, but a doer of the word is one who looks into "the perfect law of liberty and continues in it" (1:25). Presumably, "the perfect law of liberty" means the moral law embodied in the Ten Commandments and fulfilled through Jesus

Christ, and the doer of the word being the one who looks into the Word of God and acts upon what he sees there. James' graphic example of the doer of the word is the person who "visits orphans and widows in their trouble" and remains unpolluted by the world (1:27).

Show not Partiality

Believers in the Lord Jesus Christ must not show partiality. If a finely dressed person and a shabbily dressed person come into the church [James said synagogue, another indication of the early date of the letter], do not direct the rich person to a better place to sit than the poor person. In doing so, you dishonor the poor person and become a judge with evil thoughts. "Has God not chosen the poor of this world to be rich in faith and heirs of the kingdom which He promised those who love Him" (2:5) ? James believes that showing partiality violates what he calls the royal law of love: "You shall love your neighbor as yourself" (Lev. 19:18). He goes on to say, "if you show partiality, you commit sin, and are convicted by the law as transgressors, for whoever shall keep the whole law, and yet stumbles in one point, he is guilty of all" (2:9-10). So speak and do as those who are going to be judged by the law that gives mercy, "for judgment is without mercy to the one who has shown no mercy. Mercy triumphs over judgment"(2:13).

Faith without Works, Works without Faith

James is addressing believers and is focusing on how they conduct themselves, what kind of works they produce. The major theme in the letter is that faith without corresponding works is dead. "What does it profit, my brethren, if someone says he has faith but does not have works? Can faith save him" (2:14)? If you know of a brother or a sister who is destitute, without clothing or food, is it sufficient to simply say "go in peace, be warmed and filled," but not give them food and clothing? What is gained? "*Thus, also faith by itself, if it does not have works, is dead*" (2:17).

James says there are not those of faith and those of works. "Show me your faith without works, and I will show you my faith by my works" (2:18). James insists that faith and works are not independent of each other, but that they are interdependent. To illustrate he says that one may say "I believe that there is one God," but even the demon may say that and tremble all the while. James believes faith to be justified by works and gives Abraham as prime example. "Was not Abraham our father justified by works when he offered Isaac his son on the altar? Do you see that faith was working together with his works, and by works faith was made perfect? And the Scripture was fulfilled which says, *'Abraham believed God, and it was accounted to him for righteousness.'* And he was called the friend of God" (2:21-23).

James sees Abraham confirming his faith in offering his son Isaac, the one through whom the covenant promise was to be fulfilled. His faith was not a faith without works. It may seem that James and Paul are at odds on the point of faith and works, for Paul emphasizes the faith factor when referencing Abraham. But Paul is arguing that the law does not save, works do not save; it is belief that saves, it is faith not works. See Romans, chapter four. And Paul points out that Abraham's faith long preceded the law and emphasizes his point by referencing the same Scripture that James references: "Abraham believed God, and it was accounted to him for righteousness" (Gen. 15:6). James is arguing the need for works in confirming faith and emphasizes his point by pointing to Abraham's unmistakably confirmation of his faith through works, the prime example being his placing Isaac on the altar. As Paul argues that works without faith are dead, so James argues that faith without works is dead. James insists that faith must be accompanied by works to be genuine, "for as the body without the spirit is dead, so faith without works is dead" (2:26).

Necessity of Bridling the Tongue

In a sense, believers are teachers in that they should be instructive to non-believers and other believers. Thus, be aware of the tongue for it is the cause of many a stumble and a most difficult thing to control. Yet, it is imperative to control it. Note that by putting bits in the mouth of a horse, we can control this large animal, and that a large ship can be turned by a small rudder. So the tongue is a small part of the body, but can make great boasts as a small fire can kindle a great forest. "The tongue is a fire, a world of iniquity. The tongue is so set among our members that it defiles the whole body and sets on fire the course of nature; and it is set on fire by hell" (3:6). James continues his tongue dissertation saying that man has tamed all kinds of beasts, but that "no man can tame the tongue; it is an unruly evil full of deadly poison" (3:8). With the tongue we bless God and then curse those made in His image. Out of the same mouth comes both blessings and curses, and it should not happen. No doubt, controlling the tongue is a necessary step toward wisdom.

Wisdom and Good Works

If one is wise, "let him show by good conduct that his works are done in the meekness of wisdom" (3:13). If the heart harbors bitterness, envy, and self-seeking, do not boast against truth. That is not wisdom from above, for wisdom "from above is first pure, then peaceable, gentle, willing to yield, full of mercy and good fruits, without partiality and without hypocrisy" (3:18).

Shun the World

James suggests that their quarrels and battles come from their desire for fleshly pleasures. What you get does not satisfy because you ask for the wrong things. You ask for things of self indulgence. He calls them adulterers and adulteresses and asks, "Do you not know that friendship with the world is enmity with God? Whoever therefore wants to be a friend of the world makes himself an enemy of God" (4:4). Lusting after worldly pleasures is spiritual adultery that can be avoided: "Resist the devil and he will flee from you. Draw near to God and He will draw near to you . . . . Humble yourselves in the sight of the Lord and He will lift you up" (4:7-8, 10).

Caution against Slandering and Boasting

James cautions his brethren not to slander one another, for in doing so they presume to judge one another, and in judging one another they presume to judge the law. They should be doers of the law and not judges. Presumably, the law he refers to is the royal law he mentions earlier (see 2:8), the law of love: "You shall love your neighbor as yourself." Sitting in judgment of the law rather than carrying out the law is like faith without works. There is only one Lawgiver and Judge, he tells them, the One able to save and destroy. Thus, who are they to judge their neighbors? And what do they know in order to be able to boast about what they will do tomorrow, "for what is your life? It is a vapor that appears for a little time and then vanishes away" (4:14). Therefore, one should say, "If the Lord wills, we shall live and do this or that" (4:15). Boasting is evil arrogance, but one who knows to do good and does not do it commits a sin, a sin of omission.

Woe to the Rich Exploiters, Patience to the Believers

Presumably, the brethren, the believers were suffering at the hands of the rich, or were wondering why the evil rich were allowed to profit, or both, for James condemns the rich and counsels patience for the believers. "Come now, you rich, weep and howl for your miseries that are coming upon you!" (5:1). He accuses the rich of cheating the laborers of their wages and living in luxury at the laborers' expense, of having condemned and murdered the just who opposed them. But ironically, like a dumb beast they have fattened themselves for the day of slaughter. To the believers, he calls for patience like the farmer who patiently waits for the harvest and then assures them that judgment is at hand: "Behold, the Judge is standing at the door" (5:9).

Patience and Prayer

Keep the prophets who spoke for the Lord in mind, how they suffered with patience. Recall the perseverance of Job and the end intended by the Lord, how He was merciful. Those are blessed who endure. Then there is a word of caution about swearing by oath, not by heaven or by earth. "But let your 'Yes' be 'Yes,' and your 'No' be "No,' lest you fall into judgment" (5:12). James is most insistent against judging seeing it as leading to presumptuousness on the part of man who needs to focus on obeying God, especially the "royal law" of loving neighbor as self, and doing that requires good works. If one is suffering, let the person pray. If one is cheerful, let the person sing hymns. If one is sick, call the elders to anoint the person and pray over him. "Confess your trespasses to one another, and pray for one another, that you may be healed. The effective, fervent prayer of a righteous man avails much" (5:16). Elijah is given as a prime example of the power of prayer.

And so James ends the letter on this note of patience and prayer and works, and last mentioning a most excellent work, that of turning someone back who has wandered from the truth; turning "a sinner from the error of his way will save a soul from death and cover a multitude of sins" (5:20).

James Poetic Summary
Faith without Works

Which James authored the epistle by that name is left to conjecture and scholarly fuss
Maybe James the apostle or James leader of the Jerusalem church and brother to Jesus
Both knowing and well known believers of authority capable of instructing brethren abroad
Both knowing and committed believers who would want to counsel against all spiritual fraud
And it is known that James leader of the Jerusalem church chaired their first Council decisive:
Whether circumcision a necessary prerequisite for Gentile converts or whether caveat divisive.

Some scholars claim to recognize stylistic affinity between the epistle and the Jerusalem Council
For the speech of James the Council leader is recorded in Acts and there can be scrutinized still.
Whereas, what there is to read concerning James the apostle says Herod Agrippa had him killed
And he had him executed early on making it less likely the apostle got to exercise writing skill
Yet the epistle does seem to have been penned fairly early at least before the Jerusalem Council
For it mentions not Gentile believers; only to Jewish believers scattered abroad it makes appeal.

Now let us conjecture concerning the believers scattered abroad, how related to Stephen's stoning:
After the first martyr fell Jewish Jesus believers began a Jerusalem exodus, exorbitant fear owning

The Jerusalem church on Pentecost born three thousand
strong and adding daily in days to come
Led by Peter and the apostles, the Holy Spirit, and the
Seven strong, this preceding its persecution
Jews from the known world to Jerusalem had come and
thousands believed Jesus the expected One
But many seeing the fate of Stephen and James did not martyr
wish to be and thus exited Jerusalem.

Now let us conjecture that James the leader of the Jerusalem
church circulates epistle instructive
Long distant pastor paternal shepherding through epistle a
scattered flock in foreign regions respective
"A servant of God and of the Lord Jesus Christ to the twelve
tribes which are scattered abroad"
Begins the James epistle, be it James the brother of Jesus or
James the apostle we choose to laud
But author and time frame conjecture end at the point for
prayerful perusal of the epistle to begin
Author and time frame take a back seat as we peruse lines
saying faith without works is dead end.

And we further read that the testing of faith produces
patience, so rail not against trials that come
Let patience run its course, let it have its perfect work that
you may be perfect in suffering done
"Blessed is the man who endures temptation," says James,
"for when proven the crown receives
The crown of life the Lord has promised to everyone who
loves Him and in Him truly believes."
Thus, for believers trial is reality whether in Jerusalem or
whether in lands across desert and sea
And let there be no misconstruing from whence trial comes,
think not God, think Satan and "me."

A person is tempted when drawn away by his own desires
and then "when desire is conceived

It gives birth to sin, and sin when full-grown brings forth
death; know this and be not deceived."
James' epistle at times may remind the reader of O. T.
wisdom writings, Proverbs for example
Where gems of wisdom packaged in memorable statements
succinct serve to guide the people.
Certainly, James seeks to guide his people telling them that
every perfect gift comes from above
From "the Father of lights, with whom there is no variation or
turning," there only steadfast love.

And this Father of lights "brought us forth by the world of
truth that we may first fruits be"
That these early Jewish believers may be the first fruits
promising a fuller harvest yet to see
But the harvest will not come without work and wisdom: be
swift to hear and slow to speak
"Receive with meekness the implanted word, which is able to
save your souls if you so seek"
You must be both a hearer of the word and a doer; otherwise
it is like looking in the mirror
And then going away and forgetting what you are like; hearer
and doer constitute superior.

"The doer of the word looks into the perfect law of liberty
and continues in it consistently then"
Presumably, "the perfect law of liberty" is the moral law
embodied in the Commandments Ten
And fulfilled through Jesus Christ, the word being
completed through the Word made flesh
Thus, James instructing that only in the doing of the word
does the hearing and doing mesh.
And in case his abstract theology may not be clear, a concrete
example he throws in
The doer "visits orphans and widows in their troubles and
distances himself from sin."

Then there is the problem of showing partiality, for in Jesus
Christ there is only equality
And James pushes his point on this subject making it
abundantly clear: show no partiality.
Should a finely dressed and a shabbily dressed person enter
the church, do not discriminate
Do not find an exalted seat for the finely dressed and for the
shabbily dressed a lowly seat.
"Has not God chosen the poor to be rich in faith and heirs
to the kingdom, all who love Him?"
In dishonoring the poor you become judge and evil commit,
offending God who loves them.

"In showing partiality you are convicted by the law as
transgressor, for he who keeps the whole law
And stumbles on one point is guilty of all"; know the mercy
deeply embedded in the royal law
The royal law that says, "You shall love your neighbor as
yourself," making mercy supreme
Join with those who are going to be judged by the law that
gives mercy, given at the final scene
Know that mercy over judgment triumphs, love neighbor as
self, and never neighbor demean.
Consistently focusing on Christian conduct James works his
way to the epistle's major theme.

"What does it profit, my brethren, if someone says he has
faith but works he hath not?"
Rhetorical question then follows rhetorical question: "Can
faith save him, what is his lot?"
If you know of a brother or a sister who is destitute without
clothing and with food none
Is it sufficient to say to them, "go in peace, be warmed and
filled, prosper under the sun"?
Wonderful words, but what is gained? "Thus, also faith
without works is dead!"
Faith presupposes love of the Lord and love of the Lord
presupposes a heart led.

James declares there are not those of faith and those of
works, separate entities no
"Show me your faith without works and I will show my faith
by my works, thus so"
For illustration listen, one may say he believes that there is
one God, but so a demon too
And tremble all the while; no, faith is justified by works as
our Abraham was wont to do
Was he, our father, not justified by works when on the altar
he offered his son Isaac?
Was not faith and works working together in this act, and by
works faith made perfect?

Isaac the son through whom the covenant promise was to be
fulfilled, that Abraham knew
Yet, through faith he prepared the altar believing this the
work that God wanted him to do
In this act of faith with works, Scripture was fulfilled,
nothing was amiss
"Abraham believed in God, and it was accounted to him for
righteousness."
Now, are James and the apostle Paul at odds on the faith and
works issue
Since Paul uses the same scriptural quote to clarify the faith
factor, to construe?

The apostle declares that the law does not save, works do not
save, on faith rely
And references Abraham whose faith long preceded the law
given Moses on Sinai
"Abraham believed God, and it was accounted to him for
righteousness," in Genesis read.
As James emphasizes faith without works dead, so Paul
emphasizes works without faith dead.
Paul argues that faith comes through grace not works, see
Romans chapter four
James argues that belief is not faith without works to validate,
need we say more.

Faith demonstrated through good works, yes, and always
done in the spirit of humility
By example believers should teachers be, constantly
monitoring the tongue a necessity
For the tongue, James warns, is cause of many a stumble, an
intractable thing to control
"The tongue is a fire and sets on fire the course of nature,
and it is set on fire by hell bold."
Man can tame all breeds of beasts, but no man can tame the
tongue, full of deadly poison
For out of the mouth come both blessings and curses, hardly
indicative of godly wisdom.

To be wise, show good conduct, show good works done in
the meekness of wisdom
When the heart holds bitterness and envy, do not boast
against truth, bridle the tongue
Pray for that wisdom from above, wisdom peaceable, full of
mercy and partiality none
Shun the world, for friendship with the world is enmity with
God, cast off worldly lust
Lusting after worldly pleasures is spiritual adultery; resist
the devil and he flees from us
Draw near to God and He will draw near to you, humbling
yourself in His sight, a must.

James cautions against slandering one another, for that
presumes judging one another
We should be doers of the law, not judges, not presuming to
judge sister and brother
The law he references is presumably the royal law, the law of
love: love thy neighbor
Love your neighbor as yourself, and remember there is only
one Judge and Lawgiver
The One who is able to save and destroy, who are we to
judge, we the ephemeral?
Can we boast what we will do tomorrow, should we not say,
"If it be God's will"?

Hear this counsel concerning the rich and powerful
exploiting the impoverished poor
To the poor patience, to the exploiters warning, "Behold, the
Judge stands at the door.
The royal law of loving neighbor as self guides, patience with
prayer propels
Job perseveres and prevails, Elijah, facing odds enumerable,
prays and prevails
And on this triadic note—patience and prayer and
works—James brings counsel to end
Hoping to turn his hearers from death eternal having
counseled against a multitude of sin.

I Peter Prose Summary Letter Encouraging Scattered Believers

Authorship Questioned

Some scholars have questioned Peter's authorship of the letter claiming that its style is too elegant to have been written by a Galilean fisherman. Though Peter may have had a speaking knowledge of Greek, they reason, he would not have had literary mastery of the language. And they point to the less elegant style of II Peter. The prevailing counter argument notes that Peter acknowledges Silvanus (Silas) as one who helps with the letter (5:12). The Silas that Peter mentions is conjectured to be the prominent leader of the Jerusalem church designated to accompany Paul and Barnabas in delivering the famous circumcision letter from the Jerusalem Council to the church at Antioch, and who later accompanied Paul on his second missionary journey. This Silas, a Jew and a Roman citizen like Paul, was supposedly well educated and, as amanuensis, could have furnished the excellent style of I Peter. Furthermore, it is noted that I Peter echoes the history and terminology of Peter's speeches in the gospels and in Acts.

Time, Place, and Concern

Although time and place of the writing is mostly conjecture, the letter was probably written during the reign of Nero (A.D. 54-68), possibly following the great fire of A.D. 64. Peter identifies the place as Babylon, supposedly a symbolic name for Rome, and addresses the epistle "to the pilgrims of the Dispersion in Pontus, Galatia, Cappadocia, Asia, and Bithynia" (1:1). Concerned about believers in these areas who are experiencing trials and suffering, Peter offers them encouragement and comfort.

Comfort that transcends Trials

Peter reminds his fellow believers of the hope and comfort in knowing that God the Father has offered great mercy and abundant living hope "through the resurrection of Jesus Christ from the dead" (1:3). Belief in the resurrection offers an inheritance incorruptible and eternal and reserved for them in heaven. This is the sustaining comfort in the face of present suffering. Thus, in your faith you can "greatly rejoice, though now for a little while, if need be, you have been grieved by various trials, that the genuineness of your faith . . . may be found to praise, honor, and glory at the revelation of Jesus Christ, whom having not seen you love. Though now you do not see Him, yet believing, you rejoice with joy inexpressible and full of glory, receiving the end of your faith—the salvation of your souls" (1:6-9).

Prophecy Fulfilled

Peter exclaims that the wonder of this salvation is such that the prophets inquired about it and searched for it and even the angels desired to look into it. The Spirit of Christ that was in the prophets told them about Christ, about His sufferings and the glories to follow (e.g., Isa 52:13-53:12). "To them it was revealed that, not to themselves, but to us they were ministering the things which now have been reported to you through those who have preached the gospel to you by the Holy Spirit sent from heaven" (1:12). Peter himself was present and moved to preach on the Day of Pentecost when Christ sent the Holy Spirit. (See Acts 2:14-47, and especially note verse 33.)

Grace and Holiness and Testimony

"Therefore gird up the loins of your mind," exhorts Peter, "be sober, and rest your hope fully upon the grace that is to be brought to you at the revelation of Jesus Christ; as obedient children, not conforming yourselves to the former lusts, as in your ignorance; but as He who called you is holy, you also be holy in all your conduct, because it is written, 'Be holy for I am holy'" (1:13-16). This exhortation, capped by the passage from Leviticus (11:44), is the first of several exhortations throughout the letter addressing the necessity of testifying to the true grace of God.

Live in Reverent Fear

Knowing that the Father judges impartially, conduct yourself in reverent fear in your earthly sojourn. Know that you were not redeemed with corruptible things such as silver and gold "but with the precious blood of Christ, as of a lamb without blemish and without spot" (1:19). And know that Jesus Christ "was foreordained before the foundation of the world, but was manifest in these last times for you who through Him believe in God, who raised Him from the dead and gave Him glory, so that your faith and hope are in God" (1:20-21).

Love One Another and Grow in Salvation

Having been purified through the truth of the Spirit, love one another with a pure heart knowing that you have been born again through the incorruptible word of God. Know that all flesh is as grass and all glory of man as the flower of grass which withers and falls away, but that "the word of the Lord endures forever" (1:25). Love one another putting aside malice and guile and hypocrisy, and "as newborn babes, desire the pure milk of the word, that you may grow thereby" (2:2). Come to the Lord as a living stone rejected by men, but chosen by God as precious, "you also, as living stones, are being built up a spiritual house, a holy priesthood to offer up spiritual sacrifices acceptable to God through Jesus Christ" (2:5). Know that Jesus is the chief cornerstone and that you build on this foundation. He is a stumbling stone for those who do not believe, but the chief cornerstone for those who believe. You who believe "are a chosen people, a royal priesthood, a holy nation, His own special people, that you may proclaim the praises of Him who called you out of darkness into His marvelous light; who once were not a people but are now the people of God who had not obtained mercy but now have obtained mercy" (2:9-10). As in the Old Testament the Israelites were called the chosen people, now in the New Testament believers, Christians, are being called the chosen. Through salvation in Jesus Christ they become the chosen people.

Submit to Civil Authority

Know that while here on earth you are sojourners and pilgrims, heaven is your homeland; therefore, conduct yourselves prudently abstaining from fleshly lusts maintaining honorable conduct so that pagans may not speak of you as evil doers but may see your good works and glorify God. Submit yourselves to civil authority that is set up to punish evil doers and praise those who do good. Do not use "your liberty as a cloak for vice, but as servants of God. Honor all people. Love the brotherhood. Fear God. Honor the king" (2:16-17).

Submit to Masters

Servants are to be submissive to their masters whether the master is gentle or harsh. There is no credit in being punished for your faults, but patiently enduring punishment undeserved is commendable before God. For in doing so you are following the example of Christ who when reviled did not revile in return, "but committed Himself to Him who judges righteously; who Himself bore our sins in His own body on the tree, that we, having died to sins, might live for righteousness—by whose stripes you were healed" (2:24-25).

Husband and Wife Relationship

Wives are to be submissive to husbands even though the husband may not be a believer, for submissive, chaste conduct may lead the husband to believe. Wives must not concentrate on outward beauty involving fine apparel, rich adornments, or hair arrangement; their concern should be with inward beauty involving a gentle and quiet loving spirit. Sarah, wife of Abraham, is cited as an exemplary wife. Husbands are counseled to be understanding, "giving honor to the wife, as the weaker vessel, and as being heirs together of the grace of life, that your prayers may not be hindered" (3:7).

Relationships Generally

Everyone should have compassion for every other loving one another as brothers, courteous and respectful, never returning evil for evil or reviling for reviling remembering always that you are called to be follows of Jesus Christ. And as an aide for keeping proper conduct in mind, Peter quotes lines from a Psalm (34:12-16). "He who would love life / And see good days, / Let him seek peace and pursue it. / For the eyes of the Lord are on the righteous, / And His ears are open to their prayers; / But the face of the Lord is against those who do evil."

Suffering for Doing Good

"Even if you should suffer for righteousness' sake you are blessed" (3:14), so fear not threats or be troubled as the prophet Isaiah counseled. Keep the Lord in your heart and with meekness and fear always be ready to defend when asked the reason for the hope that is in you. And keep a clear conscience that those reviling you for good behavior in Christ may be shamed for their slander. "It is better, if it is the will of God, to suffer for doing good than doing evil, for Christ also suffered once for sins, the just and the unjust, that He might bring us to God, being put to death in the flesh but made alive by the Spirit" (3:17-18). And we know that He is at the right hand of God and with all angels and powers and authorities subject to Him. "Therefore, since Christ suffered for us in the flesh, arm yourselves also with the same mind . . . for we have spent enough of our past lifetime in doing the will of the Gentiles [unbelievers]—when we walked in licentiousness, lusts, drunkenness, revelries, drinking parties, and abominable idolatries" (4:1,3).

Love and Suffering

Believing the end is near, Peter again exhorts them to be serious and watchful and to be in prayer and to love one another. "Above all things have fervent love for one another, for love will cover a multitude of sins" (4:8). Be hospitable to one another, and do not grumble. According to your gifts, minister to one another utilizing the talent supplied by God so that He will be glorified. And "do not think it strange concerning the fiery trial which is to try you, as though some strange thing happened to you; but rejoice to the extent that you partake of Christ's sufferings that when His glory is revealed, you may also be glad with exceeding joy" (4:12-13). On the other hand, "let none of you suffer as a murderer, a thief, and evildoer, or as busybody in other people's matters; yet if anyone suffers as a Christian, let him not be ashamed, but let him glorify God in this matter" (4:15-16).

Grace and Humility

Humbly referring to himself as also an elder, Peter exhorts the elders to shepherd their flocks humbly and willingly not by constraint and certainly not for gain, and not as lords but as examples. "And when the Chief Shepherd appears, you will receive the crown of glory that does not fade away" (5:4). The younger people are counseled to submit themselves to the elders, and in turn all should "be submissive to one another, and be clothed in humility" (5:50). Peter then quotes a passage from Proverbs (3:34) to highlight his exhortation: "God resists the proud, / But gives *grace* to the *humble*." Peter's counsel echoes the teaching of Jesus concerning the kind of conduct valued in heaven where the greater the service the higher the marks. "Therefore, humble yourselves under the mighty hand of God, that He may exalt you in due time" (5:6).

All the while beware of that old adversary the devil who "walks about like a roaring lion, seeking whom he may devour" (5:8). Though resisting evil may very well cause suffering, remain steadfast knowing that believers everywhere suffer with you. "May the God of all grace, who called us to His eternal glory by Christ Jesus, after you have suffered a while, perfect, establish, strengthen, and settle you" (5:10). The believer may expect suffering while earthly bound, but by the grace of God the faithful servants will share in the eternal glory of their Savior, Jesus Christ.

I Peter Poetic Summary Letter Encouraging Scattered Believers

Some scholars say the style of this letter too elegant for a
Galilean fisherman
Though Greek he might be able to speak no cultured literary
style command
And then note the second letter's rough style as more likely
Peter's brand
Yet they disregard Peter's acknowledgement Silvanus lent a
helping hand
Surely Silvanus who accompanied Paul and Barnabas from
Jerusalem to Antioch
Carriers of the Council's circumcision letter freeing Gentiles
from Judean hock.

Surely the same Silas accompanying Paul on his second
missionary journey
Obviously an educated man who as amanuensis could for
Peter the stylist be
The letter's content and Peter's history in the gospels and
Acts, no discrepancy.
Therefore, let us join with those scholars accepting the letter
as Peter's primarily
And think of it in the time frame of Nero's rule, most likely
around 65 A.D.
The place is Rome though referred to as Babylon for purposes
symbolically.

The letter's recipients reside in Galatia, Cappadocia, Asia,
Bithynia and Pontus

Recipients he calls pilgrims of the Dispersion and addresses
their need for solace
Reminding them that God the Father offers great mercy and
living hope abundant
Through the resurrection of Jesus Christ: death defeated,
faith forever triumphant.
Belief brings inheritance incorruptible and eternal, heavenly
reservation assured
Though trials presently persist, take comfort knowing
salvation forever secured.

Within trial lies the genuineness of your faith that glories in
the resurrection sure
Though you do not see Him, yet believing, you rejoice with
joy inexpressibly pure
You rejoice full of glory receiving the end of your faith:
salvation that sustains the soul
The wonder of this salvation the prophets old inquired and
even angels desire to unfold.
The Spirit of Christ in the prophets told them of the Christ
to be, first suffering then glory
To them revealed that not to themselves but to us they were
ministering, relating our story.

They were revealing the things which have been reported to
you by ministers of the gospel
Those guided by the Holy Spirit sent from heaven, and first
on the apostles at Pentecost fell
In Jerusalem they awaited, by Jesus commanded, there the
Spirit of the Trinity to receive
The Holy Spirit come to comfort and instruct, the Son
sacrificed taking an earthly reprieve.
The Word made flesh ascended, the Spirit guides the
apostles in their earthly acts of faith
Witnessing first in Jerusalem then Judea and Samaria and
then on to the ends of the earth.

As in sermon so Peter in epistle exhorts, here saying "gird up the loins of your mind
Be sober, and rest your hope fully upon the grace brought you because of Jesus divine
As obedient children give up all your former lusts, for He who called you is holy
You also be holy in all your conduct; know it is written, 'Be holy for I am holy.'"

This exhortation becomes the first of several concerning testimony to the true grace of God
Know the Father judges impartially and conduct yourself in reverent fear gets second nod
Know you are redeemed by the blood of Christ as lamb without blemish and without spot
Know that Christ was foreordained before creation but manifest in these last times, our lot
Our lot that through Him we believe in God who raised Him from the dead and glorified
That we might believe placing in Him our faith, Jesus Christ resurrected though crucified.

Having been purified through the truth of the Spirit, love one another with heart pure
Knowing that you have been born again through the incorruptible word of God sure
Know that all flesh is as grass and all glory of man as the flower of grass that withers away,
Yet know that the word of the Lord endures forever, endures today, tomorrow and in that day
Know to love one another putting aside malice and guile and hypocrisy, and as babes new
Desire the pure milk of the word that you may grow thereby, may thrive thereby, all of you.

Come to the Lord as a living stone rejected by men, but chosen by God as a precious one

A building stone for a house spiritual and a priesthood to
offer up sacrifice perfectly done
Know that Christ Jesus is the chief cornerstone; know that
He is the foundation to build on
He the stumbling stone for the believer not, but the chief
cornerstone for the believer known
Know that you who believe are a chosen people, a royal
priesthood, a holy nation, His own
You are His special people to proclaim Him who called you
out of darkness into the dawn.

You who were once not a people are now the people of God,
you having mercy obtained
As in the O. T. Israelites were called the chosen people, so in
the N. T. believers the same
Through the salvation in Jesus Christ believers become the
chosen people, chosen to proclaim
Chosen to proclaim the gospel to the ends of the earth,
chosen to praise the Savior's holy name
But know that while on earth you are sojourners and
pilgrims, that heaven is your homeland
And thereby your conduct must exemplary be that the
unbeliever may profit from your stand.

Submit yourselves to civil authority set up to punish evil
doers and to praise doers of good
Do not use your liberty as a cloak for vice but as servants of
God who honor all as should
Servants be submissive to masters whether they govern with
hand gentle or hand heavy
Being punished for faults brings no credit, but punishment
undeserved, a different levy
Then you follow the example of Christ who when reviled
returned it not, retaining love
He committed Himself to the One who judges righteously, to
the heavenly Father above.

Wives, be submissive to your husbands even though some
may not believers be
Yet may be won without words when your purity and
reverence they daily see
Seeing you concentrate not on outward beauty, style
frivolous, but inward ornament
Seeing beauty radiated by a gentle and quiet spirit emulating
the Lord's temperament.
Likewise husbands show your wives proper honor and
respect, though they weaker be
You are partners in the gracious gift of life and must through
prayer strive for harmony.

Everyone, have compassion for every other, loving one
another as sisters and brothers.
Rather than return evil for evil return good for evil
demonstrating God's grace to others.
You are called to be followers of Christ Jesus which means
manifesting conduct exemplary
Consequently, commit this Psalm to mind, a steadfast guide
whatever circumstance may be:

"He who would love life and see good days let him refrain
his tongue from evil speech
And his lips from speaking guile; let him turn away from evil
and good never breach
Let him seek peace and pursue it for the eyes of the Lord are
on the righteous one
And His ears open to their prayers, but the face of the Lord is
against all evil done."

Fear not to suffer for righteousness sake, for in so doing you
are by the Lord blessed
Keep Him in your heart and with meekness and fear ever
ready to suffer and profess
Thus, a conscience clear when reviled will shame those who
slander you for behavior good

Know it better to suffer for doing good than doing evil, for
you are doing what Jesus would
And He though put to death in the flesh was made alive by
the Spirit so all believers could
And now sits at the right hand of God with all angels and
powers subject to his power good.

Therefore since Christ suffered for us in the flesh, arm
yourselves also with attitude same
For he who has suffered in his body is with sin done, no
longer ruled by that human bane
No longer willing to walk in licentiousness, in idolatry and
in lust, in transgressions inane
Believers true become earnestly watchful and pray for one
another, prayers of brotherly love
Above all things they show fervent love for each other and
doing so please their Father above
According to their given gifts each ministers to another
thereby glorifying God, for He is love.

Do not think it strange when fiery trial comes, for it is your
chance to partake of Christ's suffering
It is your chance to rejoice when His glory is revealed, joy in
knowing with Him you share offering.
And forget not humility says the apostle addressing the
elders, meekly calling himself an elder too
Shepherd your flocks humbly and willingly, not by constraint
and not ever for gain shepherding do
"And when the Chief Shepherd comes, you will receive the
crown of glory that does not fade away"
Hear passage from Proverbs: "God resists the proud, but gives
grace to the humble." Heed His say.

Then connecting Proverbs with Jesus' first last and last first
paradox, Peter hails humility prime
"Therefore, humble yourselves under the mighty hand of
God that He may exalt you in due time"

Until then beware of Satan, adversary who stalks the earth
seeking whom he may devour
Even so, believers everywhere are resisting evil and in doing
so inevitably suffer their hour
Suffering is sure for those who in faith and humility await
the Second Coming glorious
And whether alive or dead matters not for all believers,
graved or no, rise to meet Jesus.

II Peter Prose Summary
Beware of False Teachers

Authorship Questioned

Some scholars question the authorship of this letter noting that its style is different than the style of I Peter, that it has little historical support, and that its comment on Paul's letters suggests it was written after Peter's lifetime. Other scholars point out that the difference of style between I Peter and II Peter may be the result of Peter's having used a different amanuensis for each letter. He actually mentions that Silvanus (Silas) aided in the writing of the first letter (5:12). As for the time frame of the letter, Peter's reference to Paul's letters (3:15-16), does not presuppose they had become canonical. It is obvious from reading Acts and Galatians that Peter and Paul had early contact with each other, thus Peter may very well have been familiar with Paul's letters long before they were collected and canonized. It may also be noted that Peter witnessed in favor of the stance held by Paul and Barnabas in the circumcision issue adjudicated by the Jerusalem Council (Acts 15).

Actually, there is nothing in the letter that conclusively militates against its being authored by Peter. His claim of apostleship, of having witnessed the Transfiguration (1:17), of Jesus having predicted his untimely demise (1:14), are all recorded in the gospels. See Matthew 17:2 for the Transfiguration and John 21:17-18 for Jesus' prediction of Peter's untimely demise.

Time, Place, and Concern

If I Peter was written around A. D. 64 and Peter was martyred around A. D. 67/68 during the reign of Nero, as tradition has it, a probable date for this second letter is around A. D. 66.

Whereas the first letter was addressed to believers scattered throughout Asia Minor, this letter mentions no specific area but is simply addressed "to those who through the righteousness of our God and Savior Jesus Christ have received a faith as precious as ours" (1:1). It may, however, be inferred that this letter took the same route as the first letter, for near its end Peter says, "dear friends, this is now my second letter to you, [and] I have written both of them as reminders" (3:1).

Neither does Peter identify the place where he composes the letter, not even in symbolic terms as in the first letter where he calls the place Babylon, presumably code name for Rome. And Rome may very well be the location for the composition of this second letter.

Regardless of the time and place of its composition, this letter is concerned primarily with false teachers and evil doers within the church. Judging from Peter's response, the false teachers and evil doers addressed were probably persons of Gnostic persuasion who were distorting the gospel and casting doubt on the divinity of Jesus and on the validity of the promised Second Coming.

Reviewing the Basic Gospel Teachings

Before focusing on the false teachers and evil doers, Peter reminds the churches what they believe as purveyors of the gospel, as followers of Jesus Christ. Jesus had revealed to His apostles divine truth and in this epistle Peter, the premier apostle, reviews the basics of this truth with the churches receiving the epistle: "His [Jesus Christ] divine power has given us all things that pertain to life and godliness through the knowledge of Him who called us by glory and virtue, by which have been given to us exceedingly great and precious promises, that through these you may be partakers of the divine nature, having escaped the corruption that is in the world through lust. But also for this very reason, giving all diligence, add to your faith virtue, to virtue knowledge, to knowledge self-control, to self-control perseverance, to perseverance godliness, to godliness brotherly kindness, and to brotherly kindness love. If these things are yours and abound, you will be neither barren nor unfruitful in the knowledge of our Lord Jesus Christ. He who lacks these things is shortsighted, even to blindness, and has forgotten that he was purged from his old sins. Therefore, brethren, be even more diligent to make your calling and election sure, for if you do these things you will never stumble; ultimately, you will receive an abundant welcome into the kingdom of our Lord Jesus Christ" (1:3-11).

Peter is careful to point out that the essentials "to life and godliness" come through the divine power of Jesus Christ and that it is through His promises that we become "partakers of the divine nature." Thus, faith vested in the acts and teachings of Jesus Christ as witnessed by the apostles is the basis of salvation. Any distortion of these is distortion of truth. And distortion is what is being advocated and practiced by the false teachers and evil doers.

Need to Remind them of the Gospel and to Preserve the Gospel

Peter says though they know these things he feels the need to remind them and to continue reminding them "knowing that shortly I must put off my tent as our Lord Jesus Christ showed me" (1:14). And then he makes a mystifying statement saying, "Moreover I will be careful to ensure that you always have a reminder of these things after my decease" (1:15). The intent is clear: since he, a witness to the acts and teachings of Jesus Christ, will soon not be around to expound and confirm these truths, the apostle intends, in some manner, to preserve the true story he has witnessed. The mystery, of course, is how. Is he setting down the gospel story or, as has been conjectured, is he telling the story to John Mark who is recording it? Mark's gospel is believed to have been based on Peter's preaching.

Whatever the case, the apostle recognizes the need to preserve the gospel story as witnessed to serve as a bulwark against distortions by false teachers, "for we did not follow cunningly devised fables when we made known to you the power and coming of our Lord Jesus Christ, but were eyewitnesses of His majesty" (1:16). The gospel the apostle preaches is based on an eye witness account of having seen the acts of Jesus, of having heard His words, and of having heard, on the holy mountain of the transfiguration, God the Father glorify Jesus the Son by voicing His confirmation and approval: "This is My beloved Son, in whom I am well pleased" (1:17). These truths needed to be preserved as witnessed, and so they were, perhaps even better than Peter imagined, not merely in one telling but in four: Mark, Matthew, Luke, and John.

Truth of the Gospel and Prophecy of Scripture versus False Prophets and False Teachers

The transfiguration reference serves as a link between the gospel and the Scripture [Old Testament] and between true teaching and false teaching. At the transfiguration Moses and Elijah join Jesus as He is transfigured, symbolically revealing the law and the prophets fulfilled in the Son, and thus the voice of God from heaven confirming both the prophecy and the gospel. Peter's point is that the true prophecy of the Scripture is confirmed and fulfilled in the coming of the Son and that he, as apostle, is an eye witness to this truth.

Furthermore, he declares that "prophecy of the Scripture is not given to private interpretation, for it never came by the will of man, but holy men of God spoke as they were moved by the Holy Spirit" (1:21). Therefore, neither the prophecy of the Scripture nor the gospel story is cunningly devised fables as false teachers would have one believe. But as there were false prophets among the people of old, so "there will be false teachers among you, who will secretly bring in destructive heresies . . . and many will follow their destructive ways and bring the way of truth into dispute" (2:1-2). Thus, Peter prefaces his attack on the false teachers and evil doers.

God Does Not Spare the Unjust

In the long term God will not tolerate false teachers and evil doers Peter insists and cites examples as evidence: His casting the rebellious angels into hell there in chains of darkness to await judgment, His destroying by flood the ungodly ancient world of Noah's time saving only the righteous Noah and his family, His turning to ashes the cities Sodom and Gomorrah as example to those who would live ungodly lives saving only the righteous Lot. Thus, "the Lord knows how to deliver the godly out of temptations and to reserve the unjust under punishment for the day of judgment, especially those who walk according to the flesh in the lust of uncleanness and despise authority" (2:9-10).

Peter reminds the churches to be ever vigilant against false teachers and evil doers describing those at work in the churches he addresses. "These men are springs without water and mists driven by a storm. Blackest darkness is reserved for them. For they mouth empty, boastful words and, by appealing to the lustful desires of sinful human nature, they entice people who are just escaping from those who live in error. They promise them freedom, while they themselves are slaves of depravity—for a man is a slave to whatever has mastered him. If they have escaped the corruption of the world by knowing our Lord and Savior Jesus Christ and are again entangled in it and overcome, they are worse off at the end than they were at the beginning. It would have been better for them not to have known the way of righteousness, than to have known it and then to turn their backs on the sacred command that was passed on to them. Of them the proverbs are true: 'A dog returns to its vomit and a sow that is washed goes back to her wallowing in the mud'" (2:17-22).

"These men," these false teachers and evil doers may very well have been a type of early Gnostics distorting the gospel by claiming to possess special, esoteric knowledge. By taking an antinomian view that only the spirit mattered, they declare themselves free of any moral law and thereby use their bodies as they please. And by mouthing their distorted view they appeal to man's sinful nature thereby leading prior believers astray, especially the weaker ones. Outraged, Peter condemns them saying, "they are blots and blemishes, reveling in their pleasures while they feast with you. With eyes full of adultery, they never stop sinning; they seduce the unstable; they are experts in greed—an accursed brood" (2:13-14)! They are false teachers who "blaspheme in matters they do not understand" (2:12); despising authority, they are "bold and arrogant . . . [and] not afraid to slander celestial beings" (2:10). But they will receive their just deserts declares Peter: "These men blaspheme in matters they do not understand. They are like brute beasts, creatures of instinct, born only to be caught and destroyed, and like beasts they too will perish" (2:12).

Second Reminder

This is my second letter to you, says Peter, "both as reminders to stimulate you into wholesome thinking," to stimulate you "to recall the words spoken in the past by the holy prophets and the command given by our Lord and Savior through your apostles" (3:1-2). He tells them they must understand that in the last days there will come scoffers "scoffing and following their own evil desires" (3:3). The scoffers will question the Lord's promised return tauntingly asking where is He? But be not deceived counsels Peter. Keep in mind that "with the Lord a day is like a thousand years, and a thousand years are like a day" (3:8).

Warning: Destruction by Fire the Second Time

Peter goes on to deliver a little prophetic eschatology. It was by God's word that the earth was created out of the waters, and later because of man's wholesale evil the earth was deluged and destroyed by His word, and "by the same word the present heavens and earth are reserved for fire, being kept for the day of judgment and destruction of ungodly men . . . the heavens will disappear with a roar; the elements will be destroyed by fire, and the earth and everything in it will be laid bare" (3:10). Let this warning be a bulwark against the scoffers and a reminder of the kind of people you ought to be. "You ought to live holy and godly lives as you look forward to the day of God and speed its coming, [for] we are looking forward to a new heaven and a new earth, the home of righteousness" (3:11-13).

Heed Our Warning

"So then, dear friends, since you are looking forward to this, make every effort to be found spotless, blameless and at peace with the Lord. Bear in mind that His patience means salvation, just as our dear brother Paul also wrote you with the wisdom that God gave him . . . therefore, dear friends, be on your guard so that you may not be carried away by the error of lawless men and fall from your secure position. But grow in the grace and knowledge of our Lord and Savior Jesus Christ" (3:14-15, 17-18).

II Peter Poetic Summary
Beware of False Teachers

Some scholars question whether Peter actually wrote this
second letter ascribed to him
Its style differing from letter one and its controversial time
frame raise doubts for them
But style difference may merely be amanuensis difference,
the hand of Silas in letter one
While no amanuensis mentioned in the second letter
supports conjecture there was none
Or if there were it was not Silas; either way the style of letter
two would surely differ some.
And the reference to Paul's letters need not presuppose a later
time frame, one Peter beyond.

Any reader of Acts can readily discern that Peter and Paul to
each other are known well
Hear Peter witness for Paul in the circumcision issue
adjudicated by the Jerusalem Council.
Knowing Paul's mission Peter surely knew of his letters long
before their canonization
And consequently referenced them in this epistle penned
prior to his Nero martyrization.
Actually nothing in the letter conclusively countervails
against its belonging to Peter the apostle
Even the Transfiguration and martyrdom prediction
references can be confirmed by gospel.

If Peter's first letter were written around A. D. 64 and he
were martyred around A. D. 68
Victim of the nefarious Nero, letter two belongs between, A.
D. 66 being a probable date.

Letter one is specifically addressed to those believers
scattered throughout Asia Minor
Also letter two implicitly for therein he says "this is my
second letter and both reminders are"
Reminders of who they are and whose they are and of their
Lord's great commission
This from Peter penned, the foremost apostle walking with
Jesus from baptism to ascension.

From whence Peter penned letter two he does not say but
probably the same place as letter one
Which he cryptically called Babylon meaning Rome where
in these his latter years he is undone
Regardless of place or time, the letter primarily concerns
false teacher and evil doer enmity
Most probably persons of Gnostic persuasion casting doubt
on the Parousia and Jesus' divinity
But before concentrating on the evil at hand Peter reviews
the churches' role once more:
They are followers of Jesus Christ and as such must be vigilant
against all insidious lore.

"It is through Jesus that divine power has given us all things
that pertain to life and godliness"
Says Peter, "and through knowledge of Him comes
exceedingly great and precious promises
Through which you may become partakers of His divine
nature; therefore, give all diligence:
Add to faith virtue, to virtue knowledge, to knowledge
self-control, to self-control perseverance
To perseverance godliness, to godliness brotherly kindness,
to brotherly kindness love
If these things are yours and abound, you will be neither
barren nor unfruitful thereof
For you have the knowledge essential, the knowledge of our
Lord Jesus Christ above."

"He who lacks these things is amiss having forgotten he was
purged for his old sins
Therefore, my brethren, be ever diligent in making your
calling sure, make amends
For in doing so you thereby assure your welcome into
Christ's kingdom to come."
Thus, the apostle affirms: the essentials of life come through
Christ, no other One.
Faith vested in the teachings of Jesus as witnessed by the
apostles is the only salvation:
Know then that the acts of the false teachers and the evil doers
are acts of abomination.

Though they know these things Peter feels need to remind
them and continue reminding them
For the apostle knows he "must shortly put off his tent" as
the risen Jesus had revealed to him
And thereby makes a mystifying statement saying, "moreover
I will be careful to ensure
That you will always have a reminder of these things after
my decease"—but how procure?
Therein the mystery, the intent so clear the method
unmentioned causing conjecture to soar:
How can this prime witness to Jesus' acts and teachings
continue refuting all fallacious lore?

Is this apostle, perceiving death nearby, intent on patently
penning for posterity the gospel story?
Tradition has it Mark's gospel comes from Peter's preaching
and witnessing to the Lord's glory
Could it be that Peter knows Mark his associate is shaping
the story's core for circulation and more
Most say Mark furnishes the foundation for Matthew and
Luke and thereby aligns three of the four
The so called synoptic gospels that along with John's round
out the gospel story for all times
Thus, Peter's mystifying statement may cryptic prophecy be
becoming clear as time unwinds.

Whatever the case the apostle recognizes the need to
preserve the gospel story as witnessed
To saliently serve as bulwark against distortions false teacher
fostered and by them finessed
"For we did not follow cunningly devised fables," says Peter,
"when we made known to you
The power and coming of our Lord Jesus Christ, but were
eyewitnesses of His majesty true."
The gospel the apostle preaches is based on eye witness
account of having seen Jesus' act
Having witnessed, having seen, and having heard God at the
Transfiguration confirm fact.

"This is My beloved Son . . . listen to Him," commands the
Father at Transfiguration
Watching and witnessing are three chosen apostles: Peter,
James and John, each one.
Peter perceives these truths imperative must be penned to
preserve and so they were
No doubt surpassing the apostle's perception, not once
recorded but four times occur.
Peter's Transfiguration reference serves to link the gospel
story to the Scripture old
True teaching of the old linked to true teaching of the new
exposing the false twofold.

Moses and Elijah join Jesus at Transfiguration for law and
prophecy in the Son are fulfilled
And the voice of God forever confirms condemning all
teaching to the contrary as pure evil
Scripture is fulfilled in the coming of the Son and the
apostle Peter to this truth is eye witness
Furthermore, "prophecy of the Scripture is not given to
private interpretation, to man's guess
It never came by will of man, but holy men of God spoke as
they were moved by the Holy Spirit
Neither prophecy of Scripture or of Gospel is cunningly
devised fables as false teachers declare it.

"As there were false prophets among the people of old so
among you there will false teachers be
They will secretly bring in destructive heresies and many will
follow these destructionists blindly
Bringing truth into dispute," says the apostle prefacing his
false teacher/evil doer alert.
He warns that God will not long tolerate evil doers, finding
evidence in Scripture to assert:
Did He not turn to ashes licentious cities Sodom and
Gomorrah—does evil not reap His outrage?
Did God not cast the rebellious angels into Hell, and destroy
the ungodly world of Noah's age?

"And does not God the righteous save, consider Noah from
flood and Lot from fiery Sodom?
He knows how to rescue the godly and how to hold the
unrighteous for judgment day to come
Those who walk according to the flesh in the lust of
uncleanness and who authority despise
These false teachers are springs without water, mists driven
by storm, fountains of lies
And blackest darkness awaits them for their empty, boastful
words appeal to lustful human nature
They entice people who live dangerously close to error,
through promise of freedom they ensnare."

"Yet they themselves are slaves of depravity, for a man is slave
to what ever has mastered him, amen
And those having escaped the corruption of this world by
knowing our Savior Jesus Christ, but then
Again becoming entangled in this world and overcome are
worse off at the end than at the beginning
It would have been better for them not to have known than
to have known and knowing turn again
For turning their backs on the sacred command passed on to
them, the Savior they did not follow
Of them the proverb is true, 'a dog returns to its vomit; a
washed sow returns to her mud wallow.'"

These false teachers and evil doers whom Peter condemns
may well have been a type of early Gnostic
Who distorted the gospel claiming to possess special
knowledge, by taking an antinomian view toxic:
Since only the spirit mattered they were free of moral law
and could use their bodies in whatever way.
By mouthing their distorted view they appeal to man's sinful
nature thus leading prior believers astray.
Peter condemns: "they are blots and blemishes, reveling in
their pleasures while with you they feast
Eyes full of adultery they never stop sinning; they seduce the
unstable being experts in greed—beasts."

"They, an accursed brood, are arrogant false teachers who
blaspheme in matters they do not understand
They are brute beasts, creatures of instinct, born only to be
caught and destroyed, they cannot stand."
Thereafter, Peter says, "this is my second letter, both
reminders to stimulate you into thinking righteous
That you might recall the words past spoken by the holy
prophets and commands given by Lord Jesus
Given through the apostles," and he their apostle tells them
that in the last days scoffers will come
Scoffers following their own evil desires questioning the
Lord's promised return, predicting none.

"Be not deceived, with the Lord a day is like a thousand
years and a thousand years a day,"
Says Peter providing a succinct eschatological prophecy as
confirmation of the Lord's say.
"It was God's word that created the earth out of the waters,
and later because of man's wholesale evil
God's word destroyed the earth by water; by the same word
the present heavens and earth will quail
Being reserved for fire, being kept for judgment day the
destruction of ungodly men, of violators all
The heavens will disappear; the elements will be destroyed by
fire, wholesale destruction to appall."

"The earth and everything in it will be laid bare," concludes
Peter's prophecy in dramatic dénouement
Then addendum adds, "let this warning be bulwark against
scoffers and timeless reminder to everyone
What kind of people you ought to be: live holy and godly
lives looking forward to the Lord's Day
And speed its coming for with it comes a new heaven and
new earth: new home for those of the Way."
Then Peter exhorts affectionately, "so dear friends, since you
are looking forward to this new home
Strive constantly to be found blameless and at peace with the
Lord whose patience is salvation known."

"Know the patience of our Lord, the delay of our Lord, is
intended opportunity for more to learn of Him
As our dear brother Paul has written to you, so allow not the
untaught to take his words and twist them.
Dear friends, be on guard that you may not by lawless men
be led into error losing your position secure
Grow in the grace and knowledge of our Savior, Lord Jesus
Christ; hold fast His words true and sure."

I John Prose Summary Stand Fast Against False Teachers

Time, Place, Concern

This epistolary sermon, probably written near the end of the first century, sometime between A.D. 85 and 95, is traditionally attributed to the same John who wrote the fourth gospel, the apostle John, brother to James and son of Zebedee. Supposedly, he lived out his latter years at Ephesus ministering to churches in this area of Asia Minor.

John, unlike most authors of New Testament letters, does not identify himself by name. Neither does he identify a specific audience but simply says, "these things we write to you that you may be full" (1:4), probably because he intends the letter to circulate among several churches. Though he does not identify himself by name, the reader who has perused the gospel of John can readily recognize the stylistic affinity between this letter and his gospel.

Concerned with the false teaching taking place, John reminds the congregations that there is one true gospel, the one that was from the beginning taught by the apostles, eye witnesses to the words and acts of the Lord Jesus Christ. After reviewing the basics of the true gospel taught by the apostles, he warns the churches that the Antichrist is coming and that "even now many antichrists have come, by which we know that it is the last hour" (2:18). Thus, the letter is both warning and exhortation.

Who Are the False Teachers?

The false teachers, the antichrists, to whom John refers appear to be early proponents of Gnosticism, a heresy that plagued Christianity through its first two centuries. Viewing spirit as totally good and matter as totally evil, the Gnostics questioned the incarnation, thus casting doubt on the divinity of Jesus. Cerinthus, an influential Gnostic and contemporary of John, conjectured that the divine spirit entered Jesus at his baptism and left him at the cross. Tradition reports that John upon entering a bathhouse in Ephesus and learning that Cerinthus was within cried out, "let us flee lest this bathhouse falls upon us." The anecdote rings true for not only is this letter a strong refutation of Gnostic teaching but so is his gospel in which, exercising great rhetorical skill, he affirms that the Son, the Word, was present at the beginning and that the Word was with God and that the Word was God (divine) and that the Word became flesh (Jesus Christ) and dwelled among us. See John 1: 1-14.

Furthermore, the dualistic view of Gnostics that spirit was totally good and that matter was totally evil led them to the heretical stance that the body (matter) could engage in licentiousness without harm to the spirit, a view that condoned rampant immorality. Since matter was the evil, the breaking of God's laws was of no consequence; esoteric knowledge (gnosis) led to salvation not faith through Jesus Christ. It is hardly surprising that John calls these false teachers antichrists.

True Gospel, True Fellowship

Hoping to thwart these antichrists, John addresses his "little children" the congregations of the churches where he and possibly other apostles have taught the gospel as they had received it from the Lord Jesus Christ. He knows that only if they believe and hold fast to this the true gospel can they experience the fellowship of full joy. They must hold fast to "that which was from the beginning, which we have heard, which we have seen with our eyes, which we have looked upon, and our hands have handled, concerning the Word of life . . . . that which we have seen and heard we declare to you, that you also may have fellowship with us; and truly our fellowship is with the Father and with His Son Jesus Christ. And these things we write to you that your joy may be full" (1:1-4). John wishes to establish there is only one true message: the message the apostles heard from Jesus Christ.

Reviewing the Message

"This is the message which we heard from Him and declare to you, that God is light and in Him is no darkness at all. If we say we have fellowship with Him, and walk in darkness, we lie and do not practice the truth. But if we walk in the light as He is the light, we have fellowship with one another, and the blood of Jesus Christ His Son cleanses us from all sin. If we say that we have no sin, we deceive ourselves, and the truth is not in us. If we confess our sins, He is faithful and just to forgive us our sins and to cleanse us from all unrighteousness. If we say we have not sinned, we make Him a liar and the truth is not in us. My little children, these things I write to you, that you may not sin. And if anyone sins, we have an Advocate with the Father, Jesus Christ, the righteous. And He Himself is the propitiation for our sins, and not for ours only but also for the whole world" (1:5-2:1).

John makes it quite clear that all are sinners and can only be cleansed through the blood of Jesus Christ, God's Son. Forgiveness of sin comes through faith in Jesus Christ, as taught by the apostles. God is light and has revealed His light through His Son. Those who accept this through faith walk in His light, those who do not walk in darkness. And those who teach otherwise are false teachers, antichrists. This is the message John sends to several church congregations, whom the elderly apostle affectionately calls "my little children." They are children in faith and like the children of Israel prone to be led astray.

The Test for Knowing God

How do we know that we know Him? John says we know Him if we keep His commandments: "He who says, 'I know Him,' and does not keep His commandments is a liar, and the truth is not in him. But whoever keeps His word, truly the love of God is in him. By this we know that we are in Him" (2:4-5).

John's prescriptive test puts the lie to the Gnostic claim that since matter was the evil the breaking of God's laws was of no consequence; licentiousness, for example, would be of no consequence. The apostle makes it abundantly clear that faith is the only way to know God and that the test of faith is in the following of Jesus. Any other claim for knowing God is false as is the Gnostic claim of secret, esoteric knowledge that connects one's spirit to the Spirit of God.

The Last Hour and the Antichrists

"Little children, it is the last hour; and as you have heard the Antichrist is coming, even now many antichrists have come, by which we know it is the last hour. They went out from us but they are not of us; for if they had been of us, they would have continued with us; but *they went out* that they might be made manifest, that none of them were of us. But you have an anointing from the Holy One, and you know all things. I have not written to you because you do not know the truth, but because you know it, and that no lie is of the truth. *Who is a liar but he who denies that Jesus is the Christ? He is antichrist who denies the Father and the Son.* Whoever denies the Son does not have the Father either; he who acknowledges the Son has the Father also. Therefore let that abide in you which you heard from the beginning. If what you heard from the beginning abides in you, you also will abide in the Son and in the Father. And this is the promise that He has promised us—eternal life. *These things I have written to you concerning those who try to deceive you*" (2:18-26).

John stresses the urgency of the situation in referring to the time frame as "the last hour," a reference to the nearness of the second coming of Christ as indicated by the prevalence of the false teachers denying Christ. There seems to have been a common belief that an Antichrist would assume power in "the last hour" but would be swept from power by Christ's second coming. Though John is the only writer who calls him the Antichrist, Paul's "man of lawlessness" fills the role (II Th 2:3). It sounds as if both are espousing common apostolic belief.

Whatever the case of the Antichrist concept, it is clear that John is warning his "little children" to stand fast in their belief in the gospel as heard from the beginning and not to be deceived by the new group, presumably Gnostics, who are spreading the deception that belief in Jesus is not the way to salvation.

Only Those Born of God Overcome Sin

"He who sins is of the devil, for the devil has sinned from the beginning. For this purpose the Son of God was manifested, that He might destroy the works of the devil. Whoever has been born of God does not sin [will not be a habitual sinner], for His seed remains in him; and he cannot sin because he has been born of God. In this the children of God and the children of the devil are manifest: Whoever does not practice righteousness is not of God, nor is he who does not love his brother, for this is the message that you heard from the beginning, that we should love one another" (3:8-11). John is probably responding to the view held by certain Gnostics that the indulgence of fleshly pleasure was of no consequences since only the spirit mattered. Certainly, he is responding to what constitutes righteousness: the example of Jesus Christ. And only through belief in Jesus Christ can one be born of God and only can those born of God, the children of God, overcome sin.

How We Know God Abides in Us

"And this is His commandment: that we should believe on the name of His Son Jesus Christ and love one another, as He gave us commandment. Now those who keep His commandments abide in Him, and He in them. And by this we know that He abides in us, by the Spirit whom He has given us" (3:23-24). Believe in Jesus Christ and follow the Holy Spirit sent to guide believers.

Beware of False Prophets and False Spirits

"Beloved, do not believe every spirit, but test the spirits, whether they are of God; because many false prophets have gone out into the world. *By this you know the Spirit of God: Every spirit that confesses that Jesus Christ has come in the flesh is of God, and every spirit that does not confess that Jesus Christ has come in the flesh is not of God.* And this is the spirit of the Antichrist, which you have heard was coming, and is now already in the world" (4:1-3). Thus, John prescribes the acid test for prophet or spirit.

God Is Love

"*He who does not love does not know God, for God is love.* In this the love of God was manifested toward us, that God has sent His only begotten Son into the world, that we might live, through Him. In this is love, not that we loved God, but that He loved us and sent His Son to be the propitiation for our sins" (4:8-10). As God loves us so we should love one another. John goes on to explain that he who says he loves God but hates his brother is a liar, for how can he say he hates his brother whom he has seen, yet loves God whom he has not seen? Furthermore, "this commandment we have from Him: that he who loves God must love his brother also" (4:21).

Faith Is Victory

"For whatever is born of God overcomes the world. And this is the victory that has overcome the world—our faith. Who is he who overcomes the world, but he who believes that Jesus is the Son of God" (5:4-5)? Again and again John stresses the divinity of Jesus and that belief in Jesus is the only way to become a child of God. Salvation comes through faith not esoteric knowledge as the Gnostic would have it. Victory over death comes only through faith in Jesus Christ.

Verifying Witnesses

John declares that Jesus came by both water and blood: His ministry was initiated by His baptism and his earthly life and ministry closed with His crucifixion. And witnesses in heaven and on earth verify His divinity and His purpose. "There are three who bear witness in heaven: the Father, the Word, and the Holy Spirit; and these three are one. And there are three that bear witness on earth: the Spirit, the water, and the blood; and these three agree as one" (5:7-8).

Closure and Assurance

In closing, John explains that he has written to these congregations "who believe in the name of the Son of God, that you may know that you have eternal life, and that you may *continue* to believe in the name of the Son of God"(5:13). Furthermore, the apostle assures them "that the Son of God has come and has given us an understanding, that we may know Him who is true; and we are in Him who is true, in His Son Jesus Christ. This is the true God and eternal life" (5:20).

I John Poetic Summary
Stand Fast Against False Teachers

The apostle John, brother of James, son of Zebedee, and author of the non-synoptic gospel
Puts pen to papyrus again taking on Gnostic heretics who intend the gospel story to dispel
Living out his latter days at Ephesus and ministering to churches in that Asia Minor region
As the first century A.D. neared its close and Christianity traveled roads for Roman legion
The aging apostle hearing reviled the gospel story he had witnessed and recorded for all time
Composed epistle for alerting his "little children": beware the heresy denying Jesus as divine.

Preparing his "little children" to reject this heresy he reminds them of what they already know
That there is only one true gospel, the gospel taught by the apostles from the beginning apropos
For the apostles being eye witnesses to the words and deeds of Jesus Christ thereby verify
Verify that the divine Word became flesh and dwelled on earth, any denial an atrocious lie.
"The Antichrist is coming," cries John, "and many antichrists have come already," he warns
"Falsifiers usher in the last hour, but you my children stand secure in the gospel God adorns."

These falsifiers, these antichrists come in the form of early Gnostics to John's vicinity

And viewing spirit as totally good and matter as totally evil
question Jesus' divinity
Also, their dualistic view led to the claim that the body could
engage in licentiousness
Without harm to the spirit, thereby issuing invitation to
transgress without consequence
Alarmed by these threatening Gnostic views the aging
apostle sent his epistle of advice
He exhorts congregations in his churches: hold fast to the
apostolic story of Jesus Christ.

The exhortation includes a review of the apostolic story, the
story they were witness to
"This is the message," says the apostle, "which we heard from
Him and declare to you
God is light and in Him is no darkness at all, if we say we
have fellowship with Him then
And walk in darkness, we lie and do not practice the truth,
but if we walk in the light when
He is the light, we have fellowship with one another and the
blood of Jesus Christ cleanses us
Cleanses us from all sin, but if we say we have no sin we
deceive ourselves denying truth thus."

"If we confess our sins, He is faithful and just to forgive us
our sins and to cleanse us truly
If we say we have not sinned, we make Him a liar and the
truth is not in us, not in us surely
My little children, these things I write you, that you may not
sin, and if anyone transgresses
We have an Advocate with the Father, Jesus Christ, who is
the propitiation for our excesses
And not for our sins only, but for the sins of the whole
world," explains the aging apostle John.
He certifies that all are sinners and can only be cleansed
through the blood of Jesus, God's Son.

As the apostles have taught, forgiveness of sin comes only
through Jesus Christ, faith in Him
This is the message John knows his churches know and the
message he wants secure in them
God is the light and has revealed His light through His Son
and those who believe walk in light
Those who believe not walk in darkness, and teachers who
teach otherwise teach the Antichrist.
This is the message the apostle sends forth to the churches
hoping to keep Gnostic heresy at bay
The congregations he calls "my little children" fearing they,
like the children of Israel, may stray.

The urgency of the situation is stressed in referring to the
time frame as "the last hour"
Presumably John sees the false teachers as signs that the
Antichrist is procuring power
And he is reacting to the belief that the Antichrist would
assume power in the last hour
The last hour being a figurative term for a short time frame
preceding Christ's return
Into this frame falls John's Antichrist and Paul's "man of
lawlessness," evil termed
But this evil power Christ will destroy on His second coming
the faithful to confirm.

Meantime, the faithful must live righteously recognizing sin
and abhorring it
Unlike certain Gnostics who insisted that fleshly indulgence
matters not a whit
That since only the spirit mattered the body was free to take
on what pleased it.
"He who sins is of the devil," says John, "for the devil has
sinned from the beginning
And for this purpose the Son of God was manifested: to the
devil's works put ending
Whoever has been born of God cannot continue sinning
without the Lord offending."

"Whoever does not practice righteousness is not of God, nor
is he who does not love brother
For this is the message that you heard from the beginning,
that we should love one another."
Thus, John denies Gnostic blather about separation of body
and spirit citing Jesus as example
Jesus embodies righteousness and only through His love can
we receive righteousness ample.
When we believe in Jesus Christ and love one another God's
commandment we obey
And doing so we abide in Him, and He in us, this we know by
the Holy Spirit our stay.

"But beloved, do not believe every spirit, test all the spirits,
whether they are of God
Every spirit that confesses that Jesus Christ has come in the
flesh is of God, give nod
Every spirit that confesses not that Jesus Christ has come in
the flesh is not of God
And as the spirit of the Antichrist, which you have heard
was coming, has come to you."
John prescribes the acid test: to believe that Jesus Christ
came in the flesh is spirit true
The spirit that confesses otherwise is of the Antichrist: allow
not this spirit to enter you.

"Furthermore, let it be known that he who does not love
does not know God, for God is love
He sent His only begotten Son that we might live, thereby
manifesting His love from above
In this is love, not that we loved God, but that He loved us
and sent His Son to assume our sin."
The love of God and faith through His Son is the way to
salvation John stresses again and again.
Salvation comes through faith not esoteric knowledge as the
Gnostic would have it
Hear the apostle who bears witness to faith in Jesus Christ as
the only prerequisite.

"Who is he who overcomes the world, but he who believes
that Jesus is the Son of God, amen
Whatever is born of God overcomes the world, and we
overcome the world if on faith we stand."
On this note John closes explaining he has written to his
children who believe in Jesus, Son of God
That they might know they have eternal life and that they
might continue to give to Jesus their nod.
Furthermore, the apostle assures them that the Son of God
has come and has given perception true
"That we may know Him who is true, and that we are in
Him who is true": so let no antichrist undo.

II John Prose Summary
Beware of the Antichrists

Introduction
John's second epistle, like the first, seems to have been written from Ephesus sometime between A.D. 85 and 95. According to tradition the apostle lived out his latter years at Ephesus ministering to churches in this area of Asia Minor.

Referring to himself as "the elder," John addresses this epistle "to the elect lady and her children," the elect lady and her children presumably being a figurative designation for a particular church and its congregation.

This letter, in word count, is the second shortest book in the New Testament, III John being the shortest.

The Letter's Focus
John's second epistle, like the first, is concerned with deceptive teachers who are spreading false doctrine. The apostle calls these falsifiers antichrists and exhorts the church addressed to hold fast to gospel taught by the apostles from the beginning.

Concern Registered in Commendation
From the perspective of an elderly apostle watching over churches founded and grounded in the truth of the gospel as witnessed by the apostles, John says he rejoices greatly having found "*some* of your children walking in the truth, as we received commandment from the Father" (4). However, beginning with the word *some* the apostle registers concern about those who are not walking in the truth. There is obviously division in the church, but before the apostle addresses its source he emphasizes the importance of love as a means of dealing with the problem.

Love One Another

No doubt, John passionately remembers Jesus instructing the apostles, "A new commandment I give you that you love one another as I have loved you . . . by this all will know that you are My disciples" (Jn 13:34-35). Thus, he knows that division is best healed through love, for he knows and has said that God is love and in loving one another they become more like Jesus. This he points out before addressing the source of the perceived division.

The Deceivers

In addressing the source of the division, John says "many deceivers have gone out into the world who do not confess Jesus Christ as coming in the flesh. This is a deceiver and an antichrist. Look to yourselves, that we do not lose those things we worked for, but that we may receive full reward. Whoever transgresses and does not abide in the doctrine of Christ does not have God. He who abides in the doctrine of Christ has both the Father and the Son. If anyone comes to you and does not bring this doctrine do not receive him into your house nor greet him; for he who greets him shares in his evil deeds" (7-11).

The main deceivers John pinpoints here are the Gnostics who are claiming that God's Son did not become flesh. It is the same heresy that he attacks in his first letter, I John. Deceivers, itinerant prophets or preachers, are going to the various churches declaring that the Son had not come in the flesh as preached by the apostles and that salvation comes through secret knowledge and not through faith in the Jesus, God's Son in the flesh, preached by the apostles. John warns the church against these deceivers and exhorts its congregation not to take such persons into their homes nor even greet them, for in doing so they share in the deceptive evil.

Presumably, those church members who have been rejecting these deceivers are the "*some*" in whom John greatly rejoices.

Prefers Face to Face Communication

John says he has much more to say on the subject but he prefers to visit in person and "speak face to face, that our joy may be full" (12). No doubt, the presence of this elder apostle, who walked with Jesus and recorded many of the Lord's words and deeds, would be a formidable force in dispelling deceptive doctrine concerning Him and a healing force for exemplifying His commandment to love one another.

II John Poetic Summary
Beware of the Antichrists

Whereas letter one is circular directed, letter two is
specifically directed but figuratively so
It is directed figuratively to "the elect lady and her children,"
name specific we do not know
Perhaps this particular church received letter one but its
exhortations did not fully heed
So that John assessing the situation from his Ephesus hub
discerned a second letter need
And thus put pen to papyrus a short epistle to inscribe,
thinking it would the others sway
We know there are *others* for only "*some*" walk in the truth
after receiving his first essay.

Finding some of the church's children walking in the truth
has given the apostle great joy
Yet the unspoken side of the equation, quantified as the
others, must disturb if not annoy
But seeing the solution grounded in love, the apostle
resurrects the Lord's commandment
"That you love one another as I have loved you," precedent
for which the Son was sent
As John asserts and the church well knows this is gospel
truth from the beginning taught
Though all else fails it is the spirit of love that heals, for it is
God's plan, it is our ought.

As in epistle one the problem again is itinerant teachers
denying Jesus Christ came in the flesh
"Such deceiver," cries the apostle, "is an antichrist whose
message and the gospel do not mesh

Look to yourselves that we do not lose those things we
worked for, but receive full reward
Whoever transgresses and does not abide in the doctrine of
Christ does not have the Lord
He who abides in the doctrine of Christ has both the Father
and the Son, the essential needs
Thus, never receive an antichrist into your home nor greet for
then you share in his evil deeds."

Presumably, *some* in the church addressed did as bid in
epistle one while *others* disobeyed
The obedience of some made the apostle rejoice while the
disobedience of others dismayed
For the particular deceivers pinpointed are Gnostics denying
the divinity of Jesus Christ
And the others are greeting them and receiving them against
the aged apostle's advice
Thus, he sends a second letter explicit and succinct but love
filled hoping to persuade
If it does not he will visit and face to face deliberate why the
gospel truth must not fade.

III John Prose Summary
Itinerant Teachers

Introduction

John's third epistle, like the first and second, appears to have been written from Ephesus sometime between A.D. 85 and 95. Tradition has John living out his latter years at Ephesus ministering to churches in this area of Asia Minor.

This third epistle is addressed to Gaius, an individual who accommodates itinerant teachers that travel from place to place for purposes of spreading the gospel. As in the second epistle, John presents himself as "the elder."

In word count, III John is the shortest book in the New Testament. It is a few words shorter than II John though it has one verse more. The original letter probably filled no more than one sheet of papyrus.

The Situation

John, calling the itinerant teachers brethren, commends Gaius for accommodating them. "I rejoiced greatly when brethren came and testified of the truth that is in you, just as you walk in the truth, I have no greater joy than to hear that my children walk in truth" (3-4). The apostle especially commends Gaius for reaching out to them although they were strangers to him. Gaius has fulfilled the commandment to love one another and John makes it a point to praise him.

In this same church, however, there is Diotrephes, a powerful person who rejects the traveling brothers and castigates those who accommodate them. John mentions that he has written the church but Diotrephes, "who loves preeminence among them, does not receive us" (9). Consequently, the apostle says, "if I come, I will call to mind his deeds which he does, prating against us with malicious words, and not content with that, he himself does not receive the brethren, and forbids those who wish to, putting them out of the church" (10). Diotrephes, unlike Gaius, has not fulfilled the commandment to love another. In fact, John points to Diotrephes' love of "preeminence."

The Extent of the Conflict

In the second epistle John assumes the authority as an elder apostle to instruct the church addressed to reject deceptive itinerant teachers; in this third epistle he assumes the authority to instruct the church addressed to receive and accommodate legitimate itinerant teachers, whom he calls brethren. However, Diotrephes, a powerful individual in this particular local church ignores John's instruction [John has written previously] and rejects not only the legitimate itinerant teachers, the brethren, but stops any member of the congregation who wishes to do so by putting him out of the church. It appears that Diotrephes sees the solution to the problem of itinerant teachers is simply to receive none of them regardless of their message. And behind his stance may be resentment toward outside authority, even the authority of the revered apostle John. Traditionally, the apostles were viewed as the preeminent authorities on matters of doctrine, but as the church grew out of its infancy and the apostles began to die off local authority gained eminence.

Whether John or Diotrephes prevails in the long run, we do not learn, but John is clear on what should happen. He tells Gaius, "Beloved, do not imitate what is evil [e.g., Diotrephes' action], but what is good: he who does good is of God, but he who does evil has not seen God" (11). Certainly, Diotrephes violates the commandment to love one another while Gaius carries it out.

Demetrius and Beyond

Presumably, Demetrius is a leader of itinerant teachers and is delivering the letter to Gaius. John simply says, "Demetrius has a good testimony from all, and from the truth itself. And we also bear witness, and you know that our testimony is true" (12). How this plays out we can only conjecture. A probable scenario would be Demetrius delivering John's letter and Gaius receiving him and his itinerant brothers as he had received other itinerant brothers for which the apostle commends him. And armed with praise and support from John he challenges and prevails over Diotrephes. Another probable scenario would be Gaius receiving Demetrius and his itinerant brothers only to be attacked and overwhelmed by Diotrephes necessitating a visit from John to try to set things right. The apostle does say earlier in the letter "if I come, I will call to mind his [Diotrephes] deeds" (10).

In Closing

John says in closing that he has much more to say but rather than write it he hopes "to see you [Gaius] shortly, and we shall speak face to face" (14). And no doubt Gaius looks forward to a visit from the elderly apostle, not only one of the last living but one of the apostles closest to Jesus.

III John Poetic Summary
Itinerant Teachers

Soon after epistles one and two, the apostle sends from
Ephesus a third epistle succinct
Of all the books of the N. T. it has the fewest words thereby
readable in hardly a blink
Whether the apostle was short of papyrus or short of time
the reader can only conjecture
Perhaps he was weary of writing messages thinking more
effective a face to face lecture.
Central to all three epistles are the itinerant ministers,
distinguishing them false or true
Epistles one and two focus on falsifies, Gnostic antichrists,
and what churches should do.

Epistle three seems to be addressing an over response to
exhortation in epistles one and two
Or in the case of Diotrephes, a would be local church tyrant,
an opportunity power to pursue
Rather than distinguish between false or true itinerant
ministers, he insists reject them all
But to reject all violates the commandment to love one
another, thus he makes a sinful call.
John approaches the problem by praising Gaius who has true
itinerant ministers taken in:
"I rejoiced greatly when brethren came and testified that you
walk in truth and not in sin."

Jesus' parting words to his apostles is to spread the gospel
beyond Jerusalem to all lands
And so at Pentecost the preaching began and traveled by
individual disciples and by bands

How could the gospel spread were there not itinerant
ministers taking it to new frontiers?
How could itinerants survive were it not for churches
supporting them, brothers and peers?
Why was the aged John in far away Ephesus shepherding
churches in Asia Minor?
Was he not carrying out the commandment "as I have loved
you, love one another"?

Though itinerants were sometimes false as were the Gnostic
ministers John warned of
The true gospel carriers were essential to the great
commission, a commission of love.
Diotrephes lost perspective in his love of preeminence over
love for things above
Gaius distinguished between itinerants false and itinerants
true knowing what to do:
Take in the true then send them on their journey forward as
the Lord would have him to.
Thus, John makes his point by citing the acts of Diotrephes
and Gaius, contrasting the two.

The letter, addressed to Gaius, is being delivered by a true
itinerant minister, Demetrius
Confirmed by John and no doubt sent to encourage Gaius
continue his work meritorious
And if Diotrephes continues in his denial mode John hints
of a visit to come, a personal one
To engage him face to face and demonstrate that not
receiving itinerant brethren is evil done.

JUDE PROSE SUMMARY
FALSE TEACHERS

Author and Date

Jude identifies himself as a brother to James, presumably the James who is also a brother to Jesus and a leader in the Jerusalem church.

Mainly because a portion of Jude's letter resembles material in II Peter, there are two common views concerning its date. If Peter borrowed material from Jude, then the letter would have been written before A.D. 67, the year generally associated with Peter's death. If, however, Jude borrowed from Peter, then the letter may have been written later. There is no evidence for identifying the place written nor the church or churches receiving the letter.

Controversial References

Some scholars have objected to Jude's epistle being a part of the New Testament cannon because on two occasions he references apocryphal literature as if it were divinely inspired Scripture. In verse nine he references The Assumption of Moses, and in verse fourteen he references The Book of Enoch.

The Situation

Jude tells the recipients of his letter that he intended to write about the salvation they shared but was diverted to writing about the threat to their faith because of the insidious intrusion of unscrupulous men who through their actions were denying faith through Christ. "Beloved, while I was very diligent to write to you concerning our common salvation, I found it necessary to write to you exhorting you to contend earnestly for the faith which was once for all delivered to the saints. For certain men have crept in unnoticed, who long ago were marked out for this condemnation, ungodly men, who turn the grace of our God into licentiousness and deny the only Lord God and our Lord Jesus Christ" (3-4).

Again, as in the letters of John and Peter, we see in Jude's letter what seems to be the church confronted by Gnostic heresy: denial of the divinity of Christ and denial of the need to control indulgence of the flesh.

Examples to Warn

As way of warning, Jude uses examples from Scripture to remind the letter's recipients what happens to those who deny and defy God. He reminds them of what happened to the angels who rebelled, of what happened to those Israelites who did not believe even after being led out of Egypt, and of what happened to the wicked cities of Sodom and Gomorrah. "I want to remind you," he says, "though you once knew this, that the Lord, having saved the people out of the land of Egypt, afterward destroyed those who did not believe. And the angels who did not keep their proper domain but left their own habitation, He has reserved in everlasting chains under darkness for the judgment of the great day; as Sodom and Gomorrah, and the cities around them in a similar manner to these, having given themselves over to sexual immorality and gone after strange flesh, are set forth as an example, suffering the vengeance of eternal fire" (5-7).

Analogous Denunciation

Jude calls the falsifiers dreamers who "defile the flesh, reject authority, and speak evil of dignitaries" (8). To emphasize the extreme actions of the falsifiers, Jude makes analogous references. Noting how readily they reject authority and speak evil of dignitaries, he references the dispute between the devil and the archangel Michael concerning the body of Moses and notes that Michael rather than delivering a reviling accusation against the devil simply says, "The Lord rebuke you" (9), thereby not even reviling a fallen angel, not to mention an angel in good standing. "But these [falsifiers, dreamers] speak evil of whatever they do not know; and whatever they know naturally, like brute beasts, in these things they corrupt themselves," says Jude (10). He goes on to say they have gone the way of Cain, of Balaam and of Korah, examples of selfishness and greed leading to murder, false prophecy, and rebellion.

Further Characterization and Denunciation

Jude says these falsifiers violate the love feasts thinking only of themselves and feeding only themselves. They are clouds without water, autumn trees without fruit, raging waves churning up rubbish; they are "wandering stars [shooting stars] for whom is reserved blackness and darkness forever" (12-13).

Jude recalls that Enoch prophesied about these falsifiers saying that the Lord with thousands of His saints will come "to execute judgment on all who are ungodly among them of all their ungodly deeds which they have committed in an ungodly way, and of all the harsh things which ungodly sinners have spoken against Him" (14-15). And there is no doubt in Jude's mind that these current falsifiers will reap this prophesied punishment, for "these [current falsifiers] are murmurers, complainers, walking according to their own lusts; and they mouth great swelling words, flattering people to gain advantage" (16).

Exhortations

Having alerted his beloved ones to the dangers posed by these falsifiers, Jude exhorts them to take defensive measures. Calling them beloved, he asks them to recall how "the apostles of our Lord Jesus Christ" had told them "that there would be mockers in the last time who would walk according to their own ungodly lusts" (17). Jude tells his beloved ones that these falsifiers are the ungodly ones of whom the apostles spoke. They are men who follow their natural instincts and do not have the Spirit within. Against these ungodly forces Jude's beloved ones are exhorted to rely on "your most holy faith, praying in the Holy Spirit, keep yourselves in the love of God, looking for the mercy of our Lord Jesus Christ unto eternal life" (20-21).

Also they are exhorted to take offensive action to rescue those already under the influence of the ungodly ones: "On some have compassion, making a distinction; but others save with fear, pulling them out of the fire, hating even the garment defiled by the flesh" (23).

Closing

Jude ends the letter with a memorable benediction confirming belief in a God who saves those who keep the faith walking in the Spirit. "Now to

Him who is able to keep you from stumbling, / And to present you faultless / Before the presence of His glory with exceeding joy, / To God our Savior, / Who alone is wise, / Be glory and majesty, / Dominion and power, / Both now and forever. Amen" (24-25).

Jude Poetic Summary
False Teachers

Jude joins Peter and John in a common concern: that of an insidious false teacher surge
For early in the second half of the first century an embryonic Gnostic heresy had emerged
Its hatchlings heading for churches far and wide intent on perverting the gospel apostolic
By denying Jesus' divinity, exalting esoteric knowledge, and indulging licentious frolic.
Fearing these false teachers their heresy would vet, gospel guardians reacted to the threat
Anon, Peter, John, and Jude put pen to papyrus thereby cautioning churches of counterfeit.

We know Peter and John as apostles called by Jesus, but Jude identifies himself as James' brother
James, brother to Jesus, headed the Jerusalem church, the three siblings knowing Mary as mother.
Jude mentions no specific place for writing his epistle neither designates its specific destination
Some think he borrowed from Peter's second epistle while others think it's the reverse situation
It matters little other than in dating the letter, earlier if Peter be borrower later if the borrower Jude
Both gospel guardians were addressing a similar heretical situation, thus sharing the same attitude.

Jude tells recipients he intended to write about their shared salvation, but was diverted therefrom
Because of an insidious surge invading the churches and fermenting perversion touching everyone.

"Dear friends, I was primed to write you concerning our
common salvation, then came restraints:
Imperative dictated that I exhort you to contend for the faith
once and for all entrusted to the saints.
Certain men have crept in unnoticed, who were long ago
marked for this condemnation, this vice
These ungodly men turn the grace of God into licentiousness
and deny our Lord Jesus Christ."

As way of warning, Jude points to examples from Scripture
of the fate of those by God denied:
He points to the rebel angels who found themselves in
depths of darkness banned from on high
He points to the Israelites who did not believe after being
led out of Egypt, thereby felt God's ire
He points to Sodom and Gomorrah and how their aberrant
sexuality brought down the eternal fire.
Then Jude focuses specifically on these ungodly men
presently invading the churches wholesale
He calls them "dreamers who defile the flesh, reject authority,
and speak evil of dignitaries as well."

He compares them to Cain and Balaam and Korah,
murderer, bought prophet, and usurper vile
He sees them lacking respect for God and man, reveling in
licentiousness, and fomenting guile
He sees them violating the love feasts thinking only of
themselves and only themselves feeding
They are clouds without water, trees without fruit,
wandering stars to eternal darkness speeding
He recalls Enoch prophesying that the Lord and His saints
will on these falsifiers judgment execute
The Lord will come judging their nefarious deeds and harsh
things uttered against Him in disrepute.

Warning given and threat characterized Jude exhorts his
beloved ones defensive measures take

Recall "the apostles of our Lord Jesus Christ telling you that in the last times beware of the fake
These ungodly following their natural instincts and having no Spirit within, of these they spake
So you must rely on your most holy faith, pray in the Holy Spirit, and love God for Christ's sake."
Jude also exhorts for offensive measures saying "on some have compassion, distinction sustained
But others save with fear; pull them from the fire, hating even their garments corrupt flesh stained."

Warning and exhortation completed, Jude ends his epistle with most memorable benediction
It is benediction that fits many occasions and thereby through centuries has held distinction:

"Now to Him who is able to keep you from stumbling and to present you faultless
Before the presence of His glory with exceeding joy to God our Savior who alone is wise
Be glory and majesty, dominion and power, both now and forever. Amen."

Revelation Prose Summary One
John's Initial Vision and the Seven Churches

Revelation in the Apocalyptic Tradition

The Book of Revelation is what the name indicates: it is revelation. It is prophetic instruction delivered to John while imprisoned on the island of Patmos. "I was in the Spirit on the Lord's Day, and I heard behind me a loud voice, as of a trumpet, saying, 'I am the Alpha and the Omega, the First and the Last, and what you see, write on a scroll and send it to the seven churches which are in Asia: to Ephesus, to Smyrna, to Pergamum, to Thyatira, to Sardis, to Philadelphia, and to Laodicea'"(1:10-11). While "in the Spirit," meaning an exalted spiritual state, John experiences a series of visions. These prophetic visions are filled with symbolic images—some glorious, some grotesque—and often followed by interpretative explanation, a characteristic of apocalyptic literature. Both the Book of Daniel of the Old Testament and Revelation of the New Testament belong to this genre, a genre that flourished from B.C. 200 to A.D. 100.

Symbolism, standard fare in apocalyptic writing, takes various forms. There are usually beasts with heads and horns, the beasts representing nations and the heads and horns representing rulers; there are usually a series of symbolic numbers examples being the number seven representing completeness, the number twelve representing the people of God, and the number three and one half representing a period of persecution; and there are usually symbolic colors, examples being white representing victory, red representing conflict such as war, and black representing a lack of such as famine.

Historical Context and Apocalyptic Writing

Periods of severe persecution furnish the context for apocalyptic writing. Daniel is written in response to the severe persecution of Jews by the Seleucid king Antiochus IV Epiphanes, and Revelation in response to the severe persecution of Christians by the Roman emperor Domitian. Revelation is believed to have been written in the last years of Domitian's reign which ended in A. D. 96. Emperor Domitian insisted on being referred to as Lord and God thus cultivating emperor worship and thereby posing a dilemma for Christians who recognized only one God, and that God was not Caesar. But refusal to recognize Caesar as god could cause serious punishment, imprisonment, and even death. Presumably, many Christians were being persecuted at this time, especially in Asia Minor, because of their refusal to recognize only one God, their own. John says that he is imprisoned on the island of Patmos "because of the word of God and the testimony of Jesus" (1:9).

John's Visions Framed in Epistolary Form

John encases his visions within a letter framework, including a salutation and benediction, and sends this revelation to the seven churches in Asia Minor as instructed. Although some scholars disagree, it is generally assumed that the John of Revelation is the apostle John who is credited with having written the gospel of his name and the three epistles of his name. Tradition places the apostle John at Ephesus in his latter years thereby making him the likely candidate for having the stature to simply use the name John in addressing the seven Asian churches.

The Prologue

John prefaces his letter-framed revelation with a prologue addressing its source, its delivery, and its purpose. Its source is "the revelation of Jesus Christ, which God gave Him to show His servants what must soon take place" (1:1). It is delivered "by sending His angel to His servant John, who testifies to everything he saw—that is, the word of God and the testimony of Jesus Christ" (1:1-2). Its purpose is to bless "the one who reads the words of this prophecy, and blessed are those who hear it and take to heart what is written in it, because the time is near" (1:3). The "time is near" in which the believer has to take a stand requiring great sacrifice, but taking the stand holds great promise for the believer as is graphically dramatized in the ensuing revelation.

The Salutation

Identifying himself as simply "John," the apostle greets the seven churches: "Grace and peace to you from Him who is, and who was, and who is to come, and from the seven spirits before His throne, and from Jesus Christ, who is the faithful witness, the firstborn from the dead, and the ruler of the kings of the earth" (1:4-5). John incorporates the trinity into the greeting: "from Him who is, and who was, and who is to come" [God the Father]; "from the seven spirits before the throne" [the Holy Spirit]; and "from Jesus Christ . . . the firstborn from the dead" [the Son].

The Initial Vision Related

Having heard a loud voice like a trumpet instructing him to write on a scroll what he sees and send it to the seven churches, John turned around to locate the voice. After turning, he "saw seven golden lampstands, and in the midst of the lampstands One like the Son of Man, clothed with a garment down to the feet and girded about the chest with a golden band. His head and His hair were white like wool, as white as snow, and His eyes like a flame of fire . . . and out of his mouth went a two-edged sword" (1:12-14, 16). The voice is that of the Son of Man, Jesus Christ, and the lampstands represent the seven churches. The Son of Man stands with the churches in their ordeal, surely a comforting thought to them. And as the symbolic connotations suggest, He stands both as protector and judge. The robe like garment suggests high priest like declared in Hebrews, and the flaming eyes and white hair like the ancient of days in Daniel come to judge. And the sword out of his mouth suggests the power of His word. And the hair is white, a color normally suggesting victory in apocalyptic writing. There are numerous connotations that could be pursued here, but the important point is that Christ stands in the midst of the churches and He is the ultimate judge, thereby trumping the Emperor of the Roman Empire. Faith in Christ's word assures salvation, not the word of the Emperor. That does not mean that suffering and sacrifice will not happen, but it does mean that suffering and sacrifice in the faith assures victory over death as Christ, firstborn of the dead, has demonstrated.

Assurance, Instruction, and Interpretation Given John

John overwhelmed by what he has seen falls at the feet of the speaker, but is assured by Him: "Do not be afraid; I am the First and the Last. I am He who lives, and was dead, and behold, I am alive forevermore. Amen.

And I have the keys of Hades and Death" (1:17-18). Next, John is given instruction: "Write the things which you have seen, and the things which are, and the things which will take place after this" (1:19). Interpretation then follows the assurance and instruction. "The mystery of the seven stars which you saw in My right hand, and the seven golden lampstands: The seven stars are the angels of the seven churches, and the seven lampstands which you saw are the seven churches" (1:20). Assured and informed, John proceeds as instructed by writing down what he is told to say to the seven churches, "the things which are."

Messages to the Seven Churches:
It should be noted that the seven churches, though actual churches located in Asia Minor, are probably intended to represent all the churches since the number seven symbolizes completeness. But there is probably no symbolic significance to their arrangement. As can be seen there is no progressive order such as best to worst, or vice versa. Looking at a map one can see that leaving from Ephesus on the coast and heading northwest toward Pergamum and then turning southeast in a kind of semicircle route one would come first to Smyrna, then to Pergamum, then Thyatira, then Sardis, then Philadelphia, and last Laodicea, which is the order listed in Revelation.

It is worth noting that the messages do follow a common format though the situation at each church is different. The messages begin with the command given the writer followed by a descriptive image of the one giving the command and, in most cases, the image being one of those from the initial Son of Man vision (1:12-16). The churches are commended for the things they are doing well except for two, Sardis and Laodicea, who are doing nothing well. Likewise, the churches are chastised for their shortcomings except for Smyrna and Philadelphia, who are doing everything well. The messages include the promise of eternal salvation to those "who overcome," expressed in different images each time but communicating the same promise. The promise in turn is highlighted by the refrain "he who has an ear let him hear." Thus, the churches are challenged to keep the faith and promised to be rewarded for doing so.

The Message to Ephesus
First, John is commanded to write to the church at Ephesus and the command giver identifies himself as "He who holds the seven stars in His

right hand, who walks in the midst of the seven golden lampstands," an image from the initial Son of Man vision revealing dramatic attributes of the risen Christ (1-17-20). The church is commended for its labor and patience in weeding out those who are not true conveyors of the gospel, especially the Nicolaitans, a heretical sect claiming spiritual liberty allowing them to indulge in immoral acts because the body was of no consequence. But as they are commended so are they chastised: "I have this against you, that you have *left* your first love" (2:4), presumably meaning they have left their earlier love for Christ and for one another. [See John 13:34-35, "A new commandment I give you: that you love one another . . . by this all will know you are My disciples."] They are told to remember from where they have fallen, to repent and do the first works, or they will be punished: "I will come to you quickly and remove your lampstand from its place" (2:5). Then comes the promise of reward for compliance. "He who has an ear, let him hear what the Spirit says to the churches: 'To him who overcomes I will give to eat from the tree of life, which is in the midst of the Paradise of God'" (2:7).

The Message to Smyrna

Second, John is commanded to write to the church at Smyrna and the command giver identifies himself as "the First and the Last, who was dead, and came to life," also an image from the initial Son of Man vision. The church is highly commended: "I know your works, tribulation, and poverty (but you are rich): and I know the blasphemy of those who say they are Jews and are not, but are a synagogue of Satan" (2:9). They are not chastised but are warned of impending persecution and encouraged to stand fast in their faith, "to be faithful unto death." Smyrna was closely aligned with Rome and a strong proponent of emperor worship. Thus, the Christians at Smyrna were faced with hostility from both Jews and Romans, yet no allowance for laxity is made because of their tribulations. Though the devil is about to throw some of them into prison where they may be severely tested they are to be "faithful until death" (2:10). They are given no slack because of persecution; it is an opportunity to witness to one's faith. It is an opportunity to follow the example of Christ, "the First and the Last, who was dead, and came to life." Yet reward is not only implied in the image of the one giving the command but is made explicit in the closing promise: "He who has an ear, let him hear what the Spirit says to the churches, 'He who overcomes shall not be hurt by the second death'" (2:11).

The Message to Pergamum

Third, John is commanded to write to the church at Pergamum and the command giver identifies himself as "He who has the sharp two-edged sword," also an image from the initial Son of Man vision. The church is commended for its steadfastness under difficult circumstances. Pergamum being a Roman administrative center for Asia was a center for emperor worship. Though "you dwell where Satan's throne is . . . you hold fast to My name, and did not deny My faith even in the days in which Antipas was My faithful martyr, who was killed among you, where Satan dwells" (2:13). Yet there are a few things held against Pergamum. Of particular concern are "those who hold to the doctrine of Balaam" and "those who hold to the doctrine of the Nicolaitans, likewise things I hate" (2:14, 15). Balaam would be a prototype of those teaching and practicing doctrines contrary to the faith as were the Nicolaitans already mentioned as a problem at Ephesus. These violators are threatened with punishment by the command giver "who has the two-edged sword" lest they repent. But assurance of reward is given to those who remain steadfast. "He who has an ear, let him hear what the Spirit says to the churches. 'To him who overcomes I will give some of the hidden manna to eat. And I will give a white stone, and on the stone a new name written which no one knows except him who receives it'"(2:17) The hidden manna is their sustaining heavenly food, and their recorded victory over evil the white stone with their new name. The white stone is their passport to heaven.

The Message to Thyatira

Fourth, John is commanded to write to the church at Thyatira and the command giver identifies himself as "the Son of Man who has eyes like a flame of fire and feet like fine brass," also an image from the initial Son of Man vision. The church is commended for its works—its love, its service, its faith, and its patience—and for increasing these works with time. Yet there are a few things held against Thyatira, primarily their allowing "that woman Jezebel, who calls herself a prophetess, to teach and beguile My servants to commit sexual immorality and to eat things sacrificed to idols"(2:20). The name Jezebel is probably epithet for an influential libertine in the congregation who is leading others astray as Jezebel of the Old Testament led Israelites away from Yahweh. And in a tone reminiscent of Yahweh it is said that this Jezebel has been given time to repent but has not; consequently, she and her children will be destroyed so that "all the churches shall know that I am He who searches the minds and hearts. And I will give to each one of you according to your works" (2:23). To those at Thyatira who are not followers of Jezebel and who "have not known the so called deep secrets of Satan I will put on you no other burden" (2:24). Knowing "the deep secrets of Satan" is probably a reference to heretical Gnostic doctrine. But those who hold fast to the faith shall overcome; they shall be given "power over the nations" and "the morning star"(2:26-27). Suffering and perishing in the faith will place them with Christ who has power over the nations and who is the morning star: in their faith they are secure in Christ. "He who has an ear, let him hear what the Spirit says to the churches" (2:29).

The Message to Sardis

Fifth, John is commanded to write to the church at Sardis and the command giver identifies himself as "He who has the seven Spirits of God and the seven stars," also an image from the initial Son of Man vision. The church has little to commend; it seems to be the worst of the seven churches for the command giver says, "I know your works, that you have a name that you are alive, but you are dead" (3:1). Chastisement for Sardis takes the form of a probationary warning: to strengthen the things that are about to die, to remember what they have heard and received, and to repent, else "I will come upon you like a thief, and you will not know what hour I will come upon you" (3:3). The tone and the message here echoes that of Old Testament prophecy with its "if clause" factor: if you do not repent and change your ways you will be severely punished in the here and now. There are, however, a few in Sardis who walk in the faith: "You have a few names even in Sardis who have not defiled their garments; and they shall walk with me in white [in victory], for they are worthy" (3:4). And last comes the promise to those who overcome, who embrace the faith regardless of persecution: "He who overcomes shall be clothed in white garments [victory garments], and I will not blot out his name from the Book of Life; but I will confess his name before My Father and before His angels. He who has an ear, let him hear what the Spirit says to the churches" (3:5-6). It is interesting to note that in the refrain—"He who has an ear, let him hear what the Spirit says to the *churches*"—repeated in each of the seven messages ends with the plural form, *churches*, another indication besides the number symbolism that the seven churches are intended to represent all the churches.

The Message to Philadelphia

Sixth, John is commanded to write to the church at Philadelphia and the command giver identifies himself as "He who is holy, He who is true, He who has the key of David, He who opens and no one shuts, and shuts and no one opens"(3:7), this time not an image from the initial vision of the Son of Man but a newly minted image of the risen Christ who has been given the key of power to judge and to rule, to open and to close. Philadelphia is commended for having kept His word and for not having denied His name. And since it has done so well, receives no chastisement, only praise and promise: "Indeed I will make those of the synagogue of Satan, who say they are Jews and are not, but lie—indeed I will make them come and worship before your feet, and to know that I have loved you. Because you have kept My command to persevere, I also will keep you from the hour of trial which shall come upon the whole world, to test those who dwell on the earth" (3:9-10). And last, as in the other messages, comes promise to everyone who overcomes: "I will make him a pillar in the temple of My God, and he shall go out no more. I will write on him the name of My God, the name of the city of My God, the New Jerusalem, which comes down out of heaven from My God. And I will write on him My new name" (3:12). Everyone who embraces the faith and remains steadfast is assured of becoming a pillar in God's temple, thus always in His glorious presence. "He who has an ear, let him hear what the Spirit says to the churches" (3:13).

The Message to Laodicea

Seventh, John is commanded to write to the church at Laodicea and the command giver identifies himself as "the Amen, the Faithful and True Witness, the Beginning of the creation of God," again not an image from the initial vision of the Son of Man but a newly minted one. The command giver offers no commendations for the tepid church at Laodicea. In fact, Laodicea runs a close race with Sardis as being the worst of the seven churches: "I know your works, that you are neither cold nor hot. I could wish you were cold or hot. So then, because you are lukewarm, and neither cold nor hot, I will spew you out of My mouth" (3:15-16). In the cosmic battle between God and Satan, between good and evil, there is no place for tepidness, ultimately you must choose one or the other for there is no in between. "I counsel you to buy from Me gold refined in the fire that you may be rich; and white garments, that you may be clothed, that the shame of your nakedness may not be revealed; and anoint your eyes with eye salve, that you may see" (3:18). Figuratively, they are told to wake up to the reality that spiritual richness and thus spiritual victory comes through suffering and sacrifice for the faith. "As many as I love, I rebuke and chasten. Therefore be zealous and repent" (3:19). And all are loved but the choice to commit is theirs: "Behold, I stand at the door and knock. If anyone hears My voice and opens the door, I will come in to him and dine with him, and he with me" (3:20). And last, the promise to him who overcomes: "I will grant to sit with Me on My throne, as I also overcame and sat down with My Father on His throne. He who has an ear, let him hear what the Spirit says to the churches" (3:21-22).

Revelation Poetic Summary One
John's Initial Vision and the Seven Churches

Of all the books of the bible Revelation is the most
misconstrued, the most read into
Faced with visions and revisions both glorious and grotesque
what is the reader to do?
Preparation, preparation, preparation: study its historical
context and its genre, yes
Know the time, the place and the people; know the situation
and the form of address
Know that apocalyptic literature was at the time a genre
quite well known
Know in O. T. Daniel and N. T. Revelation the enigmatic
genre still lives on.

Knowing much of what the author John knew renders
Revelation a lot less weird
Knowing Nero, Domitian and emperor worship and other
things Christian feared
Somewhat dissolves the two-thousand year old façade
obstructing revelation real.
And knowing how apocalyptic speaks through stock
symbols dissolves more still:
Beasts represent nations and heads rulers, numbers
represent concepts common
Color represents status; know such things and Revelation is
less a phenomenon.

Know that when persecution seemed to reign apocalyptic
writing came on scene

For the believer needed assurance that God was aware and
would soon intervene.
Daniel's apocalyptic visions came during the onerous time of
Antiochus, Seleucid king
And John's apocalyptic visions came during the onerous time
of the emperor Domitian
Thus, Jewish prophet and Christian apostle adopt
apocalyptic writing as a way to explain
Through symbol and image: in the end it is the King of Kings,
God and Messiah who reign.

In Revelation it is prescribed emperor worship that has
endangered the Christian head
Each must swear that Caesar is his god or run the risk of
being placed among the dead.
John, the aged apostle living in Ephesus, has been subjected
to arrest and imprisonment
For espousing the word of God and testifying Jesus Christ,
for not being emperor bent.
Confined to the isle of Patmos and awaiting arraignment,
the apostle is Spirit transformed
He is called to witness pageant reassuring, revelation through
image and symbol adorned.

"I was in the Spirit on the Lord's Day, and heard a
trumpet-like voice behind me say,
'I am the Alpha and the Omega, and I command you write
down what you see today.'"
Thus, the prophetic pageant begins with John called to
witness and transcribe on scroll.
In great awe the apostle complies, etching vision after vision
on papyrus prepared for roll.
The prescribed prophetic message seven churches in Asia are
designated the recipients:
To Ephesus, Smyrna, Pergamun, Thyatira, Sardis,
Philadelphia, Laodicea it is to be sent.

Symbolism: seven being completeness, the seven churches
stand for all churches therefore
Know symbol can be what it is and more, thus the seven
churches are themselves and more.
Also know that symbolic meaning is defined by context,
"read in" meaning has no validity
Yet the construer of Revelation so often ignores this truth
and thus stumbles into sophistry.
That need not be the case if the construer knows the genre,
the genre context, and the text
Thus, let us prayerfully proceed construing Revelation within
context, this genre complex.

John encases the revelation within letter framework
including salutation and benediction
Not surprising since seven Asian churches are designated
recipients, each with distinction.
For clarification he includes prologue addressing the
revelation's source and delivery and intent:
It is "the revelation God gave Christ to inform His servants
what must soon take place, the event"
It is delivered "by heavenly beings to servant John who
records all that he will see and hear"
It is intended to bless "those who read it and then take it to
heart because the time is near."

The time is near when God will intervene, and this message
comes through the Son
The King of Kings chooses to assure his suffering servants
through the apostle John.
As analysis of the seven churches reveal, more than
persecution led the saints astray
But that had always been the case and whether persecution
or other, faith was the stay.
And as had always been the case the prophet delivering the
faith message had a hard say
He had to deliver the message so his hearers would listen; he
had to find a creative way.

And so the prophecy of Revelation begins with John in the
Spirit and commanded to write
The apostle is commanded to write on scroll what he sees,
for what he sees is what is right.
Being somewhat startled by the loud and commanding voice
John inquisitively turns round
And sees in the midst of seven lampstands One like the Son
of Man in long garment down
And girded about the chest with golden band, wool white
hair and eyes of fire like flame
And feet like fine brass furnace refined and voice like the
sound many waters might claim.

The voice is that of Jesus Christ and the seven lampstands
represent the churches seven
Their Lord stands with the seven churches in their ordeal, a
comforting thought to them
He stands in long robe garment priest like, white hair and
flaming eyes judge like too
The sword is the power of His word, and white is victory, in
apocalyptic talk not new
Standing amidst the churches He is judge ultimate,
trumping Emperor of Empire Roman
His presence confirms sacrifice for the gospel, victory over
death in Christ the risen one.

Overwhelmed by what he has heard and seen, John falls at
the feet of the speaker before
Who says "be not afraid, I am the First and Last, was dead,
but now am alive evermore
And I have the keys of the grave and death and I charge you
record the things you have seen
Yes, record things which are and things which will take place
after this, record everything."
And thus the pageant begins with evaluation of the seven
churches, Ephesus heading the list.
But do not misconstrue by trying to read into this geographical
given route some silly symbolic mist.

There is no progression from best to worst or vice versa,
listing is simply a geographical one
A map reveals that leaving from Ephesus on the coast and
going northwest toward Pergamum
Then turning southeast in semicircular route one would
come first to Smyrna, then Pergamum
Then Thyatira, then Sardis, then Philadelphia, and last
Laodicea, the order listed in Revelation.
Accept no more than circular might suggest completeness,
complimenting the number seven.
Symbolism aside, the messages do follow a common format
but each situation a different one.

The message begins with command given John followed by
an image of the command giver
Usually an awesome image of the Son of Man from initial
vision given the apostle to deliver
The churches are commended for the things done well,
except for two, Sardis and Laodicea—
Who do nothing well—before being chastised for lapses,
except for Smyrna and Philadelphia
Who do everything well: Sardis and Laodicea totally
chastised, Smyrna and Philadelphia praised
But whether church does well or ill or in between, those who
sacrifice for the gospel will be raised.

Truly, the import of the prophetic message is promise of
eternal salvation to those "who overcome"
Expressed in different images each time but communicating
the same promise, the same each one.
The image enhanced promise is highlighted by resounding
refrain: "he who has an ear let him hear"
Thus, the churches are challenged to keep the faith and
promised that heavenly intervention is near.
To Ephesus write says the command giver imaged as "He who
walks amidst the lampstands seven"
This image from the initial Son of Man vision revealing
dramatic attributes of Jesus Christ risen.

Ephesus is commended for its labor and patience in weeding
out those who are not conveyors true
Especially the Nicolaitans who claim spiritual liberty to
indulge in immoral acts, a Gnostic coup
Then praise ends with the refrain, "but I have this against
you," you have left your first love
Their earlier love for Christ and for each other has waned
thus grieving the risen one above
Either they repent or face punishment soon, yet compliance
will stay punishment and bring reward
Hear the warning refrain, "he who has an ear, let him hear
what the Spirit says," says in this regard.

Such is the message through the apostle John to Ephesus
given by the Son of Man, Jesus Christ
Promising: "to him who overcomes I will give to eat from the
tree of life amidst God's Paradise."
To Smyrna John writes that "the First and Last, who was
dead and came to life, these things say,"
He knows your works, tribulation and poverty and these
make you rich, rich in fostering the Way.
He knows the blasphemy of those who say they are Jews but
are no more than a synagogue of Satan
He knows the church there besieged by hostile Jew and
emperor worship, yet able both to withstand.

The devil is about to test them further by imprisonment, but
they are to continue their steadfastness
No slack is allowed though their persecution severe, until
death they must be resolute in faithfulness
It is opportunity to follow Christ, "the First and the Last,
who was dead and came to life," Him hear
Hear reward implied in the symbolic image and in the
closing promise hear it voiced explicitly clear
It is voiced in the warning refrain: "he who has an ear, let him
hear what the Spirit says," emphatically
He says those who overcome shall not be touched by the
second death, theirs is abundant life eternally.

To Pergamum John writes that "He who has the sharp
two-edged sword" is hereby assessing you
He wishes to commend you for steadfastness though you
reside in a region under Satan's purview
You held fast His name and did not falter when Antipas
became His faithful martyr, example prime
Yet there are a few things He holds against you: those
holding to the Balaam or Nicolaitan doctrine.
Such violators are promised punishment by the command
giver, "who has the sharp two-edged sword"
But assurance of reward is given those who remain steadfast,
those who stand together in one accord.

For assessment complete it must contain warning refrain: "he
who has an ear let him hear"
Hear what the Spirit says thematically in so many ways, "he
who overcomes need not fear."
To Thyatira John writes "the Son of Man who has eyes like
flames" is hereby assessing you
You are commended for your works, your love, your service,
your faith, your patience true
Yet there are a few things He holds against you, primarily
that woman Jezebel, pretended prophetess
Who leads the weak into sexual immorality, to eating idol
sacrifices, all in the name of righteousness.

The name Jezebel is epithet for a libertine who leads
believers astray like the O. T. female
The wife of aberrant Ahab, the wily Jezebel, led many
Israelites away from Yahweh to Baal
And in tone reminiscent of Yahweh, "He who has eyes of
flames" destruction for her asserts
To let the churches know that the Son of Man gives to each
one according to his or her works.
So those of Thyatira who do not follow Jezebel or have not
known the deep secrets of Satan
On those no other burden will come and holding steadfast
they shall overcome, the battle win.

Those who hold fast the faith shall be given power over the
nations and the morning star
Perishing in the faith they are with Christ, the power over
the nations and the morning star
And then sounds the warning refrain, "he who has an ear, let
him hear" the Spirit from afar.
To Sardis John writes that "He who has the seven Spirits of
God and the seven stars" assesses
He knows your works, that you have a name that you are
alive, but you are dead He professes
Chastisement takes the form of probationary warning:
strengthen things that are so regressive.

Remember what you originally received and repent, else He
will come upon you thief like bold
The tone of the warning echoes O. T. prophecy with its "if
clause": if you do not repent, behold
Behold, you will be punished in the here and now,
catastrophe always awaits the unrepentant
But a remnant prevails and so it is in Sardis, a few are found
who have not a soiled garment
Those shall walk with Him in white for they are worthy,
they shall in victory walk with Him
It is the promise motif: those who overcome shall be clothed
in garments white, all of them.
And their names shall not be blotted out of the Book of Life:
those who have an ear hear Him.

To Philadelphia John writes "He who has the key to David,"
He who opens and shuts exclusively
The command giver image this time not taken from the
initial vision but an image minted newly
It is an image of the risen Christ holding the key of power to
open and to shut, to judge and to rule
And in judging Philadelphia He commends them for having
kept His word, not denying the gospel
And since they have done so well chastisement they receive
none, theirs is praise and recompense

He will make the synagogue of Satan, Jews false, come to
worship before their feet in repentance.

Because they have kept His command to persevere, He will
keep them through the hour of trial
Confirming the promise that those who keep shall be kept,
for they are purified against sin vile.
Presumably, Philadelphia experienced trial severe but
through faith had emerged triumphant
Following Jesus Christ in exemplary faith, they followed the
decreed formula forever extant
And they are told to hold on to what they have, hold on to
their crown for He is coming soon
Coming soon surely means an end to their ordeal, not the
Second Coming as some presume.

The promise motif rings clear: he who overcomes will
become a pillar, a pillar in God's temple
And written on the pillar the names of God, His city, His
son: forever secure those of example
For all who hold fast to the faith are assured of becoming
pillars in God's temple, thus ever near
Despite Philadelphia's sterling example it is not warning
spared: he who has an ear let him hear.
To Laodicea John identifies the command giver as "the Amen,
the Faithful and True Witness"
Not an image from the initial vision of the Son of Man, but a
new image to judge and to assess.

The Faithful and true Witness finds no commendation for
the tepid church Laodicea
Among the seven churches it is toss up between Sardis and
Laodicea the worst to be
The command giver says he knows Laodicea and its works
are neither cold nor hot
A condition so repulsive that He spits them out of mouth, to
be lukewarm is to be not

In the cosmic battle Satan against God, evil against good,
tepidness is stance unseen
In the battle between right and wrong choice is one or the
other, there is no in between.

The command giver says "buy from Me gold refined in the
fire that you may rich be
And white garments that you may be clothed, and salve your
eyes that you may see."
Figuratively they are told to wake up to reality, spiritual
victory comes through sacrifice
"As many as I love, I rebuke and chasten, therefore be
zealous and repent," His advice:
"Behold I stand at the door and knock, if anyone opens the
door to my voice, I come in."
Repeated again, the divine promise awaits those who open
the door and overcome, amen.

"To those, I give the right to sit with Me on My throne, as I
with my with My Father sat down;
He who has an ear, let him hear the Spirit's message to the
churches," hear the message profound.

Revelation Prose Summary Two
Vision of the Throne and the Opening of the Seals

Viewing the Throne

In the first vision John sees the risen Christ walking in the mist of the seven earthly churches. Then the perspective turns heavenward as the apostle looks upward seeing a door to heaven standing open and hearing the trumpet like voice again, this time saying, "Come up here and I will show you what must take place after this" (4:1). Instantly, John is in the Spirit and a throne appears before him with someone sitting on it. The One sitting on the throne is described in terms of refracted brilliant light from the precious stones jasper and carnelian. And a rainbow of light resembling emerald encircles the throne. Surrounding the throne are twenty-four other thrones and seated on these are twenty-four elders in white robes and wearing golden crowns. From the throne come flashes of lightening, rumblings and peals of thunder; before the throne are seven blazing lamps, these being the seven spirits of God. Also before the throne is what appears to be a sea of glass, crystal clear. In the center of the throne are four living creatures front and back covered with eyes. One living creature is like a lion, one like an ox, one like an eagle, and one like a human, and each has six wings with eyes front and back, and the four creatures praise God ceaselessly saying, "Holy, holy, holy is the Lord God Almighty, who is, who was, and who is to come" (4:8). Each time the four creatures praise God with these words, the twenty-four elders fall down before Him laying their crowns before the throne and saying, "You are worthy, O Lord, to receive glory and honor and power; for You created all things, and by Your will they exist and were created" (4:11).

The One on the throne is, of course, God whose majesty is described in terms of light and his emanating power in terms of thunder and lightening. The twenty-four elders surely represent God's people; twenty-four being a multiple of twelve, and in apocalyptic literature the number twelve symbolizes God's people. Most likely, the twenty-four elders would be representative of the twelve tribes of the Old Testament and the twelve apostles of the New Testament; their being dressed in white, a symbol of victory in apocalyptic writing, signifies the victory of God's people. The four creatures represent creation, they are from the "four corners" of the earth (the lion as creature wild, the ox as creature domestic, the eagle as airborne creature, and man-like creature as man) and they are there praising the Creator. The creatures and elders join together in praising God and glorifying Him as Creator.

The Scroll

Next, John notices a scroll—written on front and back and sealed with seven seals—in the hand of the One on the throne. And he sees and hears a strong angel asking in loud voice who might be worthy to break the seals and open the scroll. When no one is found worthy to break the seals and open the scroll, John begins to weep. But he is soon comforted by one of the elders telling him, "Do not weep. Behold, the Lion of the tribe of Judah, the Root of David, has prevailed to open the scroll and to loose its seven seals" (5:5). Looking toward the throne again John sees in its midst—among the four creatures and the twenty-four elders—"a Lamb, as though it had been slain, having seven horns and seven eyes, which are the seven Spirits of God sent out into all the earth" (5:6). Obviously, the slain Lamb is the risen Christ and the seven horns and seven eyes presumably are His complete power and complete wisdom, and the seven Spirits of God the Holy Spirit. The complete power and complete wisdom are sent out to all the earth through the Holy Spirit signifying that Christ is for everyone, salvation is for everyone. The throne and scroll scene sets the stage, in this envisioned pageant, for launching the coming cosmic drama between God and Satan, between the forces of evil and the people of God.

The Lamb Takes the Scroll

When the Lamb takes the scroll the twenty-four elders and the four living creatures fall before Him, each with a harp and a golden bowl filled with incense, the incense being the prayers of the saints, and sing a new song:

"You are worthy to take the scroll, and to open its seals, for You were slain, and have redeemed us to God by Your blood out of every tribe and tongue and people and nation, and have made us kings and priests to our God; and we shall reign on the earth" (5:9-10). Next, John sees and hears angels around the throne, thousands and thousands and ten thousand times ten thousand who join the twenty-four elders and the four living creatures saying, "Worthy is the Lamb who was slain to receive power and riches and wisdom, and strength and honor and glory and blessing!" (5:12). The elders and the living creatures emphasize the worthiness of the Lamb in His death while the host of angels emphasizes the worthiness of the Lamb in His risen glory. And then John hears every creature in heaven and in the earth saying, "Blessing and honor and glory and power be to Him who sits on the throne, and to the Lamb, forever and ever!" (5:13). Thus, John hears universal praise and gratitude for God and for the Lamb and that praise and gratitude are further emphasized in the "Amen" from the four living creatures and the prostrate worship gesture of the twenty-four elders. To the Lamb who gave all in sacrificing for all, to Him belongs power and wisdom and strength and riches and blessings and honor and glory forever and ever. Unquestionably, the Lamb is worthy to open the seals.

Opening the Seals: The Four Horsemen

John sees the Lamb open the *first seal* and hears one of the living creatures call in a loud voice, "Come and see" (6:1). Looking, John sees a white horse whose rider, holding a bow, is given a crown as he goes out "conquering and to conquer" (6:2). When the *second seal* is opened, John hears a second living creature saying come and see. Looking, he sees a second horse, this one fiery red, for its rider is "to take peace from the earth and to make people kill one another" (6:4). The rider is given a great sword. When the *third seal* is opened, John hears the third living creature saying come see. Looking, he sees a third horse, this one black and its rider holding a pair of scales in his hand. Then a voice from the midst of the living creatures says, "a quart of wheat for a denarius, and three quarts of barley for a denarius" (6:6). There is to be a scarcity of food. When the *fourth seal* is opened, John hears the fourth living creature saying come and see. Looking, he sees a fourth horse, this one pale and its rider Death followed by Hades (the place of death). Death and Hades are given power "over a fourth of the earth, to kill with sword, with hunger, with plague, and by the beasts of the earth" (6:8).

Note that the first horse is white, the color of victory, and its rider is to conquer which means he will enforce his will on the conquered. But in doing so conflict and war will result, thus the red horse representing bloodshed, the black horse representing famine, and the pale horse representing death. And the people to whom John is writing would no doubt identify the conqueror on the white horse to be the Roman emperor Domitian. In forcing his will concerning who is God he is causing bloodshed, famine, and death as Christians oppose his will.

Opening the Seals: The Martyrs

When the *fifth seal* is opened, John sees "under the altar the souls of those who had been slain for the word of God and for the testimony they held" (6:9). These souls of the slain cry out in a loud voice saying, "How long O Lord, holy and true, until You judge and avenge our blood on those who dwell on the earth?" (6:10). Each of them is given a white robe and told to rest a while longer until the number of those like themselves to be killed is completed. These martyrs, thinking of the people of God below facing bloody persecution, want justice to be done; in this cosmic struggle, they want good to triumph over evil, God over Satan. They are eager for judgment and justice. Confirming the justness of their cry, they are counseled patience while given assurance. There is more suffering to come—*until the number is completed*—but judgment and justice will come. They are given white robes, white the color of victory, in this case victory for these slain martyrs, for slain martyrs to be, and for all people of God.

Opening the Seals: The Earthquake

When the *sixth seal* is opened, John sees a great earthquake with the sun becoming black as sackcloth of hair and the moon becoming like blood. The stars fall from heaven and the sky recedes like a scroll rolling up, and every mountain and island are moved from their places. And persons from kings to slaves hide themselves in caves and among rocks in the mountains saying to the mountains and rocks, "Fall on us and hide us from the face of Him who sits on the throne and from the wrath of the Lamb! The great day of His wrath has come, and who is able to stand?" (6:16-17). This earthquake scene is further assurance that judgment will come, that no one will escape it, that judgment will take place, and that justice will be served.

Opening the Seals: The Interlude

Following the earthquake scene and prior to the opening of the *seventh seal* there is an interlude in which John sees "four angels standing at the four corners of the earth holding the four winds of the earth, that the wind should not blow on the earth, one sea, or on any tree" (7:1). Next, he sees another angel with God's seal ascending from the east and crying out to the four angels holding the four winds: "Do not harm the earth, the sea, or the trees till we have sealed the servants of our God on their foreheads" (7:3). Then John hears the number sealed, it being one hundred and forty-four thousand from all the tribes of the children of Israel. No doubt, this is a symbolic number and not meant literally. The number, multiples of a combination of ten (completeness) and twelve (God's people), is surely meant to stand for all of the people of God. Next, John sees a great multitude, too vast to number and from all nations and tribes and tongues, wearing white robes and holding palm branches standing before the throne and before the Lamb. They cry out in a loud voice, "Salvation belongs to our God who sits on the throne and to the Lamb" (7:10). All the angels stand around the throne behind the elders and the living creatures; there they fall prostrate before the throne and seconding the white robed multitude say, "Amen! Blessing and glory and wisdom, thanksgiving and honor and power and might, be to our God forever and ever" (7:12). Next, one of the elders identifies, for John, the great multitude arrayed in white robes praising God and the Lamb: "These are the ones who have come out of *the great tribulation,* and who have washed their robes and made them white in the blood of the Lamb. Therefore, they are before the throne of God, and serve Him day and night in His temple. And He who sits on the throne will dwell among them. They shall neither hunger anymore nor thirst anymore . . . for the Lamb who is in the midst of the throne will shepherd them and lead them to living fountains of waters. And God will wipe away every tear from their eyes" (7:14-17). They have come out of "the great tribulation" to be with God and the Lamb, forever comforted and forever secure. Having remained faithful through persecution and suffering, they are now secure with their God and Savior. That much is clear, but what is "the great tribulation"? Some interpreters of Revelation argue it is that period of conflict in which the Antichrist reigns before being dethroned by Christ's thousand year reign, all to take place in the future end times. Other interpreters argue that "the great tribulation" referred to here is the tribulation experienced by Christians under the Roman emperor Domitian and the multitude in "their robes made white in the blood of the Lamb" are those who have sacrificed their lives in opposing the will of the Emperor over the will of God. The second argument makes more sense if John is writing to comfort his fellow Christians who are under severe persecution and who he wishes to reassure by revealing his apocalyptic visions.

This is not to say that Revelation is only for John's contemporaries, for what holds true for persecuted Christians in John's day would certainly hold true for persecuted Christians beyond John's day. The pageantry presented in John's visions reveals that God through His Son, the risen Lamb, the prevailing power in the cosmic conflict between good and evil and as the prevailing power will never allow Satan and the forces of evil to destroy the saints, the saints being those who keep the faith. In the on going cosmic conflict the saints may at times suffer severely, even to facing the martyr's death, but as long as they keep the faith tribulation for them is transitory. Death is merely passage to the heavenly realm, and the martyr's death places a saint closer to the throne of God.

Revelation Poetic Summary Two Vision of the Throne and the Opening of the Seals

After recording what the Son of Man had said about the seven earthly churches near
John looks up to see a door in heaven open and hears a voice saying "come up here."
Instantly, he is in Spirit mode beholding a throne with Being indescribable sitting on it
Indescribable except as refracted light from precious stones of rainbow colors explicit
And surrounding the throne of brilliant light are twenty-four other thrones, each an elder on
Who, in white robes and golden crowns attired, often fall in praise before the radiant throne.

From the radiant throne come flashes of lightning and peals of rumbling thunder periodically
And also seen are seven blazing lamps, the seven spirits of God, the Holy Spirit symbolically.
In front of the throne is what appears to be a sea of glass, crystal clear, and at its center stand
The four living creatures: one like a lion, one like an ox, one like an eagle, and one like a man
Each has six wings covered with eyes front and back, such are the living creatures everyone
Singing, "Holy, holy, holy is the Lord God Almighty, who is, who was, and who is to come."

Each time the living creatures praise God with these words the twenty-four elders fall face down

Laying their crowns before the throne and saying, "You are
 worthy, O Lord God most renowned
To receive glory and honor and power, for You created all
 things, and they so exist by Your will."
Thus, the Lord God is presented symbolically: He in terms
 of emanating light and His power real
In terms of emanating thunder and lightning; the
 twenty-four elders represent God's people sure
For twenty-four is multiple of twelve, symbolic number for
 God's people in apocalyptic literature.

Surely the twenty-four elders symbolize the O. T. twelve
 tribes and the N. T. twelve apostles called
And they are dressed in white, symbol of victory in
 apocalyptic scrip, victory for God's people all.
The four living creatures from the four corners of the earth
 represent creation: the lion creature wild
The ox creature domestic, the eagle creature of the air, and
 the man-like creature man, total profile.
The living creatures join the twenty-four elders in praising
 God and glorifying Him as Creator
In praise and song God's people and God's creatures pay
 homage to their glorious Benefactor.

Next, John notices a scroll, written on front and back and
 sealed with seven seals, and held
And held by the One on the throne where an angel loudly
 asks who is worthy the seals peal.
When no one comes forward to peal the seals and open the
 scroll, John in sadness tears
But soon is comforted by an elder who reveals to him
 information to assuage his fears:
From the tribe of Judah, the Root of David, One has
 prevailed worthy to open the sealed
Looking toward the throne again John beholds nearby a
 Lamb, as though having been killed.

The Lamb had seven horns and seven eyes signifying the
Spirit of God sent out the world over
The slain-like Lamb is Christ risen, and the seven eyes and
horns complete wisdom and power
These being sent out to the whole world through the Holy
Spirit signifies Christ for everyone
Christ intended for everyone, that is, everyone who believes;
no other way can salvation come.
And thus the throne and scroll scenes set the stage for
forthcoming dramatically drawn pageantry.
On cosmic screen, good and evil dressed in grotesque symbolic
imagery will battle for ascendancy.

The Lamb takes the scroll and the twenty-four elders and
the four creatures fall before Him
Each with harp and bowl of incense—saints' prayers—they
sing a *new* song, each of them:
"You are worthy to take the scroll and open its seals, for
being slain You have redeemed us to God
Through Your blood redemption comes to every tribe and
every tongue who believe and give nod
Your blood made them a kingdom of priests to reign upon the
earth; You purchased them for God."

Next, John sees and hears myriad times myriad of angels
who join the elders and creatures in praise
Singing, "worthy is the Lamb slain to receive honor and
blessing; to power and glory was He raised."
Thus, the elders and living creatures praise the worthiness of
the Lamb in His death given
And the host of angles around the throne praise the Lamb's
worthiness in His glory risen.
Then John hears every creature in heaven and in earth
singing, "blessing and honor and power
Be to Him who sits on the throne, and to the Lamb, forever
and forever from this selfsame hour."

Such John sees and hears, seeing and hearing universal praise
and gratitude for God and the Lamb
Praise and gratitude capped by the prostrate elders and the
living creatures in their "Amen" resound.
Unquestionably, the Lamb who gave all in sacrificing for all
is worthy to open these seals bound.
And when He opens the first seal, one of the living creatures
calls in voice loud, "come and see"
Looking, John sees a white horse whose rider holds a bow
and is crown given, a conqueror to be.
When the second seal is opened a second living creature calls
out in voice loud, "come and see."

Looking, John sees a second horse, this one fiery red, for
"from the earth its rider is to take peace
And to make people slay each other, so to him is given a
large sword" weapon opposed to peace.
As the third seal is broken John hears the third living
creature voice loudly, "come and see"
Looking, John sees a third horse, this one black and its rider
holding a pair of scales handily
Then he hears from the midst of the living creatures these
words, "a denarius for a quart of wheat
And three quarts of barley for a denarius," words denoting
there is to be a scarcity of food to eat.

As the fourth seal is broken John hears the fourth living
creature voice loudly, "come and see"
Looking, he sees a fourth horse, this horse pale and its rider
followed by Death and by Hades
Who are given power over a fourth of the earth to kill by
hunger, plague, beast and sword
So John sees four horses of different colors symbolic of their
roles in the pageant forward.
The first horse is white, color of victory, and its rider
conqueror to be who will force his will
And cause conflict and war, thus the red horse, color of the
blood that conflict and war spill.

War brings on hunger, thus the black horse of famine followed
by the pale horse of death real.

John's audience would identify the white horse conqueror as
Domitian, Roman emperor bold
Who in forcing his will concerning who is God brings
bloodshed and famine and death untold.
The opening of the fifth seal reveals "under the altar the
souls of the saints who had been slain"
The saints who had been slain "for the word of God and for
the testimony they had maintained."
And John hears the souls of these slain saints cry out, "How
long O Lord, most holy and true
How long until You judge and avenge our blood on those who
dwell on the earth defying You?"

Each of the slain is given a white robe and told to rest a
while longer until their number complete
These martyrs, thinking of the people of God below facing
bloody persecution, want justice replete
In this cosmic struggle they cry for good to triumph over
evil, God over Satan, and for victory anon
The justness of their cry is confirmed, but to practice
patience in assurance that judgment will come.
They are given white robes, white being the color of victory,
here victory for these martyrs slain
Also victory for the slain martyrs yet to be, and for all the
people of God who their faith maintain.

As the sixth seal is opened John sees a great earthquake in
motion, sees the sun turn deep black
Sees the moon turn blood red, the stars fall from heaven,
and the sky roll up like a scroll, alack!
Every mountain and island are moved from their places, and
persons from kings to slaves hide anon
They hide themselves in caves and among rocks in the
mountains and cry out imploringly, everyone

"Fall on us and hide us from the face of Him who sits on the throne and from the wrath of the Lamb!
The great day of His wrath has come, and who is able to stand?" The martyrs now see justice abound
They can rest assured that judgment is coming and, none will escape: hidden or no, the unjust found.

Following the earthquake scene and preceding the opening of seal seven, an interlude begins
In which John sees "four angels standing at the four corners of the earth holding the four winds
Holding them so that they should not blow on the earth, one sea, or on any tree," waiting to hear
Then he sees an angel with God's seal ascending from the east and crying out instructions clear:
"Do not harm the earth, the sea, or the trees till we put seal on God's servants' foreheads bald."
The number sealed is one hundred and forty-four thousand from Israel, the tribes of Israel all.

Reason dictates the number meant symbolically not literally, a combination of twelve and ten
Think number ten (completeness) and number twelve (God's people), then factor multiples in
Surely the number stands for all God's chosen people beginning with the Israelites historically
For did not Paul claim a true Israelite as one circumcised of heart, Abrahamic faith universally?
And does not John now see a multitude too vast to number from all nations and tongues known
Who wear white robes, hold palm branches and stand before the Lamb, the Lamb and throne?

In unison they cry out, "Salvation belongs to our God who sits on the throne, and to the Lamb."
Now all the angels are standing behind the elders and the living creatures in semicircle round

They fall prostrate before the throne and add a joyous "amen"
to the vast multitude's acclaim
Then an elder identifies for John the white robed multitude
who both God and Lamb proclaim
These are the ones who have come out of tribulation severe
and washed their robes clear
They washed them white in the blood of the Lamb, thus they
stand before the throne near.

They have come out of "the great tribulation" and now stand
with their God and Savior
Having remained faithful through persecution and suffering
they are now forever secure
That much is clear, but what is "the great tribulation," this
term so oft interpreted differently
One interpreter may say it is the period of conflict in which
the Antichrist reigns temporarily
Before being dethroned by Christ in a thousand year reign to
take place in end times to come
Another interpreter may say no: "the great tribulation" is that
taking place in the time of John.

The second interpreter is assuming that "the great
tribulation" refers to the Roman persecution
Specifically, the great tribulation Christians experienced
under the Roman Emperor Domitian.
Think of the multitude in "robes made white by the Lamb's
blood" having sacrificed their all
Opposing will of Emperor over will of God. Dear reader,
review and pray, then make *your* call.
This reader has so done and concludes the second
interpretation the more judicious one because
John writes to comfort his fellow Christians who are severely
suffering under the Emperor's laws.

He provides much needed assurance through his apocalyptic
vision so dramatic, cryptic and true

Still, this is not to say Revelation is for John's contemporaries
only; that would be to misconstrue
For what is true for the persecuted Christians of John's day
holds true for those beyond John's day
Have not centuries come and gone while John's Revelation
lives on, to comfort those of the Way?

Revelation Prose Summary Three
The Trumpet Judgments

The Seventh Seal Opened

Contrary to what the reader might expect at this point, the opening of the seventh seal does not end the pageant. Instead, the opening of this seal brings silence in heaven for about half and hour and then a new series begins: the series of the seven trumpet judgments. John sees the seven angels who stand before God given seven trumpets, and then another angel holding a golden censer standing before the throne. This angel is given incense, along with prayers of all the saints, to be offered upon the golden altar before the throne. Thus, the smoke of the incense and the prayers of the saints go up before God. Then the angel fills the censer with fire from the altar and hurls it to the earth, the result being rumbling thunder, lightning, and an earthquake, indicative of God's omnipotence.

The Trumpet Judgments:

The First, Second, Third, and Fourth Trumpets

Then the seven angels prepare to sound their trumpets, beginning the series of trumpet judgments. As the seals series reveal aspects of the persecution showing how the evil becomes self-destructive while imposing its will upon the saints, so the trumpets series reveal how the natural world is involved in God's judgment.

At the sound of the *first* angel's trumpet, hail and fire, mixed with blood, are hurled down upon the earth burning a third of it, a third of the trees and all the green grass. At the sound of the *second* angel's trumpet something like a huge mountain ablaze is thrown into the sea killing a third of its creatures and destroying a third of its ships. At the sound of the *third* angel's trumpet a great star, blazing like a torch, falls from the sky onto a third of the rivers and the springs of water on the earth. The name of the star is wormwood, and it turns a third of the waters bitter killing many people. At the sound of the *fourth* angel's trumpet a third of the sun, moon, and stars are struck so that a third of each is darkened. Thus, a third of the day did not shine, and likewise the night.

Then John sees and hears "an eagle flying through the midst of heaven saying with a loud voice, 'woe, woe, woe' to the inhabitants of the earth, because of the remaining blasts of the trumpet of the three angels who are about to sound" (8:13)!

The Fifth Trumpet

At the sound of the *fifth* angel's trumpet a star falls from heaven to the earth. The star is given a key to the Abyss, the bottomless pit, which when opened sends forth smoke, like from a great furnace, darkening the air and the sun. Then out of the smoke come locusts who are given power like that of scorpions. The locusts are commanded to harm nothing green—the grass or trees—only those men who do not have "the seal of God on their foreheads" (9:4). They are not given the power to kill, but only to torment and that limited to five months; furthermore, the torment is to be like that of a scorpion sting, heinous enough so that those tormented will desire death though it will not come. The locusts are like horses prepared for battle, but their faces are like the faces of men and on their heads are gold-like crowns. Their hair is like the hair of women and their teeth like the teeth of lions. They have iron-like breastplates and their wings sound like many horse-drawn chariots racing into battle. And the king over them is the angel of the bottomless pit, "whose name in Hebrew is Abaddon, but in Greek has the name Apollyon" (9:11). Thus, it appears the first woe has come leaving two to follow.

The Sixth Trumpet

At the sound of the *sixth* angel's trumpet, John hears "a voice from the four horns of the golden altar which is before God, saying to the sixth angel who had the trumpet, 'Release the four angels who are bound at the great river Euphrates'" (9:13-14). Immediately, the four angels prepared especially for this hour are released to kill a third of humanity. Their mounted army for this task is two hundred million (e.g., innumerable) says John, "and thus I saw the horses in the vision: those who sat on them had breastplates of fiery red, hyacinth blue, and sulfur yellow; and the heads of the horses were like the heads of lions; and out of their mouths came fire, smoke, and brimstone" (9:17). Thus, a third of humanity is killed by these three plagues: fire, smoke, and brimstone. Even so, "the rest of mankind, who were not killed by these plagues, did not repent of the works of their hands, that they should not worship demons, and idols of gold, silver, brass, stone, and wood which can neither see nor hear nor walk; and they did not repent of their murders or their sorceries or their sexual immorality or their thefts" (9:20-21).

A Parenthesis Between the Sixth and Seventh Trumpet: 10:1-11:13

(The Mighty Angel and the Seven Thunders)
Then John sees another mighty angel robed in a cloud coming down from heaven with a rainbow above his head, a face like the sun and fiery feet. Holding a little scroll he plants his right foot on the sea and his left foot on the land and voices a loud shout like the roar of a lion. Then the seven thunders speak and John prepares to write it down, but a voice from heaven tells him, "Seal up the things the seven thunders uttered and do not write them" (10:4). At this point the angel who stood with right foot on the sea and left foot on the land, raises his right hand and swears by Him who made heaven and earth and everything in them saying, "there should be delay no longer, but in the days of the sounding of the seventh angel, when he is about to sound, the mystery of God would be finished, as He declared to His servants the prophets" (10:6-7). Presumably, the voice from heaven tells John not to write down what the thunders say because doing so would mean seven more judgments as with the seven seals, the seven trumpets, and the seven bowls thereby prolonging the suffering of the faithful. Note that the mighty angel, related to the throne in heaven (4:3) by the rainbow above his head and to the Son of Man (1:15) by his fiery feet, declares there will be delay no longer but at the sounding of the seventh trumpet. A characteristic of the apocalyptic is shortened suffering for the faithful.

(The Little Scroll)
Next, the voice from heaven speaks again and instructs John, "Go, take the little scroll that lies open in the hand of the angel who stands on the sea and the earth" (10:8). When John approaches the angel to take the little scroll,

the angel commands, "Take and eat it; and it will make your stomach bitter, but it will be as sweet as honey in your mouth" (10:9). It was just as the angel said.

One familiar with the Old Testament will inevitably think of Ezekiel (2.8-3:3) who finds the scroll he is commanded to eat sweet as honey. The word of God is sweet even when the content is bitter: judgment severe on those turning a deaf ear to God's will.

The eating of the scroll presumably prepares John for further prophesying, for the angel informs him that he "must prophesy again about many people, nations, languages and kings" (10:11). Thus, the pageant continues with John measuring the temple.

(Measuring the Temple)

Next, John is given a measuring rod to "measure the temple of God, the altar, and the people who worship there" (11:1). Since measuring in biblical writings is usually intended for preservation or protection, presumably that is the case in this instance. Note that the court outside the temple, that given to the Gentiles (read symbolically the non-believers), is not to be measured. Thus, only the believers will be protected while the Gentiles, the non-believers, "tread the holy city underfoot for forty-two months" (11:2). The forty-two months (3 ½ years, 1260 days) is not meant literally but used figuratively meaning a short period of time. Symbolically, the worshippers in the temple are God's people and they will be protected during the treading of the holy city.

(The Two Witnesses)

Then the Lord tells John, "I will give power to My *two witnesses*, and they will prophesy one thousand two hundred and sixty days, clothed in sackcloth" (11:3). The two witnesses represent God's people and symbolically span both the Old and New Testaments. Symbolically representing the Old Testament the two witnesses are Moses and Elijah, law and prophecy. John implicitly identifies them when he describes their power: "if anyone wants to harm them, fire proceeds from their mouth and devours their enemies [and they] . . . have power to shut heaven so that no rain falls in the days of their prophecy; and they have power over waters to turn them to blood, and to strike the earth with all plagues, as often as they desire" (11:5-6).

Symbolically representing the New Testament is the church established by Jesus Christ whose coming fulfilled the law and prophecy as depicted in the Transfiguration (Matt. 17:1-13). Thus, God's people as witnesses may be martyred, as was Jesus, but they will be resurrected and glorified in heaven as he was and as are the two witnesses in John's vision. The two witnesses will be overcome temporarily by "the beast that ascends out of the bottomless pit . . . [to] make war against them, overcome them, and kill them, and their dead bodies will lie in the street of the great city which spiritually is called Sodom [figuratively Jerusalem/Rome] and Egypt [figuratively Jerusalem/Rome], where our Lord was crucified" (11:7-8). The non-believers will rejoice, make merry and not allow the two witnesses' dead bodies to be buried, but "after three and a half days the breath of life from God entered them, and they stood on their feet, and great fear fell on those who saw them. Then a loud voice from heaven calls to the two witnesses "and they ascended to heaven in a cloud and their enemies saw them" (11:11). In the same hour a great earthquake came destroying a tenth of the city and killing seven thousand men; "the rest were afraid and gave glory to the God of heaven" (11:13). No doubt, the preservation and glorification of the two martyred witnesses offer comfort and assurance to the persecuted believers that John is addressing.

The Seventh Trumpet

Between the parenthesis (10:1-11:13) and the sounding of the *seventh* angel's trumpet (11:15), John includes an enigmatic statement: "The second woe is past. Behold, the third woe is coming quickly" (11:14). Earlier, after the fourth trumpet, John tells us he saw and heard an eagle flying through midair, "saying with a loud voice, 'woe, woe, woe' to the inhabitants of the earth, because of the remaining blasts of the trumpet of the three angels who are about to sound"(8:13)! Then after the fifth trumpet he writes, "One is past. Two more woes are coming after these things" (9:12). Thus, reading 11:14 it is logical to assume that a third woe is coming with the sounding of the seventh trumpet, but that seems not the case. Upon the sounding of the seventh trumpet, "there were loud voices in heaven, saying, 'The kingdoms of this world have become the kingdoms of our Lord and of His Christ, and He shall reign forever and ever!'" (11:15). This hardly sounds as if the seventh trumpet heralds the third woe although the twenty-four elders in their worshipping of God at this point do say, "The nations were angry and Your wrath has come, / And the time of the dead, that they should be judged, / And that You should reward Your servants the prophets and the saints, / And those who fear Your name, small and great, / And should destroy those who destroy the earth" (11:18). Perhaps the meaning of the three woes is dual, referring to the woe heralded by trumpets five and six, and the woe continuing after the seventh trumpet, namely the woe of the seven bowls judgment that begins with chapter sixteen as well as the woe of the seals judgment rendered earlier in chapters six, seven, and eight. Thus, there are three series of woe each series including seven judgments: the seals judgment, the trumpets judgment, the bowls judgment.

Whatever the case, the trumpet series ends with a glimpse of the temple of God: "Then the temple of God was opened in heaven, and the ark of His covenant was seen in His temple. And there were flashes of lightning, rumbling, peals of thunder, an earthquake, and a great hailstorm" (11:19). The ark of covenant is a reminder of God's steadfastness, the keeping of covenant with His people. The lightning, thunder, earthquake, and hail are reminders of God's omnipotence. The faithful can rest assured that God keeps his covenants, His promises, and that He possesses the ultimate power to overcome evil forces arrayed against His people.

The appearance of the ark of covenant prepares the reader for the next portion of the pageant which shows, figuratively of course, the flow of history leading up to the present situation, a staple in apocalyptic writing. For example, see chapter eight of Daniel.

Revelation Poetic Summary Three: The Trumpet Judgments

Contrary to reader expectation opening of the seventh seal
does not the pageant end
No, a dramatic interlude, half an hour of silence in heaven,
then action begins again
Another series of seven, this time a series of seven trumpet
blasts by angels blown
John sees seven angels with trumpets in hand, and all
standing tall before the throne
And with them another angel holding a golden censer and
given incense and prayer
Incense mixed with prayers of the saints to be offered upon
the golden altar there.

After incense smoke and saints' prayers go up to God, the
angel fills the censer with fire
And hurls it to earth where thunder, lightning, earthquake
speak God's omnipotence dire
Then the seven angels prepare to sound their trumpets a
new series of judgments to begin
A series revealing how the natural world can be involved in
God's judgment on evil men
Seen as the sound of the *first* angel's trumpet sends hail and
fire, blood mingled, to earth
There a third of the trees were burned, all the green grass,
leaving mere ashes and dearth.

Sounding the *second* angel's trumpet something like a
mountain ablaze into the sea is thrown

Whose simmering blaze destroys a third of its creatures and
a third of its ships sailing thereon.
Sounding the *third* angel's trumpet a blazing star called
Wormwood falls on a third of the rivers
And the springs of water on the earth, killing many people
for the waters became poison bitters.
Sounding the *fourth* angel's trumpet a third of the sun,
moon, and stars are struck on site
A third of each thus darkened that a third of the day did not
shine, and likewise the night.

Then comes the cryptic scene of the eagle flying through
heaven's midst crying "woe, woe, woe"
Warning the inhabitants of the earth, whether only about
the next three trumpets we cannot know.
Is it double entendre, as later seems, also meaning seals,
trumpets, bowls, the three series of woe?
Sounding the *fifth* angel's trumpet a star from heaven falls to
earth and is given a key to the Abyss
From the bottomless pit comes forth smoke darkening the
air and the sun like furnace driven mist
And out of the smoke come locusts possessing the power of
scorpions and momentum relentless.

The locusts torment only those without God's seal and only
for a limited time, like a locust season
The torment though is like that of a scorpion sting so
heinous it drives the tormented beyond reason
Desiring death though it will not come, only the horse-like
locusts prepared for battle, men's faces
And heads with gold-like crowns, hair like that of women,
teeth like that of lions, multifaceted cases
They have iron-like breastplates and wings sounding like
horse-drawn chariots racing into battle long
Their king is angel of the bottomless pit, in Hebrew known as
Abaddon, but Apollyon in Greek known.

We hear that two more woes will follow and we wonder only
trumpets or bowls too, again dual tone?
Sounding the *sixth* angel's trumpet elicits a voice from the
horns of the golden altar of God's throne
The voice commands release of the four angels bound at the
great river Euphrates, them unbind
Immediately, the four angels are released for their special
mission: killing one third of mankind
And for this task they possess a mounted army of two
hundred million says John who sees them pass
He sees breastplates fiery red, hyacinth blue, sulfur yellow,
and also horses' with lion like heads, alas!

And out of the horses' mouths came fire, smoke, and
brimstone, three plagues decimating men
But despite the killing of mankind, one third, the survivors
did not repent of incriminating sin
They continued to worship demons and works of their
hands: senseless idols dumb and bereft
They would not repent of their murders, their sorceries,
their sexual immorality, or their theft.
Now, rather than the sounding of trumpet seven we seem to
see a sidebar or parenthesis
We see action involving a mighty angel, seven thunders, a little
scroll, and two witnesses.

A mighty angel robed in a cloud comes down from heaven
with a rainbow above his head
His face resembles the sun, fiery are his feet and in his hand
he holds a little scroll unread.
Placing his right foot on the sea and his left on the land the
mighty angel roars like a lion
Then seven thunders speak and John prepares to write it
down, but is instructed to decline
"Seal up the things the seven thunders uttered, do not
record" was heaven's quick command
"There should be delay no longer," swears the mighty angel
with deference raised right hand.

Supposedly, recording the thunders would prolong the
suffering of the faithful ones
Beyond the present trumpet series, the coming bowl series,
and the seals already done
The mighty angel declaring "there should be delay no longer"
possesses authority implicitly
He connects to the throne of God by rainbow and to the
Son of Man by fiery feet, figuratively
And when he speaks, one foot planted on the sea and one on
the land, speaks authoritatively
He qualifies the no delay saying "but in the days surrounding
the seventh angel" prophetically.

He says when the seventh trumpet is about to sound "the
mystery of God would be finished"
Presumably the angel means God's plan for good plainly
prevails nothing having diminished
More conflict and battle are yet to come, but the outcome is
known, God and good will win
Such is confirmed in John's cosmic vision: the forces of good
triumph over the forces of sin.
Although this visionary pageant tends to take enigmatic
turns, its major motif is never lost
That is, if readers remember to put themselves in John's time
frame when supplying gloss.

In the hand of the mighty angel lies the little scroll, and John
is told to receive it therefrom:
"Eat it," says the angel, "it will make your stomach bitter, but
will taste sweet as honeycomb."
John's audience will think of Ezekiel commanded to eat a
scroll both bitter and honey sweet:
The word of God is sweet, but to those in defiance its
content turns bitter in judgment meet.
The eating of the scroll prepares the visionary John for
further prophetic duty it seems
For he is told he must prophesy again about many people,
nations, languages and kings.

Next, John is given a measuring rod to measure God's temple
and the people who worship there
Figuratively, the measuring means that the people of God
will be protected from Satan's snare
The court outside the temple is not to be measured, for there
warning signs the Gentile confronts
Thus, symbolically, only believers will be protected when the
holy city is tread forty-two months.
Then John is told about *two witnesses* who will, clothed in
sackcloth, prophesy for 1,260 days
Though not named the two witnesses are identified implicitly
through description of their ways.

God gives power to His two witnesses who symbolically
represent the Old Testament and the New
As Old Testament representatives, they are Moses and
Elijah, the law and the prophets, these two
Who but Moses had the power to turn the waters into blood
and strike the earth with plagues all?
Who but Elijah had power to devour enemies with fire and
close up heaven so rain does not fall?
As New Testament representatives they become the Church
established by Jesus Christ the head
His coming fulfilled the law and prophecy as the
Transfiguration scene in the gospels clearly said.

God's people may be martyred as was Jesus, but they will be
resurrected and in heaven glorified
As was Jesus and as are these witnesses who are in
prescribed time attacked by evil personified
The beast from the bottomless pit ascends to make war on
them, kill them, and let their bodies lie
The non-believers rejoice and will not allow the bodies to be
buried, but in the street pass them by
They in the great city spiritually called Sodom and Egypt,
figures fingering Rome and Jerusalem
These two cities actively persecuted God's people and had a
hand in the crucifixion, both of them.

After three and a half days when the breath of life from God
entered the two witnesses they stood
Then a loud voice from heaven called and they ascended in a
cloud as their enemies turned wood
Their fear soared as a great earthquake destroyed a tenth of
the city killing seven thousand men
The survivors promptly gave glory to the God of heaven not
daring to defy His witnesses again.
Thus ends the parenthetical scene, but before the seventh
trumpet can sound enigma enters in
It is loudly announced, "the second woe is past, behold, a third
woe is coming quickly," amen.

Enigmatic is the seeming discrepancy between the woe
announcements and actual circumstance
After the fourth trumpet an eagle flew thru midair crying,
"woe, woe, woe to earth's inhabitants"
Woe because of the remaining blasts of the remaining three
angels who are yet to sound?
Then after the fifth trumpet we hear, "one is past, but two
more woes are coming around?
Is it not logical to assume when the second woe is past and
the third woe announced, it is so?
Yet upon the sounding of the *seventh trumpet* voices from
heaven proclaim, but hardly woe!

For the voices from heaven proclaim, "the kingdoms of this
world become our Lord's domain
And the domain of His Christ and that He shall reign
forever, and forever He shall be our king."
This hardly seems as if the seventh trumpet heralds a third
woe, yet the twenty-four elders declare:
"The nations were angry and your wrath has come that the
time of the dead should be judged there
That You should reward Your servants the prophets and the
saints and those who fear your name
Both small and great, and should destroy those who destroy
the earth," the elders boldly proclaim.

Perhaps it is assurance boldly proclaimed before more woes
are poured upon the earth forsooth
Perhaps the meaning of the three woes is dual, as
conjectured before, the double entendre truth:
The woe heralded by trumpets five and six, and the woe
continuing after trumpet seven sounds
Namely the woe of the judgments initiated in chapter
sixteen, the woe of the seven bowl rounds.
Counting the seals woe of chapters six thru eight, the total
three series of judgments:
The seals, the trumpets, the bowls, each a judgment of woe,
and all three heaven sent.

Double entendre woe or no, the trumpet series ends in a
glimpse of God's temple pure
"Then the temple of God is opened in heaven, and the ark of
His covenant seen secure"
Also flashes of lightning, peals of thunder, an earthquake
and a great hailstorm appear.
The ark of covenant is a reminder of God's steadfastness, the
keeping of covenant dear
The lightning, thunder, earthquake, and hail are reminders
of God's omnipotent sheen
The faithful can rest assured that all His promises are
preserved in His power supreme.

Furthermore, the appearance of the ark of covenant prepares
the reader for the portion next
Figuratively, the flow of history leading up to the present
situation now constitutes the text.

REVELATION PROSE SUMMARY FOUR
HISTORICAL OVERVIEW

Introduction

At this point of the pageant, John includes a historical overview showing events leading up to the present condition of God's people and the outcome of their present difficulties. It is, of course, revealed indirectly through symbolic action rendered through highly figurative language. Chapters twelve, thirteen, and fourteen comprise this historical overview.

The Woman and the Fiery Red Dragon

A great sign appears in heaven: "a woman clothed with the sun, with the moon under her feet, and on her head a garland of twelve stars [and] being with child, she cried out in labor and in pain to give birth" (12:1-2). The child to be born is obviously the Messiah. And dedicated to destroying the Child is "a great fiery red dragon having seven heads and ten horns" (12:3). The dragon has to be Satan, the seven heads suggesting complete evil and the ten horns suggesting great power: "His tail drew a third of the stars of heaven and threw them to the earth. And the dragon stood before the woman who was ready to give birth, to devour her Child as soon as it was born" (12:4). The dragon, of course, is not successful in devouring the "male Child who was to rule all nations with a rod of iron. And her Child was caught up to God and to His throne" 12:5). And "the woman fled into the wilderness, where she has a place prepared by God, that they should feed her there one thousand two hundred and sixty days" (12:6). The woman with the garland of twelve stars (twelve the symbol for God's people) now represents the new people of God needing His protection as did the Israelites in Exodus. It is interesting to note that the time of protection (the feeding) corresponds to the time of persecution, the symbolic 1,260 days. It should be further noted that the wilderness besides being a place of refuge can also be a place of danger and evil.

War in Heaven and the Consequences

War breaks out in heaven whereby Michael and his angels battle the dragon and his angels. The dragon and his angels lose and no place is found for them in heaven any longer "so the great dragon was cast out, that serpent of old called the Devil and Satan, who deceives the whole world; he was cast to the earth, and his angels were cast out with him" (12:9). The earlier figurative statement "his tail drew a third of the stars of heaven and threw them to earth," no doubt, portends the war in heaven and the casting out of Satan (the dragon) and his angels.

Upon the casting out of Satan and his angels a loud voice from heaven announces that "now salvation, and strength, and the kingdom of our God, and the power of His Christ have come, for the accuser of our brethren [see Job 1:9-11], who accused them before our God day and night, has been cast down" (12:10). Heaven is rid of Satan and his angels, but earth becomes the new battlefield. Yet even on earth Satan can be defeated as assured by the loud voice from heaven who goes on to say that believers overcome him (Satan) "by the blood of the Lamb, and the word of their testimony," and by remaining faithful in the face of death (12:11). Though believers are given the sure plan for triumph, the earthly battle will not be easy as the loud voice from heavens warns, "Woe to the inhabitants of the earth . . . for the devil has come down to you having great wrath, because he knows that he has a short time" (12:12). His time is short because he will be restricted when the earth is transformed.

When the dragon realizes that he has been cast to the earth, he begins to persecute "the woman who gave birth to the male Child, but the woman was given two wings of a great eagle, that she might fly into the wilderness to her place, where she is nourished for a time and times and half a time, from the presence of the serpent" (12:13-14). The serpent/dragon spews water out of his mouth thinking to cause the woman to be carried away by the flood, but the earth opens up and swallows the flood spewed from the serpent/dragon's mouth. "And the dragon was enraged with the woman, and he went to make war with the rest of her offspring, who keep the commandments of God and have the testimony of Jesus Christ" (12:17). Thus, the pageant provides an explanation of the evil persecution of God's people (the dragon cast to earth takes revenge against God by persecuting the woman and her offspring), an explanation of limits to the power of evil against God's people (the woman is protected "for a time and times and half a time" from the serpent), and an explanation of the means of preservation for God's people against evil ("by the blood of the Lamb, and the word of their testimony").

The Dragon and the Beast Out of the Sea

John sees the dragon standing on the seashore and rising out of the sea a beast "having seven heads and ten horns, and on his horns ten crowns, and on his heads a blasphemous name" (13:1). No doubt, the beast is Rome and the seven heads represent emperors with total power. The beast is further described as being like a leopard but having feet like a bear and a mouth like a lion. This image echoes Daniel (7:2-7) who uses these three animals to describe three powerful empires and John, by allusion, is attributing these powerful attributes to Rome: "and the dragon gave him [the beast] his power, his throne, and great authority" (13:2).

"So they worshipped the dragon who gave authority to the beast; and they worshipped the beast, saying, 'Who is like the beast? Who is able to make war with him?' And he was given a mouth speaking great things and blasphemies" (13:4-5). They worship the dragon through the beast who mouths blasphemies. The Roman emperors at the time were declared to be divine and emperor worship was encouraged and at times forced. An emperor claiming to be god and demanding worship would, of course, be blasphemous to Christians.

"And it was granted him [the beast] to make war with the saints and to overcome them. And the authority was given him over every tribe, tongue, and nation. And all who dwell on the earth will worship him, whose names have not been written in the Book of Life of the Lamb slain from the foundation of the world" (13:7-8). Thus, the saints are informed that evil will be allowed to run its course (forty-two months, the symbolic indefinite period), and to emphasize John sounds again the earlier refrain used in the seven letters: "If anyone has an ear let him hear" (13:9). But the saints are given dual assurance: "He who leads into captivity shall go into captivity; he who kills with the sword must be killed with the sword. Here is the patience and the faith of the saints" (13:10). The saints can take comfort in knowing that evil will receive its just punishment, and that their names are written in the Book of the Lamb. Thus, the saints are comforted and assured that their salvation is secure in their patience and faith.

The Beast Out of the Earth

Then John sees "another beast coming up out of the earth, and he had two horns like a lamb and spoke like a dragon, and he exercises all the authority of the first beast in his presence, and causes the earth and those who dwell in it to worship the first beast, whose deadly wound was healed" (13:11). This beast out of the earth is subservient to the beast out of the sea for, as the "horns like a lamb" suggests, he represents the religious priesthood that serves emperor worship (symbolically the beast out of the sea represents the emperors). "He [the beast out of the earth, the religious priesthood serving emperor worship] performs great signs, so that he even makes fire come down from heaven on earth in the sight of man, and he deceives those who dwell on the earth by those signs which he was granted to do in the sight of the beast [the beast out of the sea, the emperors], telling those who dwell on the earth to make an image to the beast who was wounded by the sword and lived" (13:13-14).

The reference to "the beast who was wounded by the sword and lived" is, no doubt, a reference to Nero, the emperor who most cruelly persecuted the Christians and around who, after his death, a myth developed foretelling of his return to life and to power. The myth or no, Nero became synonymous with Christian persecution and a symbolic name for it as Babylon had become a symbolic name for Jewish persecution and for idol worship. Domitian, reigning emperor at the time of the writing of Revelation, was considered by many to be fulfillment of the Nero reincarnation myth. He insisted on being viewed as god and actively persecuted Christians who refused to recognize him as such. Yet, by extension all the emperors claiming deity would symbolically be Nero as John indicates when revealing the number that identifies the beast out of the sea (the emperor beast).

The beast out of the earth (the priesthood beast) "was granted power to give breath to the image of the beast [the emperor beast] that its image should both speak and cause as many as would not worship its image to be killed, and he [the priesthood beast] causes all, both small and great, rich and poor, free and slave, to receive a mark on their foreheads, and that no one may buy or sell except one who has the mark or the name of the beast [the emperor beast], or the number of his name" (13:15-17). Then

John reveals the number saying, "let him who has understanding calculate the number of the beast, for it is the number of a man: his number is 666" (13:18).

The Number 666

The most logical explanation for the number 666 is the following. In early times peoples had no system of figures so that each letter had a designated number, therefore, the letters of one's name could be expressed by the total of the numbered letters. To illustrate, scholars sometimes give the example of a preserved line written on the wall of a building in Pompeii (the ancient Roman city deluged by a volcano in 79 A.D.): "I love her whose number is 545." Thus, the writer could both conceal and reveal his beloved. Likewise, John conceals and reveals the name of the beast. According to scholars, the name Nero fits the number 666 and the number 616 which is used in some ancient manuscripts. The name is spelled two different ways: Nero Caesar and Neron Caesar. When written in Hebrew the designated numbers for the letters in Nero Caesar total 616; the designated numbers for Neron Caesar total 666. Thus we have a logical explanation of John's cryptic identification of the beast.

The 144,000

"Then I looked, and behold, a Lamb standing on Mount Zion, and with Him one hundred and forty-four thousand, having His father's name written on their foreheads" (14:1). John also hears a voice from heaven "like the voice of many waters and like the voice of loud thunder," figurative rendering of the voice of God. And to the harmonious sound of harpists a new song is sung that no one could learn "except the hundred and forty-four thousand who were redeemed from the earth" (14:3), those who have remained faithful and have not worshipped the beast. The hundred and forty-four thousand must be a symbolic number representing God's people: think multiple of twelve (God's people) and multiple of ten (completeness). Also figurative is the reference to their being virgins not having defiled themselves with women, meaning they have maintained their fidelity to the Lord. The fidelity figure is used on occasion by the prophets of the Old Testament in describing the relationship between the Israelites and God. Later, John writes, "in their mouth was found no guile, for they are without fault before the throne" (14:5).

Babylon Fallen

Next, John sees "another angel flying in the midst of heaven, having the everlasting gospel to preach to those who dwell on the earth—every nation, tribe tongue, and people—saying with a loud voice, 'fear God and give glory to Him, for the hour of His judgment has come; and worship Him who made heaven and earth, the seas and springs of water'" (14:6-7). The gospel having been carried world wide, it is now time for judgment. John witnesses still another angel proclaiming judgment at hand in saying, "Babylon is fallen, is fallen, that great city because she has made all nations drink of the wine of wrath of her fornication" (14:8). The hundred and forty-four thousand, the people of God, are exalted because of their fidelity while Rome (Babylon) is fallen and destined to receive God's wrath because of its infidelity.

Contrasting the Fate of Those Who Worship the Beast and Those Who Worship the Lord

A third angel announces, "if anyone worships the beast and his image, and receives his mark on his forehead or on his hand, he himself shall also drink of the wine of the wrath of God, which is poured out full strength into the cup of His indignation. And he shall be tormented with fire and brimstone in the presence of the holy angels and in the presence of the Lamb. And the smoke of their torment ascends forever and ever; and they have no rest day or night, who worship the beast and his image, and whoever receives the mark of his name" (14:9-11). The fate of those who worship the beast and those who worship the Lord becomes abundantly clear in the contrast between the eternal punishment of the people of the beast and the eternal preservation of the hundred and forty-four thousand, the people of God. It is interesting to note at this point in the pageant what might be called an aside: John hears a voice from heaven saying, "Write: 'Blessed are the dead who die in the Lord from now on'" (14:13). The saints to whom John is writing are being warned of the likelihood of facing martyrdom but at the same time are being assured of great reward for holding fast to their faith.

The Harvest

John looks and beholds "a white cloud, and sitting on the cloud One like the Son of Man, having on His head a golden crown, and in His hand a sharp sickle" (14:14). Since the earth is ripe, the "One like the Son of man" reaps the earth taking His own. Then a second divine being, an angel, also holding a sharp sickle is instructed to "thrust in your sharp sickle and gather the clusters of the vine of the earth for her grapes are fully ripe. So the angel thrust his sickle into the earth and gathered the vine of the earth, and threw it into the great winepress of the wrath of God, and the winepress was trampled outside the city and blood came out of the winepress, up to the horses' bridles, for one thousand six hundred furlongs" (14:18-20). In this harvest metaphor we see the gathering of the faithful for preservation and reward, and the gathering of the followers of the beast for confinement and punishment. The faithful are secure inside the city while the followers of the beast are trampled in the winepress outside the city with blood coming "out of the winepress, up to the horses' bridles, one thousand six hundred furlongs." No doubt, the sixteen hundred furlongs is intended figuratively like other numbers in the script. It has been purposed the sixteen hundred number being a multiple of four (representing the created world) and of ten (representing inclusiveness) portends that God's judgment reaches to anywhere in the world, and that here it is primarily focused on the beast and his followers. Such seems to be a reasonable explanation.

Revelation Poetic Summary Four
Historical Overview

Inserted into the pageant is historical overview, events
leading up to time present
Time when prevailing emperor worship poses for God's
people an ominous event
All revealed indirectly through symbolic action carried by
language highly figurative
A woman, a dragon, and two beasts provide narrative both
historical and imaginative.
First, appearing is the woman all clothed with the sun and
with the moon under her feet
With garland of twelve stars on her head, with child and in
labor both painful and sweet.

Waiting to destroy her Child is a great fiery red dragon
having seven heads and ten horns
The child being born must Messiah be and the red dragon
Satan sure, sounding all alarms
Symbolizing total evil are his seven heads and massive power
his ten horns, yet he fails
And failing to destroy her Child who is caught up to God on
His throne, the dragon wails.
The woman flees to the wilderness to a place prepared by
God and there for 1,260 days fed
She symbolizes God's new people needing protection as did
the Israelites when Moses led.

War breaks out in heaven, Michael and his angels battle the
dragon and his angels unsound
The dragon and his angels lose and are thereby cast out, no
longer is place in heaven found

"So the great dragon was cast out, that serpent of old called
Satan, that deceiver of the world
Now the power and strength and kingdom of our God and
Christ have come, have unfurled
For the accuser of our brethren, night and day accuser before
our God, has been cast down"
So announces a heavenly voice confirming the old accuser and
his angels no longer around.

The war in heaven whereby Satan and his angels are cast
down is metaphorically portended:
"The dragon's tail drew a third of heaven's stars and threw
them down to earth suspended."
Heaven rid of Satan, earth becomes the new battlefield, yet
there he can be defeated as well
So declares an assuring voice from heaven: "by the blood of
the Lamb, and by testimony tell"
Yet his defeat with difficulty comes: "woe to the inhabitants
of the earth, beware of his wrath"
The old serpent roams earth bent on destroying God' people,
revenge for the short time he hath.

John writes, "the dragon enraged with the woman went to
make war on her offspring, all
He warred on those who keep the commandments of God
and who testify to Christ's call."
Thus, the pageant provides explanation for the evil
persecution of the people of God true
(Dragon cast down takes revenge against God, persecuting
the woman and offspring too).
It provides explanation of limits to the power of evil: (the
woman protected, time indefinite)
Explained also is the preservation of God's people: (the blood
of the Lamb, testimony right).

Joining the woman and dragon is a beast with seven heads
and ten horns, a beast out of the sea

"On the beast's ten horns were crowns and on his seven
heads a name, a name of blasphemy."
No doubt the beast represents Rome and the seven heads
emperors with power complete
The beast is further described as being leopard-like, but with
lion's mouth and bear's feet
These three animals, powerful empires in Daniel, by allusion
here become powerful Rome
In confirmation, we hear "and the dragon gave the beast his
power, his authority, his throne."

"So they worshipped the dragon who gave authority to the
beast, and the beast too
Saying there is no one like the beast, no one can war on him,
no one him construe."
Furthermore, the beast "was given a mouth speaking great
things and blasphemies"
Thus, subjects worship the dragon through the beast who
mouths seductive infamies.
Roman emperors of the time were cast as divine and their
worship sometimes forced
To the Christian such procedure could only be perceived a
most blasphemous course.

John writes, "it was granted the beast to make war with the
saints and to overcome them
And authority was given him over every tribe, tongue, and
nation; all will worship him
All will worship him whose names have not been written in
the Book of Life of the Lamb."
Now the saints know evil will be allowed to run its course,
for an indefinite time abound
And for emphasis John sounds refrain: "if anyone has an ear
let him hear," ear inclined
For there is more to hear and it concerns assurance, assurance
against evil of any time.

"He who leads into captivity shall go into captivity; he who kills with sword dies by sword
And here is the patience and the faith of the saints:" here they are assured thru God's word.
The saints can take comfort in knowing that evil will receive its just punishment in due time
That security resides in their names written in the Book of Life, in their patient faith sublime.
But with assurance comes more challenge, again in the form of a beast, a second one
This beast, rising out of the earth, "had two horns like a lamb and spoke like a dragon."

"He exercises all the authority of the first beast in his presence and commands his worship
All are to worship the first beast, whose deadly wound was healed," it is official prescript.
The beast out of the earth is subservient to the beast out of the sea, (emperors symbolically)
Perpetuating emperor worship is the beast of the earth's purview, (priesthood symbolically).
This beast in lamb disguise deceptively performs great signs, signs of great appeal
And tells all subjects make an image to the beast "whose deadly wound was healed."

"The beast who was wounded by the sword and lived" surely references the emperor Nero
Whose name became synonymous with persecuting emperor like sinful city with Gomorrah.
Following Nero's death a myth spread foretelling of his return to life and to Caesar reinstated
And Domitian, emperor at Revelation's writing, was perceived by many as Nero reincarnated
But myth aside, several god pretending, persecuting emperors fit the prototype of Nero Caesar
As John so indicates when he reveals by number the symbolic identity of the sea beast bizarre.

The earth beast was granted power to give breath to the
image of the sea beast, emperor real
That its image should both speak and cause as many as
would not worship that image killed
And this earth beast (read priesthood) causes all, free or
slave, rich or poor, strong or frail
All to receive a mark on their forehead; anyone without the
mark could neither buy nor sell
Without the mark or name of the beast or the number of his
name, buying and selling is nixed
"Let him with understanding calculate the beast's number, for
it is the number of a man: 666."

Speculation runs wild about this cryptic number, but one
reasoned, logical explanation prevails:
Preceding the Arabic numeral system, each letter had a
designated number to weight the scales
And letters spelling the name Nero Caesar in Hebrew added
together tip the scales at 616
Which, of course, without further explanation would not
suffice, would not speculation nix
Yet scholars know that some early manuscripts of Revelation
used the number 616 as name
But most spelled the name Nero*n* Caesar, adding an "*n*" and a
weight of 666: man the same.

Then, John looks seeing a Lamb standing on Mount Zion,
standing with Him 144,000 souls
All with His father's name written on their foreheads, and
then from heaven a voice unfolds
The voice unfolds like the sound of many waters and like the
voice of loud thunder, like God
And to the harmonious sound of harps he hears a new song
sung, but only one group gets nod
Only the 144,000 redeemed from the earth, the 144,000
that remained faithful to the Lord
They had remained faithful never worshipping the beast, they
had remained of one accord.

The hundred and forty-four thousand is a number symbolic,
a multiple of twelve and of ten
They represent God's people whose faith is complete,
thereby reaching their journey's end.
But there is much more pageant to witness as John's
apocalyptic vision continues to unfold
More angels more announcements more prophecies, most
pointing ahead to judgments bold
There is the angel flying through the midst of heaven having
the eternal gospel to spread
Saying to all those who dwell on the earth, "God's judgment
has come, judgment dread."

Then another angel proclaims judgment at hand saying,
"Babylon is fallen, great the fall
She is fallen for making the others drink of the wine of
wrath of her fornication, cities all."
Of course, Babylon stands for Rome and the worshippers of
the beast are subjects of Rome
And contrasting the people of God and the worshippers of
the beast becomes warning strong
"If anyone worships the beast and his image he shall drink
the wine of God's wrath infinite
He shall be tormented with fire and brimstone in the presence
of the Lamb, eternal plight."

"And the smoke of their torment ascends forever and ever;
they have no rest night or day"
Thus, the pageant contrasts the fate of those worshipping
the beast versus those of the Way
It is eternal damnation for those of the beast but eternal
preservation for those of the Way
For the hundred and forty-four thousand, the people of
God, it is eternal joy night or day.
Then in an aside a warning comes: "Blessed are the dead who
die in the Lord from now on"
Assurance is theirs, the people of God, but only if they keep
the faith even thru martyrdom.

Looking up, John beholds "a white cloud, and sitting on the cloud One like the Son of Man"
Ready to reap the ripe earth taking His own, and for so doing He holds a sharp sickle in hand.
Looking again, John sees a second divine, an angel who also holds in his hand a sickle sharp
The angel has instructions to thrust his sickle gathering the vine of the earth, grapes fully tart
When done, throw it "into the great winepress of the wrath of God," there to be trampled on
And so it was, outside the city, and blood came out bridle deep for sixteen hundred furlongs.

In this harvest metaphor we see the gathering of God's people for preservation and reward
In the gathering of the people of the beast, we see confinement and punishment their card.
Figuratively, God's people are secure inside the city while the beast's people suffer outside
And, no doubt, the 1,600 furlongs is figurative too as are most numbers in this pageant wide.
One reasonable conjecture is that being a multiple of four and of ten suggests its significance:
Think four for created world, think ten for inclusiveness, then think God's judgment limitless.

Revelation Prose Summary Five
The Bowl Judgments, and the Harlot and Beast

Prelude to the Bowl Judgments
"Then I saw another sign in heaven, great and marvelous: seven angels having the seven last plagues, for in them the wrath of God is complete" (15:1). Thus, the pageant continues, the figurative and symbolic rendering of the message of Revelation. The sight is "great and marvelous" to John for he perceives victory for the persecuted saints whose unshakable faith in the Lamb has lifted the martyred among them to the throne of God where they sing His praises preceding the final series of judgments. John "saw something like a sea of glass mingled with fire [fire now because of judgment] and those who have victory over the beast, over his image and over his mark and over the number of his name, standing on the sea of glass, having harps of God. And they sing the song of Moses, the servant of God, and the song of the Lamb" (15:2-3). As the Israelites safely cross the Red Sea before the closing waters destroyed Pharaoh's pursuing army sang praises to God, so those having victory over the beast now sing praises to Him. It is also interesting to note that several of the plagues involved in the bowls judgment echo the plagues visited upon Egypt to persuade Pharaoh to let the Israelites depart.

John looks again and this time sees that "the temple of the tabernacle of the testimony in heaven was opened. And out of the temple came the seven angels having the seven plagues, clothed in pure bright linen, having their chests girded with golden bands. Then one of the four living creatures gave to the seven angels seven golden bowls full of the wrath of God who lives forever and ever"(15:5-7). John further notes that the temple was filled with smoke from God's power and glory and that no one was allowed to enter the temple until the completion of the seven bowls judgment.

The Seven Bowls Judgment

A loud voice from the temple tells the seven angels, "Go and pour out the bowls of the wrath of God on the earth" (16:1). The *first* angel "poured his bowl out upon the earth, and a foul and loathsome sore came upon the men who had the mark of the beast and those who worshipped his image. Then the *second* angel "poured out his bowl on the sea, and it became blood as of a dead man; and every living creature in the sea died. Then the *third* angel poured out his bowl on the rivers and springs of water, and they became blood" (16: 2-4). The angel of waters responds to the blood plague saying, "You are righteous, O Lord, / The One who is and who was and who is to be, / Because You have judged these things. / For they have shed the blood of saints and prophets, / And you have given them blood to drink. / For it is their just due" (16:5-6). The angel is pleased that the punishment fits the crime: the persecutors who have shed so much blood now must drink blood to their detriment.

The *fourth* angel poured out his bowl on the sun giving him the power to scorch men with fire, and so they were. Yet, instead of repenting, they blasphemed God, the all powerful One. "Then the *fifth* angel poured out his bowl on the throne of the beast, and his kingdom became full of darkness; and they gnawed their tongues because of the pain. And they blasphemed the God of heaven because of their pains and their sores, and they did not repent of their deeds" (16:10-11). Despite the judgments against the people of the beast, they continue to blaspheme God; repentance is not on their minds.

The *sixth* angel pouring out his bowl on the river Euphrates dries up its waters thus preparing the way for the kings of the east. As a matter of history, Parthia, a land of fierce fighters and a formidable enemy of the Roman Empire, lay to the east of the Euphrates. But the implications of the judgment go beyond the historical, John sees "three unclean spirits like frogs coming out of the mouth of the dragon, out of the mouth of the beast, and out of the mouth of the false prophet [the second beast]. For they are spirits of demons, performing signs, which go out to the kings of the earth and of the whole world, to gather them to the battle of that great day of God Almighty" (16:13-14). Out of the mouths of this reverse and perverse trinity come demonic spirits directed to persuade and summon kings of the earth to join together at a particular place, later identified as Armageddon (16:16), prepared to do battle against God Almighty.

At this point is interjected a parenthetical element in the form of a prophetic announcement from the Son of Man (see Matt 24:43-44): "Behold, I am coming as a thief. Blessed is he who watches, and keeps his garments, lest he walk naked and they see his shame" (16:15). Presumably, this statement is interjected to remind the people of God to remain vigilant and hopeful though surrounded by evil forces. Following the prophetic interjection the narrative returns to the demonic spirits: "And they [the demonic spirits] gathered them [the kings] together to the place called in Hebrew, Armageddon" (16:16).

"Then the *seventh* angel poured out his bowl into the air, and a loud voice came out of the temple of heaven, from the throne, saying, 'It is done'" (16:17). The pouring out of the seventh bowl ends not only the bowl plagues but the series of judgments: seals, trumpets, and bowls. Each of the three ends punctuated by thunderings, lightnings, and an earthquake (8:5; 11:19; 16:18), and the earthquake punctuating the completion of the series, the bowl plagues, is a great and mighty earthquake "as had not occurred since men were on the earth." The next verse seems to indicate that the mighty earthquake severely damaged Babylon (Rome): "Now the great city was divided into three parts, and the cities of the nations fell. And great Babylon was remembered before God, to give her the cup of the wine of the fierceness of His wrath" (16:19).

Following the great earthquake is a mighty hail storm: "And great hail from heaven fell upon men, every hailstone about the weight of a talent [one-hundred pounds]. And men blasphemed God because of the plague of the hail" (16:21). Despite the punitive plagues, men continue in their blasphemy.

The Great Harlot and the Beast

One of the bowl angels approaches John saying, "Come, I will show you the judgment of the great harlot who sits on many waters, with whom the kings of the earth committed fornication, and the inhabitants of the earth were made drunk with the wine of her fornication" (17:1-2). For this portion of the pageant John is carried away in the Spirit to the wilderness where he sees "a woman sitting on a scarlet beast which was full of names of blasphemy, having seven heads and ten horns" (17:3). We soon perceive that the great harlot represents Rome, especially the political arm of Rome which is persecuting Christians, for the harlot is "drunk with the blood of the martyrs of Jesus" (17:6). And we should note that the scarlet beast on which she is sitting is "full of names of blasphemy." Presumably, the beast is the Roman Empire with its many gods, including certain emperors, whose names would register blasphemy to Christians. This would especially be true in the case of decreed emperor worship.

On the forehead of the great harlot is written, "*Mystery,* Babylon the Great, the Mother of Harlots and the Abominations of the Earth" (17:5). When John marvels upon seeing the great harlot, the angel tells him, "I will tell you the *mystery* of the woman and the beast that carries her, which has the seven heads and the ten horns" (17:7). The angel then reveals that the seven heads are seven mountains on which the harlot sits and that also the seven heads are seven kings. The seven heads as mountains surely mean the seven hills that Rome was built on and presumably the seven kings represent Roman emperors. Thus, Rome, like Babylon before her, is persecuting God's people and, with its seductive power and wealth is, like a harlot, corrupting the world. The seven heads as rulers is not so clear and trying to designate seven actual emperors presents problems. Does one begin with Julius Caesar or with Augustus, and does one count or not count the three excessively short term reigns between Nero and Vespasian? What seems clearer is that seven, the seven heads as rulers, indicates something coming to completion: "five have fallen, one is, and the other has not yet come, and when he comes, he must continue a short time" (17:10). This seems to predict that the persecution of God's people by the beast will be ending in a short time.

But John, not finished with the beast symbolism, says "the beast that was, and is not, is himself also the eighth, and is of the seven, and is going to perdition"(17:11). Is John figuratively implying, as scholars have suggested, that the demonic character of the beast, as it now exists, is taken from one of the past rulers who has been reborn? If so, that would, of course, be Nero, the first emperor to vigorously persecute the Christians, and whose spirit is reborn in the person of Domitian, the emperor vigorously persecuting Christians at the time Revelation was written. Then there is the symbolism of the ten horns of the beast: "And the ten horns which you saw are ten kings who have received no kingdom as yet, but they receive authority for one hour as kings with the beast" (17:12). It sounds as if the ten kings are allies of the beast, and give their power to the beast for a short time, but will "hate the harlot, make her desolate and naked, eat her flesh and burn her with fire" (17:16). Presumably, the beast and the ten allies turn on the harlot and destroy her. In this case we have evil destroying evil, a characteristic of evil that John perhaps wants to emphasize. Ironically, it is God who "has put it into their hearts [the ten kings] to fulfill His purpose, to be of one mind, and to give their kingdom to the beast, until the words of God are fulfilled" (17:17). It appears at this point that the harlot Rome is separated from the beast Rome as the persecutor of Christians, and though she is destroyed Rome as an empire lives on. If that is the case, then the destruction of the harlot symbolically portends the end of the Christian persecution.

Babylon Fallen (Rome Doomed)

As the pageant continues, John sees another angel, one of great illumination and of great authority come down from heaven crying loudly, "Babylon the great is fallen, is fallen and has become a habitation of demons, a prison for every foul spirit . . . for all the nations have drunk of the wine of the wrath of her fornication, the kings of the earth have committed fornication with her, and the merchants of the earth have become rich through the abundance of her luxury" (18: 2-3). Of course, Babylon is the symbolic name for Rome in this announcement that may remind the reader of prophetic funeral dirges in the Old Testament referencing the destruction of notorious cities such as Babylon and Nineveh. And in this pageant scene Rome joins those notorious cities as her destruction is described: "Her plagues will come in one day—death and mourning and famine. And she will be utterly burned with fire, and strong is the Lord God who judges her" (18:8). This second voice from heaven also sends warning to God's people: "Come out of her, my people, lest you share in her sins, and lest you receive her plagues, for her sins have reached to heaven, and God has remembered her iniquities" (18:4-5). God's people are warned to flee in order that they are not caught in the judgment thereby experiencing further suffering.

The kings and merchants and traders affiliated with Rome though not directly included in the judgment are greatly impacted by the judgment as they "standing at a distance" lament their loss. On the one hand, Rome was the world's commercial center to which and through which the products of the world came for sale and distribution—no doubt, a beneficial service—but, on the other hand, Rome's accumulated wealth and power resulted in abusiveness in the form of luxurious excess and trafficking in human lives which in turn led to her judgment: "In her was found the blood of prophets and saints, and all who were slain on the earth" (18:24). The pageant calls for rejoicing as she is destroyed: "Rejoice over her, O heaven and you holy apostles and prophets, for God has avenged you on her" (18:20). In the cosmic war between good and evil, between God's people and Satanic evil, God's people win another battle.

Revelation Poetic Summary Five
The Bowl Judgments, and the Harlot and Beast

"Then I saw another sign, great and marvelous: seven angels each with a plague filled bowl
And in the seven bowls the wrath of God complete," says John, seeing more pageant unfold.
Great and marvelous is the sight to John who perceives victory for the saints persecuted
Especially so seeing the martyred ones standing near God's throne and there constituted
Where with harps in hand they sing His praises preceding the final series of judgment
Triumphant they stand on the sea of glass, now fire mingled signifying God's intent.

Those with the harps sing the song of Moses, the servant of God, and the song of the Lamb
As the triumphant Israelites, seeing Pharaoh's power perish via the Red Sea, praised I Am
So now those triumphant over the beast, over his image, his mark and number, praise Him.
Looking again John sees this time the temple of the tabernacle of the testimony opening
And through its opening he sees seven angels with the seven bowls of plagues emerging
Further he notes the temple filled with smoke, signifying God's power and glory surging.

A loud voice instructs the seven angels to pour upon the earth their bowls of God's wrath:

The *first* angel pours his bowl causing foul sores to arise on
those following the beast's path
The *second* angel pours out his bowl on the sea so that it
turns to blood killing its creatures all
The *third* angel pours out his bowl on the rivers and springs
turning them to blood each and all.
Then the angel of waters cries that the Lord is righteous:
punishment fits the crime committed
They have shed the blood of saints and prophets and You give
them blood to drink unremitted.

The *fourth* angel pours out his bowl on the sun that it scorch
men with fire, and so they are
Yet they repent not but blaspheme the Lord God Almighty,
thus becoming the more bizarre
Then the *fifth* angel pours out his bowl on the throne of the
beast turning his kingdom dark
And causing subjects of the beast to gnaw their tongues
engulfed in pain and darkness stark
Despite the plagues of judgments poured upon them, the
people of the beast will not desist
They think not of repentance but continue to spew forth
blasphemy like a blanket of mist.

The *sixth* angel pours out his bowl on the river Euphrates
drying up its waters for trespass
Bridging the way for eastern kings, perhaps Parthia and
others, to march across en masse
And in preparation demon spirits like frogs come out of the
mouths of the grisly three—
The dragon, the beast and the false prophet—come out to
perform a mission of perfidy
These demon spirits send out signs to kings worldwide
heralding a much hyped foray
Earth's kings, persuaded by this perverse trinity, come together
to defy God Almighty.

At this point is interjected a parenthetical element in form of
prophetic announcement:
Christ says He is coming as a thief and blessed is he who
remains dressed and vigilant.
Presumably, this interjection is exhortation: people of God
remain vigilant and prepared
Though surrounded by evil forces, for the narrative picks up
where parenthetically pared
"And the demonic spirits gathered the kings together at
Armageddon," a seeming nonevent
For the place, Hebrew named, is mentioned not again, but
resuming is the bowls judgment.

The *seventh* angel pours out his bowl into the air and a voice
from the throne says, "It is done"
And thus ends the bowls judgment and the series
three—seals, trumpets, and bowls—it is done.
Each ended with thunderings, lightnings, and earthquakes:
all manifestations of God's power
But the quake punctuating this series' ending measures the
mightiest ever, incalculable power
"The great city [Rome] was divided into three parts, and
cities of the nations tumbled in its path
And the great Babylon [Rome] was remembered before God"
receiving His cup of fierce wrath.

Following earthquake is hailstorm mighty: hailstones huge
falling from heaven in rounds
But men do not repent; still they blaspheme as stones fall
weighing one hundred pounds.
Next, a bowl angel calls to John, "come so that you may see
judgment of the great harlot
She is one who sits on many waters and with kings of the
earth engages in fornication hot
And inhabitants of the earth are made drunk with the wine
of her fornication wholesale"
So John is spirited to the wilderness for the pageant scene
starring this symbolic female.

There John sees "a woman sitting on a scarlet beast which
was full of names of blasphemy
Having seven heads and ten horns," and providing us
another scene of symbolic pageantry.
Supposedly, the harlot represents Rome, particularly its
political arm persecuting the saints
For we note that the harlot is "drunk with the blood of the
martyrs of Jesus," no restraints.
Next, we note the scarlet beast she rides, a beast heralded as
"full of names of blasphemy"
And we think: this the Roman Empire with its many gods, its
emperor worship especially.

"*Mystery, Babylon the Great, Mother of Harlots, Earth's
Abominations*," the harlot's headliner
So an angel tells John he will explain the mystery of the
woman on the beast, he is the definer:
The seven heads of the beast are seven mountains and seven
kings, substitute hill and emperor
Rome, like Babylon, persecutes God's people and seduces the
world with its wealth and power
Thus, Rome with power and wealth, like a harlot, the world
seduces seems clear enough
But the seven heads/emperors symbol seems somewhat fuzzy,
posing explication tough.

Does one begin count with Julius Caesar or Augustus and
does one count the ephemeral three
The three whose reigns, if reigns, between Nero and
Vespasian were short lived exceedingly?
Problematic identifying seven actual rulers, but easy to see
"seven" as symbolic of completion:
"Five have fallen, one is and the other not yet come, and
coming his rule being of short duration."
Phrased thus, the prediction seems to be that persecution of
God's people by the beast ends soon
But let us listen to more of the angel's figurative explanation
before we more explication presume.

"The beast that was, and is not, is himself also the eighth,
and is of the seven and is going to perdition"
Says the angel, and in his indirect way reveals about the
demonic beast certain essential information.
Surely, the angel suggests the beast's demonic character as it
now exists is taken from a ruler past
Making him a reborn, a reincarnated Nero, first emperor to
vigorously persecute Christians, alas!
Thereby, Nero's spirit is reborn in the person of Domitian
persecutor of the saints John knew
But there is more for the angel to explain: why the ten horns;
what is the purpose of this crew?

We are told that the ten horns of the beast represent ten
kings, and all ten allies of the beast
And they "hate the harlot, make her desolate and naked,
burn her and then on her flesh feast."
Presumably, the beast and his allies, the ten kings, turn on
the harlot thereby putting her away
Thus, we have evil destroying evil, a phenomenon that John
sees fit to emphatically convey
For it is made clear that it is God who "put it into their
hearts [the ten] His purpose to fulfill"
The ten kings give themselves to the beast but in doing so
they unwittingly fulfill God's will.

Thereby, the harlot Rome is separated from the beast Rome
as persecutor of Christian lives
And though the harlot, "drunk with the blood of martyrs," is
destroyed the empire survives
This being the case, the destruction of the harlot portends
the end of Christian persecution.
At this point a change of scene occurs heralded by an angel
imbued with great illumination
From heaven comes this illumined and authoritative angel
crying, "Babylon the great is fallen
She is fallen having become a habitation of demons, a prison
for every foul spirit, all walled in."

"All the nations have drunk of the wine of wrath of her
fornication, the world's kings immense
They committed fornication with her, and world merchants
were enriched by her abundance."
Babylon, of course, is the symbolic name for Rome in the
angel's descriptive announcement
An announcement echoing prophetic funeral dirges for
notorious cities of the Old Testament
And in this pageant scene Rome joins these notorious cities,
her destruction to come about
So prophesies the voice from heaven, "her plagues will come
in one day," her plagues stout.

"And she will be utterly burned with fire, strong is the Lord
God who judges her," amen.
God's people are warned to come out before judgment
begins lest they share in her sin.
Kings, merchants, and traders affiliated with Rome but not
directly in her judgment included
Stand at a distance lamenting their loss, and in their lament
reveal Rome's good not precluded.
On one hand, Rome served as the world's commercial center
thus rendered a service beneficial
But luxurious Rome, wealth and power corrupted and
trafficking in human lives, city despicable.

The pageant calls for rejoicing in the destruction of Rome,
that sinful city of moral dearth
"For in her was found the blood of prophets and saints, and
all who were slain on the earth
Rejoice over her, O heaven and you holy apostles and
prophets, for you are avenged," amen.
Thus, in the God and Satan cosmic war as scripted in John's
pageant, God's people win again.

Revelation Prose Summary Six
Rejoicing in Heaven, and the Warrior Messiah

The Alleluia Chorus

After the destruction of the great harlot, there is rejoicing in heaven. John hears "a loud voice of a great multitude in heaven, saying, '*Alleluia!* Salvation and glory and honor and power to the Lord our God, for true and righteous are His judgments, because He has judged the great harlot who corrupted the earth with her fornication; and He has avenged on her the blood of His servants shed by her'" (19:1-2). The twenty-four elders and the four living creatures fall down worshipping God, saying, "Amen! Alleluia!" (19:4). And a voice from the throne says, "Praise our God, all you His servants those who fear Him, both small and great!" (19:5). And then John hears what sounds like a great multitude, "as the sound of mighty thunderings, saying, 'Alleluia! For the Lord God Omnipotent reigns! Let us be glad and rejoice and give Him glory, for the marriage of the Lamb has come and His wife [bride] has made herself ready'" (19:6-7). Thus, this alleluia chorus praises God to the highest rejoicing in His glory and for the marriage of Christ and His Church. The promise of God to His people, the redeemed in Christ, is made abundantly clear in this triumph of the martyrs. The great harlot has been destroyed; the redeemed have been called to the marriage supper.

Staying Focused

First, the angel instructs John to write, "Blessed are those who are called to the marriage supper of the Lamb!" Then he tells John, "These are the true sayings of God" (19:9). At this point, John falls at the feet of the angel to worship him, but is given an instructive rebuke: "See that you do not do that! I am your fellow servant, and of your brethren who have the testimony of Jesus. Worship God" (19:10)! Blessed indeed is it to be called to the "marriage supper of the Lamb" and thus encompassed in the Savior's steadfast and eternal love. But blessed not is it to worship angels, only God is to be worshipped as John dramatically emphasizes at this opportune point in the pageant. Presumably, he perceived angel worship a serious problem and took this opportunity to discourage it. Even though angels were glorious beings delivering God's words, they were never to be worshipped.

The Conquering Christ

John now sees heaven open and beholds a white horse, "and He who sat on him was called Faithful and True, and in righteousness He judges and makes war. His eyes were like a flame of fire, and on His head were many crowns. He had a name written that no one knew except Himself. He was clothed with a robe dipped in blood, and His name is called the Word of God" (19:11-13). The image is of the conquering Christ: the white horse is a symbol of victory, the rider is the Messiah, the One who is Faithful and True and thus triumphs over all the unfaithful and the untrue, for His name is the Word of God. He wears many crowns because He is the "King of Kings and Lord of Lords" as written on His blood dipped robe. Armies in heaven clothed in clean white linen and riding white horses follow Him, this One out of whose mouth "goes a sharp sword, that with it He should strike the nations" (19:15). The tone of this image, perhaps more Old Testament than New Testament reflective, dramatizes the power of Christ in the ultimate triumph of God's Word over falsehood, righteousness over unrighteousness, good over evil. The winner of the cosmic war between God and Satan, between good and evil is being made clear in this pageant image and becomes dramatically clearer in the next image, that of the carnage strewn triumph of the conquering Christ.

Christ and His Armies Triumph over the Beast and His Armies

An angel standing in the sun alerts all birds that fly in the midst of heaven to "come and gather together for the great supper of the great God" (19:17). Then John sees "the beast, the kings of the earth, and their armies, gathered together to make war against Him who sat on the horse and against His army. Then the beast was captured, and with him the false prophet who worked signs in his presence, by which he deceived those who received the mark of the beast and those who worshipped his image. These two were cast alive into the lake of fire burning with brimstone. And the rest were killed with the sword which proceeded from the mouth of Him who sat on the horse. And all the birds were filled with their flesh" (19:19-21). The first beast (symbol of the self deified emperors), and the false prophet (second beast and symbol of the false priests of the first beast) are cast alive into the lake of fire, eternal damnation, and their followers are slain and their bodies left for the birds of the air. No doubt, John's audience who is living through the Domitian persecution takes heart from this triumphant image of the conquering Christ.

Satan Bound

Next, John sees an angel from heaven come down with a key to the bottomless pit and in his hand a chain. He lays hold of Satan and binds him for a thousand years (not literal years), and casts him into the bottomless pit setting a seal on him "so that he should deceive the nations no more till the thousand years were finished" (20:3). Let us note that it is an angel who binds Satan and that the thousand years is used figuratively and not literally. Again, it is a symbolic number with a multiple of ten, thus indicating completeness and meaning Satan is bound completely for a time, perhaps a long time, after which he will be released for a while.

Let us further note that the binding of Satan and the faith of the martyrs are related. John sees thrones "and they sat on them" (20:4), and judgment was *given* them. The "they" and the "them" are the martyrs: "And I saw the souls of those who had been beheaded for their witness to Jesus and for the word of God, who had not worshiped the beast or his image, and had not received his mark on their foreheads or on their hands, and they lived and reigned with Christ for a thousand years" (20:4). The implication here is that the faith of these martyrs, their steadfastness in the face of persecution, brings about the binding of Satan. It is a powerful and assuring message that John communicates to his audience, God's people, who were currently being severely persecuted under the reign of Domitian. The martyrs are of the "first resurrection," probably meaning they are the closest to God: "Blessed and holy is he who has part in the first resurrection . . . [for] they shall be priests of God and of Christ, and shall reign with Him a thousand years" (20:6).

Satan, Gog and Magog

John says that *whenever* the thousand years is ended Satan will be released from his confinement and that he "will go out to deceive the nations which are in the four corners of the earth, Gog and Magog, to gather them to battle, whose number is as the sand of the sea. They went up on the breadth of the earth and surrounded the camp of the saints and the beloved city and fire came down from God out of haven and devoured them" (20:8-9). Here John uses Gog and Magog as he has used Babylon. Co-opted from Ezekiel, the figures Gog and Magog fit neatly into this new context where, as in the Old Testament, they are used here as formidable enemies marshaled against God's people and they meet the same fate as there: destruction by the fire power of God. Satan who deceived them is "cast into the lake of fire and brimstone where the beast and the false prophet are. And they will be tormented day and night forever and ever" (20:10).

Judgment

Then John sees "a great white throne and Him who sat on it from whose face the earth and heaven fled away . . . And I saw the dead, small and great, standing before God, and books were opened. And another book was opened, which is the Book of Life. And the dead were judged according to their works [deeds], by the things which were written in the books" (20:11-12). This image confirms judgment for everyone; at some juncture all persons must answer to God for their deeds. Here there is no mention of Christ or of a specific gathering of the dead, but simply a confirmation that all will be judged. One's life appears in one book and one's evaluation in the other. This judgment image is more reflective of the Old Testament than the New.

The image continues: "Then Death and Hades were cast into the lake of fire . . . and anyone not found written in the Book of Life was cast into the lake of fire" (20:14-15). Thus, the judgment image is completed: Death and Hades and all those whose names do not appear in the Book of Life are cast into the lake of fire, the second death. Thus, judgment would be completed. Those who chose God and lived accordingly would be with Him eternally; those who chose evil and lived in denial of God would experience the second death, eternal separation from God.

Revelation Poetic Summary Six
Rejoicing in Heaven, and the Warrior Messiah

Announcement of the great harlot's destruction triggers
thunderous rejoicing, heaven's nod
A mighty multitude sings out: "*Alleluia*! Salvation and glory
and honor to the Lord our God"
True and righteous are His judgments; true and righteous is
His judgment against the harlot
The harlot's horrid fornication corrupted the earth and
spared the blood of His servants not.
The twenty-four elders and the living creatures fall with a
worshipful "Alleluia," all of them
And from the throne a voice cries out, "Praise Him, all servants
who fear Him, praise Him."

John then hears a voice of a great multitude "as the sound of
mighty thunderings saying,
'Alleluia! For God the Lord God Omnipotent reigns,'" praise
with announcement relaying
"Rejoice, for the marriage of the Lamb has come and His
bride has made herself ready sure."
This alleluia chorus praises God and rejoices in the marriage
of Christ and His Church pure
For God's promise to His people, the redeemed in Christ, is
fulfilled in the marriage supper
The great harlot destroyed, and now the redeemed have been
called to the marriage supper.

Presumably, this portion of the pageant trumpets the
triumph of the martyrs' steadfast stand

That is assuming the faithfulness of the martyrs brings
about the intervention of God's hand
Why else the pure white linen of the bride declared the
righteous acts of the saints bold?
Why else to write "blessed those called to the marriage
supper of the Lamb" is John told?
And then to be overwhelmed hearing "these are the true
sayings of God," and falling derelict
Having to be angel reminded: never think of worshipping
anyone other than the Lord direct?

Now heaven opens and John beholds sitting on a white
horse One called Faithful and True
One who in righteousness judges and makes war and whose
eyes are like flames of fire too
On His head were many crowns His robe dipped in blood
and the Word of God the name
The image is that of the conquering Christ and the white
horse the symbol of victory same
It is the Messiah sent to preside over the funeral dirge of the
fallen great harlot gone
This is conqueror legitimate, not conqueror who goes out for
conquering sake alone.

This is the conqueror Faithful and True who triumphs over
the unfaithful and the untrue
He wears many crowns for He is King of Kings and Lord of
Lords, on His robe construe.
Armies in heaven all clothed in white linen clean and riding
on white horses follow Him
Out of His mouth goes sword sharp, the word of God, for
striking the nations, all of them.
This image, Old Testament toned, dramatizes Christ's
power in the triumph of God's word
The ultimate triumph of God's word in Testament New
revealed, though in O.T. tone heard.

And the O.T. tone continues in the carnage strewn image of
the conquering Christ victorious
Symbolically, nature celebrates the triumph of the word of
God in the bird's feast glorious
An angel in the sun alerts all birds flying in heaven's midst
come for God's great supper to be
Come see the beast and kings of the earth armies facing the
King of Kings and His great army
See the beast captured with the false prophet who worked
deceptive signs the people to hold
Who deceived them to the mark of the beast and to his image
worship, except for saints bold.

These two, the beast and the prophet false, were cast alive
into the lake of the burning brimstone
The rest were killed with the sword proceeding from the
mouth of Him as Kings of Kings known
And all the birds were filled with the flesh of those who
opposed the King of Kings and Lords too
The first beast, symbol of self defied emperors, and false
prophet symbol of second beast construe
These two thrown in the lake of fire, eternally damned, their
slain followers food for birds of the air.
Should not John's hearers, Domitian persecuted, take heart in
the conquering Christ and not despair?

Next, John sees an angel from heaven descend with chain in
hand and key to the bottomless pit
He binds Satan setting a seal on him that he should not, for
a time, the nations deceive or outwit
The time is termed a thousand years, a symbolic number
with multiple of ten, meaning completeness
Satan is bound and bound completely for a time, perhaps a
long time, before loosed to deceptiveness.
Let it not go unnoted that the binding of Satan and the faith
of the martyrs are connected inextricably
John sees thrones and they sat on them, and judgment was
given them: the *they* and *them* martyrs be.

"And I saw the souls of those who had been beheaded for
their witness to Jesus for God's word
Who had not worshipped the beast or his image, nor had
received his mark on hand or forehead
Now they lived and reigned with Christ for a thousand
years," the figurative time for Satan's stay.
Did the martyrs' steadfast faith not bind Satan's power; is
evil not overcome when facing the Way?
Surely so, and surely John intends this powerful and assuring
message to bolster the besieged saints
Surely he intends to bolster God's people who are experiencing
Domitian persecution sans restraints.

Seemingly the message is that total faith of God's people
binds old Satan, and lack thereof unbinds:
For "*whenever* the thousand years ends Satan will be released
from his confinement," John reminds,
"And he will go out to deceive the nations which are in the
four corners of the earth, Gog and Magog."
Presumably lack of faith will loose Satan to roam the earth
again, but time and situation are left in fog.
Co-opted from Ezekiel, Gog and Magog represent
formidable enemies marshaled against God's own
And like their O. T. namesake they meet the same fate:
destruction from the fire power of God's throne.

Thus, God's enemies gathered by Satan from earth's four
corners could hardly be a battle called
As they "surrounded the camp of the saints and the beloved
city" heaven's fire devoured them all.
Is the "camp of the saints and the beloved city" the church,
the spiritual Jerusalem, writ figuratively?
And is this old Satan's last venture against the saints; is his
being cast into the fire intended literally?
One cannot say for sure for fog pervades this pageant scene,
but there is for sure a sense of finality
We see Satan join the beast and false prophet in the lake of
fire, be it figuratively or be it literally.

Yet, is this intended to depict the world's end? If so, why is
Christ not there in power and glory?
There is a judgment scene but without Christ there it seems
more message sent than actual story.
John sees "a great white throne and Him who sat on it from
whose face earth and heaven fled
And I saw the dead, small and great, standing before God,
and books were opened to be read
And another book was opened, the Book of Life, and the
dead were to be judged according to deed."
Thus, judgment is confirmed for everyone; at some juncture
everyone must answer to God, indeed!

Though there is no mention of Christ or of a specific
gathering of the dead, there is confirmation
There is confirmation that all will be judged, that the lives of
all will be recorded for determination
Into the lake of fire, the second death, is cast anyone whose
name in the Book of Life appears not
And the casting of Death and Hades into this selfsame lake
thereby completes the image and the lot.
The message is clear: those who choose the Lord and live in
steadfast faith reign eternally with God
Those who choose evil and live in denial of God are second
death assigned, the lake of fire to trod.

Revelation Prose Summary Seven
The Grand Finale

The New Jerusalem Descending

John now sees a new heaven and a new earth for the first heaven and first earth had passed away and with them the sea out of which came the persecuting beast. Continuing to look, John sees "the holy city, New Jerusalem, coming down out of heaven from God, prepared as a bride adorned for her husband" (21:2). Then he hears a loud voice from heaven saying, "Behold, the tabernacle of God is with men, and He will dwell with them, and they shall be His people, and God himself will be with them and He will be their God" (21:3). These words echo words spoken by prophets of the Old Testament prophesying a time of reconciliation between God and His people when He would be their God and they would be His people (e.g., Jer 32:38). Such proves to be the case in the New Jerusalem where "God will wipe away every tear from their eyes; there shall be no more death, nor sorrow, nor crying; and there shall be no more pain, for the former things have passed away" (21:4).

Historical Time Frame

The meaning of this symbolic image is a debatable matter, but surely in the context of John's historical time frame, the severe persecution of Christians under the rule of Domitian, the image promises relief from this persecution, a reality that occurred with his death.

And would not John's contemporary audience be further relieved and assured upon hearing John reveal that "He who sat on the throne said, 'Behold, I make all things new'" (21:5), and then tells John, "Write, for these words are true and faithful"? And would John's contemporary audience not be even more relieved and assured upon hearing these further revelations? "I am the Alpha and the Omega, the Beginning and the End.

I will give of the fountain of the water of life freely to him who thirsts. *He who overcomes* shall inherit all things, and I will be his God and he shall be My son, but *the cowardly*, unbelieving, abominable, murderers, sexually immoral, sorcerers, idolaters, and all liars shall have their part in the lake which burns with fire and brimstone, which is the second death" (21:6-8). Certainly, persecuted believers of later times reading John's Revelation would no doubt be relieved and assured as well, but first and foremost John is addressing his contemporaries, his fellow Christians under emperor Domitian's persecution.

Higher View

Presumably to give him a higher view, a greater spiritual perspective, one of the seven bowl angels tells John, "Come, I will show you the bride, the Lamb's wife," and then carries him "in the Spirit" to a high mountain and shows him "the great city, the holy Jerusalem, descending out of heaven from God, having the glory of God" (21:9-11).

The Holy Jerusalem Described

Describing the holy Jerusalem, John says "her light was like a most precious stone, like a jasper stone, clear as crystal. Also she had a great and high wall with twelve gates, and twelve angels at the gates, and names written on them, which are the names of the twelve tribes of the children of Israel: three gates on the east, three gates on the north, three gates on the south, and three gates on the west. Now the wall of the city had twelve foundations, and on them were the names of the twelve apostles of the Lamb" (21:11-14). Obviously, this is the city of God's people: the Israelites, the chosen people of the Old Testament, represented in the names of the twelve tribes inscribed on its gates and the Christians, the chosen people of the New Testament, represented in the names of the twelve apostles inscribed on its foundations. The angel carries a gold reed to measure the city which is laid out as a square, "and he measured the city with the reed: twelve thousand furlongs, its length, breadth, and height being equal" (21:16). Its wall measures "one hundred and forty-four cubits . . . and the construction of its wall was of jasper; and the city was pure gold, like clear glass. And the foundations of the wall of the city were adorned with all kinds of precious stones: the first foundation was jasper, the second sapphire, the third chalcedony, the fourth emerald, the fifth sardonyx, the sixth sardius, the seventh chrysolite, the eight beryl, the ninth topaz, the tenth chrysoprase, the eleventh jacinth, and the twelfth amethyst. And the twelve gates were twelve pearls: each individual gate was of one pearl. And the street of the city was pure gold like transparent glass. But I saw no temple in it, for the Lord God Almighty and the Lamb are its temple" (21:17-22). This is truly the holy city where God and the Lamb have come to dwell with their people. It is called the Bride of the Lamb (21:9), suggesting the Church in the sense of God's people all, the people of faith before and after Christ's crucifixion and resurrection. The city is four square and cubed, symbol of perfection. The Holy of Holies in the tabernacle and the temple were cubed, but the New Jerusalem is itself the Holy of Holies; it is the dwelling place of God and the Lamb and will be the dwelling place of all the redeemed, the people who have kept the faith and whose names have been written in the Book of Life. Twelve, symbol for God's people as number or multiple, permeates the description of the New Jerusalem, the city of God and the city for God and His people: the twelve tribes written on its gates, the twelve apostles written on the foundations of its wall, the twelve thousand furlongs comprising the length, breadth, and height of the city, the one hundred and forty-four cubits comprising the height of its wall, twelve different precious stones adorn the foundations of its wall, and twelve pearls comprise its twelve gates.

The city had no need of sun or moon, "for the glory of God illuminated it, and the Lamb is its light . . . its gates shall not be shut . . . but there shall by no means enter it anything that defiles, or that causes an abomination or a lie, but only those who are written in the Lamb's Book of Life" (21:23, 25, 27). In the middle of its street and "proceeding from the throne of God and the Lamb" runs a pure and crystal clear river of water; "on either side of the river was the tree of life, which bore twelve fruits, each tree yielding its fruit every month. And the leaves of the tree were for the healing of nations. And there shall be no more curse, but the throne of God and the Lamb shall be in it, and His servants shall serve Him. They shall see His face, and His name shall be on their foreheads. And there shall be no night there: They need no lamp nor light of the sun, for the Lord God gives them light. And they shall reign forever and ever" (22:1-5). Thus, John describes his vision of the holy city to come, the New Jerusalem, but the pageant is not yet ended. There is the epilogue.

The Epilogue

(Besides John and the angel, there is a third speaker in the epilogue: the Lord. To differentiate the Lord's words I have used italics.) Following the description of the New Jerusalem, the angel tells John "these words are faithful and true" and that "the Lord God of the holy prophets sent His angel to show His servants the things which must shortly take place: '*Behold, I am coming soon! Blessed is he who keeps the words of the prophecy of this book*' "(22:6-7). John, again overwhelmed, falls down to worship the angel and is again rebuked: "See that you do not do that, for I am your fellow servant .... Worship God" (22:9). Then the angel tells John, "Do not seal the words of the prophecy of this book, for the time is at hand" (22:10).

The nearness time factor is strongly emphasized in the epilogue. Clearly, decisive action is soon to take place, but just what that decisive action is to be is not so clear. The reader's first thought may be that the Second Coming is at hand. But is that what John intended? Surely, that is not what he intended, for it did not happen. Almost two-thousand years later, it has not happened. So let us assume that is not what John intended and look for a more probable explanation. And we need look no further for probable explanation than that provided by James M. Efird in his book *Revelation for Today*: "If one consistently applies apocalyptic interpretative procedure to these visions and teachings, the very real possibility is that John did not understand himself to be describing Jesus' *final* return. He may have been using the apocalyptic idea of God or God's agent (in this case, clearly Jesus) in a symbolic way to describe the end of a period of persecution and the establishment of a new age with the persecution gone" (p. 125). He goes on to point out that John wrote Revelation about A.D. 94 or 95, and that when Domitian died in A.D. 96, the persecution ended.

Now, this is not to imply that Revelation was written only for John's contemporaries, for his visions, what we have referred to as the pageant, make it abundantly clear that in the cosmic battle between good and evil that good will triumph, that Satan will be defeated, that through the Lamb there will be a new heaven and a new earth for all those who keep the faith: they "have the right to the tree of life and may go through the gates into the city," the New Jerusalem (22:14). And those who have made the supreme sacrifice of giving their lives for the faith, the martyrs, are promised the special relationship of reigning as "priests of God and of Christ" (20:6).

Revelation then, through its apocalyptic pageant, offers hope and assurance not only to John's contemporaries who were suffering severe persecution under the emperor Domitian, but to believers suffering persecution in any age since. Furthermore, it dramatizes the cosmic battle between good and evil, between God and Satan, and assures all believers that God and good will ultimately triumph over Satan and evil, and that all believers in Jesus Christ who keep the faith will share in this triumph. And does not this blessed assurance, as dramatically presented in Revelation, seem most appropriate for the concluding book of the New Testament, and thereby of the Bible?

Revelation Poetic Summary Seven
The Grand Finale

John now sees a new heaven and a new earth for the first had passed away, and so the sea
He sees the holy city, the New Jerusalem, coming down from God, prepared as bride to be
He hears a loud voice from heaven saying, "The tabernacle of God is with men, all behold!
For He will dwell with them, and they shall be His people and He shall be their God," untold.
Echoes from the prophets of old seeing reconciliation between God and His people to come
And so it comes as holy city new, the city without tears or pain or death, the New Jerusalem.

For the saints of John's day this symbolic image surely rayed out hope against Satan's lies
Would they not see it as prophecy fulfilled when persecution ended with Domitian's demise?
Would their ears not ring in recall, "I am the Alpha and the Omega, the Beginning and the End
He who overcomes shall inherit all things, for I will be his God and he shall be My son," then?
The image would, of course, speak to the persecuted saints of later times and of today as well
But first of all John is addressing his fellow saints, the ones Emperor Domitian seeks to dispel.

This holy city being such a sight to behold John finds himself repositioned for a better view
In the Spirit he is carried by one of the bowl angels to a high mountain to view the city new:

Called "the bride, the Lamb's wife, the great city, the holy
Jerusalem from heaven descending"
And from his prime perspective it is left to John this glorious
view describe, on him depending.
John says "her light was like a most precious stone, like a
jasper stone, crystal clear the same
She had a great and high wall with twelve gates, and at each
gate an angel and also a name."

The names of the twelve tribes of the children of Israel were
written on the twelve gates:
On the east three gates, the north three gates, the south
three gates, the west three gates.
The wall of the city had twelve foundations, thereon names
of the twelve apostles inscribed
Yes, it is the city of God's people: the Israelites the chosen
ones of the O.T., the twelve tribes
Represented by the names of the twelve tribes inscribed on
the twelve gates, like nations
And the chosen of the N.T. represented by the apostles' names
on the wall's foundations.

An angel carries a reed of gold to measure the holy city, a city
laid out four square
Twelve thousand furlongs, its length, breadth, and height,
being equal everywhere
Its wall measures one hundred and forty-four cubits, it of
jasper but the city pure gold
Twelve precious stones forms the foundations of the wall of
this city John saw unfold
This city with street of transparent gold and with twelve
gates, each gate a pearl whole
But John sees no temple "for the Lord God Almighty and the
Lamb are its temple" untold.

It is a city four square and cubed, symbolic perfection, no
need for a Holy of Holies here

As in the tabernacle or temple, for in this New Jerusalem
God's presence is everywhere
This city, the dwelling place of God and the Lamb, is
prepared for people redeemed
Prepared for those who keep the faith and whose names in
the Book of Life are seen.
Twelve, symbol for God's people as number or multiple,
permeates the New Jerusalem
And by focusing on this number so profusely surely John is
attempting to assure them.

The names of the twelve tribes are written on the city's
twelve gates, one and all
The names of the twelve apostles are written on the twelve
foundations of its wall
Twelve thousand furlongs comprise its length, breadth, and
height, equal all
One hundred and forty-four cubits comprise the height of
its four square wall
Twelve precious stones adorn the twelve foundations of its
four square wall
And twelve pearls comprise the twelve gates, each a pearl
whole, one and all.

The city hath no need of sun or moon for the glory of God
and the Lamb illuminate it
And though its gates are never shut, by no means shall enter
it anything that defiles it
Or causes an abomination, but only those who are written in
the Lamb's Book of Life.
Down its street's middle runs a crystal clear river, and on
each side is the Tree of Life
Each Tree bears twelve fruits yielding its fruit every month,
and its leaves heal nations
The curse is gone, for the throne of God and the Lamb is
there: now perfect relations.

Seeing His face His servants shall serve Him for on their
foreheads His name bright
And there shall be no night, no need of light from lamp or
sun, the Lord God is light.
Thus, John describes the holy city, the New Jerusalem; then
the pageant in epilogue ends
John and the angel engage in dialogue while the Lord
interjects statement that portends
The angel, sent by the Lord God of the holy prophets,
asserts the words of the pageant true
The Lord says He is coming soon and blessed is he who keeps
these prophetic words true.

John falls down again to worship the angel only to be
rebuked again to worship God only
And told not to seal the words of the prophecy of this book,
for the time is at hand, surely.
Thus, the epilogue says one thing clearly, decisive action is
coming and its coming is near
But as throughout Revelation the message is indirect: it is
figurative, never direct and clear.
Many readers interpret the action near to be the Second
Coming, but is that what it is?
It did not happen in John's day nor has it happened
two-thousand years later: gee whiz!

Should we then assume that the immediate Second Coming
was not the message intended?
Surely so, surely we should look for other explanation, one
fitting and logically defended.
Suppose we keep in mind this is apocalyptic writing and
John is not communicating directly
The message is in pageant form meaning presented
figuratively, which is to say not literally.
John is using the apocalyptic idea of God intervening in the
emperor inspired persecution
So surely he uses the second coming of Jesus as only symbolic
frame for that intervention.

Why can we not assume that he uses it figuratively to
prophesy a new age free of persecution?
Literally, that is what happened closely following the death
of persecution emperor Domitian
Certainly, a new age did begin with his death in A. D. 96, a
year or so after John's Revelation
Thus, who can conscientiously argue the logical explanation
above not truly a valid explication?

This is not to say John wrote Revelation for his
contemporaries only, only for their knowing
His visions, the pageant scenes, make it abundantly clear
there is a cosmic battle on-going
Furthermore, that in this cosmic battle between good and
evil that good will triumph sure
That Satan will be defeated, that heaven and earth will be
created new, a holy city pure
That those who keep the faith shall enter its pearly gates and
of the tree of life partake
And that faith's martyrs shall live closest to God, having given
their all for Christ's sake.

Though figurative Revelation focuses on the persecuted of
John's day, is it not still today reliable?
And is its dramatic assurance to believers who keep the faith
not the perfect ending for the Bible?